Migration and Restructuring in the United States

Migration and Restructuring in the United States

A Geographic Perspective

EDITED BY
KAVITA PANDIT
AND
SUZANNE DAVIES WITHERS

ROWMAN & LITTLEFIELD PUBLISHERS, INC.
Lanham • Boulder • New York • Oxford

ROWMAN & LITTLEFIELD PUBLISHERS, INC.

Published in the United States of America
by Rowman & Littlefield Publishers, Inc.
4720 Boston Way, Lanham, Maryland 20706
http://www.rowmanlittlefield.com

12 Hid's Copse Road
Cumnor Hill, Oxford OX2 9JJ, England

British Library Cataloguing in Publication Information Available

Library of Congress Cataloging-in-Publication Data

Migration and restructuring in the United States : a geographic perspective /
edited by Kavita Pandit and Suzanne Davies Withers.
p. cm.
Includes bibliographical references and index.
ISBN 0-8476-9392-9 (alk. paper). — ISBN 0-8476-9393-7 (pbk. : alk. paper)
1. Migration, Internal—United States. 2. Rural-urban migration—Economic aspects—United States. 3. Regional planning—United States. 4. Labor mobility—United States. I. Pandit, Kavita, 1956– . II. Withers, Suzanne Davies, 1963– .
HB1965.M56 1999
304.8′0973—dc21 99-10342
CIP

Printed in the United States of America

♾ The paper used in this publication meets the minimum requirements of American National Standard for Information Sciences—Permanence of Paper for Printed Library Materials, ANSI/NISO Z39.48–1992.

Contents

Preface

In the past few decades the United States has seen rapid and fundamental changes in its economic and demographic structures. Economic restructuring is exemplified by the decline of manufacturing jobs, the rise of the service economy, the downsizing of firms, and the related reskilling of the workforce. Demographic restructuring is seen in the aging of the population, as well as in its increasing cultural and ethnic diversity.

Migration is fundamentally linked to the spatial processes of economic and demographic restructuring. Internal migration patterns are dynamically linked to the rise and fall of regional economies. At the same time, aging of the population has contributed to the transformation of factors driving migration and the choice of destinations. Immigration to the United States has similarly profound implications for the economic and demographic restructuring of society. Immigration has been responsible for the redirection of federal spending at the national level and has triggered regional economic changes. On the social front, the ongoing patterns of immigration have sparked national debates on the nature of U.S. society and the future assimilation of incoming migrants. These changes, taken together, have challenged migration scholars to reexamine traditional research and identify research frontiers.

In response to this challenge, in May 1997 a group of geographers, demographers, and economists engaged in migration research convened in a three-day roundtable entitled "Migration and Restructuring in the U.S.: Towards the Next Millennium." The roundtable was hosted by the University of Georgia in Athens and was supported under the university's State-of-the-Art Conference initiative. This volume brings together a selection of papers presented and discussed at the conference.

The interconnections between restructuring and migration are complex and recursive, and no book, including this one, can boast of covering all dimensions of the relationship in totality. The contributions in this volume, however, succeed in providing a depth and breadth of coverage that will be welcomed by scholars in migration studies across disciplines. The individual chapters provide a desirable combination of theoretical and empirical analyses that we hope will make this volume an invaluable guide for both researchers and policymakers.

We would like to thank Jodie Guy who provided invaluable editorial help and Sally Kroehnke for her assistance with many of the figures and maps in the book. The financial support of the University of Georgia is also gratefully acknowledged.

1

Introduction: Geographic Perspectives on Migration and Restructuring

Kavita Pandit and Suzanne Davies Withers

Patterns of migration in the United States have long been intertwined with deep-rooted economic and demographic changes within society. Looking back at the nation's history, the westward population movement in the nineteenth century was linked to the colonization of the periphery, development of rich farmland, and the industrialization of the Northeast. Over time, successive waves of migration of Europeans from increasingly diverse parts of the continent revolutionized the demographic makeup of the U.S. population. In the early twentieth century, the migration of blacks from the economically depressed South to the industrializing North corresponded with the transformation of the nation from a primary, rural-based economy to a secondary, urban-based one (Johnson and Campbell 1981). Simultaneously, it succeeded in further transforming the ethnic makeup of the North.

The latter twentieth century was no exception. Beginning in the 1950s, an unprecedented movement of people occurred out of central cities into adjoining suburban areas that was closely linked to economic and demographic forces. The rapid increase in economic prosperity in the post–World War II era, together with the restructuring of transportation through improved highways and advances in automobile engineering, made car ownership and longer-distance commuting economically feasible for most Americans (Hall 1988; Knox 1994). This period was also characterized by high rates of family formation leading to a significant demographic event—the birth of the baby-boom generation. This, in turn, created a housing boom in the suburbs, fueled in part by cheap government mortgages (Knox 1994; Cadwallader 1996).

Another spatial transformation was seen in the 1970s and 1980s when the

Northeast and Midwest regions that had long experienced net in-migration began to lose population to the rest of the country, particularly the South and the West. Once again, this movement was closely related to a fundamental shift in the economy, viz. from manufacturing-based to service-based production and employment. This restructuring of industry had the most adverse effect in the Northeast "Snowbelt" region, historically associated with manufacturing activity. In contrast, restructuring toward a service economy favored the growth of the "Sunbelt" states in the South and West (Biggar 1979). Snowbelt to Sunbelt shifts were also magnified by demographic changes, viz. the entry of the large baby-boom generation into their prime years of mobility and a rise in the size of the retirement-age population.

At the turn of the twenty-first century, we are once again confronted by significant economic and demographic changes inextricably intertwined with migration patterns and processes. The trend toward globalization and the emergence of "global cities" have triggered huge flows of migrants across international boundaries (Castells 1989; Sassen 1991, 1994). International migration to the United States, after several decades of relative dormancy in the middle part of the twentieth century, has grown in volume and come to occupy the forefront of the national agenda. The geographic and ethnic specificity of immigration streams to the United States have, in turn, brought about far-reaching economic and demographic shifts within the country. Other factors such as the aging of the populace, the emergence of poverty concentrations at the urban and regional scales, and the shift to high-technology production collectively influence and are influenced by migration processes.

Given this, there is an urgent need to reexamine the interconnections between migration and the economic and demographic restructuring under way in the United States and to confront the implications for migration research. Particularly useful in this regard is a *geographic* perspective, that is, one that recognizes that migration and the economic and demographic processes with which it is associated are spatially contingent. This perspective runs through this volume, which is organized into three sections: Migration and Economic Restructuring, Migration and Demographic Restructuring, and Methodological Frontiers in Migration Research.

Migration and Economic Restructuring

The term *economic restructuring* has its root in the concept of "structural change" in development theory (Webber et al. 1992), which refers to the fundamental alterations in a national economy as it is transformed from a less developed to a more developed one (Chenery and Syrquin 1975). These changes are seen in areas as varied as employment and production (Clark 1957; Graham et al. 1988), government structure and services (Pinch 1989; Winckler

1990), international trade and capital flows (Jackson 1990), and urban structure (Longcore and Rees 1996). Recent conceptualizations pay greater attention to theoretical frameworks, with economic restructuring variously defined in terms of accumulation patterns, class and gender relations, technological options, corporate strategies, or phases of capitalist development (Webber et al. 1992). Further, restructuring is now examined at various scales, ranging from households to social networks, corporations, industries, and regions. Regardless of the theoretical conceptualization or scale of analysis, however, restructuring is commonly regarded as an irrevocable shift from one order to another.

In the United States the economic restructuring terminology became commonplace in the aftermath of the oil price shocks of the 1970s and the consequent global economic recession. Restructuring referred primarily to the restructuring of industry, specifically the shift of production and employment from manufacturing-dominant to service-dominant activities. The shift was attributed by some to the loss of America's competitive edge in manufacturing necessitating a shift to services, particularly producer and financial services (Lawrence 1984). Others such as Bluestone and Harrison (1982) argued that major industries were made vulnerable by poor management and the lack of federal policy guidance. Yet others viewed the 1970s as signaling the end of the Fordist regime of capitalist accumulation and the beginning of a post-Fordist era.

The restructuring of the 1970s had a number of dimensions. The first was the increase in the demand for skilled workers and the concomitant deskilling of many operations. Indeed both of these trends were central to the emergence and growth of what Sassen (1991) referred to as "global cities": major metropolitan areas in which global financial and business services are concentrated. These cities created a simultaneous demand for high-skilled managers and professionals, as well as low-skilled, low-wage service personnel. Consequently, the second aspect of economic restructuring was a new social polarization, a rise in wage and income disparities, and an overall decline in job security (Bluestone and Harrison 1982; Harrison and Bluestone 1988; Massey and Meegan 1982). A third consequence of restructuring was seen in the shifting priorities of government programs. In particular, the declining tax revenues and escalating fiscal deficits brought about government downsizing and federal spending cuts in the 1990s. Finally, given that the process of economic restructuring was inherently uneven over space, it brought with it new geographic alignments and patterns (Clark 1993).

The links between regional economic conditions and migration patterns have long been recognized in the literature. Migration, particularly long-distance migration, has been found to increase during economically prosperous times and to decline in times of economic decline (Milne 1993). Further, economic upswings are associated with expanding migration regions, suggesting greater integration and interdependence in the national labor market. Conversely, migration regions shrink during times of worsening economic conditions, suggesting segmentation and localization of labor markets (Clark 1982). Regardless of economic conditions, however, migration flows between regions are for the most part mutually compensating, resulting from routine job turnovers within an established spatial arrangement of economic functions (Plane 1984).

In contrast, periods of economic restructuring precipitate abrupt, systemwide shifts in population movement that represent sharp departures from established patterns. Migration flows during such period are associated with changing spatial arrangements of economic functions (Plane 1984). They also cease to be compensating; that is, a mobility flow in one direction is not necessarily balanced by a reverse flow. As a result, migration streams during periods of economic restructuring become highly focused or unidirectional. Thus, for example, the restructuring of the U.S. economy from agriculture to manufacturing in the first half of the twentieth century precipitated a nationwide exodus of people from rural to urban areas. Likewise, the shift from manufacturing to service activities in the 1970s fueled a massive shift from the old industrial states in the Northeast and Midwest to the Sunbelt states of the South and West (Plane 1989) and gave new impetus to the flow out of central cities to suburbs and exurbs.

Although patterns of migration may be transformed by economic restructuring, they themselves often define the nature of restructuring. Current trends in immigration to the United States, seen as the natural outcome of the restructuring of global financial activity, are resulting in an ethnic restructuring of the country. Regions faced with massive depopulation, such as the northeastern and midwestern states in the 1970s, have to drastically modify patterns of government spending and employment generation. Regions with heavy in-migration may find their economies transformed as certain sectors (construction, transportation) grow more rapidly than others. At the urban scale, the movement of wealthy, largely white populations from the inner city to the suburbs has created a largely minority "underclass" in the central cities, a group whose economic options are severely limited by its inability to move (Wilson 1987; Hughes 1995).

Given this, a number of interesting substantive questions emerge. For example, if economic restructuring is inherently uneven over space, has migration served to equilibrate differences over the long run? Is net out-migration inevitable in regions undergoing deindustrialization? Do the economic impacts of internal and external migration at the national scale reveal what is going on at the regional scale? What are the likely effects of government downsizing, such as through welfare reform, on the volume of immigration to the United States? Issues such as these are inherently geographic in their scope and lie at the heart of the economic restructuring-migration relationship.

Migration and Demographic Restructuring

Migration also fundamentally alters the characteristics of the population of the origin and destination regions. We refer to these changes as demographic restructuring because, like economic restructuring, they represent a qualitative shift from one order to another. Specifically, we consider two types of demographic restructuring: changes in the age structure of the population and changes in the ethnic composition of the population.

The restructuring of the U.S. population age structure is evident in the steady aging of the population. This trend is a result of underlying changes in the vital processes of fertility and mortality. In the United States, declining fertility of the U.S.-born population combined with rising life expectancies is contributing to a steady aging of the population, a trend only partially counteracted by the higher fertility of the U.S. foreign-born population. Consequently, the share of the U.S. population over age 65 rose from 7 percent in 1940 to 13 percent in 1998, and the median age of the population over the same time period went from twenty-nine years to thirty-four years (Soldo and Agree 1988; Population Reference Bureau 1998).

Although there is an unmistakable rise in the share of the older population and the median age in the United States, the pace of this change is extremely uneven over time and space. The size of the elderly population at any given time is determined largely by the number of births in the country 65 or more years earlier. Thus the large elderly cohort in the 1970s and 1980s can be traced to the high fertility in the late 1800s and early 1900s. The growth rate of the elderly population at the turn of the twenty-first century is slowing down as the smaller cohort born during the Depression years reaches age 65. The growth rate will pick up again between 2010 and 2030, however, as the post–World War II baby-boom generation begins to enter the ranks of the elderly (Soldo and Agree 1988; Bouvier and De Vita 1991). There are also enormous regional and subregional variations in the pace of population aging. For example, in the late 1980s it was the Snowbelt states of the Northeast and Midwest and the popular retirement destinations in Florida and Arizona that had the highest shares of elderly in the nation (Rogerson 1996).

Migration and population age composition are intricately linked. Migration is a process that is highly selective by age: the highest rates of migration are generally experienced during young adulthood and decline thereafter (Rogers, Raquillet, and Castro1978). Consequently, a typical migrant stream will tend to increase the median age of population at the origin and lower the median age at the destination (as evidenced by the higher elderly concentrations in the Snowbelt states compared with the Sunbelt states). This effect is amplified by the fact that migrants are in their prime reproductive years, and their subsequent fertility will also render the destination region more youthful. Specific streams of migration, however, may vary significantly in age composition: flows from colder regions to warmer retirement destinations (such as Florida and Arizona) typically have a much higher representation of older persons. In summary, this means the pace of aging in a particular region is a joint consequence of the age structure of net migration to the region and the age structure of the regional population as a whole, the latter determining the size of cohorts entering old age over time (Rogerson 1996).

Just as migration influences the age structure of a region, the population age structure can affect migration through its influence on regional economic conditions. For example, a number of studies have shown that the migration rates of a cohort are powerfully influenced by the relative size of the cohort. Large cohorts such as the baby-boom generation have notably lower mobility rates than small cohorts (Rogerson 1987; Plane 1992) because the entry of large cohorts into the labor force increases competition for jobs and housing (Easterlin 1968), which, in turn, tends to inhibit mobility rates throughout their lifetime (Wilson 1983; Rogerson 1987). Indeed, the Snowbelt to Sunbelt migration can be attributed in part to age composition effects because the migrants were largely composed of the baby boomers who came of age in the Northeast and Midwest during the 1970s and 1980s. Even though this generation was moving at lower than expected rates, the sheer volume of migrants greatly magnified the significance of the Snowbelt to Sunbelt shifts (Plane 1992; Pandit 1997).

The second type of demographic restructuring under way is that of the ethnic composition of the U.S. population. Since 1960 there has been a steady decline in the proportion of the population that identifies itself as "white" and an increase in the share of people of other racial and ethnic groups (Taylor 1994). If these rates were to continue, it is expected that by the middle of the twenty-first century today's minorities will comprise nearly half of all Americans, with Hispanic Americans surpassing African Americans as the nation's largest ethnic minority (O'Hare 1992; del Pinal and Singer 1997). Migration, viz. immigration to the United States, has played the dominant role in this ethnic restructuring (although many ethnic minority groups are also characterized by higher fertility rates than the white population). Between 1960 and 1990, almost half of all immigrants to the United States were of Hispanic origin, and almost one-quarter were of Asian origin (O'Hare 1992).

Like aging, the process of ethnic restructuring is not even across space. Spatial differences are strongly related to geographic patterns of immigration: the vast majority of immigrants enter the United States through a small number of "gateway" cities and states (Frey 1995a; Wright, Ellis, and Reibel 1997). This has two significant implications for subsequent internal migration flows. First, immigrants often undertake a secondary move shortly after entering the United States (see chapter 12 in this volume). A highly influential factor in this secondary move is the location of preexisting concentrations of the ethnic minority group to which the immigrant belongs (Bartel 1989), thereby creating ethnically and geographically "channelized" migration streams (see chapter 11 in this volume). Second, the internal migration patterns of native-born Americans appear to be associated with immigration patterns. Studies consistently show that the cities and states receiving high numbers of immigrants experienced a net out-migration of low-skilled, native-born white residents (Filer 1992; Frey 1995b). This trend has been variously attributed to substitution in the labor market (Filer 1992; Borjas, Freeman, and Katz 1992), competition in housing markets (Frey 1995a), the social and psychological responses of natives to immigrants (Frey 1994), and the consequence of economic restructuring and the emergence of global cities (Wright, Ellis, and Reibel 1997).

Once again, a series of interesting questions arises. In the case of the age restructuring of the population, the question arises as to the relative role of migration versus vital processes (fertility and mortality) in the restructuring of a region's age composition. How will the interplay among regional trends in migration, fertility, and age composition today shape the geography of aging in the coming decades? In the case of ethnic restructuring, the central debate addresses whether migration is contributing to the assimilation of ethnic minorities or is further polarizing the geography of ethnicity. Answering this question requires a close examination of the links among immigration, internal migration, and ethnic population distribution.

Methodological Frontiers in Migration Research

There is little doubt that the content, outlook, and scale of migration research over time have been influenced by the prevailing migration patterns and social and economic conditions. We have moved from the heroic narratives of westward migration in the early 1900s to the problematic perception of rural-to-urban migration in the 1950s to the focus on shorter-distance city-to-suburb movement in the 1960s. Today, migration scholars are devoting increasing attention to the social and economic impacts of elderly migration and U.S. immigration (Long and Nucci 1997).

Whereas the prevailing social trends may define the substantive questions asked by migration scholars, it is the availability of data that has greatly influenced the empirical work. In this regard, 1940 was a defining year for migration research because, for the first time, the U.S. Census included a question to measure the extent of mobility of the resident population and retained it in subsequent years. The 1940s also marked the initiation by the Census Bureau of the Current Population Survey, which solicited information on migration and mobility once a year. Consequently, migration data became available at regular intervals for geographically disaggregated areas. Since then we have seen a progressive growth in the availability of migration data through the Internal Revenue Service records, the Social Security Administration records, and the Census Bureau's Public Use Micro Samples. There has also been a rise in the availability of longitudinal datasets, such as the Panel Study on Income Dynamics and the Survey of Income and Program Participation, which allow new and exciting questions to be posed.

The growth of migration data has been accompanied by the refinement and broadening of analytical methods. The availability of standardized migration data has allowed the use of standard demographic techniques such as survival-rate methods to estimate and project interregional migration flows (Long and Nucci 1997). Increased data have also made it possible to test hypotheses about the causes and consequences of migration using inferential techniques such as regression analysis. The proliferation of longitudinal datasets in the past few decades has allowed hazard models to be used in migration studies. Paradoxically, the heightened use of quantitative analysis has brought about a greater awareness of the kinds of questions our statistical data and methods cannot address; this, in turn, has led to a growth in ethnographic and narrative analyses of migration.

Apart from the substantive questions regarding the relationship between migration and restructuring, therefore, several conceptual and methodological questions are worth posing. The first relates to the issue of scale: Are the linkages between restructuring and migration constant at all scales of analysis, or does the spatial resolution make a difference? In other words, do relationships at the national level necessarily hold at the state and regional levels? A second set of questions arises with respect to research methodology. The rapid growth of data availability and computing capabilities has expanded the resources and analytical methods available to migration scholars. At the same time, advances in the conceptualization of the migration process and its links to broader societal changes have drawn attention to alternative methods for migration research. These are vital to consider as we seek to refine our understanding of the relationship between migration and restructuring.

Scope and Organization of This Volume

This volume focuses on the interactions between migration (both internal and external), economic restructuring (specifically shifts in the composition of employment and production, and shifts in government programs and spending), and demographic restructuring (specifically changes in the population age structure and changes in the ethnic makeup of the population). The conceptual framework for this book is outlined in Figure 1.1, which highlights several key points. First, the relationship between migration and restructuring is recursive: economic and demographic restructuring influences migration, and vice versa. Second, the links between the restructuring processes and migration are mediated by a spatial "filter." Specific changes associated with economic and demographic restructuring are spatially uneven in their occurrence, which, in

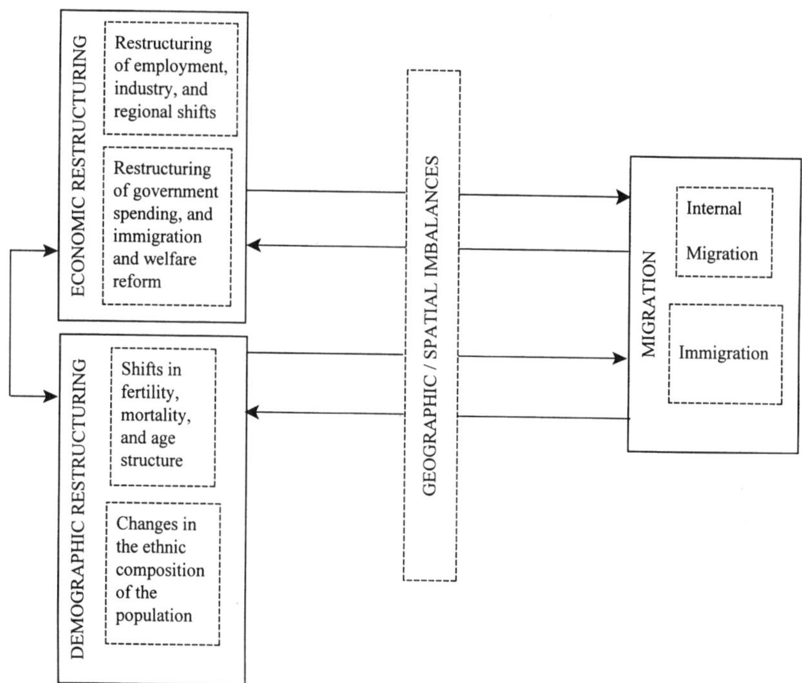

Figure 1.1 Conceptual Linkages among Economic Restructuring, Demographic Restructuring, and Migration

turn, trigger specific migration flows. At the same time, migration flows modify the economic and demographic characteristics of regions in ways that either accelerate or retard the restructuring under way. Finally, several other sets of linkages exist but fall outside the scope of this book. These include connections among the various economic restructuring processes, amongst the various demographic restructuring processes, and between economic and demographic restructuring.

The chapters in this book have been carefully selected to be integral to the theme. Individually, the chapters are carefully crafted studies that address contemporary issues and debates in migration studies. Taken together, however, they shed light on various aspects of the complex links between migration and restructuring and set the conceptual context for future studies. They incorporate an explicit geographic perspective in that the regional and local implications of larger-scale economic and demographic restructuring are explored. They provide a balanced coverage of the dynamics of U.S. internal migration and immigration.

No volume is capable of dealing comprehensively with all possible aspects of the restructuring-migration relationship. Instead, we present a range of studies that explore different aspects of the relationship at various spatial scales and geographic contexts to highlight the types of substantive and methodological issues that underlie the migration-restructuring linkage.

References

Bartel, Ann. 1989. "Where Do the New U.S. Immigrants Live?" *Journal of Labor Economics* 7: 371–391.

Biggar, Janet. 1979. "The Sunning of America: Migration to the Sunbelt." *Population Bulletin* 34, 1. Washington, D.C.: Population Reference Bureau.

Bluestone, Barry, and Bennett Harrison. 1982. *The Deindustrialization of America*. New York: Basic Books.

Borjas, George, Richard Freeman, and Lawrence F. Katz. 1992. "On the Labor Market Effects of Immigration and Trade." In George J. Borjas and R. B. Freeman (eds.), *Immigration and the Work Force: Economic Consequences for the United States and Source Areas*. Chicago: University of Chicago Press.

Bouvier, Leon F., and Carol J. De Vita. 1991. "The Baby Boom-Entering Midlife." *Population Bulletin* 46, 3. Washington, D.C.: Population Reference Bureau.

Cadwallader, Martin. 1996. *Urban Geography*. Upper Saddle River, N.J.: Prentice-Hall.

Castells, Manuel. 1989. *The Informational City*. Oxford: Basil Blackwell.

Chenery, Hollis, and Moises Syrquin. 1975. *Patterns of Development, 1950–1970*. New York: Oxford University Press.

Clark, Colin. 1957. *The Conditions of Economic Progress*, 3rd ed. London: Macmillan.

Clark, Gordon. 1982. "Volatility in the Geographical Structure of Short-Run U.S. Interstate Migration." *Environment and Planning A* 14: 145–167.

———. 1993. "Costs and Prices, Corporate Competitive Strategies and Regions." *Environment and Planning* 25: 5–26.

del Pinal, Jorge, and Audrey Singer. 1997. "Generations of Diversity: Latinos in the United States." *Population Bulletin* 52, 3. Washington, D.C.: The Population Reference Bureau.

Easterlin, Richard A. 1968. *Population, Labor Force and Long Swings in Economic Growth*. New York: Columbia University Press.

Filer, Randall. 1992. "The Effect of Immigrant Arrivals on Migratory Patterns of Native Workers." In George J. Borjas and R. B. Freeman (eds.), *Immigration and the Work Force: Economic Consequences for the United States and Source Areas*. Chicago: University of Chicago Press.

Frey, William H. 1994. "The New White Flight." *American Demographics* (April): 40–48.

———. 1995a. "Immigration and Internal Migration 'Flight': A California Case Study." *Population and Environment* 16, 4: 353–375.

———. 1995b. "Immigration Impacts on Internal Migration of the Poor: 1990 Census Evidence for U.S. States." *International Journal of Population Geography* 1: 51–67.

Graham, Julie, Katherine Gibson, Ronald Hovarth, and Don Shakow. 1988. "Restructuring in U.S. Manufacturing: The Decline of Monopoly Capitalism." *Annals of the Association of American Geographers* 78: 473–490.

Hall, Peter. 1988. *Cities of Tomorrow*. New York: Basil Blackwell.

Harrison, Bennett, and Barry Bluestone. 1988. *The Great U-Turn*. New York: Basic Books.

Hughes, Mark A. 1995. "A Mobility Strategy for Improving Opportunity." *Housing Policy Debate* 6, 1: 271–297.

Jackson, J. H. 1990. *Restructuring the GATT System*. London: Royal Institute of International Affairs.

Johnson, Daniel, and Rex Campbell. 1981. *Black Migration in America: A Social Demographic History*. Durham, N.C.: Duke University Press.

Knox, Paul. 1994. *Urbanization*. Englewood Cliffs, N.J.: Prentice-Hall.

Lawrence, Robert Z. 1984. *Can America Compete?* Washington, D.C.: Brookings Institute.

Long, Larry, and Alfred Nucci. 1997. "Socioeconomic Trends and the Next Stages of Migration Research." Paper presented at the Migration and Restructuring: Toward the Next Millenium Conference, Athens, Georgia, May.

Longcore, Travis R., and Peter W. Rees. 1996. "Information Technology and Downtown Restructuring: The Case of New York City's Financial District." *Urban Geography* 17: 354–372.

Massey, Doreen, and Richard Meegan. 1982. *The Anatomy of Job Loss*. London: Methuen.

Milne, William J. 1993. "Macroeconomic Influences on Migration." *Regional Studies* 27: 365–373.

O'Hare, William P. 1992. "America's Minorities—The Demographics of Diversity." *Population Bulletin* 47, 4. Washington, D.C.: Population Reference Bureau.

Pandit, Kavita. 1997. "Cohort and Period Effects in U.S. Migration: How Demographic and Economic Cycles Influence the Migration Schedule." *Annals of the Association of American Geographers* 87, 3: 439–450.

Pinch, S. P. 1989. "The Restructuring Thesis and the Study of Public Services." *Environment and Planning A* 21: 905–926.

Plane, David A. 1984. "A Systemic Demographic Efficiency Analysis of U.S. Interstate Population Exchange." *Economic Geography* 60, 4: 294–312.

———. 1989. "Population Migration and Economic Restructuring in the United States." *International Regional Science Review* 12: 263–280.

———. 1992. "Age-Composition Change and the Geographical Dynamics of Interregional Migration in the U.S." *Annals of the Association of American Geographers* 82: 64–85.

Population Reference Bureau. 1998. *World Population Data Sheet*. Washington D.C.: Population Reference Bureau.

Rogers, Andrei, R. Raquillet, and L. J. Castro. 1978. "Model Migration Schedules and Their Applications." *Environment and Planning A* 10: 475–502.

Rogerson, Peter A. 1987. "Changes in U.S. National Mobility Levels." *Professional Geographer* 39: 344–351.

———. 1996. "Geographic Perspectives on Elderly Population Growth." *Growth and Change* 27: 75–95.

Sassen, Saskia. 1991. *The Global City: New York, London, Tokyo*. Princeton: Princeton University Press.

———. 1994. *Cities in a World Economy*. Thousand Oaks, Calif.: Pine Forge Press.

Soldo, Beth J., and Emily M. Agree. 1988. "America's Elderly." *Population Bulletin* 43, 3. Washington, D.C.: Population Reference Bureau.

Taylor, Ronald L. (ed.). 1994. *Minority Families in the United States*. Englewood Cliffs, N.J.: Prentice-Hall.

Webber, Michael, Gordon Clark, John McKay, and Geoff Missen. 1992. *Industrial Restructuring: Definition*. Working Paper 92–2, Universities of Monash and Melbourne Joint Project on Comparative Australian-Asian Development.

Wilson, Franklin D. 1983. "Cohort Size Effects and Migration." *International Migration Review* 17: 485–504.

Wilson, William J. 1987. *The Truly Disadvantaged: The Inner City, the Underclass, and Public Policy*. Chicago: University of Chicago Press.

Winckler, V. 1990. "Restructuring the Civil Service: Reorganization and Relocation, 1962–1985." *International Journal of Urban and Regional Research* 14: 135–157.

Wright, Richard, Mark Ellis, and Michael Reibel. 1997. "The Linkage between Immigration and Internal Migration in Large Metropolitan Areas in the United States." *Economic Geography* 73, 2: 234–254.

SECTION I

MIGRATION AND ECONOMIC RESTRUCTURING

The chapters in this section, each with a different geographic focus, address the explicit connections between migration and economic restructuring. Of prime importance is the fact that these processes have very distinct regional and local articulation. Figure A summarizes how the individual contributions fit into the general scheme of the book as presented in the introduction.

The chapter by Cushing examines the role of migration and economic well-being in Appalachia, a region persistently suffering from deindustrialization, population out-migration, and long-term regional stagnation. Cushing shows that whereas migration spurs economic growth in some settings, it contributes to long-term economic decline in others. His focus on persistent poverty brings to the fore the importance of related issues of welfare policy, economic renewal, and population movement.

In contrast, Brown, Lobao, and Digiacinto examine the local influences and outcomes of economic restructuring in a well-established industrial region, the Ohio River Valley. Their chapter reveals striking geographic variations in the migration effects of economic restructuring even in an old manufacturing region. They emphasize the recursive relationship between restructured economies and population change, stressing the responsive, adaptive nature of local economies to the larger economic changes.

Morrill and Falit-Baiamonte explore the connections between socioeconomic structure and mobility at the metropolitan scale, using Atlanta and Minneapolis as case studies. The authors examine issues of income polarization by assessing the impact of population redistribution processes on the concentration of poverty in metropolitan areas. The issues of income inequality and polarization are of national concern, yet they have significant local influences and outcomes.

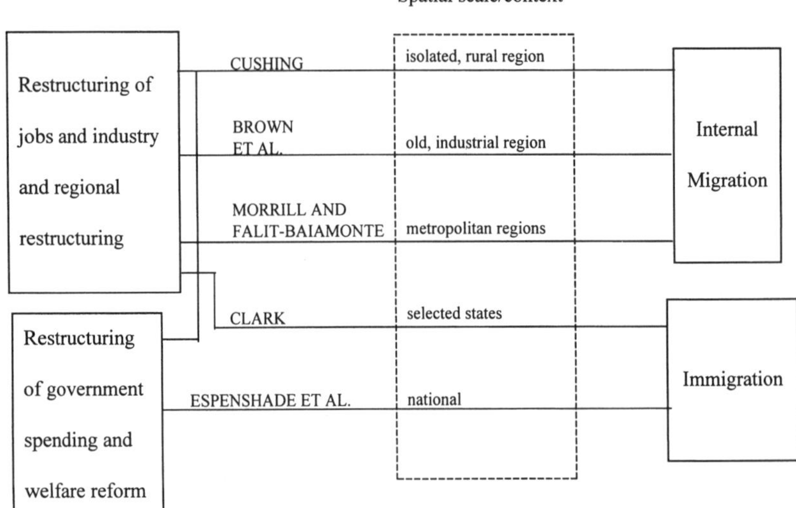

Figure A Economic Restructuring and Migration: Location of Individual Contributions

Public policy at the national level has also witnessed fundamental changes, but implementation of national public policies has specific and varied regional and local outcomes. Clark contrasts the opportunity paths of more recent waves of immigrants relative to previous waves as a result of the restructuring of both the economy and immigrant population flows. He finds wide disparities in the skill and poverty levels of natives and immigrants at the state level. He further indicates that research at the national level masks important variations in the regional impacts of these processes.

Espenshade, Baraka, and Huber discuss the impacts of the restructuring of welfare and immigration policy on the future of immigration and examine some unintended consequences of changes in national policy, specifically the 1996 Welfare Reform Act and Immigration Reform Act. The authors argue that the combined effects of these two reform measures on people's incentives to migrate to the United States will be the opposite of what is intended. They project reduced levels of legal immigration, a higher average level of skill and income among future legal immigrant streams, and at the same time expanded incentives for illegal immigration. These projections have profound implications for traditional port-of-entry cities as well as border communities and may precipitate a new era of immigration.

2

Migration and Persistent Poverty in Rural America

Brian Cushing

Population migration constitutes an integral part of economic growth and change. Many households use migration as the primary means for improving economic well-being. For regions and the nation, migration provides a potentially effective way of fighting poverty and increasing economic growth. Since resources tend to move toward areas perceived to have better economic opportunities, labor migrates from areas with surplus labor to those with relatively high labor demand. For many regions, migration spurs economic restructuring and regeneration over time. Eventually, periods of decline lead to renewed economic growth, as predicted by neoclassical economic theory.

This process of factor mobility spurring renewal, however, breaks down in some cases. Instead of spurring renewal, factor mobility contributes to long-term regional stagnation and decline, that is, it becomes part of the problem instead of a solution. The mobile population leaves the region along with the jobs. The declining employment base inadequately supports the region's remaining, predominantly immobile population, which, in turn, lacks the skills needed to attract new employment. In short, the remaining people cannot reasonably get to the jobs, and the jobs will not come to the people.

This scenario resembles a classic case of urban spatial mismatch with results on poverty concentration similar to those discussed by Morrill and Falit-Baiamonte in chapter 4 (this volume). It applies equally, however, to many nonmetropolitan regions in the United States. The process of regeneration and renewal continually unfolds even in large central cities with serious economic problems, although pockets of long-term poverty remain. Economic stability, not to mention regeneration and renewal, eludes many rural areas even after several decades of economic decline and out-migration.

Because metropolitan areas house most people and economic activity in the United States, research on population migration and its relationship to phenomena such as economic growth and poverty has focused on metropolitan areas, at least since the mid-1960s. Those studies that have looked at nonmetropolitan areas have mainly pointed out the workings of marginal productivity theory in rural areas as legions of displaced farmworkers relocated to urban industrial America. The "nonmetropolitan-metropolitan migration turnaround" in the mid-1970s revived interest in nonmetropolitan areas, but this related more to the metropolitan fringe than to truly rural America. Unfortunately, statistical data typically group counties into central city, suburban, and nonmetropolitan. This masks the important distinction between nonmetropolitan and rural, as well as the different types of rural areas. The concentration of research and policy on metropolitan areas and the aggregation of all other counties into nonmetropolitan have obscured the serious economic problems of many rural areas, such as extraordinarily high poverty. The Task Force on Persistent Rural Poverty (1993) stated that "rural poverty is 'out of sight, out of mind' from a policy perspective" (p. 40).

Recently, several studies have brought the economic problems of declining rural areas to the forefront, especially the phenomenon of persistent rural poverty.[1] This coincides with a growing literature on the causes and effects of out-migration from declining rural areas.[2] Beaulieu (1988), Brown and Warner (1991), and Evensky (1991) focused on those who remained in declining nonmetropolitan areas, an approach equally important for understanding the causes and effects of long-term decline. Chapter 14 in this volume illustrates how "seemingly modest population change in terms of size and composition can have far-reaching consequences" for rural areas.

This chapter presents a case study of a six-county region in southern West Virginia, a part of Central Appalachia. Historically, the economy of this small, isolated region has depended on resource extraction, making it highly susceptible to the economic implosion and persistently high poverty described earlier (Brown and Warner 1991; Task Force on Persistent Rural Poverty 1993). This region exemplifies the diversity of experiences regarding nonmetropolitan growth and change. The region is also more isolated than the declining rural Ohio River Valley counties examined in chapter 3 in this volume. Learning more about population mobility in this kind of region is a precondition for understanding some of the severest, most chronic poverty in the nation. It also illustrates the need for flexibility in designing policies, such as recent welfare reform initiatives, to deal with scenarios that defy the norm and often elude the comprehension of most people, including policymakers and politicians.

The chapter begins with a brief overview of the region, focusing particularly on employment and population change since the mid-1970s. Following this I analyze the patterns of in- and out-migration for the region during the 1985–1990 period and the demographic changes in the region between 1980 and 1990. The discussion then focuses on the characteristics of the region's poverty population, particularly the working-age poor. I end by considering implications for the future prospects of the region, as well as for the success of recent welfare reform initiatives.

Economic Distress in Central Appalachia

In 1964 the President's Appalachian Regional Commission (PARC) concluded, "'real' Appalachian standards of living are below national norms" (PARC 1964: 10). In the three and a half decades since the PARC report, much of Appalachia has made significant gains relative to the rest of the United States with respect to income, poverty, and housing quality. Central Appalachia, particularly its nonmetropolitan portion, however, "is the one part of Appalachia where living standards and poverty rates are at levels that we assumed were features of the past. With respect to the standard of living, this part of Appalachia may still be 'a region apart'" (Cushing and Rogers 1996: 35).

Cushing and Rogers (1996: 33) suggested that population migration might be both cause and effect of the persistently high rates of poverty in Central Appalachia: "Those most likely to migrate out of declining and distressed areas, however, are the young, the well-educated, and the affluent individuals. In cases of severe distress and decline, those that remain will disproportionally be those who are immobile, and therefore stuck in poverty with little choice but to muddle through. High psychic costs and unaffordable financial costs of moving, lack of information about alternatives, obsolescence of job skills (structural unemployment), and often age substantially reduce mobility for these individuals."

This type of situation has important implications for the new welfare system, which implicitly assumes that in the absence of the welfare crutch individuals will either find employment locally or relocate to secure an appropriate job. Some areas, however, lack employment opportunities and have a population that cannot feasibly opt to relocate. "Two years and you are off" and similar welfare programs that limit the amount of time a person receives public assistance are not workable in such areas, even with allowances for a small proportion of long-term recipients among the welfare caseload.

In the case of Central Appalachia, Cushing and Rogers (1996: 34) noted the poor prospects for returning many of the region's displaced workers to the labor force and suggest restructuring public policy accordingly: "Public policy is not likely to yield much additional adjustment in some impoverished counties that have been in decline and have suffered from economic distress for at least a decade, in some cases a few decades. In these cases, provision of adequate public welfare support, especially to the elderly and the long-term unemployed, may be the only realistic policy option." The southern portion of West Virginia, analyzed in the next section, furnishes a classic example of economic distress in Central Appalachia.

Economic Change in Southern West Virginia

This study focuses on the six-county region of southern West Virginia that includes McDowell, Mercer, Monroe, Raleigh, Summers, and Wyoming Counties. This area is an Appalachian Regional Commission (ARC) local development district and is part of the Central Appalachia subregion of Appalachia, as defined by the ARC. It also constitutes a Public Use Microdata Area (PUMA) for the 1 percent Public Use Microdata Sample from the 1990 Census of Population and Housing, which facilitates the migration analysis later in this chapter. As of July 1, 1994, the area had an estimated population of 231,900, comparable to a medium-sized metropolitan area.

Even within nonmetropolitan Central Appalachia, economic growth varies significantly. Although most counties near metropolitan areas, especially those in Tennessee and central Kentucky, are growing, the more isolated coal counties of southern West Virginia and eastern Kentucky continue to stagnate. The southern West Virginia region encompasses the majority of the isolated southern West Virginia coal counties. Raleigh County touches on the southern tip of Kanawha County, the dominant county of the Charleston, WV MSA (Metropolitan Statistical Area), but is distant from the majority of the metropolitan population.[3]

The southern West Virginia region has experienced dramatic economic change during the past two and a half decades, particularly McDowell County (Table 2.1). Driven by a surge in the coal mining industry in the aftermath of the 1973 OPEC oil embargo, southern West Virginia flourished during the mid-1970s, with employment peaking in 1977. Major labor strikes in the coal mining industry and the introduction of long-wall mining ended the growth prematurely, but the regional economy remained fairly stable through the end of the decade. After 1980 the bottom dropped out. Whereas the national economy experienced a deep recession in the early 1980s, the southern West Virginia economy began a long-term economic decline. Employment declined by 10 percent between 1980 and 1983. The decline continued through the decade, with employment bottoming out in 1989 at a level 18 percent below its 1977 peak. By 1994 total employment had recovered to its highest level since 1985 but was still 12 percent below its 1977 peak.

The decline of mining employment, the traditional economic base of the region, during this time was stunning. Employment declined by 19 percent between 1976 and 1980 and by another 35 percent by 1983. With the rapid switch to long-wall mining, the decline in mining employment continued through the

Table 2.1 Trends in the Southern West Virginia Economy, 1973–1994

	Region				McDowell County			
	Population (thousands)	Total Employment	Mining Employment	Unemployment Rate (%)	Populations (thousands)	Total Employment	Mining Employment	Unemployment Rate (%)
1950	340.0	—	—	—	98.9	—	—	—
1960	279.5	—	—	—	71.4	—	—	—
1970	238.5	—	—	—	50.7	—	—	—
1973	251.4	81,659	17,314	—	50.3	14,866	7,450	—
1974	253.9	83,058	18,050	—	50.5	14,841	7,562	—
1975	259.3	87,769	20,224	—	51.2	16,127	8,451	—
1976	268.1	92,875	22,788	—	52.0	17,127	9,520	—
1977	274.2	94,230	22,374	—	52.2	16,964	9,240	—
1978	276.4	93,851	20,337	—	51.8	15,660	7,941	—
1979	277.5	93,686	18,913	—	51.2	15,811	7,858	—
1980	275.5	93,416	18,477	10.4	49.7	15,801	7,601	13.0
1981	273.9	89,810	15,806	11.6	48.9	14,084	6,236	14.7
1982	272.9	89,176	15,697	15.9	48.2	13,301	5,874	27.2
1983	270.7	83,906	11,925	22.7	47.6	11,788	4,555	37.1
1984	265.9	84,879	11,775	18.2	46.0	11,561	4,408	28.4
1985	261.7	83,829	10,734	15.0	44.6	11,311	4,323	23.0
1986	257.2	81,181	9,202	15.1	43.2	10,549	3,764	24.6
1987	249.1	78,567	7,140	15.2	41.0	8,018	1,452	32.8
1988	241.6	77,521	6,263	12.9	38.6	7,835	1,411	23.2
1989	236.1	77,311	5,975	10.7	36.6	7,782	1,630	17.4
1990	232.2	78,818	6,076	9.4	35.0	7,919	1,682	13.0
1991	231.6	79,625	5,568	11.4	34.4	7,690	1,434	18.0
1992	232.0	80,139	5,143	12.4	34.0	7,853	1,413	16.1
1993	232.1	81,075	4,469	12.2	33.6	7,765	1,356	15.0
1994	231.9	83,366	4,198	9.8	33.1	7,772	1,094	14.0

Sources: Regional Economic Information System, U.S. Bureau of Economic Analysis except 1950, 1960, and 1970 populations, which are from the *Census of Population,* 1950, 1960, and 1970, respectively; West Virginia Department of Employment, Bureau of Employment Programs.

first half of the 1990s. By 1994 mining employment had declined by 82 percent from its 1976 peak. In terms of its relative importance in the region, it declined from 25 percent of total employment in 1976 to just 5 percent in 1994. In the case of McDowell County, economic collapse is a more fitting term than economic decline, as illustrated in Table 2.1. Total employment in 1994 stood 55 percent below and mining employment 89 percent below their 1976 peaks.

Unemployment data are just as startling for the early 1980s.[4] The unemployment rate increased from 10.4 percent to 22.7 percent between 1980 and 1983, more than double the peak national unemployment rate of 9.7 percent. The unemployment rate remained above 10 percent until 1990 and then increased substantially during the early 1990s before declining to 9.8 percent in 1994. The rapid decline in the unemployment rate by 1990 and its rise and fall by 1994 suggest some long-term population adjustment to the economic change. Population estimates imply substantial net out-migration from the region. Population declined from a peak of 278,000 in 1979 to 232,000 by 1990, a drop of 17 percent. It has remained stable since then. This percentage decline in population parallels the percentage decline in employment. In McDowell County, unemployment increased from 13 percent in 1980 to 37 percent in 1983 and remained above 20 percent until 1989. It declined to 13 percent in 1990 before increasing sharply and then falling again to 14 percent in 1994. In the meantime, population fell continuously from a high of 52,000 in 1977 to 33,000 in 1994, a drop of 37 percent. Population declined by about one-third less than the percentage decline in employment for the county, some indication of an incomplete population adjustment to the drastic economic changes.

The analysis that follows considers the population adjustment in more detail. I first discuss migration for the region during the 1985–1990 period and the demographic changes resulting from migration during the decade. The migration period coincided with a period of stagnation in the regional economy and closely followed the sharp economic decline of the early 1980s, making it a prime period to observe population adjustment in an economically distressed area.

Population Migration and Demographic Change

During the 1985–1990 period, southern West Virginia experienced net out-migration of 20,000 persons, a net loss of 8.3 percent relative to the 1985 base population of 243,000 (Table 2.2).[5,6] The region had an out-migration rate of 15.2 percent and an in-migration rate of just 7.0 percent. Virginia and the remainder of West Virginia were the primary origins for in-migrants; they accounted for 20 percent and 29 percent of in-migrants, respectively. Most other in-migrants came from Ohio (10 percent), North Carolina (8 percent), Pennsylvania (6 percent), Missouri (5 percent), and Kentucky (4 percent). North Carolina (29 percent) and Virginia (27 percent) dominated the destination

Table 2.2 Migration and Demographic Change by Age

A. Migration, 1985–1990

	Nonmovers		In-Migrants		Out-Migrants		Net Migration		Migration Rates (%)		
Age	Number	Percent	Number	Percent	Number	Percent	Number	Percent	In Rate	Out Rate	Net Rate
5–9	53,550	25.9	3,258	19.2	9,241	24.9	−5,983	29.7	5.2	14.7	−9.5
20–24	11,430	5.5	2,466	14.5	8,046	21.7	−5,580	27.7	12.7	41.3	−28.7
25–29	10,656	5.2	2,520	14.8	5,416	14.6	−2,896	14.4	15.7	33.7	−18.0
30–34	14,310	6.9	2,124	12.5	5,066	13.7	−2,942	14.6	11.0	26.1	−15.2
35–44	32,256	15.6	2,448	14.4	4,403	11.9	−1,955	9.7	6.7	12.0	−5.3
45–54	25,236	12.2	1,782	10.5	2,694	7.3	−912	4.5	6.4	9.6	−3.3
55–64	24,336	11.8	612	3.6	945	2.5	−333	1.7	2.4	3.7	−1.3
65 and over	34,614	16.8	1,764	10.4	1,286	3.5	478	−2.4	4.9	3.6	1.3
Total	206,388	99.9	16,974	99.9	37,097	100.1	−20,123	100	7.0	15.2	−8.3

Note: Migration rates are relative to the 1985 base population (nonmovers + out-migrants)

B. Age Distribution, 1980–1990

	Region				McDowell County				United States			
	1980		1990		1980		1990		1980		1990	
Age	Number	Percent	Number	Percent	Number	Percent	Number	Percent	Number	Percent	Number	Percent
0–19	93,848	34.1	67,739	29.1	18,932	37.9	11,247	31.9	72,458,463	32.0	71,321,886	29.9
20–34	67,512	24.5	45,947	19.8	11,764	23.6	6,896	19.6	58,400,543	25.8	62,196,244	26.1
35–49	40,097	14.6	48,894	21.0	6,568	13.2	6,917	19.6	36,724,465	16.2	51,451,476	21.6
50–64	42,154	15.3	34,558	14.9	7,484	15.0	4,966	14.1	33,412,907	14.7	32,498,436	13.6
65 and over	31,792	11.5	35,494	15.3	5,151	10.3	5,207	14.8	25,549,427	11.3	21,241,831	8.9
Total	275,403	100.0	232,632	100.0	49,899	100.0	35,233	100.0	226,545,805	100.0	238,709,873	100.0

choices for out-migrants, with large numbers also going to the remainder of West Virginia (13 percent), Florida (7 percent), Ohio (4 percent), Tennessee (3 percent), and Maryland (3 percent). The migration exchange with North Carolina and Virginia accounted for 79 percent of the region's net out-migration, with Florida accounting for another 10 percent.

Native West Virginians dominated the population of the southern West Virginia region. Natives comprised 82 percent of the 1985 base population, 85 percent of nonmovers, and 48 percent of in-migrants. The high proportion of natives among in-migrants suggests the possible importance of return migration. Unfortunately, the data do not permit identification of place of birth at the substate level.

Migration by Age

Migration significantly depleted the population under age 35 (Table 2.2). The highest rates of net out-migration were for those aged 20–24 (29 percent), 25–29 (18 percent), and 30–34 (15 percent). All three of these typically mobile age groups experienced rates of out-migration exceeding 25 percent, including a rate of 41 percent for the 20–24 age group.[7] The region also suffered a disproportionate net loss of children, not surprising given the net out-migration of the 20–34 age group. The net loss of those over age 34 was fairly small, especially in light of the extraordinary changes in employment during the 1980s. As expected, migration patterns differed for the elderly, with net in-migration of those aged 65 and older. In total, the age pattern of migration for southern West Virginia resembles that described by Fuguitt and Heaton (1995) for nonmetropolitan agricultural communities. Compared with this agricultural prototype, however, southern West Virginia experienced exaggerated net out-migration for those under age 34 and a relatively low net loss of those over 45 years of age.

The changing age distribution of the region's population during the decade corresponded with the patterns of migration and resulted in a much older age distribution of the population. The percentage of the population below age 35 declined from 59 percent in 1980 to 49 percent in 1990 (Table 2.2). The other striking feature was the increase not only in the proportion but also in the absolute number of persons in the 35–49 and 65 years and over age groups. This contrasted sharply with the significant decline in the region's total population.[8] The much lower proportion of young working-age individuals (20–34 years old) and the higher proportion of elderly individuals (65 and over) differed markedly from the U.S. population, which shifted toward the middle of the age distribution. Loss of young workers poses a serious obstacle to future economic growth.

Migration by Educational Attainment

As with age, migration by educational attainment (for those aged 25 and over) has hampered southern West Virginia's ability to attain economic stability and self-sufficiency. Net out-migration increased with educational attainment, includ-

Table 2.3 Migration and Demographic Change by Educational Attainment for Those Aged 25 and Over

A. Migration, 1985–1990

	Nonmovers		In-Migrants		Out-Migrants		Net Migration		Migration Rates (%)		
Education	Number	Percent	Number	Percent	Number	Percent	Number	Percent	In Rate	Out Rate	Net Rate
0–8 years	29,772	21.1	1,368	12.2	1,305	6.6	63	−0.7	4.4	4.2	0.2
9–12 years	30,474	21.6	2,448	21.8	3,161	16.0	−713	8.3	7.3	9.4	−2.1
H.S. diploma	64,602	45.7	5,958	53.0	10,336	52.2	−4,378	51.1	8.0	13.8	−5.8
Assoc. degree	5,022	3.6	630	5.6	1,398	7.1	−768	9.0	9.8	21.8	−12.0
College degree	11,538	8.2	846	7.5	3,610	18.2	−2,764	32.3	5.6	23.8	−18.2
Total	141,408	100.2	11,250	100.1	19,810	100.1	−8,560	100.0	7.0	12.3	−5.3

Note: Migration rates are relative to the 1985 base population (nonmovers+out-migrants).

B. Educational Attainment, 1980–1990

	Region				McDowell County				United States			
	1980		1990		1980		1990		1980		1990	
Education	Number	Percent	Number	Percent	Number	Percent	Number	Percent	Number	Percent	Number	Percent
0–8 years	50,948	32.2	32,132	21.2	11,322	42.5	7,048	31.8	24,257,683	18.3	16,502,211	10.4
Some high school but no degree	30,229	19.1	30,772	20.3	5,767	21.6	5,718	25.8	20,277,514	15.3	22,841,507	14.4
H.S. diploma	64,527	40.7	74,668	49.3	8,195	30.7	8,354	37.7	66,742,010	50.2	87,214,465	54.9
Bachelor's degree	12,698	8.0	13,998	9.2	1,381	5.2	1,015	4.6	21,558,480	16.2	32,310,253	20.3
Total	158,402	100.0	151,570	100.0	26,665	100.0	22,135	100.0	132,835,687	100.0	158,868,436	100.0

ing a net loss of 18 percent of the population with a college degree (Table 2.3). Gross out-migration followed the expected pattern of increasing mobility with educational level, including high rates of out-migration for the highly educated. Nearly one-quarter of those with a college degree left the region during the five-year period. This pattern of increasing mobility did not hold for in-migration. The in-migration rate of 5.6 percent for those with a college degree lagged all except those with an eighth-grade education or less (4.4 percent). Migration appears to have both lowered the average educational level of the population and significantly reduced the number of college-educated individuals residing in the region.

Given these migration patterns, some changes in educational attainment of the population between 1980 and 1990 may be surprising.[9] The percentage of the population with eight or fewer years of education decreased substantially (from 32 to 21 percent), the percentage with at least a high school degree increased sharply (from 49 to 59 percent), and the percentage with a bachelor's degree increased modestly (from 8 to 9 percent) (Table 2.3). These changes reflect an ongoing transition toward a population raised during the modern era of compulsory basic education. The region still lagged well behind the United States as a whole, however, in which three-quarters of the population had at least a high school degree in 1990 and 20 percent had a bachelor's degree. For McDowell County, the change in the percentage of college degrees differed from that in the rest of the region. In 1990 nearly one-third of its population had eight or fewer years of schooling, just 42 percent had at least a high school degree, and less than 5 percent had a bachelor's degree. Given the loss of jobs requiring little formal education, such as in the extraction industries, the continued low educational attainment of the region's adult population places the region and its people at a great disadvantage in competing for jobs.

Migration by Labor Force Attachment

Labor force status data for 1990 must be interpreted carefully. Given migrants' age and educational composition and southern West Virginia's economic decline, the substantial net out-migration of individuals employed at the end of the migration period is not surprising (Table 2.4). Comparing the status of in-migrants and nonmovers, that is, those who resided in the region at the beginning and the end of the five-year period, reveals more. Just 43 percent of working-age in-migrants were employed in 1990, compared with 52 percent of nonmovers. Forty-eight percent of in-migrants were not in the labor force, with another 9 percent unemployed. The latter implies an unemployment rate for in-migrants equal to 17 percent. Only half of the working-age in-migrants had worked during the first quarter of 1990 (not shown in tables). One-third of working-age in-migrants had worked previously but not in more than a year (since 1988). More than 5 percent had never been employed. As a whole, in-migrants to the region had weak labor market attachment.

A. Migration, 1985–1990

Labor Status	Nonmovers		In-Migrants		Out-Migrants		Net Migration		Migration Rates (%)		
	Number	Percent	Number	Percent	Number	Percent	Number	Percent	In Rate	Out Rate	Net Rate
Military	180	0.2	324	2.7	876	3.3	−552	2.7	30.7	83.0	−52.3
Civilian employed	61,488	52.0	4,806	40.2	19,502	73.4	−14,696	73.0	5.9	24.1	−18.1
Unemployed	5,706	4.8	1,062	8.9	949	3.6	113	−0.6	16.0	14.3	1.7
Not in Labor Force	50,850	43.0	5,760	48.2	5,243	19.7	517	−2.6	10.3	9.3	0.9
Total	118,224	100.0	11,952	100.0	26,570	100.0	−14,618	72.6	8.3	18.4	−10.1

Note: Migration rates are relative to the 1985 base population (nonmovers+out-migrants).

B. Labor Force Status, 1980–1990

Labor Status	Region				McDowell County				United States			
	1980		1990		1980		1990		1980		1990	
	Number	Percent	Number	Percent	Number	Percent	Number	Percent	Number	Percent	Number	Percent
Military	122	0.0	223	0.2	16	0.0	36	0.2	1,384,964	1.1	1,540,541	1.1
Civilian employed	77,255	51.6	67,425	52.1	11,216	43.5	6,976	37.2	87,617,950	68.1	106,242,733	72.6
Unemployed	7,531	5.0	8,606	6.6	1,413	5.5	1,849	9.9	5,461,984	4.2	6,399,217	4.4
Not in labor force	64,923	43.3	53,163	41.1	13,163	51.0	9,906	52.8	34,166,217	26.6	32,136,057	22.0
-institutional	(2,268)	(1.5)	(2,828)	(2.2)	(78)	(0.3)	(202)	(1.1)	(3,616,131)	(2.8)	(3,232,910)	(2.2)
Total	149,831	100.0	129,417	100.0	25,808	100.0	18,767	100.0	128,631,115	100.0	146,318,548	100.0
Unemployment Rate		8.9		11.3		11.2		20.9		5.8		5.6
Employed-population ratio		52.4		53.4		43.7		37.8		71.2		75.3

Despite southern West Virginia's substantial out-migration and its decline in the working-age population (aged 20 to 64) during the 1980s, more individuals were unemployed in 1990 than in 1980. This resulted in an increased unemployment rate, from 8.9 to 11.3 percent (Table 2.4).[10] The latter was twice the U.S. unemployment rate, which declined in 1990 compared with 1980. The employment-population ratio remained fairly constant at a very low level, rising slightly to 53.4 percent of the working-age population in 1990. This compared poorly with the U.S. rate of 75.3 percent, which had risen by more than 4 percentage points since 1980. The changes in McDowell County are stunning. Despite a 28 percent decline in the noninstitutional working-age population during the 1980s, the unemployment rate increased from 11 percent in 1980 to 21 percent in 1990, nearly four times the U.S. level. The employment-population ratio declined to 38 percent, about half the U.S. level.

Migration by Work Disability Status

The high level of work disabilities contributed to in-migrants' poor labor force attachment. Of working-age in-migrants, 38 percent had a work disability, including 17 percent with a total work disability, that is, one that completely prevented them from working (Table 2.5). These percentages matched those of nonmovers but exceeded the figures for out-migrants; only 8 percent of the latter had a work disability. The region experienced net in-migration of individuals with limited and total work disabilities and substantial net out-migration of those with no work disability. Once again, the exchange of population through migration worked to the disadvantage of the region's economy because of a net loss of able-bodied adults and a net gain of adults likely to require partial or complete support from the social welfare system.

Consistent with the migration data, southern West Virginia experienced an increase between 1980 and 1990 in the proportion of individuals with a work disability, from 15 to 18 percent of the noninstitutional working-age population (18 to 64 years old) (Table 2.5). The absolute and percentage increase in those with a disability preventing them from working was particularly important. McDowell County endured dramatic change, with the rate of work disabilities increasing to 25 percent; disabilities prevented nearly one in five individuals from working. Work disabilities are a severe problem for the region compared with the United States as a whole, where just 8 percent of the working-age population had a work disability in 1990, down slightly from the 1980 level. Disabilities prevented just 4 percent of the U.S. working-age population from holding a job.

Migration by Poverty Status

The poverty rate among in-migrants is astonishing, even given the disadvantageous age, educational, labor force, and disability profile of in-migrants and the poor condition of the regional economy. About half of the region's in-

Table 2.5 Migration and Demographic Change by Work Disability Status for Those Aged 20–64

A. Migration, 1985–1990

Disability	Nonmovers		In-Migrants		Out-Migrants		Net Migration		Migration Rates (%)		
Status	Number	Percent	Number	Percent	Number	Percent	Number	Percent	In Rate	Out Rate	Net Rate
Limited	25,146	21.3	2,556	21.4	1,690	6.4	866	−5.9	9.5	6.3	3.2
Cannot work	18,792	15.9	1,980	16.6	509	1.9	1,471	−10.1	10.3	2.6	7.6
None	74,286	62.8	7,416	62.0	24,371	91.7	−16,955	116.0	7.5	24.7	−17.2
Total	118,224	100.0	11,952	100.0	26,570	100.0	−14,618	100.0	8.3	18.4	−10.1

Note: Migration rates are relative to the 1985 base population (nonmovers+out-migrants).

B. Work Disability Status, 1980–1990

	Region				McDowell County				United States			
Disability	1980		1990		1980		1990		1980		1990	
Status	Number	Percent	Number	Percent	Number	Percent	Number	Percent	Number	Percent	Number	Percent
Limited	6,761	4.0	6,194	4.3	1,913	6.5	1,076	5.1	6,011,090	4.2	6,232,420	4.0
Cannot work	18,881	11.3	19,037	13.3	3,879	13.2	4,118	19.4	6,308,461	4.4	6,594,029	4.2
None	141,741	84.7	117,885	82.4	23,663	80.3	16,019	75.5	132,347,081	91.5	144,497,473	91.8
Total	167,383	100.0	143,116	100.0	29,455	100.0	21,213	100.0	144,666,632	100.0	157,323,922	100.0

migrants had incomes below the poverty level in 1989 (Table 2.6), double the poverty rate of nonmovers in a poor region and almost four times the national poverty rate. The poverty rate of in-migrants was high for all age groups, generally far above the rate for nonmovers and out-migrants. In-migrants aged 65 and older or 30 to 34 fared much better than other in-migrants, with poverty rates of only 24 percent and 33 percent, respectively. Poverty rates for the other in-migrant age groups ranged from 41 percent (55 to 64 years old) to 65 percent (20 to 24 years old). The poverty profile of in-migrants runs counter to the scenario of individuals moving to improve their economic well-being.

Consistent with migrant characteristics and demographic changes during the decade, poverty in southern West Virginia increased markedly between 1980 and 1990 (Table 2.6). Despite the decline in total population, the number of persons classified as poor increased by about 17 percent and the poverty rate jumped from 17 percent in 1980 to 24 percent in 1990, nearly twice the U.S. poverty rate.[11] The U.S. poverty rate increased by less than one percentage point between 1980 and 1990. In 1990 the region's poverty rate came close to the nation's only for those 65 years and over (Table 2.7). The poverty rate was nearly twice the national level for those under 35 years of age and was more than twice the national level for those aged 35 to 64. The latter group typically has high earning power and a low poverty rate.[12] McDowell County's situation was more severe initially and deteriorated more sharply. The poverty rate increased from 24 percent in 1980 to 38 percent in 1990. In 1990 half of the children, 43 percent of young workers, and nearly one-third of those of those aged 35 to 64 were poor.

Migration Summary

On the whole, migration to and from southern West Virginia during the 1985–1990 period did not favor future economic stability and growth in the region. The region's long and severe economic decline predestined the substantial net out-migration, generally a necessary component of regaining economic stability. The region's out-migrants, however, included a large proportion of those best suited to adjust to economic change and provide the base for the region's labor force—the young, the well educated, and those well connected to the labor force. In contrast, the region's in-migrants included a disproportionate number of older and less educated individuals. A large proportion of working-age in-migrants were not connected to the labor force, with work disabilities holding many back. The differing labor market success and poverty rates of in-migrants and out-migrants reveal the great imbalance in the region's migration exchange.

The migration exchange during the 1980s, along with the continued economic decline, has left southern West Virginia in a very disadvantageous, perhaps desperate, economic situation. Other than some improvement in the high

Table 2.6 Migration and Demographic Change by Poverty Status

A. Poverty Status of Movers and Nonmovers by Age, 1985–1990

	Nonmovers		In-Migrants		Out-Migrants	
Age	Number of Poor	Poverty Rate (%)	Number of Poor	Poverty Rate (%)	Number of Poor	Poverty Rate (%)
5–19	18,810	35.9	1,242	47.3	1,936	24.0
20–24	2,538	22.8	1,458	65.3	1,596	21.0
25–29	3,708	34.8	1,278	57.7	240	4.5
30–34	4,806	34.1	630	33.0	962	19.6
35–44	6,354	19.8	1,386	56.6	494	11.4
45–54	4,806	19.0	756	49.4	255	10.0
55–64	4,266	17.5	252	41.2	249	26.3
65 plus	5,958	18.0	324	24.0	126	12.3
Total	51,246	25.2	7,326	49.1	5,858	16.9

B. Poverty Status, 1980–1990

	1980		1990	
	Number	Percent	Number	Percent
Region				
Poor	46,914	17.3	54,974	24.1
Nonpoor	224,864	82.7	173,317	75.9
Total[1]	271,778	100.0	228,291	100.0
McDowell County				
Poor	11,715	23.5	13,195	37.7
Nonpoor	38,060	76.5	21,790	62.3
Total	49,775	100.0	34,985	100.0
United States				
Poor	27,392,580	12.4	31,742,864	13.1
Nonpoor	193,453,186	87.6	210,234,995	86.9
Total	220,845,766	100.0	241,977,859	100.0

Note: 1. Population for whom poverty status was determined.

school completion rate, the key characteristics of the population and the labor force were less amenable to economic recovery in 1990 than in 1980, when the region began its economic collapse. In 1990 the population had an older age distribution, a lower college completion rate, a greater rate of work disabilities, less attachment to the labor force, and much greater poverty than in 1980. Rather than help the region to restructure its economy and regain economic stability, population migration severely depleted its productive workforce. The

Table 2.7 Poverty Status by Age, 1990

Age	Number of Poor	Percentage of Poor	Poverty Rate (%)
Region			
0–17	20,184	36.7	33.6
18–34	14,214	25.9	27.8
35–44	6,630	12.1	18.6
45–64	8,450	15.4	17.9
65 plus	5,496	10.0	16.1
Total	54,974	100.0	24.1
McDowell County			
0–17	5,095	38.6	50.3
18–34	3,416	25.9	43.2
35–44	1,620	12.3	30.9
45–64	2,012	15.2	30.4
65 plus	1,052	8.0	20.7
Total	13,195	100.0	37.7
United States			
0–17	11,428,916	36.0	18.3
18–34	9,479,824	29.9	14.3
35–44	3,207,376	10.1	8.6
45–64	3,846,163	12.1	8.3
65 plus	3,780,585	11.9	12.8
Total	31,742,864	100.0	13.1

Source: U.S. Bureau of the Census, *1990 Census of Population and Housing,* STF-3 file.

remaining workforce will have difficulty attracting new employment, especially given the rural, relatively isolated nature of the region. Unemployment, including discouraged workers who drop out of the official labor force, will probably remain high into the next millennium.

Characteristics of the Poor, 1990

Besides the implications for the regional economy, the long-term economic decline and consequent demographic changes brought on by the extensive exchange of out-migrants and in-migrants raise important policy issues regarding southern West Virginia. One important issue, welfare reform, is designed to reduce welfare rolls by pushing more able-bodied adults into the labor force. New programs set short-term and lifetime limits on the length of time an individual may receive welfare benefits. The new welfare structure permits states to have a certain percentage of long-term welfare cases, with this allowance decreasing over time. Welfare reform's advocates assume the vast majority of current welfare recipients can either find work locally or relocate to secure a job. The stagnant economy, large proportion of unemployed working-age adults, and high poverty level are not conducive to this type of adjustment by southern West Virginia's population. The characteristics of the region's poverty population also make this a difficult task.

We have seen that southern West Virginia's poverty rates exceed the nation's for all age groups, more than doubling the nation's rate for those aged 35 to 64 years (Table 2.7). The region's poor are concentrated more in the 35–64 age group (28 percent for the region, 22 percent for the nation) and less in the younger working ages (26 percent for the region versus 30 percent for the nation). This probably reflects a greater proportion of displaced workers, many of whom will have difficulty retraining for other employment.

Census data support this notion. As of the 1990 census, only one-quarter of the region's working-age (20–64) poor were employed, about 11 percent were officially unemployed, and almost two-thirds were out of the labor force (Table 2.8). For the United States, 41 percent of the working-age poor were employed and 11 percent were officially unemployed. Of the region's poor of ages 35 to 54, about 30 percent had participated in the labor force during the past but had not held a job since 1984; another quarter had last worked between 1985 and 1988. For the United States, the corresponding figures are 21 percent and 13 percent. For those aged 55 to 64, more than half had participated in the labor force previously but had not worked since 1984, compared with 43 percent for the nation. In short, a large proportion of the poor aged 35 to 64 have experienced chronic unemployment, indicating a significant structural unemployment problem. Work disabilities explain part of this long-term unemployment. Of the working-age poor, 27 percent had a disability that prevented them from working (compared with 14 percent for the nation), and another 7 percent had a disability that limited the type of work they could undertake.

Relatively low educational attainment typifies the poverty population; however, it more seriously limits southern West Virginia compared with the nation. In the region nearly half of the working-age poor had not attained a high school degree as of 1990, and only 3 percent had either an associate or a bachelor's degree. For the nation, the proportion of poor without a high school degree was similar, but 12 percent of the poor held an associate or higher degree.

Some housing characteristics also distinguish southern West Virginia's poor from the remainder of the nation. We assume the vast majority of the poor live in rental housing. In 1990 that was true for the nation, where 66 percent of the working-age poor resided in rental housing. Southern West Virginia reversed the situation, with nearly 60 percent of the working-age poor residing in owner-occupied housing. This makes the region's poor population relatively immobile. Much of this owner-occupied housing is of poor quality and holds little market value. In 1990 about a third of the region's owner-occupied structures were mobile homes. Regardless of the quality, however, these owner households

Table 2.8 Distribution of Characteristics of Working-Age Poor (aged 20–64), 1990 (%)

	Region	United States		Region	United States
Labor Force Status			*Work Disability Status*		
Military employment	0.7	0.2	Limited	6.6	6.3
Civilian employment	24.5	40.6	Cannot work	27.0	13.6
Unemployed	10.7	11.4	No work disability	66.4	80.1
Not in labor force	64.1	47.8			
Year Last Worked (35–54-year-olds)			*Year Last Worked (55–64-year-olds)*		
1989–90	30.2	55.9	1989–90	11.2	29.7
1985–1988	24.1	12.8	1985–1988	11.6	15.9
1984 or earlier	31.4	21.1	1984 or earlier	55.4	43.4
Never worked	14.3	10.1	Never worked	21.9	11.0
Education			*Housing Tenure*		
No high school diploma	46.0	42.2	Owner-occupied	57.4	34.4
Only high school diploma	51.2	46.1	Rental	42.6	65.6
Postsecondary degree	2.8	11.7			
Telephone in Housing Unit			*Automobile Available*		
Yes	66.3	80.0	Yes	80.7	74.1
No	33.7	20.0	No	19.3	25.9

Source: One percent file of the Public Use Microdata Sample from the *1990 Census of Population and Housing*.

have a piece of property and some housing security. Relocating in search of employment would mean giving up the security of home ownership, which protects them from eviction, for what may be more costly, less secure, and less desirable rental housing.

Other characteristics rendering the region's poor less mobile and less able to obtain employment include poor access to a telephone and absence of an automobile. One-third of the region's working-age poor lack a telephone in their housing unit, compared with 20 percent for the United States. One in five lives in a housing unit without an automobile. This proportion is somewhat less than that for the nation (one in four), but it affects a region such as southern West Virginia more seriously. Job search in sparsely populated rural areas, which rarely have much public transportation, requires access to a phone and a car.

In sum, the characteristics of southern West Virginia's poverty population differ from the nation's poverty population. The region's poor tend to be older, much less attached to the labor force, and somewhat less educated. This reflects a relatively large group of displaced workers, including many former coal miners, who would be difficult to retrain and place in new jobs. Many of these former workers have disabilities and therefore receive disability benefits. The economic benefits of trying to retrain and place the rest of these older individuals in jobs may not justify the costs. Given the short time horizon for older individuals, policymakers should consider simply providing adequate public welfare support to most of them and concentrating retraining and job placement efforts elsewhere.

In addition, southern West Virginia's poverty population more likely resides in owner-occupied housing, albeit relatively low-quality housing with low market value. The region's poor are also more isolated because of low access to phones and automobiles and almost no access to public transportation because of the region's spread-out rural nature. Greater isolation reduces the ability to search regionally for employment, and both housing tenure and isolation reduce mobility out of the region. These characteristics reduce information on opportunities elsewhere, as well as the ability to reach those opportunities. Relocation may exact great expense, considering not only moving costs but also the likelihood of a substantial increase in housing costs. For most of these people, a major move would impose considerable psychic costs. It would entail leaving home and family for the first time and moving from a small rural area to the "big city." Relocating to a city of just 25,000 people would be a shock to many of these individuals.

Conclusion

Population migration is an inevitable and integral part of economic change for any region. For some regions, migration enables growth and prosperity to continue. For others, it is a sometimes painful but necessary part of adjusting to economic decline, a process that eventually brings about economic stability and renewed prosperity. For some declining regions such as southern West Virginia, this self-correcting mechanism does not fully work. Ultimately, it increases instability and prolongs economic stagnation. Instead of continually relocating the unemployed to reduce the surplus labor pool, migration leaves a large group of hard-core unemployed and a population that becomes increasingly more impoverished as economic decline continues.

The situation in a declining, isolated rural region differs from that in a densely populated urban area. The former exhibits less diversity in employment, fewer opportunities for retraining and placing dislocated workers, and less opportunity for local development, combined with much greater attachment to home. In urban areas some economic regeneration always occurs, with some industries growing and others declining. In an area such as southern West Virginia, the situation differs notably even from that in most other declining rural areas. In many farm communities the employment decline has primarily affected young workers. As technology changed or large conglomerates bought up family farms, few opportunities remained for young workers. As young people left, the population declined and age distribution changed. Unemployment often stayed low or rose only during a brief period of transition. The remaining farming community often prospered. Even during crisis years, when financial institutions foreclosed on family farms, communities adjusted accordingly, although painfully. Those who lost their farms also lost their homes and had to relocate, finding another means of employment. The usually successful transition in rural agricultural communities led Davis (1977) to conclude that "rural out-migration appears to contribute to the development and well-being of sending regions" (p. 165). The large number of middle-aged and older workers who lost their jobs, the low educational attainment of those workers, and the stronger attachment to home differentiate southern West Virginia from the typical Midwest farm community where the hard-to-place workers lost their jobs but not their homes.

This distinction raises important concerns regarding recent welfare reform, concerns rather different from the immigrant issues discussed in chapter 6 (this volume). In an impoverished area subsidized private employment, government employment, local development initiatives, and relocation constitute the primary alternatives for getting most poor individuals off welfare and into jobs. An area like southern West Virginia has few opportunities to apply the first three options. To meet goals for reducing welfare roles and placing welfare recipients in jobs, the region would have to rely primarily on relocation. For many of the region's poor, however, relocation is not viable. Characteristics such as high age and low educational attainment would yield a small financial return to migration, even for those who succeeded in securing a job at a new location. Those owning their own house and land would incur especially high migration costs. Taking all expected private and social benefits and costs into account, the only rational and ethical solution to poverty and economic distress in southern West Virginia may consist of providing long-term public welfare support to the immobile and allowing the region to adjust slowly through aging, mortality, and continued out-migration of the mobile population. Eventually, demographic change will bring about the adjustments necessary to stabilize southern West Virginia's economy and reduce the large number of individuals not strongly connected to the labor force.

Notes

1. For example, see Pigg (1991); Task Force on Persistent Rural Poverty (1993); and Obermiller and Philliber (1994).

2. See Swanson and Butler (1988); Fuguitt, Brown, and Beale (1989); Garkovich (1989), Fitchen (1991); Lichter (1992); and Lichter, McLaughlin, and Cornwell (1992).

3. Kanawha County's population declined significantly during the 1980s.

4. Prior to 1980, consistent unemployment data at the substate level are unavailable for West Virginia.

5. All migration data come from the 1 percent file of the Public Use Microdata Sample from the *1990 Census of Population and Housing*. Unless otherwise noted, all other data are from published volumes from the *1990* and *1980 Census of Population and Housing*.

6. The 1985 base population equals the number of nonmovers (those at least 5 years of age on April 1, 1990, who resided in the PUMA on both April 1, 1985, and April 1, 1990) plus the number of out-migrants (those at least 5 years of age on April 1, 1990, who resided in the PUMA on April 1, 1985, but resided elsewhere in the United States on April 1, 1990).

7. Of the out-migrants aged 20–24, 31 percent attended school in 1996. Excluding those attending school, the out-migration rate for this group was only slightly lower (38 percent), with a net out-migration rate of 23 percent.

8. The population decreased in all six counties between 1980 and 1990.

9. Because of changes in categories of educational attainment used in the *Census of Population and Housing,* the educational distribution of the population in 1980 and 1990 cannot be perfectly compared. The earlier data only report number of years of schooling, not degrees actually received. For this comparison I consider four years of high school to mean a high school degree and four or more years of college to mean at least a bachelor's degree.

10. The discussion of the unemployment rate to this point reported "official" U.S. Bureau of Labor Statistics data. The data cover those aged 16 and over and are annual averages based on a small monthly survey (Current Population Survey), state insured employment-unemployment data, and some population benchmarks, such as the decennial census. The data in this section are for the reference week (typically late March) of the census year and are based on the roughly 20 percent of households who filled out the census long form questionnaire.

11. The poverty rate reported in the census is based on income and official poverty lines for the prior year (1979 for the 1980 census and 1989 for the 1990 census).

12. Comparable county-level data were not readily available for 1980.

References

Beaulieu, Lionel. 1988. *The Rural South in Crisis: Challenges for the Future*. Boulder: Westview.

Brown, David, and Mildred Warner. 1991. "Persistent Low-Income Nonmetropolitan Areas in the United States: Some Conceptual Challenges for Development Policy." *Policy Studies Journal* 19, 2: 22–41.

Cushing, Brian, and Cynthia Rogers. 1996. "Income and Poverty in Appalachia." *Socio-Economic Review of Appalachia* (papers commissioned by the Appalachian Regional Commission), Regional Research Institute, West Virginia University, Morgantown.

Davis, Kingsley. 1977. "The Effect of Outmigration on Regions of Origin." In Alan Brown and Egon Neuberger (eds.), *Internal Migration: A Comparative Perspective*. New York: Academic.

Evensky, Jerry. 1991. "The Neoclassical Model Enriched by the Structure of Control: A Labor Market Illustration." *American Journal of Economics and Sociology* 50, 2: 207–222.

Fitchen, Janet. 1991. *Endangered Spaces, Enduring Places: Change, Identity and Survival in Rural America*. Boulder: Westview.

Fuguitt, Glenn, David Brown, and Calvin Beale. 1989. *Rural and Small Town America*. New York: Russell Sage Foundation.

Fuguitt, Glenn, and Timothy Heaton. 1995. "The Impact of Migration on the Nonmetropolitan Age Structure, 1960–1990." *Population Research and Policy Review* 14: 215–232.

Garkovich, Lorraine. 1989. *Population and Community in Rural America*. New York: Greenwood.

Lichter, Daniel. 1992. "Migration, Population Redistribution, and the New Spatial Inequality." In D. L. Brown, J. J. Zuiches, and D. R. Field (eds.), *The Demography of Rural Life*. University Park, Md.: Northeast Regional Development Center.

Lichter, Daniel, Diane McLaughlin, and Gretchen Cornwell. 1992. "Migration and the Loss of Human Resources in Rural America." In Lionel Beaulieu and David Mulkey (eds.), *Investing in People: The Human Capital Needs of Rural America*. Boulder: Westview.

Obermiller, Philip, and William Philliber (eds.). 1994. *Appalachia in an International Context: Cross-National Comparisons of Developing Regions*. Westport, Conn.: Praeger.

PARC. 1964. "Appalachia: A Report by the President's Appalachian Regional Commission." Washington, D.C.: U.S. Department of Commerce.

Pigg, Kenneth (ed.). 1991. *The Future of Rural America: Anticipating Policies for Constructive Change*. Boulder: Westview.

Swanson, Linda, and Margaret Butler. 1988. "Human Resource Base of Rural Economies." In *Rural Economic Development in the 1980's: Preparing for the Future*. Washington, D.C.: Economic Research Service, USDA.

Task Force on Persistent Rural Poverty (Rural Sociological Society). 1993. *Persistent Poverty in Rural America*. Boulder: Westview.

3

Economic Restructuring and Migration in an Old Industrial Region

Lawrence A. Brown, Linda Lobao, and Scott Digiacinto

Conceptualizations of the migration process have assumed either that changing location represents individual choice or that structural characteristics are a major directive force. The latter extreme is represented by Friedmann and Wulff (1976: 26–27) who observed that, "Migration . . . reflects merely a demographic adjustment to changes in the spatial structure of economic and social opportunities. . . . [It] is a derived phenomenon, a symptom of urbanization and not the thing itself. . . . Demographers and others insisted on treating migration as a major policy variable when it was, in fact, dependent on the major structural features of the economy."

The other extreme, that migration represents individual choice, is best represented by utility maximization frameworks wherein individual (or family) migration is a response to the perception that the future earnings stream will be greater elsewhere (Sjaastad 1962). Close to this perspective is the labor force adjustment model wherein migration choices reflect place-to-place differences in wage levels, job opportunities, and information about such conditions (Lowry 1966). Although these models were originally stated in terms of individual choice, considering these conventional models more critically—beyond their stated precepts—leads to the conclusion that socioeconomic structure is a critical component, the determinant of place-to-place differences in wages, job opportunities, and information flows (Brown 1991).

Accordingly, directly incorporating structural effects has proven important. For example, spatially uneven development in Third World settings gives rise to dramatically different structural conditions from place to place, creating distinct spatial variation in the migration process (Brown 1991).

A similar approach could be applied to North America and Europe, which are also characterized by spatially uneven development. In the post–World War II era, however, one is more compellingly drawn to socioeconomic restructuring, a particular form of development that has been studied in its own right as a distinct phenomenon and that, like Third World development, varies both temporally and spatially. Further, post-1960s restructuring presents a socioeconomic scenario that, rightly or wrongly, is widely accepted as a dramatic change from the past (Brown and Lobao 1997). Accordingly, this provides an appropriate opportunity for seriously rethinking the study of migration.

To address this issue, we proceed in four steps. First, we consider post-1960s socioeconomic restructuring and some of its implications for migration systems. Attention then turns to empirical analysis. Our study area is the Ohio River Valley (ORV), which, as a portion of the American Manufacturing Belt, exemplifies an *old industrial region* (Brown and Lobao 1997; Brown, Lobao, and Verheyen 1996; Hudson 1989; Page and Walker 1991). In this regard, the chapter's second section describes the ORV region, its characteristics, and its evolution. Third, focus turns to patterns of net migration, their spatial attributes, and their relationship to structural characteristics of the economy at the county level. The final section presents a discussion of findings, general observations, and conclusions.

Economic Restructuring in the Post-1960s and Migration Processes

Conceptualization of the migration process has changed little since the 1960s. Models continue to be formulated around concepts of, for example, wage, job opportunity, and information differentials from place to place; migration chain and socioeconomic bond effects; and income maximization strategies. In the mid-1970s structural forces were given more attention, in part reflecting Marxist approaches to social science and offsetting the theretofore strong assumption of individual choice. Representative are conceptualizations spotlighting development effects on migration (Brown and Sanders 1981; Brown 1991), which blend structural and individual behavior perspectives.

Linking development and migration is, however, a modest task in light of today's world and dramatic changes over the past thirty years. There have emerged clearly demarcated spatial divisions of labor; an array of production systems from traditional assembly lines to flexible manufacturing to cottage-type, labor-intensive enterprise; decomposition of the production process, leading to spatial variation in economic function and complexity; economic initiatives ranging in focus from mass to niche markets; transnational circulation as a central and increasingly pervasive element of population movements and settlement systems; shifts in the social organization of labor markets, communities, families, and interpersonal relationships; and underlying these many changes, transportation-communications-information systems that have experienced a revolution from, seemingly, Stone Age to Cyber Age. In this regard, one must keep in mind that such variation and economic restructuring have always been with us, an ongoing phenomenon (Brown and Lobao 1997; Brown 1999). Nevertheless, the post-1960s form of restructuring is more visible and more visibly ongoing and has received extraordinary attention (e.g., Bluestone and Harrison 1982; Scott 1988a).

There is good reason, then, to rethink and reconceptualize migration. To illustrate the potential of this exercise, consider five aspects of socioeconomic restructuring that are significant in North American settings.

1. Downsizing of economic activity and increasingly flexible production systems have been major aspects of restructuring. Hence, economic growth per se, a fundamental variable of the conventional model, may not be correlated with in-migration since fewer workers are needed and labor supply is a less important component of production processes.

2. Change in the significance of economic sectors, such as the shift from manufacturing to service activities, could lead to job change without migration, out-migration by some population segments, and in-migration by others. This highlights at the very least the importance of considering distinct population segments and, likewise, distinct economic sectors.

3. A similar conclusion follows from the need for different labor force attributes. Higher skills are required in some instances; in others deskilling or a shift to activities requiring less ability, which also command lower wages, has occurred.

4. These changes have a distinct spatial component. In broad terms, economic decline, deskilling, and the like are associated with areas characterized by Fordist-type manufacturing, generally referred to as *old industrial regions* (Hudson 1989). Economic growth is associated with global cities (Sassen 1991), territorial production complexes (Piore and Sable 1984), and locales distinguished by high-technology enterprise, producer-business-financial-professional services, and other lead industries (Scott 1988a, 1988b; Soja 1989)—areas often referred to as undergoing a post-Fordist transition.

But such abstract categories elude the ground-level reality of most North American locales, including especially counties constituting the Ohio River Valley, our study area. More pertinent is the general, less systematic translation of broad national-regional trends into differentiated local effects for areas where the space-economy features a dense network of medium-sized towns and trade centers, large urban complexes, rural areas distant from metropolitan ones, or dominance of extraction and durable manufacturing employment. Such settings are rather different from, and considerably more common than, those that have received the most attention in the post-Fordist transition literature

(Brown and Lobao 1997; Brown, Lobao, and Verheyen 1996; Clark 1989; Florida 1996). How does contemporary economic growth emerge in these types of settings? And how, then, is migration affected?

5. Another spatial component is decentralization of the workforce, a delinking of labor from place of employment facilitated by the post-1960s transportation-communications revolution. This decentralization is especially relevant for major urban areas, which have experienced urban sprawl, dramatically expanding their spatial reach.

Because of delinking, employment factors (e.g., wages, job availability) may remain central to migration decisionmaking but not to choosing a specific place of residence. Hence, a two-step process evolves wherein a broad area is chosen on the basis of conventional migration factors (wages, job availability, economic growth) but residence is chosen on the basis of factors such as accessibility, amenities, and residential preferences.

Ohio River Valley Study Area

An opportunity to consider these points in more concrete terms is provided by the Ohio River Valley. This region is a portion of the American Manufacturing Belt, an example of an old industrial region (Hudson 1989; Page and Walker 1991), and a cross-section of North America that has been recognized as a distinct socioeconomic entity since the late eighteenth century (Reid 1991). Anchored at one end by Pittsburgh-Wheeling-Youngstown and encompassing Columbus-Cincinnati-Louisville and a multitude of smaller cities, towns, and rural areas as far west as the Mississippi, this region epitomizes the Midwest's industrial heartland, its agricultural-energy reserve, the "true path to capitalist growth" (Page and Walker 1991: 281).

The ORV's settlement and development patterns were initially bound to the river, which connected Upper Midwest iron and steel industries and Midwest farmers with the Mississippi and broader markets. Railroads and highways deepened economic integration, also linking Ohio River Valley cities and rural hinterlands to national and global markets but at a much greater magnitude than before. From the early twentieth century to the 1970s, regional specialization in steel, other durable manufacturing, chemicals, and natural resource extraction gave an outward appearance that the ORV was a center of Fordist development with concentrated industry, large-scale firms, and blue-collar jobs. Indeed, this aspect and centrality to external markets made the region an important engine of national growth throughout the twentieth century. The Ohio River Valley's economic structure, however, has been and remains diverse. Whereas large national corporations were predominant in steel, electrical power, and some mining operations, small locally owned firms characterized industries such as glass, pottery, lumber, and wood processing.

The ORV study area is defined as counties three deep on each side of the Ohio River, from its head in Allegheny County, Pennsylvania, to its Mississippi end point. Also included are counties comprising a Metropolitan Statistical Area (MSA) of which only a portion was included under the original criteria—Canton, Columbus, Dayton-Springfield, and Lexington-Fayette. The result is 222 counties in six states (Illinois, Indiana, Kentucky, Ohio, West Virginia, Pennsylvania). The counties include major urban areas, smaller towns whose prominence coincided with fortunes of the American Manufacturing Belt, areas of mineral extraction, and rural farm areas (Figure 3.1).

Between 1980 and 1990, ORV counties experienced two types of change pertinent to net migration, the concern of this chapter.

Change in Employment Level

One type of change is that in the overall employment level, a surrogate for labor demand. Employment change is calculated as the civilian labor force employed in 1990 divided by the civilian labor force employed in 1980, with the result converted to z-scores and mapped in three categories (Figure 3.2). A z-score greater than 0.75 indicates high employment growth, between +0.75 and −0.75 indicates average growth, and less than −0.75 indicates low or negative growth.

High employment growth occurs in a corridor stretching from Evansville, Indiana, through Louisville-Lexington, Kentucky, and on to Cincinnati-Dayton-

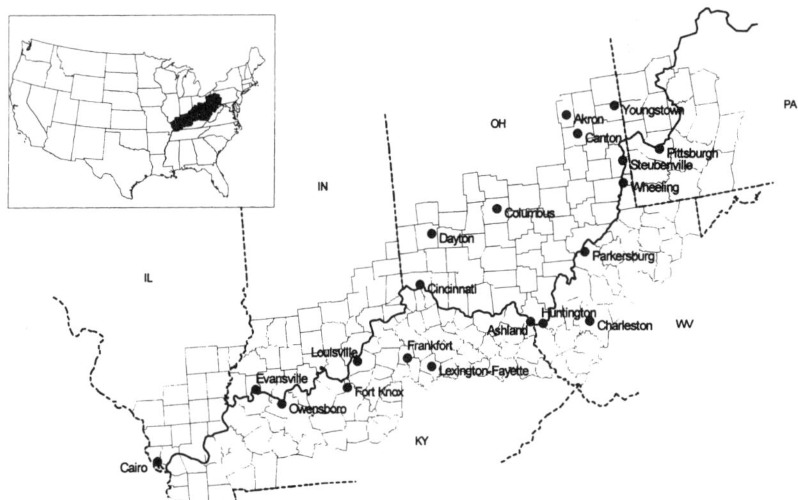

Figure 3.1 The Ohio River: States, Counties, and Selected Cities

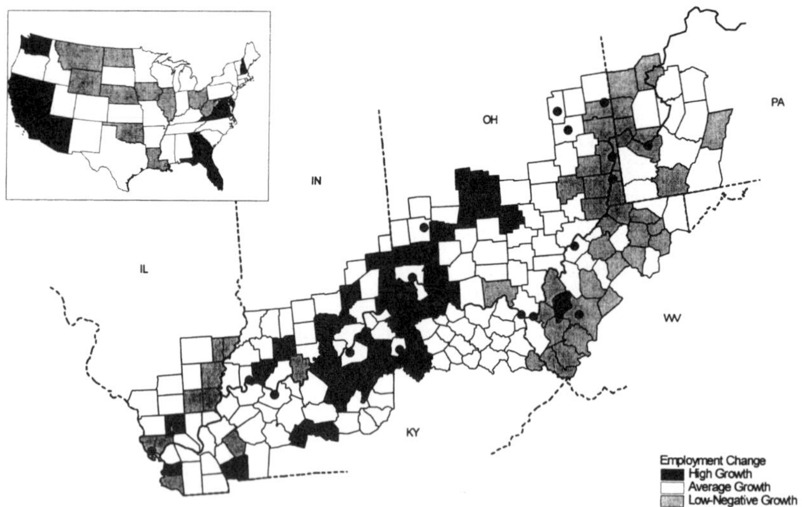

Figure 3.2 Employment Change in Ohio River Valley Counties, 1980–1990

Columbus, Ohio—an area that might be described as composed of "New Age" locales. With the exception of Columbus, growth is around, not within, the central portion of these urban areas. Similarly evident is low or negative employment growth in most of West Virginia, eastern Ohio, southwestern Pennsylvania, and southern Illinois (Figure 3.2).

Hence, areas that were central to Fordist economic activity—for example, centers of steel, automotive, and extractive industries with production facilities that were dated by the 1980s and earlier—experience low or negative growth and decline relative to other locales. High growth is found in areas that were less significant in the American Manufacturing Belt era and that today contain more contemporary, post-Fordist economic structures.

Especially striking is the marked clustering of employment change patterns. There is a distinct subregional pattern wherein the ORV is trifurcated into declining western and eastern counties on either side of a growing set of central counties (Figure 3.2). Low or negative growth in employment is highly prevalent in southern Illinois, western Kentucky, southeastern Ohio, southwestern Pennsylvania, and West Virginia. These areas, at the western and eastern extremities of the Ohio River Valley, were characterized the most by Fordist activities, particularly durable manufacturing and mineral extraction. High employment growth is found at the ORV's center, particularly in a more or less continual band stretching from Evansville through Louisville-Lexington-Cincinnati-Dayton-Columbus, areas that represent New Age contemporary economies and have prospered significantly since the 1970s. Outside the umbrella of these metropolitan areas (but still in the ORV's central section), the more rural counties tend to experience average employment growth.

Also relevant is the geographic scale of analysis, which affects considerably what one sees in terms of employment change. If state-level data are used, for example, the American Manufacturing Belt (AMB) appears to lose ground relative to other parts of the nation beginning with the end of World War II and persisting into 1980–1990, when Illinois, Ohio, and West Virginia experience low or negative employment growth and other AMB states are neutral (Figure 3.2 inset). But if the focus is not on states but on ORV counties, a more local scale, the picture is dramatically different (Figure 3.2).

Another important observation is that ORV employment growth is not dependent on new economic activity. This link is real, but it is considerably less significant than one would glean from the corpus of post-Fordist transition research. Examples of new economic activity include a Fidelity Investment printing and mailing facility in Covington, Kentucky (Hirsch 1996), a distribution and light industry park in Washington Courthouse, Ohio, numerous outlet malls along I-71 between Cincinnati and Columbus, Ohio, and an extensive corridor of contemporary manufacturing and service activity along I-79 south of Pittsburgh, Pennsylvania. More common, however, is growth in older industry that has simply expanded over time, usually accompanied by a shift in focus. Examples of traditional industry in this category include Chillicothe's Mead Paper and Pittsburgh Plate and Glass plants; Marble King of Paden City, West Virginia; Rocky Shoes of Nelsonville, Ohio; Longaberger Baskets of Dresden, Ohio; aluminum plants in the vicinity of Wheeling, West Virginia; chemical processing (for example, G.E. and DuPont) near Parkersburg, West Virginia; and power plants dotting the Ohio River between Cincinnati and Marietta, Ohio. These establishments have been in place for well over half a century, but there are also more recent enterprises such as the Pillsbury plant in Wellston, Ohio, which began as Gino's Pizza in the 1970s. Another set of older organizations epitomizes post-Fordist transitions and has expanded accordingly (for example, BancOne, Cardinal Health, Compuserve, the Limited, and Nationwide Insurance in Columbus, Ohio).

These observations draw on field reconnaissance by the authors but are also supported by statistical evidence. For example, the 1993 share of new jobs from existing businesses in ORV counties ranged from 56 percent to 100 percent, with most at the upper end of this continuum (Kraybill 1995).

Change in Economic Activity

The second type of change involves the mix of economic activity within a county (Brown, Lobao, and Verheyen 1996), which may affect migration in its own right, as noted earlier. One type of economic activity change within a county mirrors change in the region and the nation. Areas identified with a single traditional industry often encountered sharp employment decline in that industry between 1980 and 1990. Generally, these declines are in durable manufacturing and mineral extraction and represent a continuation of trends outlined by the *deindustrialization* thesis—areas characterized by intense Fordist-type development wherein durable manufacturing and its mineral extraction engine were central.

In many counties employment grew consistently in retail trade and in personal and social–health services. This follows broad regional–national trends, except that retail employment expanded at a higher rate than nationally. Ground-level field reconnaissance indicates growth of outlet malls and national retail distribution centers in many ORV locales that have major highway and interstate connections.

The ORV also experienced locally differentiated change in economic activity. Although durable manufacturing employment declined overall during the 1980s, its importance increased in new locales, making that sector one of the most robust in the ORV. An explicit examination of employment regeneration through flexibly organized, new manufacturing firms is not possible with presently available data, but the spatial dispersion of durable manufacturing, posited by the post-Fordist transition thesis, clearly occurred.

Nondurable manufacturing employment also increased in many locales, even though its importance in the ORV and the nation declined slightly. Increases often occurred in regionally indigenous subsectors, highlighting the Midwestern Manufacturing Belt's varied industrial structure in which nondurables such as furniture and lumber-wood are important historically as well as today. Also, the fact that nondurable manufacturing is a lead industry, probably elsewhere as well as in the ORV, tends to be overlooked by analysts focused on durable manufacturing as a dominant sector in old industrial regions.

What manufacturing subsectors are associated with these shifts? In durable manufacturing, employment losses were most pronounced throughout the ORV in stone, clay-glass, primary metal, fabricated metal, and industrial machinery; rubber-plastics and transportation equipment grew. Electronics employment declined in urban areas and counties characterized by durable manufacturing but grew elsewhere. Nondurable manufacturing throughout the ORV suffered employment losses in the food, tobacco, and apparel sectors but experienced gains in the lumber-wood sector. Furniture employment gained in all except urban counties and counties with durable manufacturing; sporadic gains also occurred in paper, instrument, and textile industries. More generally, employment shifts in durable and nondurable manufacturing benefited all counties except those characterized by urban, durable manufacturing, or small-town economies that were centers of Fordist-era manufacturing and were economically robust in the 1940–1970 era.

Some counties show marked evidence of transition to a new economic base. This is especially apparent where specialized manufacturing had been strong, with a turn toward consumer sectors and trade; elsewhere, shifts in economic structure were more incremental, often toward construction and transportation.

Some counties show little or no change in economic activity. Relevant to our portrayal of the ORV is a recent report on Chillicothe, a small urban place at the southern edge of the Columbus MSA (Gibbs 1997: 36–37). This urban area

> has usually mirrored the country's fortunes. . . . [There has been] about one [ribbon-cutting ceremony] every month . . . yet the mood . . . is as much superstition (cynicism) as celebration. . . . The most successful businesses are ones that can read the new economy and exploit its moods. . . . For the big industrial manufacturers that ring Ross County [Chillicothe], the challenge is to convert the old economy into the new, which often means better profits but less hiring. . . . Workers who can't keep up with changing technology are finding fewer and fewer plants that will hire them. . . . There are more jobs than good people. . . . City officials . . . are planning a center . . . with an incubator incentive package . . . to attract high-tech businesses . . . the right kind of business for the future.

Chillicothe, then, provides a vivid illustration of the broad trends enumerated thus far, as would any number of other places.

Returning to the general, giving attention to the Ohio River Valley—a real and representative area—leads to the conclusion that empirical, ground-level evidence more strongly supports the old industrial region thesis, wherein intraregional differentiation is both acknowledged and paramount, rather than the deindustrialization thesis, wherein regions are viewed as homogeneous and suffering uniformly from the socioeconomic restructuring of the post-1960s. A second conclusion is the importance of geographic scale in shaping one's view of the impact of socioeconomic restructuring. In the present instance, for example, a state-based view of unemployment presents a considerably more pessimistic view than does a county-based view; the scourge of deindustrialization identified with post-Fordist transitions is limited only to selected counties of the Ohio River Valley. A third important conclusion is that present-day economic growth is a reinvention of, rather than a sharp break from, the past and its economic heritage.

Research Design and Findings

We now turn to the relationship between migration and economic restructuring, an issue that typically focuses on net migration. Following conventional thinking, net migration should vary directly with economic opportunity, wage levels, and amenities, and these effects will be amplified (positively or negatively) by information levels.

To measure net migration we use the migration efficiency ratio (MER), which provides a standardized statistic and thus avoids problems related to size differences in county population (Gober 1993: 14–15). This is stated as:

(In-Migration − Out-Migration) / (In-Migration + Out-Migration)

where all in-migration yields a value of 1, all out-migration yields a value of −1, and 0 indicates that in- and out-migration are equal.

MERs are computed for each of the 222 ORV counties, using the entire population of in-and out-migrants. This set of statistics is referred to as Overall MERs. In addition, following earlier observations on the importance of considering population segments in a situation of economic restructuring, MERs are computed for subgroups based on education (Low—no high school diploma; Medium—high school diploma and some college; High—college degree), age (Younger—25–34; Older—35–44), and poverty status (In-poverty—below the poverty line; Not-in-poverty—above the poverty line). These are commonly used dimensions, and categories therein, for sample stratification. They link directly to economic structure at the county level, and they represent categories likely to be differentially impacted by the socioeconomic restructuring of recent decades.

Data are from a special run of county-to-county migration streams from the 1990 U.S. Census of Population. This tabulates place of residence in 1985 and 1990 for those population segments listed earlier (and others). Two types of analysis are reported. The first examines spatial patterns of net migration for the population overall and for population subgroups, differences among them, and relationships to broad economic restructuring trends in the Ohio River Valley. The second analysis relates migration efficiency ratios to variables representing economic sectors of employment and to overall employment and income characteristics in 1980 and as they changed during the 1980–1990 decade.

Spatial Patterns of Net Migration

To visualize spatial patterns of net migration and to enable comparison among population groups, migration efficiency ratios are z-score standardized, with a z-score value greater than 0.75 indicating net in-migration, between +0.75 and −0.75 indicating neutral net migration, and less than −0.75 indicating net out-migration. The Overall MER, the basic point of reference, is first mapped (Figure 3.3) and shows the following characteristics.

- A band of in-migration extends continuously from Evansville through Louisville, Cincinnati, Lexington, and Columbus, but within this band central city counties experienced neutral net migration.
- Marked clustering of out-migration occurs in West Virginia, southeast Ohio, southwest Pennsylvania, southern Illinois, and western Kentucky, but within these clusters is an occasional in-migration county.
- Neutral MERs are found throughout the study area and, unlike in- and out-migration, do not form a distinct pattern.

A notable degree of association exists between overall migration and 1980–1990 employment change (Figures 3.2 and 3.3). In general, net in-migration occurs

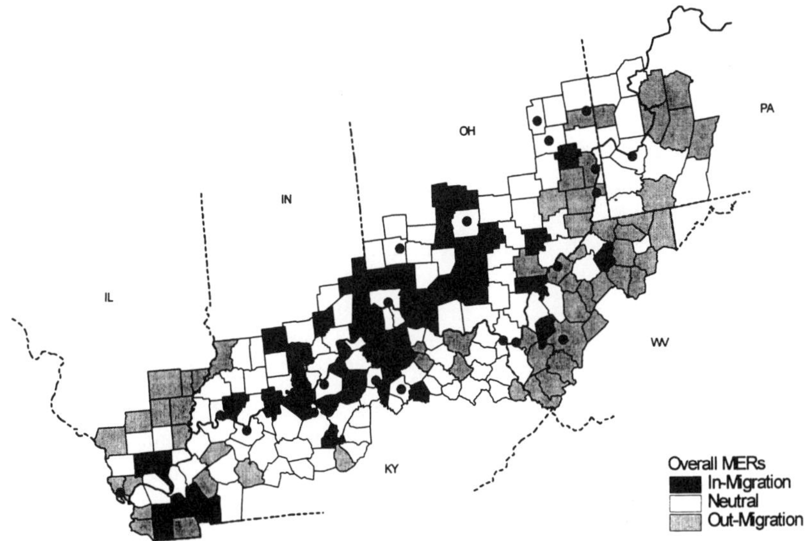

Figure 3.3 Overall Migration Efficiency Ratios

where employment growth is high, net out-migration where employment growth is low or negative. Using the three classification categories (in-/high, neutral/average, out-/low or negative), 67 percent of the counties match migration and employment growth.

To identify divergence in the spatial patterns of net migration, the MERs of population subgroups were mapped as overlays on the overall migration efficiency ratio. The spatial resemblance between overall MERs and MERs for subgroups is readily indicated by the percentage of ORV counties with corresponding in-, out-, or neutral migration.

Overall MER versus:	High Education MER	=	61.7% agreement
	Medium Education MER	=	84.3% agreement
	Low Education MER	=	60.9% agreement
	Older Age MER	=	75.2% agreement
	Younger Age MER	=	89.2% agreement
	Not-in-poverty MER	=	87.0% agreement
	In-poverty MER	=	51.8% agreement

MERs for Medium Education, Not-in-poverty, and for both age groups correspond with overall MERs in at least 75 percent of counties, a high level of conformity. There is a low correspondence in the case of High and Low Education MERs and especially for In-poverty MERs.

To capture these distinctions in a summary form, MERs for each subgroup and the population overall were subject to principal components analysis (Table 3.1). Principal Component I (PCI) includes the migration efficiency ratios for the overall population, the Medium and High Education subgroups, the Older and Younger Age subgroups, and the Not-in-poverty subgroup. When compared, 83.8 percent of ORV counties have a similar value for their overall MER and PCI (using once again the trichotomization scheme that a z- or PC-score greater than 0.75 is high, that between +0.75 and −0.75 is neutral, and that less than −0.75 is low). Principal Component II (PCII) includes migration efficiency ratios for the Low Education and In-poverty subgroups. Here, only 51.8 percent of ORV counties are concordant with the overall pattern of net migration.

Comparing the spatial patterns of PCI and PCII (Figure 3.4) reveals important differences between migrant subgroups. Net in-migration by Low Education or In-poverty migrants often occurs in counties that are neutral for others. This is seen throughout portions of Kentucky but especially in southern Ohio. Counties under the umbrella of major urban areas that are also characterized by in-migration differ in their experience with Low Education or In-poverty migrants. Those groups show out-migration in the vicinity of Louisville, Lexington, Dayton, and Columbus, in-migration around Evansville, and both in- and out-migration near Cincinnati.

An important aspect of these patterns is the ruralization of poverty, an occurrence associated with deindustrialization and the post-Fordist transition. Most research on this issue addresses the in situ conditions of rural poverty (e.g., Lichter, Johnston, and McLaughlin 1994; Lichter and McLaughlin 1995). By contrast, findings here pertain to rural poverty directly linked to migration, adding to research by Fitchen (1991, 1994), Frey (1995), Nord (1998), and Cushing (chapter 2 in this volume). This subject is discussed more extensively in the final section of the chapter.

Table 3.1 Principal Components Analysis of Migration Efficiency Ratios

Migration Efficiency Ratio	PCI	PCII	Communality
Overall	0.937	0.332	0.988
High education	0.839	−0.167	0.732
Medium education	0.871	0.355	0.885
Low education	0.499	0.650	0.671
Older age	0.853	0.274	0.802
Younger age	0.887	0.342	0.904
Not-in-poverty	0.954	0.145	0.930
In-poverty	0.017	0.900	0.810
Percent Explained:			
Each PC	69.9	14.2	
Cumulative	69.9	84.0	

Note: $n = 222$ counties

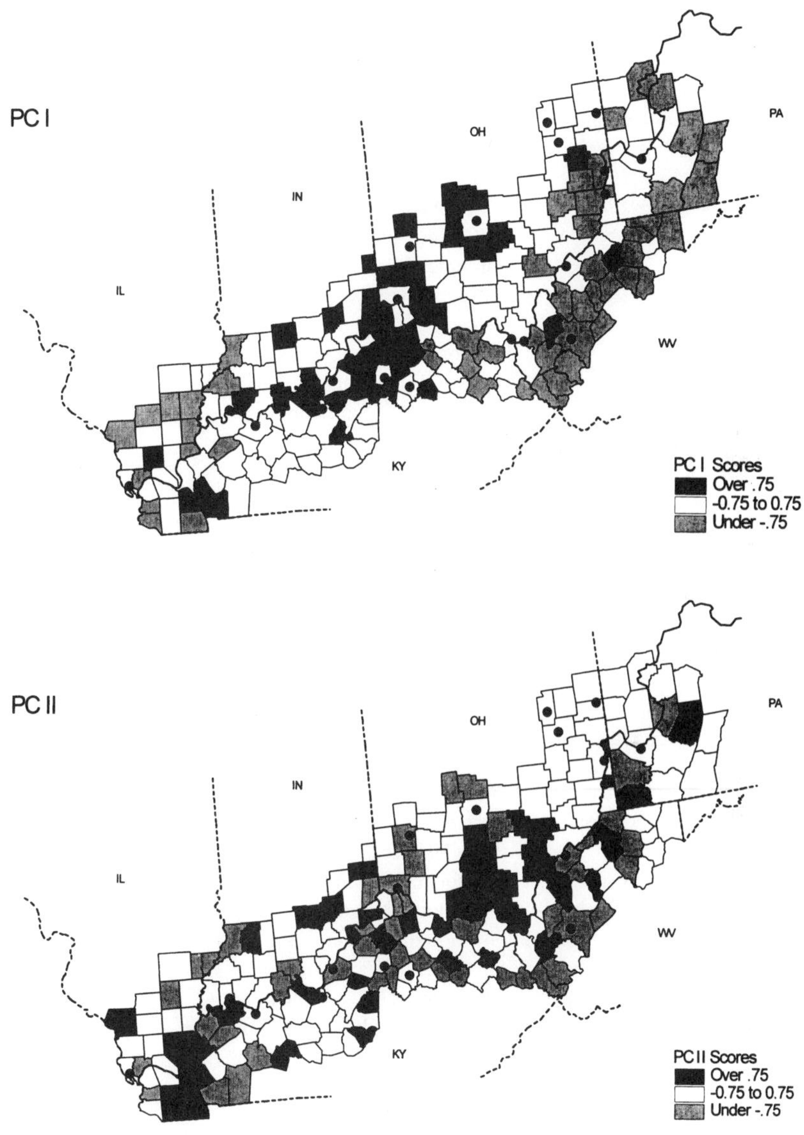

Figure 3.4 Composite Measures of Population Subgroup Migration Efficiency Ratios

Table 3.2 Definition of Independent Variables and Computation Procedures

Economic Sectors of Employment			
AGEXTRC 8	% Emplyd	Agriculture, Forestry, Fisheries, Mining (SICs 010–050)	1980
AGEXTRC Δ	% Change	Agriculture, Forestry, Fisheries, Mining	1980–1990
BUSERV 8	% Emplyd	Business, Repair Services (SICs 721–760)	1980
BUSERV Δ	% Change	Business, Repair Services	1980–1990
COMMUN 8	% Emplyd	Communications, Other Public Utilities (SICs 440–472)	1980
COMMUN Δ	% Change	Communications Other Public Utilities	1980–1990
CONSTR 8	% Emplyd	Construction (SIC 060)	1980
CONSTR Δ	% Change	Construction	1980–1990
EDUC 8	% Emplyd	Educational Services (SICs 842–860)	1980
EDUC Δ	% Change	Education, Educational Services	1980–1990
ENTER 8	% Emplyd	Entertainment, Recreation Services (SICs 761–802)	1980
ENTER Δ	% Change	Entertainment, Recreation Services	1980–1990
FINAN 8	% Emplyd	Finance, Insurance, Real Estate (SICs 700–712)	1980
FINAN Δ	% Change	Finance, Insurance, Real Estate	1980–1990
HEALTH 8	% Emplyd	Health Services (SICs 812–840)	1980
HEALTH Δ	% Change	Health Services	1980–1990
DURABL 8	% Emplyd	Durable Goods Manufacturing (SICs 230–392)	1980
DURABL Δ	% Change	Durable Goods Manufacturing	1980–1990
NONDUR 8	% Emplyd	Non-Durable Goods Manufacturing: (SICs 100–222)	1980
NONDUR Δ	% Change	Non-Durable Goods Manufacturing	1980–1990
PROF 8	% Emplyd	Professional, Related Services (SICs 841, 861–892)	1980
PROF Δ	% Change	Professional, Related Services	1980–1990
PUBADM 8	% Emplyd	Public Administration (SICs 900–932)	1980
PUBADM Δ	% Change	Public Administration	1980–1990
RETAIL 8	% Emplyd	Retail Trade (SICs 580–691)	1980
RETAIL Δ	% Change	Retail Trade	1980–1990
TRANS 8	% Emplyd	Transportation (SICs 400–432)	1980
TRANS Δ	% Change	Transportation	1980–1990
WHOLE 8	% Emplyd	Wholesale Trade (SICs 500–571)	1980
WHOLE Δ	% Change	Wholesale Trade	1980–1990
Overall Employment and Income			
EMPLOY 8	%	Total Civil Employment	1980
EMPLOY Δ	% Change	Total Civil Employment	1980–1990
INCOME 8		Median Household Income	1980
INCOME Δ	% Change	Median Household Income	1980–1990

(Cont.)

Table 3.2 Definition of Independent Variables and Computation Procedures *(Cont.)*

Overall Employment and Income			
PERCINC 8		Per Capita Income	1980
PERCINC Δ	% Change	Per Capita Income	1980–1990

Note: Computational procedures were as follows:
Economic Sectors of Employment
% Employed: numbr employees, sector (k), county (i) / total emplymnt, all sectors, county (i)
% Change: 1990 emplymnt, sector (k), county (i) / 1980 emplymnt, sector (k), county (i)
Overall Employment and Income
% Employed: civil labor force, county (i) / total civil labor force, county (i)
% Change: civil labor force 1990, county (i) / civil labor force 1980, county (i) median hshld income 1990, county (i) / median hshld income 1980, county (i) per capita income 1990, county (i) / per capita income 1980, county (i)

Economic Patterns

Earlier findings indicate a strong correspondence between overall MERs and employment change during the 1980–1990 decade. Also noted were differences among subgroup MERs in terms of spatial patterns, suggesting that economic sectors vary in their relevance to population segments. This reverberates with observations that through restructuring a shift occurred in the importance of specific economic sectors.

To examine this further, we correlate MERs (actual, not the trichotomization used earlier), PCI, and PCII with employment in a broad range of economic sectors, with overall employment, and with income characteristics in 1980 and as they changed during the 1980–1990 decade. ORV counties are observations. Variables and the way they were computed are listed in Table 3.2. Zero-order correlations are given in Table 3.3.

A relevant aspect of this analysis is its use of census data, which are tabulated at "place of residence." Accordingly, the delinking of work and residence place, associated with socioeconomic-spatial restructuring, is embodied within the data—that is, the nature of the data itself addresses the conceptual issue raised earlier.

To extract significant independent variables, 0.25 is taken as a correlation threshold. Beyond this, a variable's importance is designated as Low if it has a correlation of 0.25–0.30, Medium for a correlation of 0.31–0.40, High for a correlation of 0.41–0.50, and Very High for a correlation greater than 0.50.

As in the case of spatial patterns, zero-order correlations (ZOCs) for the In-poverty and Low Education subgroups are distinct. For others (Overall, High Education, Medium Education, Older Age, Younger Age, Not-in-poverty, PCI), the following levels of importance and direction of relationship are observed from Table 3.3.

Table 3.3 Zero-Order Correlations of Migration Efficiency Ratios and MER Principal Component Scores with Economic Indices

	Overall	Highed	Meded	Lowed	Poverty	Non-poverty	Young	Old	PCI	PCII
AGEXTRC 8	−**.322**	−.211	−**.381**	−.145	−.059	−**.349**	−**.329**	−.241	−**.325**	−.057
AGEXTRC Δ	**.358**	**.316**	**.360**	.088	.047	**.402**	**.353**	**.296**	**.384**	−.012
BUSERV 8	.169	**.264**	.164	−.064	−.143	.197	.175	.108	**.245**	−.204
BUSERV Δ	.103	.038	.075	.104	.064	.132	.104	.094	.086	.077
COMMUN 8	−.014	.003	−.047	.014	.101	−.015	−.011	−.009	−.037	.073
COMMUN Δ	**.249**	**.250**	**.246**	.120	.005	.238	**.261**	.168	**.266**	−.010
CONSTR 8	.090	−.024	.048	.104	.123	.021	.083	.094	.023	.147
CONSTR Δ	**.444**	**.325**	**.436**	**.299**	.204	**.451**	**.416**	**.420**	**.418**	.190
EDUC 8	−**.270**	−.244	−.132	−.150	.152	−**.334**	−**.327**	−.092	−**.302**	.123
EDUC Δ	**.251**	**.264**	**.236**	.090	−.059	**.262**	**.258**	.200	**.293**	−.075
ENTER 8	.064	.124	.095	−.053	.011	.094	.047	.076	.098	−.051
ENTER Δ	.125	.100	.112	.056	−.038	.127	.120	.111	.138	−.029
FINAN 8	.181	.238	.174	−.002	−.104	.237	.180	.134	**.246**	−.145
FINAN Δ	**.275**	**.264**	**.280**	.058	.025	**.300**	**.288**	.193	**.298**	−.026
HEALTH 8	−.161	−.211	−.117	−.056	.003	−.204	−.135	−.188	−.200	.045
HEALTH Δ	**.321**	**.267**	**.294**	.162	.120	**.360**	**.302**	**.306**	**.322**	.081
DURABL 8	.207	.171	.239	.086	−.014	**.286**	.243	.101	.238	−.021

DURABL Δ	.194	.037	.204	.131	.107	.182	.155	.234	.154	.132
NONDUR 8	.223	.083	.199	.135	.015	.230	.218	.186	.202	.052
NONDUR Δ	.177	.152	.178	.112	−.015	.223	.174	.151	.202	−.007
PROF 8	−.005	.010	.035	−.132	−.102	.020	−.014	.001	.033	−.128
PROF Δ	.092	.138	.050	.071	.030	.087	.094	.081	.101	.009
PUBADM 8	.228	.174	.205	.162	.059	.163	.204	.223	.207	.072
PUBADM Δ	**.338**	.193	**.313**	**.277**	−.055	**.263**	**.328**	**.294**	**.323**	.041
RETAIL 8	−.159	−.016	−.138	−.110	−.098	−.154	−.167	−.125	−.112	−.120
RETAIL Δ	**.539**	**.453**	**.512**	**.339**	.127	**.569**	**.525**	**.466**	**.546**	.113
TRANS 8	.008	−.055	−.026	.038	.075	−.023	.017	−.007	−.037	.088
TRANS Δ	.203	.219	.188	.113	−.058	**.270**	.154	**.245**	**.257**	−.063
WHOLE 8	.074	.169	.032	−.028	−.214	.153	.081	.026	.159	−.224
WHOLE Δ	.206	.129	.180	.171	**.261**	.151	.224	.165	.136	.233
EMPLOY 8	.077	.228	.130	−.129	−.221	.210	.071	.065	.211	**−.288**
EMPLOY Δ	**.721**	**.546**	**.716**	**.403**	.116	**.751**	**.688**	**.652**	**.732**	.116
INCOME 8	.237	**.303**	**.253**	.049	−.134	**.329**	**.274**	.116	**.323**	−.164
INCOME Δ	**.568**	**.402**	**.573**	**.263**	−.015	**.612**	**.533**	**.527**	**.599**	.001
PERCINC 8	.075	.175	.103	−.066	−.140	.174	.107	−.010	.160	−.185
PERCINC Δ	**.551**	**.479**	**.551**	.161	−.053	**.614**	**.518**	**.509**	**.618**	−.095

Bold indicates zero-order correlation with a value ≥ 0.250.

−	Agriculture and extractive, % employed 1980	Medium
+	Agriculture and extractive, % employment change	Medium
+	Communications, % employment change	Low
+	Construction, % employment change	High
−	Educational services, % employed 1980	Medium
+	Educational services, % employment Change	Low
+	Finance-Ins-Real Estate, % employment change	Low
+	Health services, % employment change	Medium
+	Public administration, % employment change	Low-Medium
+	Retail, % employment change	High-Very High
+	Total employment, % change	High-Very High
+	Median household income, 1980	Low-Medium
+	Median household income, % change	High-Very High
+	Per capita income, % change	Very High

These findings group into four sets of forces (or variables) that affect net migration for the overall population, for subgroups representing High Education, Medium Education, Older Age, Younger Age, and Not-in-poverty, and for the population represented by Principal Component I.

- Net migration varies directly with the growth of activities identified with contemporary economies (e.g., communications, educational services, finance-insurance-real estate, health services, public administration, retail).
- Net migration varies directly with the revival of traditional sectors (e.g., agriculture-extractive activities).
- Net migration varies directly with conventional migration forces (e.g., employment and income change).
- Net migration varies inversely with push or excess labor supply factors (e.g., agriculture-extractive 1980, educational services 1980).

For the In-poverty subgroup and PCII (capturing both Low Education and In-poverty), noteworthy variables are wholesale employment % change (+, Low) and total employment % in 1980 (−, low) for PCII. The latter corresponds with theses concerning the ruralization of poverty, also observed in findings on spatial patterns.

For the Low Education subgroup, noteworthy variables are construction employment % change (+, Medium), public administration employment % change (+, Low), retail employment % change (+, Medium), total employment % change (+, High), and median household income % change (+, Low). In general, these sectors correspond with labor market opportunities for persons with low education.

Discussion of Findings and Concluding Observations

This chapter has examined relationships between post-1960s socioeconomic restructuring and migration. There is no question that migration processes have been affected by restructuring, but the nature of this in terms of general constructs has received little attention. We began, then, by posing questions concerning the impact on migration processes of occurrences commonly associated with socioeconomic restructuring in North America—downsizing of economic activity, changes in the significance of economic sectors, shifts in the value of various labor force attributes and deskilling, and the delinking of labor from places of employment. Another aspect is the socioeconomic landscape on which migration occurs, an aspect that intersects with the restructuring debate.

One school, focusing on *deindustrialization,* views regions as homogeneous entities that suffer uniformly from socioeconomic restructuring of the post-1960s. *Post-Fordist transition* perspectives focus on specialized areas such as global cities, territorial production complexes, and particular lead sectors of the economy. The *old industrial region* focus, which we favor, considers more common settings composed of networks of medium-sized towns and trade centers, large urban complexes, rural areas distant from metropolitan ones, and places characterized by the continued importance of activities associated with Fordism such as durable manufacturing or extraction. These settings provide evidence that the translation of global, national, and regional trends is highly differentiated at a local level; they are not characterized by the uniformity indicated by research in the deindustrialization or post-Fordist transition traditions. The Ohio River Valley, our study area, mirrors the local differentiation perspective, details of which are elaborated as a foundation for subsequent analyses of migration.

One striking feature of the Ohio River Valley, illuminated by empirical analyses, is its trifurcation in terms of both employment change and net migration for the population overall. In general, low-negative employment growth and out-migration are highly prevalent in areas of southern Illinois, western Kentucky, southeastern Ohio, southwestern Pennsylvania, and West Virginia. These areas, at the western and eastern extremities of the Ohio River Valley, are characterized the most by Fordist activities, particularly durable manufacturing and mineral extraction. By contrast, high employment growth and in-migration are found at the ORV's center, particularly in a more or less continual band stretching from Evansville through Louisville-Lexington-Cincinnati-Dayton to Columbus—areas that represent *New Age* contemporary economies and have prospered significantly since the 1970s. Outside the umbrella of these metropolitan areas (but still in the ORV's central section), the more rural counties tend to experience average growth in employment and neutral net migration.

This is, of course, a generalization—the spatial demarcation is not absolute, and no perfect correlation exists between employment growth and net migration.

It is highly relevant, however, that the ravages of deindustrialization continue to appear in 1990 statistics, twenty years after the watershed of Fordism, during which adjustment to an equilibrium surely should have occurred. This observation is rendered even more relevant in light of a dramatic economic resurgence in formerly Fordist areas, which has been documented through field reconnaissance by the authors and statistically by Brown, Lobao, and Verheyen (1996). What is happening, then? Has the equilibrium not yet been reached because shifts in the relevance of economic sectors and labor force attributes, downsizing, and deskilling are still ongoing in a significant manner? Has the dramatic resurgence observed in field reconnaissance occurred since 1990? These are important questions for future research.

A second finding of significance is the set of independent variables notably related to net migration at the county level. The direct relationship between net migration and the growth of activities identified with contemporary economies (e.g., communications, educational services, finance-insurance-real estate, health services, public administration, retail) underscores a major thesis of this research—that socioeconomic restructuring and migration are highly interlinked and migration constructs should be rethought and modified to reflect this. It is not simply that activities identified with contemporary economies would not have appeared in statistical models twenty years ago. In addition, these activities, as well as more traditional migrant-drawing sectors (e.g., agriculture-extractive, durable and nondurable manufacturing), are vastly changed in their form, function, and labor demand characteristics, as noted for Chillicothe, Ohio, by Gibbs (1997).

A third important finding concerns the sharp bifurcation among migrant subgroups. One cluster is High and Medium Education, Older and Younger Age, Not-in-poverty; the second cluster is Low Education, In-poverty. Differences were expected; a more or less neat division into two groups was not. In broad terms, supported by our statistical findings, this indicates a society bifurcated between those who participate in the contemporary economy and those who do not. The observation is not new, but its manifestation in migration was a surprise nevertheless.

Relevant in the ORV context, which represents a broad swath of local settings, is the reverberation of this finding with research on the ruralization of poverty, one aspect of the socioeconomic restructuring that is a backdrop for work reported here. Rural poverty, which has long rivaled urban poverty, is a significant issue. Research tends to focus on factors such as community reliance on a single industry, falling wages, fewer employment opportunities, declining returns to agriculture and changing family structure leading to more female-headed households (Lichter and McLaughlin 1995; Lobao 1990). Considerably less attention has been given to mobility of the poor and less educated. Fitchen (1994) indicated that the rate of such mobility is notably higher than usual, on the order of 70 percent versus 20 percent and often occurring more than once per year. The major factor is a chronic gap between household income and housing costs; interpersonal disruption, such as in partnering relationships, is also important. Employment opportunity elsewhere plays a very minor role. The rural destination may reflect community or family ties, attachment to or familiarity with a place, and low-cost living in small towns, villages, or trailer housing. Nord (1998) does not completely contradict this, but he attributes more causality to labor market factors.

That these factors fall outside the purview of conventional migration constructs and related analyses is noteworthy but particularly so in light of the dramatic socioeconomic-spatial restructuring of recent decades. The norm has changed dramatically. Clearly, then, future research should more vigorously target the subgroup distinctiveness of migration processes.

Note

Research reported here was supported by the National Research Initiative Competition Grants Program, USDA, Grant 93–37401–8972. Earlier versions of this chapter were presented at the 1995 meeting of the North American Regional Science Council, as a Presidential Address, the Regional Research Institute of West Virginia University, and elsewhere. Data were provided by William H. Frey of the University of Michigan Center for Population Research.

References

Bluestone, Barry, and Bennett Harrison. 1982. *The Deindustrialization of America*. New York: Basic Books.

Brown, Lawrence A. 1991. *Place, Migration, and Development in the Third World: An Alternative View*. London: Routledge.

———. 1999. "Change, Continuity, and the Pursuit of Geographic Understanding." *Annals of the Association of American Geographers*.

Brown, Lawrence A., and Linda M. Lobao. 1997. "Regional Change As the Interplay of Global and Local." *Korean Journal of Applied Geography* 20.

Brown, Lawrence A., Linda M. Lobao, and Anthony L. Verheyen. 1996. "Continuity and Change in an Old Industrial Region." *Growth and Change* 27: 175–205.

Brown, Lawrence A., and Rickie L. Sanders. 1981. "Toward a Development Paradigm of Migration: With Particular Reference to Third World Settings." In Gordon F. DeJong and Robert W. Gardner (eds.), *Migration Decision Making: Multidisciplinary Approaches to Micro-Level Studies in Developed and Developing Countries*. New York: Pergamon.

Clark, Gordon L. 1989. "Pittsburgh in Transition: Consolidation of Prosperity in an Era of Economic Restructuring." In R. A. Beauregard (ed.), *Economic Restructuring and Political Response*. Newbury Park: Sage.

Fitchen, Janet M. 1991. *Endangered Spaces, Enduring Places*. Boulder: Westview.

———. 1994. "Residential Mobility among the Rural Poor." *Rural Sociology* 59: 416–36.

Florida, Richard. 1996. "Regional Creative Destruction: Production Organization, Globalization, and the Economic Transformation of the Midwest." *Economic Geography* 72: 314–334.

Frey, William H. 1995. "The New Geography of Population Shifts: Trends towards Balkanization." In R. Farley (ed.), *State of the Union: America in the 1990s, Volume 2, Social Trends*. New York: Russell Sage.

Friedmann, John, and Robert Wulff. 1976. "The Urban Transition: Comparative Studies of Newly Industrializing Societies." In C. Board, R. J. Chorley, P. Haggett, and D. R. Stoddart (eds.), *Progress in Geography, Volume 8*. New York: St. Martin's.

Gibbs, Nancy. 1997. "Warming to Success." *Time Magazine,* May 19: 36–37.

Gober, Patricia. 1993. "Americans on the Move." *Population Bulletin* 48, 3. Washington, D.C.: Population Reference Bureau.

Hirsch, James S. 1996. "A High-Tech System for Sending the Mail Unfolds at Fidelity: Robots at 'Kentucky Farm' Boost Output, Invigorate Back-Office Operations." *Wall Street Journal,* March 20: 1, 11.

Hudson, Raymond. 1989. "Labour Market Changes and New Forms of Work in Old Industrial Regions: Maybe Flexibility for Some but Not Flexible Accumulation." *Environment and Planning D: Society and Space* 7: 5–30.

Kraybill, David S. 1995. "Facts on Job Creation in Ohio." *Ohio's Challenge* 8, 2: 4–7.

Lichter, Daniel T., Gail M. Johnston, and Diane K. McLaughlin. 1994. "Changing Linkages between Work and Poverty in Rural America." *Rural Sociology* 59: 395–415.

Lichter, Daniel T., and Diane K. McLaughlin. 1995. "Changing Economic Opportunities, Family Structure, and Poverty in Rural Areas." *Rural Sociology* 60: 688–706.

Lobao, Linda M. 1990. *Locality and Inequality: Farm and Industry Structure and Socioeconomic Conditions*. Albany: State University of New York Press.

Lowry, Ira S. 1966. *Migration and Metropolitan Growth: Two Analytical Models*. San Francisco: Chandler.

Nord, Mark. 1998. "Poor People on the Move: County-to-County Migration and the Spatial Concentration of Poverty." *Journal of Regional Science* 38: 329–352.

Page, Brian, and Richard Walker. 1991. "From Settlement to Fordism: The Agro-Industrial Revolution in the American Midwest." *Economic Geography* 67: 281–315.

Piore, Michael J., and Charles F. Sable. 1984. *The Second Industrial Divide*. New York: Basic Books.

Reid, Robert L. (ed.). 1991. *Always a River: The Ohio River and the American Experience*. Bloomington: Indiana University Press.

Sassen, Saskia. 1991. *The Global City*. New York: Princeton University Press.

Scott, Allen J. 1988a. "Flexible Production Systems and Regional Development: The Rise of New Industrial Spaces in North America and Western Europe." *International Journal of Urban and Regional Research* 12: 171–185.

———. 1988b. *New Industrial Spaces*. London: Pion.

Sjaastad, Larry A. 1962. "The Costs and Returns of Human Migration." *Journal of Political Economy* 70: 80–93.

Soja, Edward. 1989. *Post-Modern Geographies*. London: Verso.

4

Social and Economic Change and Intrametropolitan Migration

Richard Morrill and Anthony Falit-Baiamonte

Inequality and migration have typically been pursued as two fairly distinct research and teaching endeavors, although we know that people may move to improve their well-being and that the effects of migration on origin and destination areas may be profound. In this chapter, we combine these interests directly and ask the following questions: How does internal migration influence the social and economic character of subregions of the modern American metropolis? Is there a spatial restructuring that manifests forces of social and economic restructuring in the wider society? Does migration have the net impact of equilibrating—that is, reducing polarization of well-being across the urban landscape—as in simple theory it should, or can it, in fact, aggravate and reinforce differences?

These questions will be pursued here in a fairly simple and limited way as the beginning of a larger, more complex project. We report on analyses of two cities, Atlanta and Minneapolis–St. Paul,[1] and we utilize for now just one data set and a rather crude set of geographic units: the counties constituting the two metropolitan areas. Our data are the 1985–1990 intercounty flows of migrants, even though these represent mainly residential mobility rather than true migratory flows. The two metropolitan areas are convenient for this study, as they both have a fairly large number of counties and are similar in size and dynamism and in their role as major regional economic capitals. We relate the 1985–1990 flows to characteristics of counties in 1980 and 1990 and to change across the decade.

Theory and Expectations

Our metropolitan areas have been subject to massive social and economic restructuring since World War II. This includes:

- The birth of the baby-boom generation of 1946–1964, the vast expansion of middle-class family suburbs, accompanied by the selective decline and employment losses of the central cities
- The social revolution of the 1960s and 1970s in reaction to the entry into the cities of migrant blacks or poor whites, which brought about increasing rights but also increasing instability of households headed by women and minorities
- The stagnation or decline in real wages in the 1970s and 1980s as a result of the entry of that huge baby boom into the labor force and the competitive behavior of global capital
- The selective redevelopment and gentrification of parts of the central cities and experimentation with varying forms of management of growth and development in the face of deregulation and structural change toward increasing inequality

Metropolitan evolution is a consequence of the behavior of capital, of households, of social groups, of governments and other organizations—all with varying preferences and powers. Decisions concerning the perceived necessity of businesses to decentralize and later to recentralize, in part to maintain profitability, are clearly critical, even if they are in part a response to independent household decisions. Households have diversified (i.e., husband–wife families have become less dominant) for complex reasons, as have their preferences and capabilities, with a consequence of marked spatial sorting, including widespread suburbanization of traditional families. Despite legal decisions and programs enacted to encourage racial and class integration, group consciousness continues to segregate the metropolis. Finally, households, businesses, and organizations, through the mechanism of local government and regional entities, profoundly influence the location of jobs, of services, of housing of different kinds, of transportation, and thus of households and classes.

This is a complex history. Specifically for the period 1985–1990, what might we expect? On the one hand, forces remained for continuing peripheralization: the relative shifting of jobs—especially in manufacturing, retailing and basic services—accompanying or even leading population to take advantage of lower-cost sites, external connections, a more educated labor force, and higher average suburban incomes. Households, especially husband-wife households with children, should have had strong incentives to move out for space, for affordable single-family homes, for perceived better schools, and to flee contact with blacks and poor ethnic populations. Thus, other things being equal, this should be a disequilibrating force, leading to increasing polarization between an increasingly affluent periphery and a stagnant core plagued by decreased access to appropriate jobs. Within this overly generalized suburbia, however, we might expect particularly significant change at the outer edge as suburban development displaces perhaps fairly low-income, rural, small-town settings. At the inner suburban edge, there is the possibility of stagnation or selective decline from the spillover of minority and poor populations from an overcrowded or unsafe central city and even from the suburbanization of some middle-class city households that are poorer than the middle-class households they displaced.

On the other hand, in the later 1980s there were powerful constituencies for revitalization of parts of the metropolitan cores. Downtown landowners, city unions, and political leaders—the urban growth machine—aided by federal agencies, such as the Department of Housing and the Urban Development and Urban Mass Transit Administration and legislation like Intermodal Surface Transportation Efficiency Act, cooperated to reinvest in central business districts, often with fair success as in the cases of Atlanta and the Twin Cities. The social restructuring of households—with far more single persons, roommates of the same or opposite sex, childless couples and empty nesters, and older widows—along with the shift of downtown employment to business and information services, created a new market for inner-city apartment and townhouse living. In addition, the relatively high educational levels and political liberalism of such people predisposed them toward the new urbanism of city revitalization and gentrification. Such reurbanization may result in outward displacement of the less affluent. Unfortunately, even more than with the forces for decentralization, these urbanizing forces may be difficult to discern at the county level, except perhaps through compositional changes of core county populations.

Previous Work

The literature on urban structure and residential mobility is vast. We note here just a few studies especially critical to the argument of this chapter. Some especially relevant work on urban restructuring includes, first, those who see a "dual" city, who stress occupational division of labor and social polarization. Much of this literature has a political or an economic focus—for example Mollenkopf and Castells (1991), Van Kempen (1994), Sassen (1991), and Fainstein, Gordon, and Harloe (1992). A second set of authors emphasizes the role of suburbanization and the creation of a "spatial mismatch" of people and opportunities—for example, Bourne (1993), Wilson (1987), McLafferty and Preston (1996), and Stanback (1991). Yet other authors introduce complexities such as lifestyle and demographic factors—for example Clark (1987), Bourne (1996), Hamnett (1994), and Massey (1996).

Short (1978) provides a good overview of residential mobility, whereas Frey (1985) and St. John, Edwards, and Wenk (1995) specifically investigate U.S. metropolitan mobility. Most directly relating migration and residential mobility to urban restructuring are the works by Bourne (1993) on income change within Canadian cities, Bourne (1996) on prospects for reurbanization in overcoming polarization, Hill and Wolman (1997a, 1997b) on central city–suburban income discrepancies, MacLachlan and Sawada (1997) on social inequality in Canadian cities, Nord (1996) on the role of migration in spatial concentrations of poverty, and Smith, Duncan, and Reid (1994) on gentrification in New York City. Finally, we note the valuable empirical work of Adams, Van Drasek, and Lambert (1995) on Minneapolis–St. Paul that includes comparisons with other U.S. metropolitan areas.

Methods

The strategy is fairly simple. The 1985–1990 county-to-county migration data reported in the 1990 U.S. Census contain relevant characteristics of both stayers (nonmovers) and the persons in each intercounty flow.[2] These data can therefore be used to assess whether, given the characteristics of intercounty migrants, the net impact of all local flows results in a relative improvement or deterioration of selected social and economic characteristics of county populations. We first present tables and maps indicating the characteristics of intercounty migrants for the major flows within the two metropolitan regions, the net impact of those flows, and the aggregate effects of the flows on the counties. We then undertake a limited statistical analysis, relating some characteristics of the flows to the base-period characteristics of the counties. We conclude with a review of whether the observed changes reflect the expectations outlined earlier.

Selected characteristics of counties are analyzed for 1980 and 1990, as well as for changes from 1980 to 1990. The indicators used included nonfamily share of all households, minority share of the population, proportion of college-educated persons, white-collar share of all workers, and share of the population below poverty. A measure of income inequality (skewness) is also included and is defined as the difference between mean household income and median household income divided by median household income (the standard deviation is not available). We first calculated the percentage of all of the population or of all households represented by a particular category—for example, college-educated persons—for each county relative to the metropolitan-wide average for each decade. We then then calculated the difference between the 1980 and 1990 values as a measure of change.

The migration data were similarly analyzed, but this was a little more complex. We were able to use some of the same variables: shares of the college educated, minorities, white-collar workers, persons below poverty, and nonfamily households. Household income, however, is not known for migrants but rather for persons in several income strata, a situation resulting in a less than satisfactory measure of skewness. Values for the variables were calculated for the total in- and out-migration flows to and from each metropolitan county, and the differences in character of the in- and out-migration flows were assessed and, in some cases, mapped. The results were used to answer the following questions:

- Is there evidence of core–periphery centralization and decentralization processes?
- Is there evidence of sectoral differentiation in social change?
- Is there evidence of polarization, in the sense of greater average differences across the metropolis, and of greater inequality in some subregions?
- Do the same processes and patterns appear in both Atlanta and Minneapolis–St. Paul? What is different? Does race matter?
- Does the 1985–1990 migration change pattern correspond to the 1980–1990 patterns of population change, or are there anomalies, in which the pattern of migrant characteristics differs from the pattern for the population as a whole?
- What are some of the greatest and least differences among in- and out-migration profiles?
- Do these migration and social change relationships reflect similar changes in industrial structure?

Decentralization/Centralization and Sectoral Differentiation

For both Atlanta and the Twin Cities, only one indicator—the share of nonfamily households—clearly reveals the expected tendency for family households to leave the core for the periphery and for nonfamily persons to leave the periphery for the core, irrespective of class variation. This reflects the preference or necessity of families to find single-family housing in the farther suburbs and of younger entrants to the labor force or college to find opportunities and apartments in the urban core (Figure 4.1, Table 4.1).

Is there evidence of sectoral differentiation, that is, of selective migration exchanges in certain subregions of the metropolis? Indeed, such processes seem to be dominant among the chosen indicators. Looking at two closely related variables, the college educated and white-collar occupations, for Atlanta we see a marked north–south axis of counties—including the core counties of Fulton and Cobb and the suburban counties of Cherokee and Fayette—with marked gains through in- and out-migration flows, whereas core but suburban DeKalb and

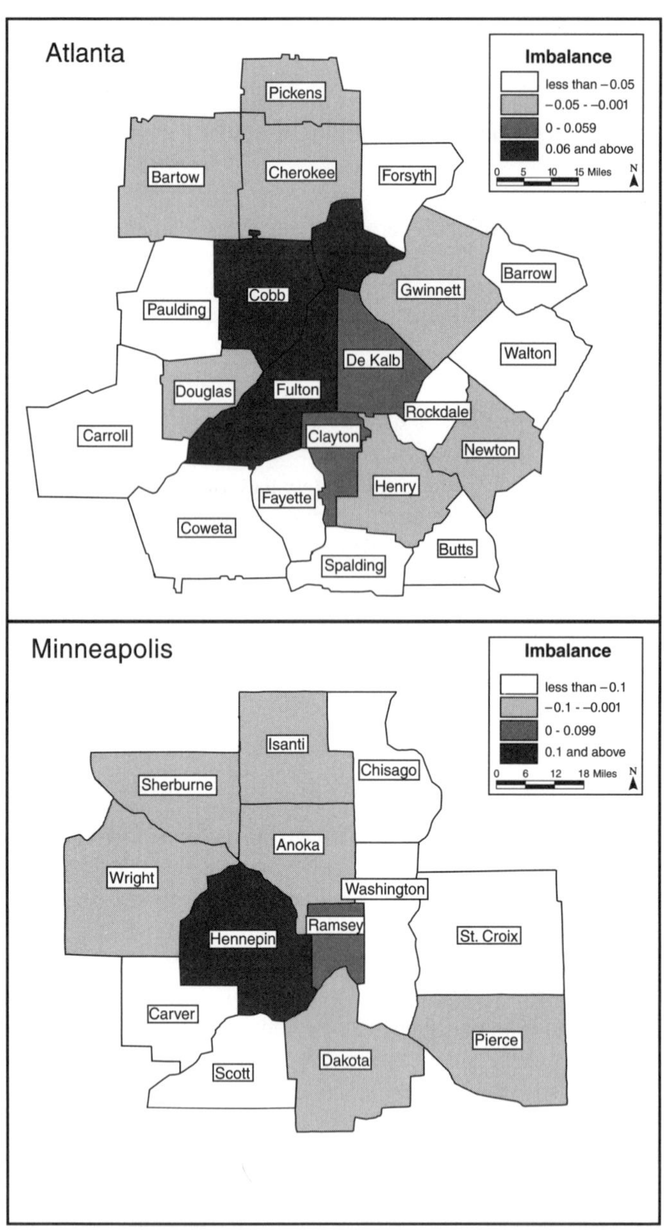

Figure 4.1 Nonfamily Household Migration Imbalance, Atlanta and Minneapolis

Table 4.1 Nonfamily and College Migration, Minneapolis and Atlanta

	(A) Nonfamily Households					
	In-Migration	Out-Migration	Effectiveness	% In	% Out	Diff %
Minneapolis	51,931	51,931	0.00	21.6	21.6	0.0
Anoka	5,309	5,978	−0.06	15.2	23.1	−7.9
Carver	860	1,417	−0.24	12.1	25.1	−13.0
Chisago	570	886	−0.22	11.0	25.8	−14.8
Dakota	7,696	5,224	0.19	19.3	23.9	−4.6
Hennepin	16,991	15,539	0.04	33.1	19.3	13.8
Isanti	349	568	−0.24	10.2	19.8	−9.7
Ramsey	12,313	12,719	−0.02	29.5	20.3	9.2
Scott	1,072	1,440	−0.15	12.8	24.2	−11.4
Sherburne	1,042	793	0.14	14.6	23.0	−8.4
Washington	3,313	4,516	−0.15	12.6	26.6	−14.0
Wright	1,010	1,308	−0.13	12.2	22.1	−9.9
Pierce, WI	688	760	−0.05	24.1	26.8	−2.7
St. Croix, WI	718	769	−0.03	17.0	27.4	−10.4
Atlanta	61,914	61,914	0.00	18.0	18.0	0.0
Barrow	312	238	0.13	8.6	15.1	−6.6
Bartow	611	341	0.28	10.5	15.1	−4.5
Butts	118	176	−0.20	5.2	13.5	−8.3
Carroll	961	728	0.14	13.1	21.9	−8.8
Cherokee	1,558	890	0.27	9.4	11.9	−2.5
Clayton	4,357	3,257	0.14	16.9	11.1	5.8
Cobb	9,606	8,330	0.07	24.7	17.8	7.0
Coweta	458	381	0.09	6.5	12.9	−6.4
DeKalb	14,694	15,864	−0.04	23.7	19.6	4.1
Douglas	1,310	1,181	0.05	13.3	14.0	−0.7
Fayette	804	1,095	−0.15	6.5	19.0	−12.5
Forsyth	723	356	0.34	10.4	17.4	−6.9
Fulton	13,916	20,840	−0.20	29.0	20.2	8.9
Gwinnett	8,368	4,757	0.28	17.8	18.7	−0.8
Henry	1,033	671	0.21	6.7	11.0	−4.3
Newton	533	372	0.18	10.8	12.2	−1.4
Paulding	609	465	0.13	6.7	14.8	−8.1
Pickens	195	67	0.49	10.2	11.0	−0.9
Rockdale	877	912	−0.02	9.1	18.2	−9.2
Spalding	336	541	−0.23	9.0	19.6	−10.6
Walton	535	479	0.06	8.9	18.7	−9.8

(Cont.)

Table 4.1 Nonfamily and College Migration, Minneapolis and Atlanta *(Cont.)*

	(B) College Educated					
	In-Migration	Out-Migration	Effectiveness	% In	% Out	Diff %
Minneapolis	52,088	52,088	0.00	26.3	26.3	0.0
Anoka	4,353	4,203	0.02	15.8	19.8	−3.9
Carver	1,729	1,041	0.25	29.8	22.5	7.3
Chisago	440	339	0.13	11.4	12.2	−0.8
Dakota	9,614	4,649	0.35	29.6	25.6	4.0
Hennepin	13,929	19,149	−0.16	31.0	29.1	1.9
Isanti	225	262	−0.08	9.3	11.2	−1.9
Ramsey	11,739	16,267	−0.16	32.6	31.4	1.2
Scott	1,475	862	0.26	21.9	17.6	4.2
Sherburne	737	475	0.22	13.3	17.0	−3.7
Washington	5,670	2,638	0.36	27.9	18.8	9.1
Wright	832	745	0.06	13.0	15.6	−2.6
Pierce, WI	372	865	−0.40	15.2	37.2	−22.0
St. Croix, WI	973	589	0.25	29.1	26.0	3.2
Atlanta	69,094	69,094	0.00	24.6	24.6	0.0
Barrow	284	164	0.27	9.6	13.6	−3.9
Bartow	473	208	0.39	10.5	11.4	−0.9
Butts	135	135	0.00	7.2	13.0	−5.9
Carroll	370	910	−3.42	6.3	32.7	−26.5
Cherokee	3,131	996	0.52	23.2	17.2	6.0
Clayton	2,774	3,007	−0.04	13.8	13.2	0.6
Cobb	10,833	10,444	0.02	33.0	26.5	6.4
Coweta	751	343	0.37	13.9	15.0	−1.2
DeKalb	15,036	21,506	−0.18	29.7	31.7	−2.0
Douglas	972	530	0.29	12.6	8.1	4.5
Fayette	2,020	735	0.47	21.6	15.7	6.0
Forsyth	1,234	293	0.62	21.4	17.9	3.4
Fulton	15,307	22,221	−0.18	37.4	26.3	11.0
Gwinnett	11,648	5,700	0.34	29.6	27.1	2.5
Henry	1,199	457	0.45	9.9	9.9	0.0
Newton	386	136	0.48	9.5	5.7	3.7
Paulding	533	274	0.32	7.2	11.6	−4.4
Pickens	174	70	0.43	11.7	14.5	−2.8
Rockdale	1,114	485	0.39	14.9	11.6	3.3
Spalding	291	337	−0.07	10.5	15.8	−5.3
Walton	429	202	0.36	9.1	10.2	−1.1

counties along the southern periphery experienced relative losses (Figure 4.2, Table 4.1). These trends presumably reflect patterns of labor force and racial change (DeKalb) and the location of high-skilled jobs and those requiring high levels of education in this north–south corridor. Similar in process but different in orientation, in Minneapolis–St. Paul a southern concentration of the college educated and white-collar jobs occurs, which includes the core counties of Hennepin and Ramsey but emphasizes the inner east and southern suburban counties. Jobs in the northwest and southeast sectors have become less oriented toward white-collar occupations and high levels of education.

The more direct outcome variable, change in the percentage below poverty, reflects all of the other indicator variables but in no simple way (Figure 4.3, Table 4.2). In Atlanta the pattern is more core–periphery than sectoral in that the four innermost counties that had net out-migration overall also experienced increasing poverty concentrations, whereas all but one outer suburban county reduced the percentage of poor through migration. The exception, Carroll County, experienced a relative loss in white-collar jobs and the college educated, but this may be an artifact of its being dominated by an undergraduate college. Inner Fulton and Cobb Counties gained in educated and white-collar workers even while becoming less familial and poorer, reflecting losses in blue-collar jobs and implying greater income polarization—an implication supported by the 1980–1990 values and changes in income inequality (skewness). Suburban Fayette and Cherokee Counties also gained in white-collar and educated populations but became relatively more familial with lower concentrations of poor.

DeKalb and Clayton Counties, in a sectoral shift or, perhaps more accurately, a spillover or extension of the inner core to the southeast, experienced a pervasive relative decline across most indicators—occupation, family status, and poverty levels. (Not surprisingly, they also gained the most through net migration of blacks out of Atlanta.) Conversely, selected outer suburban counties in the next tier or ring—Forsyth, Gwinnett, Rockdale, and Henry to the east and Douglas to the west—had the opposite experience, with decreasing poverty and increasing white-collar and college levels.

For the Twin Cities, the change in poverty through the migration interchange more closely mirrors the change in education and occupation—that is, poverty levels increased along the northwest to southeast axis but decreased to the south and inner east and also to the northeast. This situation also seems to reflect the core–periphery change in nonfamily versus family households. As with Atlanta, a suburban edge county, Pierce County, Wisconsin, experienced relative decline, as did one of the core counties, Ramsey (relative to Hennepin).

In sum, evidence reveals core–periphery centralization and decentralization forces, as well as sector-specific differentiation in both metropolitan areas. They have similar examples of counties, outer as well as inner, that declined overall, whereas several suburban counties rose in overall status. But evidence from both areas also indicates greater local polarization of income, notably in

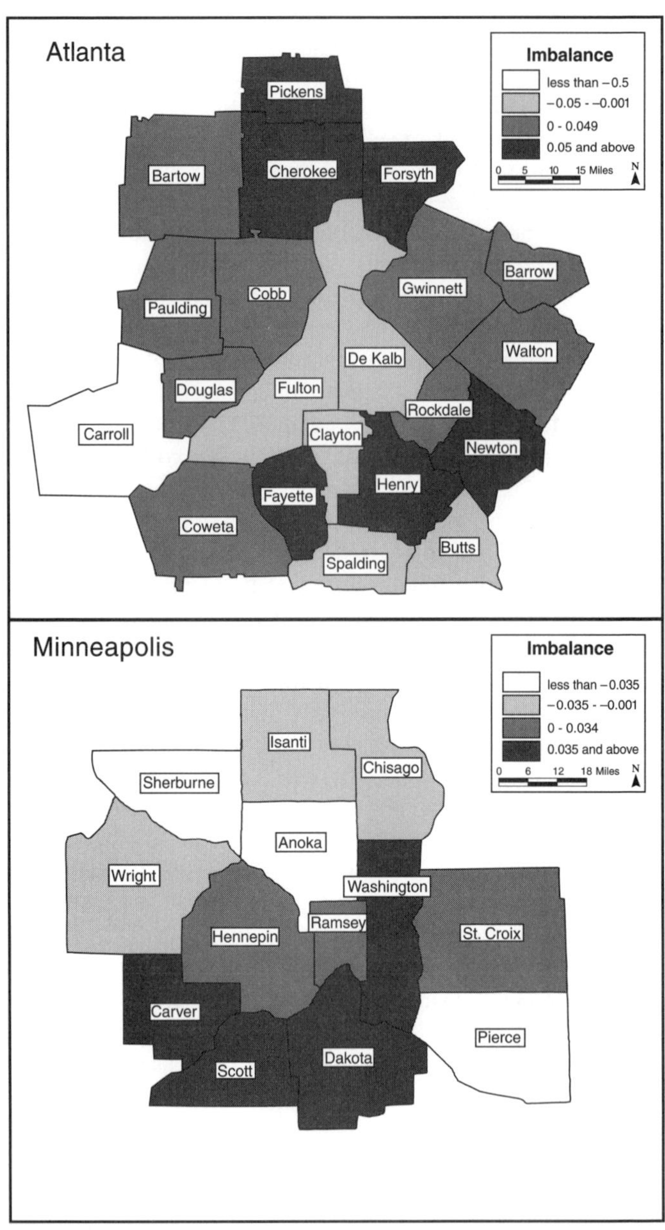

Figure 4.2 College Education Migration Imbalance, Atlanta and Minneapolis

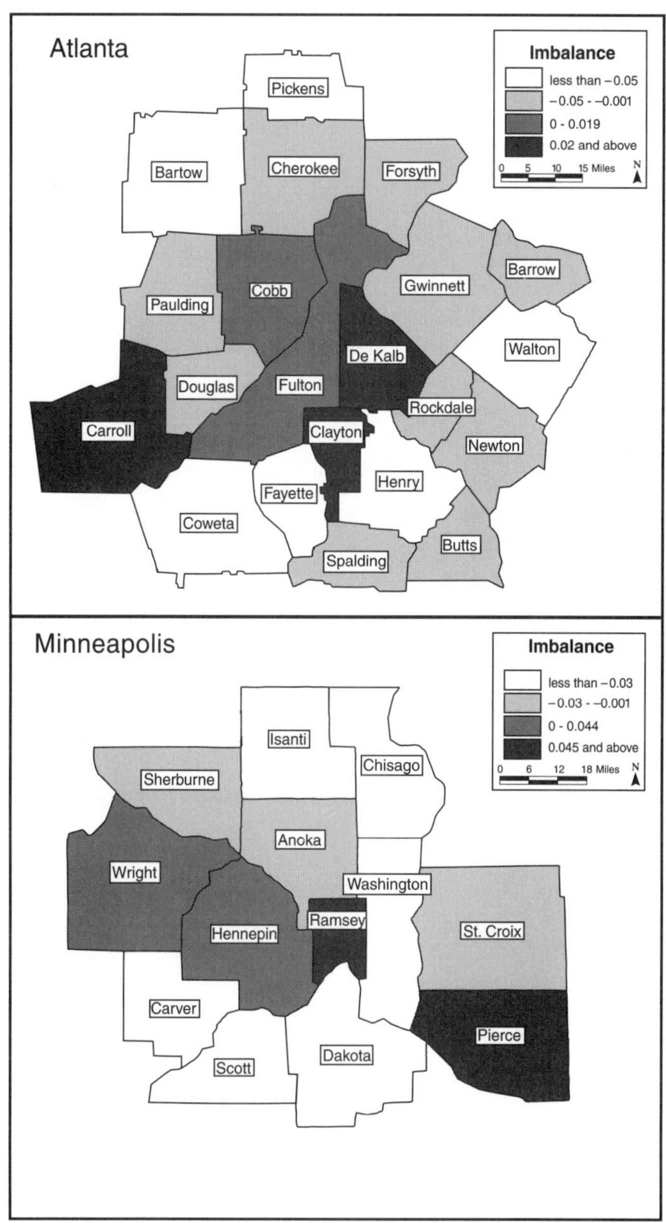

Figure 4.3 Persons below Poverty Migration Imbalance, Atlanta and Minneapolis

Table 4.2 Poverty Migration, Minneapolis and Atlanta

	Below-Poverty In-Migrants	Below-Poverty Out-Migrants	Poverty Migration Effectiveness	Percent of Poor in Out-Migrants	Percent of Poor in In-Migrants	Percent Difference
Minneapolis	18,003	18,003	0.00	7.7	7.7	0.0
Anoka	2,428	2,068	0.08	7.1	8.2	−1.1
Carver	324	457	−0.17	4.7	8.5	−3.9
Chisago	390	443	−0.06	7.7	13.4	−5.8
Dakota	1,900	1,744	0.04	4.8	8.3	−3.4
Hennepin	4,477	6,047	−0.15	9.2	7.8	1.4
Isanti	355	385	−0.04	10.6	14.2	−3.6
Ramsey	4,438	3,831	0.07	11.2	6.3	4.9
Scott	378	474	−0.11	4.6	8.4	−3.8
Sherburne	702	385	0.29	10.6	11.6	−1.1
Washington	1,370	1,434	−0.02	5.2	8.8	−3.6
Wright	524	345	0.21	6.5	6.1	0.4
Pierce, WI	454	174	0.45	20.1	6.5	13.6
St. Croix, WI	263	207	0.12	6.4	7.7	−1.3
Atlanta	28,903	28,903	0.00	8.7	8.7	0.0
Barrow	386	223	0.27	10.7	14.7	−4.0
Bartow	506	299	0.26	9.0	14.6	−5.6
Butts	270	234	0.07	17.6	18.9	−1.3
Carroll	1,050	310	0.54	17.5	10.1	7.4
Cherokee	811	511	0.23	5.0	7.0	−2.0
Clayton	3,192	1,664	0.31	12.7	5.8	6.9
Cobb	2,845	2,508	0.06	7.5	5.5	1.9
Coweta	435	530	−0.10	6.2	19.5	−13.3
DeKalb	7,283	5,747	0.12	12.2	7.3	4.9
Douglas	783	913	−0.08	8.2	11.4	−3.2
Fayette	283	510	−0.29	2.3	9.1	−6.8
Forsyth	282	169	0.25	4.2	8.5	−4.4
Fulton	4,908	10,791	−0.37	11.0	10.8	0.2
Gwinnett	1,752	1,347	0.13	3.8	5.5	−1.8
Henry	649	850	−0.13	4.3	14.4	−10.1
Newton	660	405	0.24	14.0	14.3	−0.3
Paulding	695	375	0.30	7.7	12.2	−4.5
Pickens	219	128	0.26	11.6	24.0	−12.4
Rockdale	846	545	0.22	8.9	11.5	−2.6
Spalding	592	487	0.10	16.7	19.1	−2.4
Walton	456	422	0.04	7.8	17.8	−10.0

the innermost cosmopolitan core and in suburban areas that seem to have become a little more homogeneous or at least to have experienced less than the average increase in inequality.

The migration data also permit disaggregation of flows of persons of various incomes. Although personal rather than household income is problematic for analysis, the results are of some interest (Figures 4.4 and 4.5). In Atlanta the migration of the poorest persons (with incomes below $10,000) shows that families with young children are moving to the far, more affordable edge—understandably avoiding the more affluent intermediate counties. The moderate-income group, with incomes between $10,000 and $25,000, appears to be shifting out of Fulton County (Atlanta) and into the adjacent inner counties of Cobb, DeKalb, and Clayton. Finally, the upper-middle-income group ($25,000–$50,000) clearly picks the growing, more affluent suburban counties, whereas the richest group (incomes over $50,000) is prevalent in several of the counties with high levels of college and white-collar jobs along the north–south axis. The core, Fulton County, especially stands out, corroborating the greater increase in income skewness in the county with more poor nonfamily persons and more rich persons but fewer families in the middle.

In Minneapolis–St. Paul, a similar partition of suburban counties is revealed between some that are gaining poorer persons and more affluent ones that are not. Ramsey County, like DeKalb and Clayton Counties in Atlanta, gained in the number of poor households. Many eastern and southern counties with increasing education levels and white-collar jobs also gained higher-income migrants, but unlike Atlanta the core counties did not gain in the richest persons. Relatedly, they also increased less in inequality (income skewness) between 1980 and 1990 than did Atlanta's Fulton County.

1980–1990 Change

Change in social character from 1980 to 1990 is similar but not identical to the 1985–1990 impacts of migration exchanges, in part because the periods are different and in part because the intrametropolitan migration treated here is only part of migration, which also occurs from the rest of the state, the rest of the nation, and abroad (see end of this chapter). Only one 1980–1990 map is shown (Figure 4.6), that for income inequality or skewness, since we cannot calculate this from the migration data. Overall the 1980–1990 skewness rose from 0.188 to 0.247 (a 31 percent increase) for Atlanta and from 0.144 to 0.202 (a 40 percent increase) for Minneapolis–St. Paul (Table 4.3). The basic difference in skewness between the two cities reflects in part the racial composition (Atlanta has a far higher share of blacks), as well as the traditional egalitarianism of the Upper Midwest compared with the South. The lower increase in skewness in Atlanta (which was well under the mean national increase), however, reflects the city's major education gains and the strength of its economy.

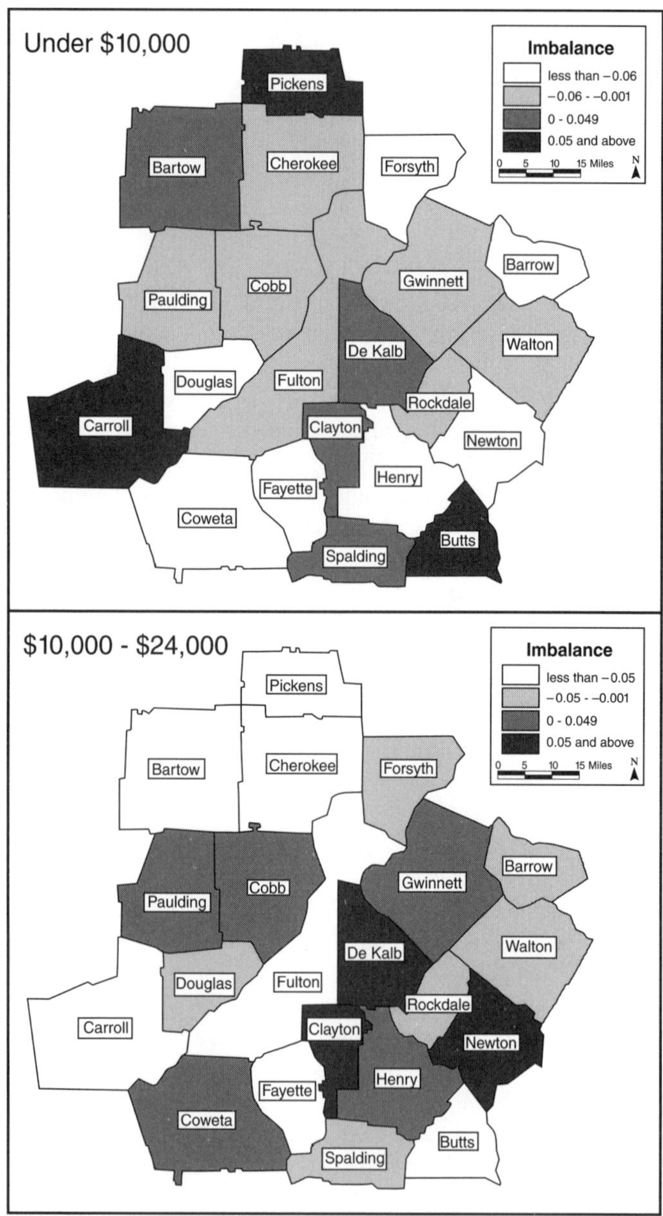

Figure 4.4 Migration Imbalance by Income, Atlanta

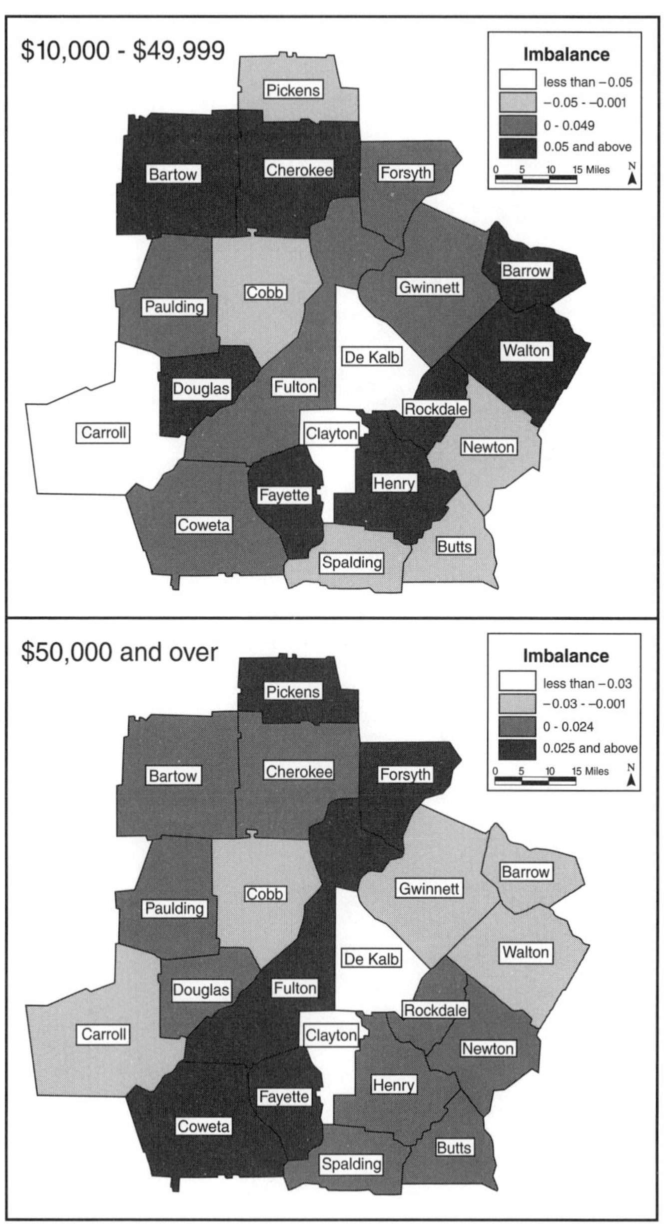

Figure 4.4 (*Cont.*)

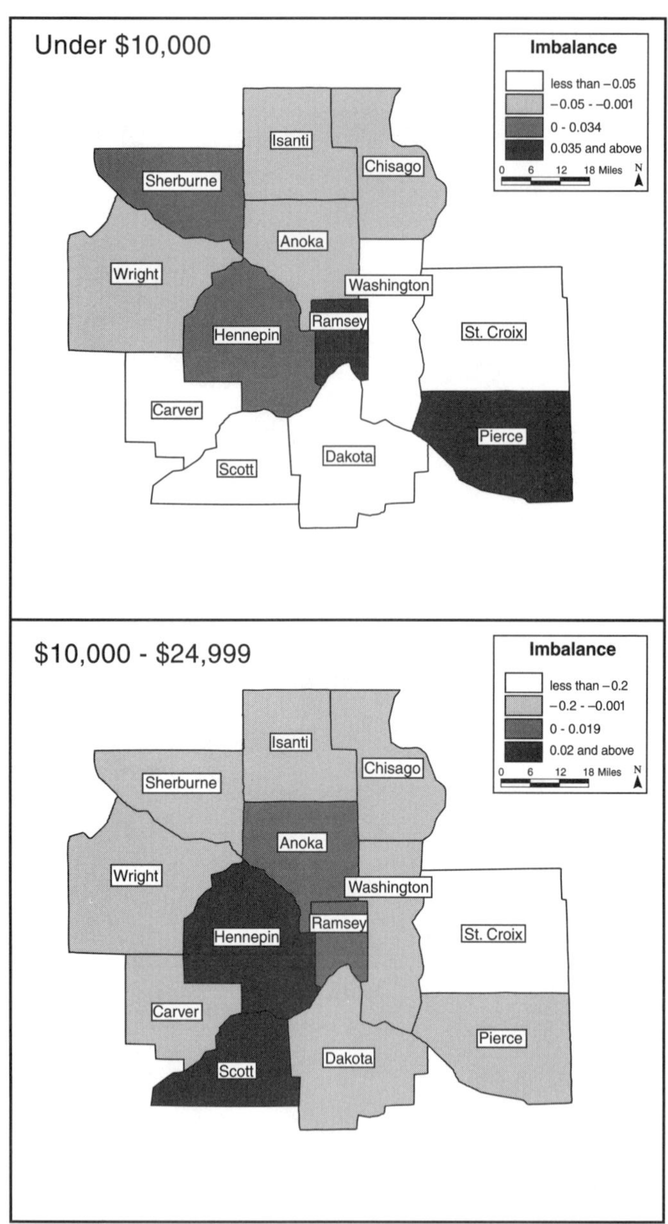

Figure 4.5 Migration Imbalance by Income, Minneapolis

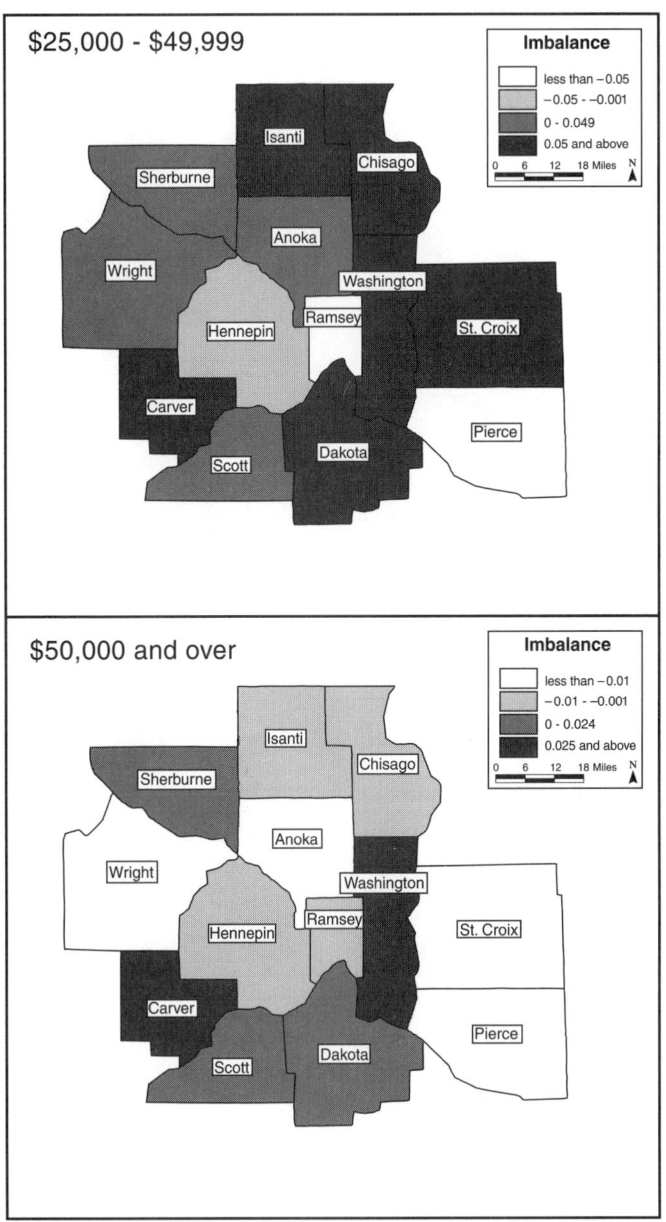

Figure 4.5 (*Cont.*)

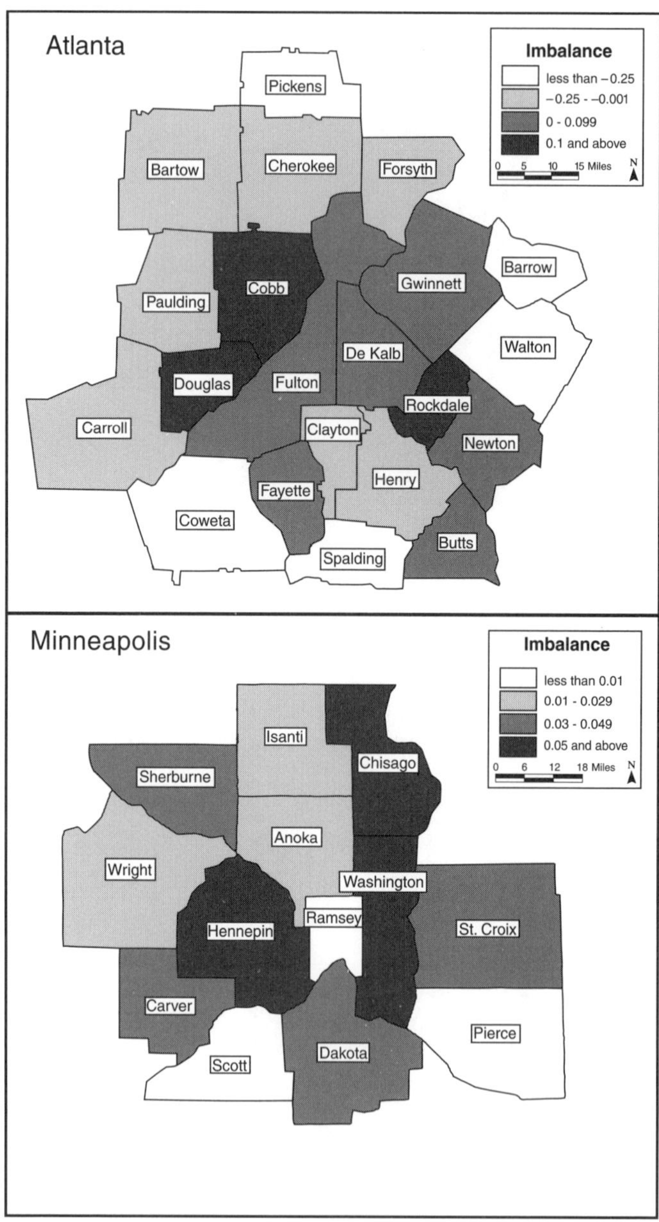

Figure 4.6 1980–1990 Change in Income Skewness, Atlanta and Minneapolis

Table 4.3 Change in Skewness, Minneapolis and Atlanta

	1980 Skewness	1990 Skewness	Change in Skewness
Minneapolis	0.144	0.202	0.058
Anoka	0.048	0.071	0.023
Carver	0.139	0.179	0.040
Chisago	0.062	0.126	0.064
Dakota	0.099	0.139	0.040
Hennepin	0.192	0.266	0.074
Isanti	0.080	0.109	0.029
Ramsey	0.165	0.172	0.007
Scott	0.114	0.121	0.007
Sherburne	0.070	0.108	0.038
Washington	0.081	0.156	0.074
Wright	0.108	0.125	0.017
Pierce, WI	0.152	0.153	0.001
St. Croix, WI	0.101	0.149	0.049
Atlanta	0.188	0.247	0.059
Barrow	0.162	0.132	−0.030
Bartow	0.157	0.182	0.025
Butts	0.193	0.308	0.114
Carroll	0.162	0.202	0.040
Cherokee	0.094	0.081	−0.013
Clayton	0.089	0.116	0.027
Cobb	0.127	0.205	0.078
Coweta	0.219	0.217	−0.002
DeKalb	0.174	0.242	0.068
Douglas	0.045	0.100	0.055
Fayette	0.089	0.124	0.035
Forsyth	0.181	0.187	0.006
Fulton	0.404	0.536	0.132
Gwinnett	0.089	0.139	0.050
Henry	0.119	0.105	−0.014
Newton	0.139	0.201	0.062
Paulding	0.086	0.078	−0.009
Pickens	0.240	0.202	−0.038
Rockdale	0.073	0.174	0.101
Spalding	0.266	0.202	−0.065
Walton	0.212	0.211	−0.001

This finding also applies generally to the South where, despite higher levels of inequality, the increase in inequality between 1980 and 1990 was much lower than for the rest of the nation.

Within the Atlanta region local (intracounty) inequality was fairly modest in both 1980 and 1990. Inequality increased only slightly or even decreased in the outer ring of more homogeneous suburban counties but increased more strongly in the metropolitan core and inner suburban counties, where from the 1985–1990 data we observed not only increasing nonfamily households and spillover of blacks from Atlanta but also the influence of educated, white-collar, higher-income persons. Inequality in Fulton County rose from a high 0.4 to an even higher 0.54, and in neighboring Cobb County it increased from 0.13 to 0.20.

In the Twin Cities the pattern is somewhat different. No county declined absolutely in skewness, although Ramsey County, which did not experience the growth in college-educated and white-collar populations and which gained poor people, had only a very low increase in income inequality, as did far suburban Pierce County, which also gained in lower-income families. The eastern suburban counties of Washington and Chisago increased the most in inequality but from low starting levels, whereas in Hennepin County (Minneapolis), which like Fulton County (Atlanta) had the highest skewness in the metropolis, inequality rose significantly from 0.19 to 0.27 (but still to a level only half that of Fulton's).

1985–1990 Change in Inequality

Although household income is unavailable for migrants, the data on persons by income categories permit a crude measure of skewness or inequality. This measure is given as the ratio of the number in the richest group (income over $50,000) to the sum of the numbers in the two lowest groups (income below $25,000). High ratios for either inflows or outflows imply greater inequality or polarization. Skewness/inequality figures for Atlanta and Minneapolis are presented in Table 4.4 and mapped in Figure 4.7.

For Atlanta a southwest to northeast (I-85) corridor had more unequal inflows than outflows—for example, middle-income families leaving and poorer nonfamily and richer professionals coming in. This relates well to the pattern of the college educated and of white-collar jobs. Conversely, adjoining inner metropolitan counties (Cobb, Clayton, DeKalb, and Gwinnett) had inflows more equal than outflows, implying that these counties were recipient to the families leaving the core counties. The outer counties experienced smaller change, with inflows usually slightly more unequal than outflows, perhaps related to general change in household structure and housing types.

For Minneapolis–St. Paul the pattern is somewhat different. Here the southern counties, which gained in white-collar jobs requiring a college degree, did experience inflows that were more unequal than outflows, whereas Ramsey

Table 4.4 Migration of Poor and Rich Persons, Minneapolis and Atlanta

	Poor[1]		Rich[2]		Rich/Poor Ratio		
	In-Migrants	Out-Migrants	In-Migrants	Out-Migrants	In-Migrants	Out-Migrants	Diff.
Minneapolis	135,132	135,132	12,801	12,801	0.091	0.093	−0.002
Anoka	19,014	15,280	1,036	1,056	0.054	0.069	−0.015
Carver	3,599	3,406	535	287	0.149	0.084	0.064
Chisago	2,868	2,172	126	108	0.044	0.050	−0.006
Dakota	20,244	12,438	2,502	1,327	0.124	0.107	0.017
Hennepin	31,769	43,263	2,641	4,294	0.083	0.099	−0.016
Isanti	1,895	1,938	47	63	0.025	0.033	−0.008
Ramsey	25,649	33,738	2,108	3,540	0.082	0.105	−0.023
Scott	4,419	3,414	508	263	0.115	0.077	0.038
Sherburne	4,105	2,181	302	98	0.074	0.045	0.029
Washington	12,555	10,269	1,903	720	0.152	0.070	0.081
Wright	4,666	3,571	273	315	0.059	0.088	−0.030
Pierce, WI	2,071	1,774	71	98	0.034	0.055	−0.021
St. Croix, WI	2,278	4,330	289	632	0.127	0.146	−0.019
Atlanta	195,149	195,149	20,708	20,708	0.106	0.106	0.000
Barrow	2,248	1,106	34	33	0.015	0.030	−0.015
Bartow	3,618	1,590	197	41	0.054	0.026	0.029
Butts	1,636	871	47	12	0.029	0.014	0.015
Carroll	5,150	2,161	163	101	0.032	0.047	−0.015
Cherokee	8,205	4,234	981	414	0.120	0.098	0.022
Clayton	16,472	16,116	493	1,273	0.030	0.079	−0.049
Cobb	21,114	24,377	2,866	4,014	0.136	0.165	−0.029
Coweta	3,833	1,763	432	83	0.113	0.047	0.066
DeKalb	37,400	43,204	2,984	6,418	0.080	0.149	−0.069
Douglas	5,598	5,430	294	242	0.053	0.045	0.008
Fayette	5,788	3,624	1,107	270	0.191	0.075	0.117
Forsyth	3,659	1,205	747	97	0.204	0.080	0.124
Fulton	25,774	61,475	5,487	5,067	0.213	0.082	0.130
Gwinnett	24,568	13,409	3,181	2,095	0.129	0.156	−0.027
Henry	8,578	3,659	606	160	0.071	0.044	0.027
Newton	3,506	2,003	104	51	0.030	0.025	0.004
Paulding	5,497	1,914	178	56	0.032	0.029	0.003
Pickens	1,224	411	105	21	0.086	0.051	0.035
Rockdale	5,376	3,319	416	121	0.077	0.036	0.041
Spalding	2,304	1,748	113	60	0.049	0.034	0.015
Walton	3,601	1,735	182	79	0.051	0.046	0.005

Notes: 1. Income less than $25,000.
2. Income greater than $50,000.

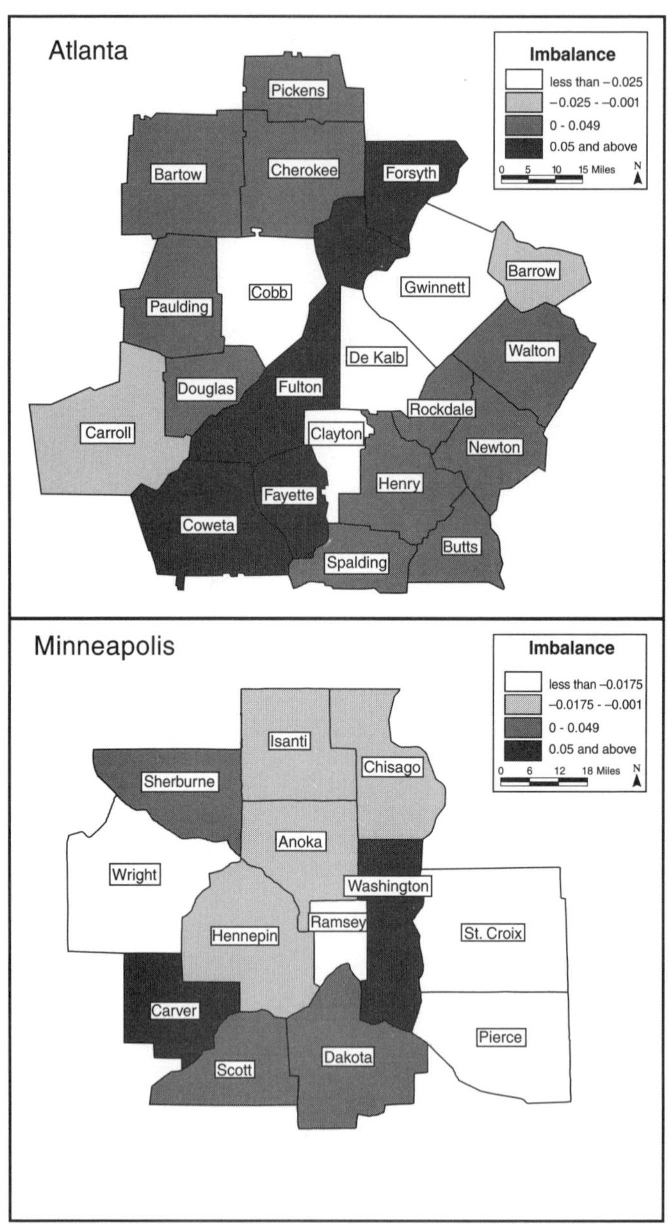

Figure 4.7 Imbalance of Flow of Rich and Poor, Atlanta and Minneapolis

County (like DeKalb and Cobb Counties in Atlanta) had the opposite pattern, as did the Twin Cities' far western and eastern (Wisconsin) counties, which provided housing opportunities for less affluent middle-class families.

1985–1990 Efficiency of Migration Imbalances

Migration efficiency is a useful alternative way of looking at migration imbalances. Figures 4.8 and 4.9 (Table 4.5) summarize the effectiveness measures for Atlanta and Minneapolis–St. Paul for in- and outflows for each county. Effectiveness is given by the ratio of net migration to gross migration (i.e., inflow − outflow / inflow + outflow), so a value of + 0.33, for example, suggests that twice as many people are coming in as are leaving (e.g., 2,000 − 1,000 / 3,000). Four indicators are examined for each city: overall migration (Minneapolis only), migration of black households (Atlanta only), and migration of nonfamily households, persons below poverty, and persons with college degrees.

For Minneapolis–St. Paul for overall migration, the core counties of Hennepin and Ramsey had fairly effective net out-migration, Dakota and Sherburne Counties had very effective in-migration, and most other suburban counties experienced moderate overall net in-migration. The pattern for nonfamily persons is rather different, with actual gains to Hennepin County and, relative to overall migration, gains in Ramsey County, whereas many suburban counties experienced losses in nonfamily persons. Even those that gained in nonfamily persons gained at a lower rate than they did overall. Whereas the more "bedroom-type" suburban counties lost the most, the "edge city" areas did gain. Ramsey County gained poor people despite overall losses; Pierce, Wright, and Hennepin Counties—the northwest to southeast corridor—gained poor people relative to all migration. The outer southwestern and northeastern suburban counties lost poor while gaining greatly overall. In the case of the college educated, the central, eastern, and southern counties tended to hold on to the educated—they either lost less or gained more relative to all migrants. In contrast, the northern and western counties (and Pierce County) gained less or even lost college-educated residents.

For Atlanta for overall migration, the core county of Fulton had a high negative (severe net out-migration) effectiveness (−0.37), whereas DeKalb's effectiveness was moderate (−0.13). Cobb and Clayton Counties had smaller losses. Eleven outer counties—more than half of all counties—had high positive (strong net in-migration) effectiveness (0.36 or more), exceeding any seen in the Minneapolis area, and six others had small to moderate gains—a fairly regular core-to-periphery pattern. For mainly black households the pattern is very different, with extreme negative effectiveness (−0.64) for Fulton and very high positive efficiency for adjoining counties (DeKalb, Clayton, Fayette, Douglas, Cobb, Forsyth, and Gwinnett). Farther suburban counties varied, some gaining in blacks through the exchange (e.g., far southern and

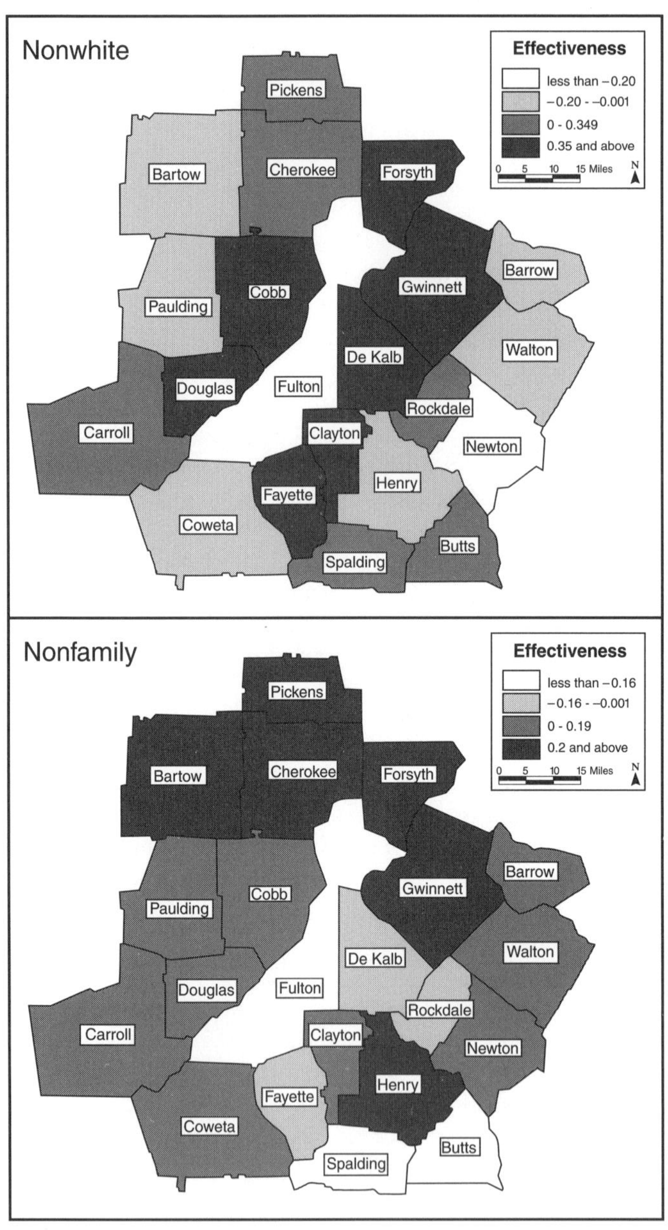

Figure 4.8 Migration Effectiveness of Selected Migration Streams, Atlanta

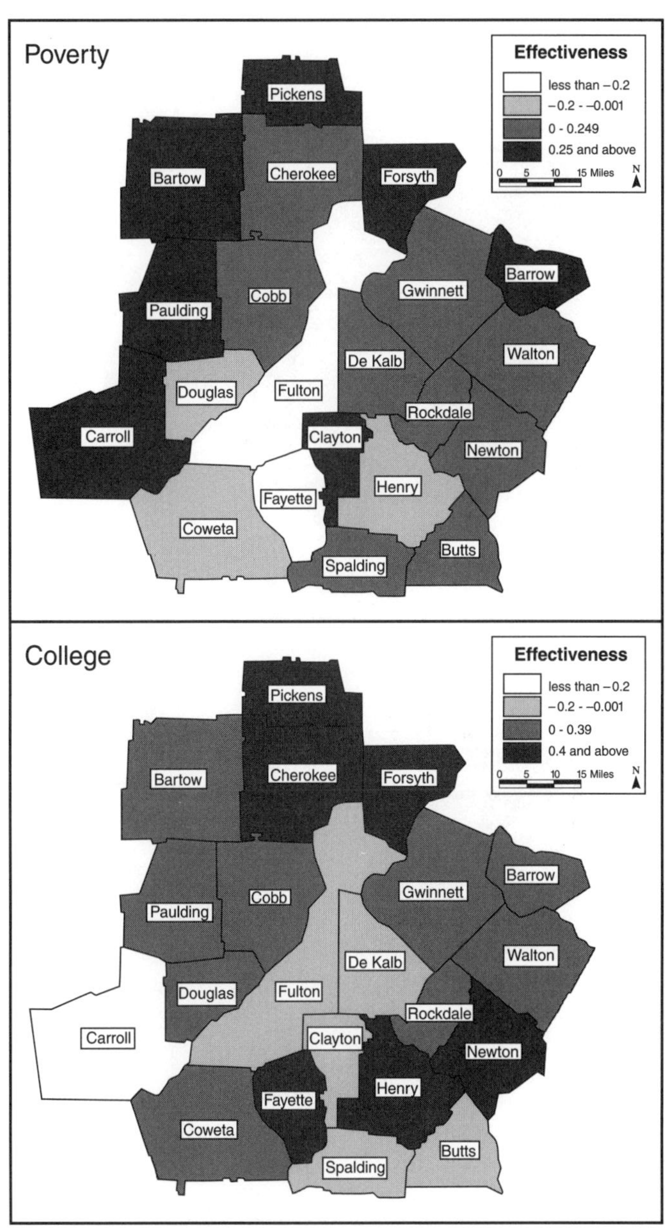

Figure 4.8 (*Cont.*)

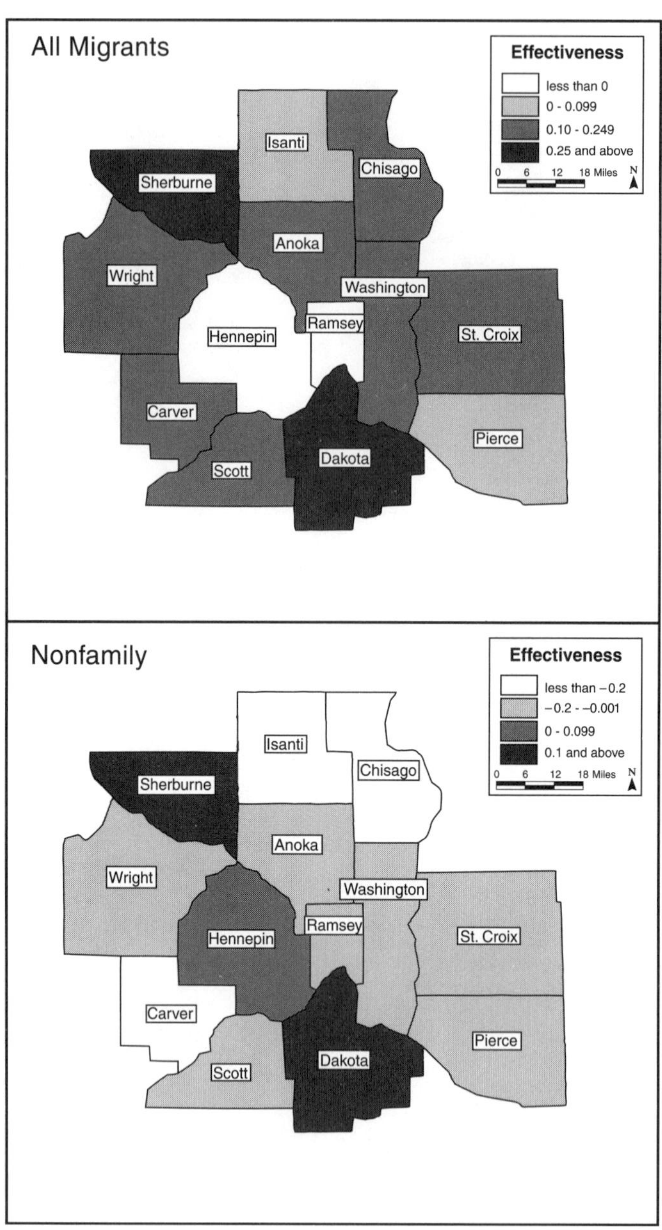

Figure 4.9 Migration Effectiveness for Selected Migration Streams, Minneapolis

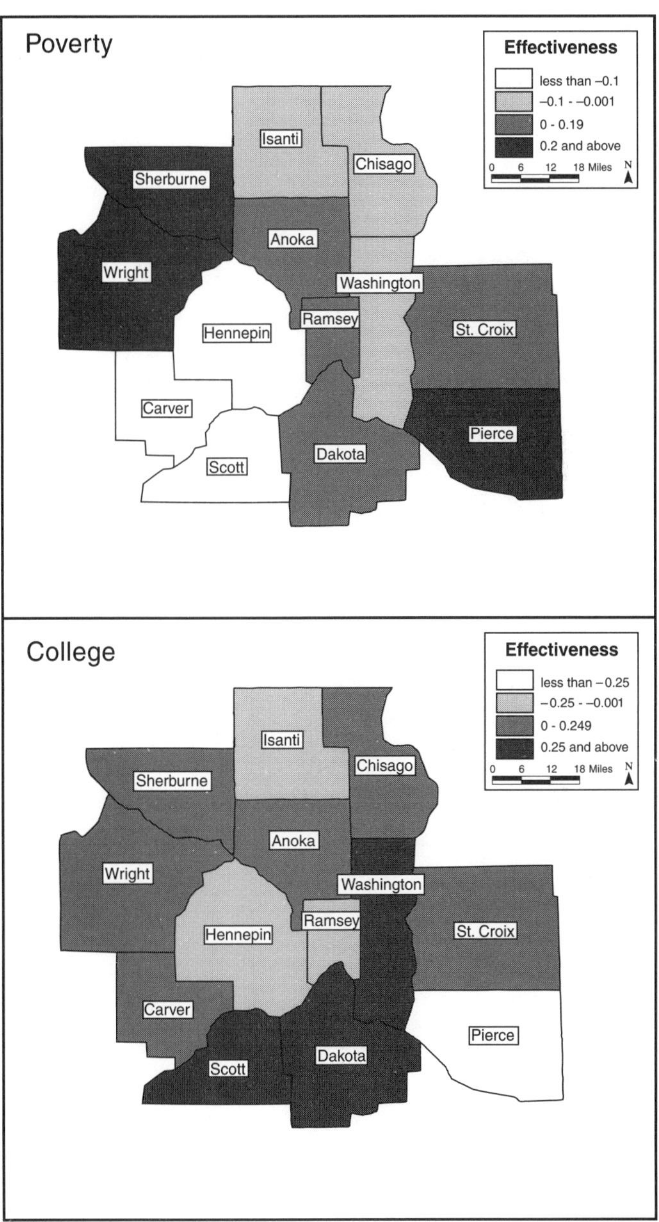

Figure 4.9 (*Cont.*)

Table 4.5 Migration Effectiveness for Minneapolis and Atlanta, 1985–1990

(A) All Migrants

	In-Migration	Out-Migration	Net Migration	Effectiveness
Minneapolis	240,680	240,680	0	0.00
Anoka	34,823	25,871	8,952	0.15
Carver	7,111	5,637	1,474	0.12
Chisago	5,176	3,437	1,739	0.20
Dakota	39,910	21,843	18,067	0.29
Hennepin	51,291	80,365	−29,074	−0.22
Isanti	3,438	2,865	573	0.09
Ramsey	41,794	62,738	−20,944	−0.20
Scott	8,387	5,952	2,435	0.17
Sherburne	7,132	3,442	3,690	0.35
Washington	26,280	16,961	9,319	0.22
Wright	8,275	5,922	2,353	0.17
Pierce, WI	2,856	2,836	20	0.00
St. Croix, WI	4,224	2,811	1,413	0.20
Atlanta	344,366	344,366	0	0.00
Barrow	3,634	1,572	2,062	0.40
Bartow	5,801	2,263	3,538	0.44
Butts	2,287	1,308	979	0.27
Carroll	7,318	3,326	3,992	0.38
Cherokee	16,609	7,465	9,144	0.38
Clayton	25,765	29,398	−3,633	−0.07
Cobb	38,825	46,902	−8,077	−0.09
Coweta	7,082	2,953	4,129	0.41
DeKalb	62,002	80,906	−18,904	−0.13
Douglas	9,837	8,438	1,399	0.08
Fayette	12,370	5,775	6,595	0.36
Forsyth	6,946	2,051	4,895	0.54
Fulton	47,937	103,283	−55,346	−0.37
Gwinnett	46,883	25,496	21,387	0.30
Henry	15,374	6,099	9,275	0.43
Newton	4,951	3,050	1,901	0.24
Paulding	9,091	3,152	5,939	0.49
Pickens	1,918	607	1,311	0.52
Rockdale	9,689	5,000	4,689	0.32
Spalding	3,742	2,763	979	0.15
Walton	5,979	2,559	3,420	0.40

(Cont.)

Table 4.5 Migration Effectiveness for Minneapolis and Atlanta, 1985–1990 *(Cont.)*

(B) Nonwhite Migrants

	In-Migration	Out-Migration	Effectiveness	% of	% of	Diff %
Minneapolis	11,024	11,024	0.00	4.6	4.6	0.0
Anoka	1,228	840	0.19	3.5	3.2	−0.3
Carver	106	92	0.07	1.5	1.6	0.1
Chisago	88	106	−0.09	1.7	3.1	1.4
Dakota	2,043	757	0.46	5.1	3.5	−1.7
Hennepin	3,107	4,824	−0.22	6.1	6.0	−0.0
Isanti	92	52	0.28	2.7	1.8	−0.9
Ramsey	2,984	3,624	−0.10	7.1	5.8	−1.4
Scott	245	87	0.48	2.9	1.5	−1.5
Sherburne	249	49	0.67	3.5	1.4	−2.1
Washington	644	440	0.19	2.5	2.6	0.1
Wright	129	111	0.08	1.6	1.9	0.3
Pierce, WI	82	5	0.89	2.9	0.2	−2.7
St Croix, WI	27	37	−0.16	0.6	1.3	0.7
Atlanta	77,570	77,570	0.00	22.5	22.5	0.0
Barrow	212	277	−0.13	5.8	17.6	11.8
Bartow	247	344	−0.16	4.3	15.2	10.9
Butts	674	481	0.17	29.5	36.8	7.3
Carroll	656	549	0.09	9.0	16.5	7.5
Cherokee	415	235	0.28	2.5	3.1	0.6
Clayton	12,866	4,086	0.52	49.9	13.9	−36.0
Cobb	7,931	3,299	0.41	20.4	7.0	−13.4
Coweta	544	696	−0.12	7.7	23.6	15.9
DeKalb	32,977	12,492	0.45	53.2	15.4	−37.7
Douglas	1,105	455	0.42	11.2	5.4	−5.8
Fayette	1,179	266	0.63	9.5	4.6	−4.9
Forsyth	41	10	0.61	0.6	0.5	−0.1
Fulton	10,823	49,241	−0.64	22.6	47.7	25.1
Gwinnett	4,106	1,647	0.43	8.8	6.5	−2.3
Henry	1,060	1,129	−0.03	6.9	18.5	11.6
Newton	389	645	−0.25	7.9	21.1	13.3
Paulding	239	356	−0.20	2.6	11.3	8.7
Pickens	74	41	0.29	3.9	6.8	2.9
Rockdale	843	444	0.31	8.7	8.9	0.2
Spalding	813	487	0.25	21.7	17.6	−4.1
Walton	376	486	−0.13	6.3	19.0	12.7

western Carroll, Spalding, and Butts), but others losing, especially toward the east and northwest. In the case of nonfamily households, Fulton and DeKalb Counties lost, but much less than for all migrants. Cobb and Clayton Counties gained (despite overall losses), whereas all outer counties lost or gained at a lower than overall rate.

With respect to poor persons, most significant were the (large) gains to DeKalb, Clayton, and Cobb from Fulton, despite overall losses and a very high net inflow to one suburban county (Carroll—i.e., students). Moderate gains of poor persons prevailed in the majority of suburban counties, but actual losses occurred in a few (Henry, Fayette, Coweta, and Douglas), all adjoining the core on the south or west, despite overall migration gains. As to the college educated, Fulton lost but at a rate much lower than for all migrants, whereas DeKalb lost at a greater rate. The majority of suburban counties gained the college educated at a rate higher than for all migrants—especially counties just beyond the inner core (e.g., Douglas, Fayette, Henry, Rockdale, Gwinnett, Forsyth, and Cherokee), whereas several far suburban counties grew at lesser rates for the college educated—Carroll being the expected extreme outlier.

For Minneapolis–St. Paul we calculate the efficiency measures for pairwise exchanges involving Hennepin County. Hennepin experienced overall losses to all other counties but especially to Sherburne and Dakota Counties. There was a loss of nonfamily households to these same two vigorous counties but a gain from all others, despite the overall population loss. With respect to poor migrants, Hennepin County lost (received fewer than it sent) to counties along the northwest-to-southeast alignment corridor (comprising the less affluent Wright, Sherburne, Anoka, Ramsey, and Dakota Counties) but gained from the richer counties (Carver, Scott, and Washington). Hennepin County lost college graduates in all exchanges. A comparison with Atlanta's Fulton County is not undertaken because Fulton's losses in pairwise exchanges were so great that it lost to most counties across all categories.

Accounting for Imbalances of In- and Out-Flows of Poor Persons

The data, although limited, permit a variety of statistical analyses. The small number of data units is not limiting since the units are counties and the variables are all mean or median values for populations—that is, we are not working with a sample. Thus although T-values and significance levels will be shown, they have no inferential meaning; the main value of the analysis is to highlight major associations. Also, especially for the 1985–1990 flow data, we do not have the kinds of data to test plausible causal relations behind the observed changes because our indicators—overall migration, nonfamily, nonwhite (black), college graduate, white-collar worker, and below poverty—are all interdependent. Still, it is of interest to report on one simple analysis undertaken for Atlanta and for Minneapolis–St. Paul: the imbalance (difference in the percentage of persons) in the flows of poor persons in and out of counties as a dependent variable and a combination of other 1985–1990 flow imbalances and the 1980 baseline conditions as independent variables. To our surprise and perhaps consternation, the results are rather different for the two cities. There seems to be an orderliness and a simplicity for Minneapolis that is absent for a more complex Atlanta. Race seems to be the major reason for this difference.

For Minneapolis–St. Paul, 90 percent of the imbalance in proportions of poor leaving or entering counties is accounted for by three variables. The results are given by:

	Dependent variable: Imbalance of poor migrants entering and leaving countries		
Independent variables	β	T	significance
College imbalance	−0.544	−7.2	0.0001
HH Inc skewness, 1980	0.056	2.3	0.0434
College %, 1980	−0.094	1.8	0.1044
R-square = 0.90			

A strong inverse correlation is found between flows of the poor and of the college educated. Yet there is a weak tendency for more poor to move to areas that were more educated in 1980. Since the correlation of the college flow imbalance and the 1980 percentage college educated is only 0.25, it is evident that the college-educated, more affluent zone is shifting outward from the core. As expected, there is a fairly strong relation as well with the 1980 skewness measure of inequality.

Other correlations of interest for Minneapolis are:

College imbalance and white-collar imbalance	0.88
College imbalance and rich/poor imbalance	0.562
White-collar imbalance and rich/poor imbalance	0.605
Nonfamily household imbalance and 1980 skewness	0.860

Both college and white-collar flow imbalances are directly associated with unequal shifts of rich and poor persons. Nonfamily flow imbalances are related to inequality in 1980, that is, nonfamily persons tend to move toward unequal places and further increase the places' inequality.

For Atlanta the relation is profoundly influenced by race. The racial flow imbalance is the strongest correlate of the imbalance in poor persons ($r = 0.53$), so in a stepwise regression the only variables to enter are race and the nonfamily percentage in 1980. The R-square is only 0.42, much weaker than and different from the result for the Twin Cities. The results are given as follows:

	Dependent variable: Imbalance of poor migrants entering and leaving countries		
Independent variables	β	*T*	significance
Nonwhite	0.196	2.90	0.0089
Nonfamily, 1980	0.090	1.94	0.0689

R-square = 0.42

If race is excluded, a stronger relation is obtained, but it is still weak compared with Minneapolis.

Independent variables	β	*T*	significance
Nonfamily, 1980	0.176	3.4	0.0031
Poverty, 1980	−0.108	−3.4	0.0035
White-collar imbalance	−0.348	−2.5	0.0209

R-square = 0.52

Now the poor are shifting to areas that were nonfamily in 1980, as earlier, but away from areas that were poor in 1980, opposite the behavior for Minneapolis–St. Paul. In both cities the poor are moving away from areas gaining in white-collar workers (Atlanta) or the college educated (Minneapolis).

Other correlations of interest for Atlanta are:

College imbalances and white-collar imbalances	0.84
Nonwhite imbalance and rich/poor imbalance	−0.53
Nonfamily household imbalance and 1980 skewness	0.76

For Atlanta, the imbalance in flows of richer and poorer persons is weakly related to college and white-collar imbalances but strongly related to the imbalance of nonwhite (black) flows, again illustrating the complex role of race. As to one question posed at the start, "Do the 1985–1990 flow imbalances correlate with the 1980–1990 change in character?" we find that the correlation of decadal change in the character of areas with the 1985–1990 imbalances in the character of in- and outflows reveals a generally weak level of association and strong differences between Atlanta and Minneapolis–St. Paul.

For Atlanta, there is a strong correlation (0.935) between change in the proportion black and imbalances in the in- and outflows. This racial dominance appears to account for a moderate correlation of change in nonfamily households (0.34) and especially of below-poverty persons (0.69) with the imbalances in nonfamily households and below-poverty persons. But in Atlanta virtually no correlation (0.09) was found between 1980–1990 change in the share with college degrees and the flow imbalances of the college educated; here the effect of nonlocal migration dominates.

For Minneapolis, very weak correlations were found between, first, the 1980–1990 change in nonfamily households and, second, persons below poverty with the 1985–1990 flow imbalances of these groups (−0.09 and −0.035, respectively). Yet there was a very strong correlation (0.803) between the 1980–1990 change in the college educated and migration flows—indicating a relative relocation of the college educated from the core that did not occur in Atlanta.

Conclusion

The research task was to discover whether and how social and economic restructuring is expressed in the urban landscape through the mechanism of intrametropolitan migration. We had a special interest in whether the nationally observed increase in income inequality is manifest everywhere or in concentrations in particular parts of the metropolis. Are patterns of change similar for our two sample cities, Atlanta and Minneapolis–St. Paul? Do the changes support the idea that migration is a force for equilibrium, disequilibrium, or both?

Imbalances or differences in the composition of flows into and out of counties strongly contributed to uneven spatial expression of social and economic conditions. Traditional core–periphery exchanges of nonfamily versus family households persist, but there was spillover of nonfamily households into inner suburban areas and concentration of less affluent younger families in selected suburban counties. College-educated persons and white-collar jobs illustrated the geographic impact of economic restructuring: in Atlanta a relative shift to the skilled and educated occurred on a south(west) to north(east) axis, in the Twin Cities in the southern and close eastern zone. Poverty change, as evidence of change both in nonfamily households and blue- versus white-collar jobs, was generally expressed concentrically—that is, more poverty in the core but in an extending core and less poverty on the periphery—although there were sectoral exceptions or exaggerations, broadly reflecting the previous changes in education and jobs.

Imbalances of flows of persons by income to and from counties contributed to differential change in income inequality in a fairly complex way. In Atlanta the core counties became more unequal, but in Minnesota (Hennepin County) did not. Race could be an intervening variable. In both areas, adjoining inner counties became relatively more unequal, recipients of lower-income families but not of higher-end jobs. In both cities rings of rapidly growing suburban counties became more unequal, in line with national trends and returns to education. And in both but especially the Twin Cities, some far suburban counties, like some inner suburban areas, provided havens for less affluent families and showed only small changes in inequality.

Certainly, Atlanta and Minneapolis shared the same broad processes, but the resulting patterns were close but not identical. Race appears overwhelmingly important in distinguishing the cities generally—to a degree we did not anticipate. Local persons from these places can undoubtedly tell us what other unique qualities of the regions and specific counties explain more particular patterns.

What might we do next or differently? Most obviously, many of the processes we want to understand call for household rather than aggregated data for persons, so the logical next step is to use Public Use Micro Samples data to obtain a richer picture of the kinds of households that are moving differentially. It will then be reasonable to try to use regression to account for observed changes and imbalances. The use of counties was necessary but creates inescapable problems of variation in size and internal variance, especially for a comparison between Atlanta and Minneapolis–St. Paul. Still, the patterns were strong enough and the data good enough to show how firms and households sorted themselves in the end-of-the-century American metropolis. A second obvious need is to consider the effect of all forms of migration—that is, of exchanges with the rest of the states, the nation, and the world—and to compare their impacts with that of intrametropolitan migration.

The internal flows treated in this chapter constitute somewhat under half of total flows. In both cities the urban core counties lose through internal migration within the metropolis but gain from abroad (the net is unknown) and from the rest of the state and nation, to leave the core close to a balance overall (Table 4.6). In both cities the inner suburban counties gain the most from migration, from both internal and external migration streams. The outer suburban counties gain mainly from internal flows within the metropolis toward the periphery. Clearly, these flows are all significant, and their effects should be compared with the structure of internal flows to gain a fuller picture of the relationship between mobility and metropolitan restructuring.

Intrametropolitan migration clearly illustrates the validity of major processes of metropolitan change—peripheral and sectoral shifts and the sorting of persons by class, education, and race with a continuing decentralization of middle-class families, continuing extensive suburbanization at the edge, the spillover of relatively poor and minority households from the core to selected inner suburbs, and partial gentrification of parts of the core by educated professionals, contributing to core income polarization. It is difficult, in the end, to argue that the main impact of migration is toward equilibrium or disequilibrium, as there is evidence for both. The most honest conclusion seems to be that whereas the migration of households to take advantage of housing and job opportunities is an equilibrating force, the power of social differences and the inherent unequal

Table 4.6 Components of Migration for Atlanta and Minneapolis–St. Paul Metro Areas (in thousands)

Zone	Migrants from Abroad	Migrants from within Metro Area			Migrants from Rest of State/Nation		
		In	Out	Net	In	Out	Net
Minneapolis							
Core[1]	23.4	93.1	143.1	−50.0	185.1	158.6	26.5
Inner[2]	3.9	101.0	64.6	36.3	74.4	553.0	21.4
Outer	1.1	46.0	33.0	13.6	36.0	34.0	2.4
All	28.3	240.7	240.7	0.0	296.0	245.5	50.4
Atlanta							
Core[3]	22.3	109.0	184.2	−74.3	213.1	157.1	56.0
Inner[4]	16.9	111.5	101.3	9.7	225.0	90.6	134.5
Outer	4.2	122.9	58.8	64.6	100.3	61.1	39.2
All	43.3	344.3	344.3	0.0	538.5	309.0	229.6

Notes: 1. Hennepin and Ramsey Counties.
2. Anoka, Dakota, and Washington Counties.
3. Fulton and DeKalb Counties.
4. Cobb, Clayton, and Gwinnett Counties.

power of people are sufficiently disequilibrating to maintain a high degree of inequality on the urban landscape.

Notes

We thank Collette Flanagan for her assistance with cartographic design.

1. Minneapolis–St. Paul will be referred to interchangeably as Minneapolis, Minneapolis–St. Paul, and the Twin Cities in this study.

2. We recognize that Public Use Micro Samples data could also have been utilized and would have had the advantage of avoiding the risks attendant on aggregation. The geography would have been different because the larger counties would be broken up and the smaller counties combined. This approach will be the subject of further research.

References

Adams, John S., Barbara J. Van Drasek, and Laura J. Lambert. 1995. *The Path of Urban Decline*. Minneapolis: Center for Urban and Regional Affairs.

Bourne, Larry S. 1993. "Close Together and Worlds Apart: An Analysis of Changes in the Ecology of Income in Canadian Cities." *Urban Studies* 30: 1293–1317.

———. 1996. "Reurbanization, Uneven Urban Development and the Debate on New Urban Forms." *Urban Geography* 17: 690–713.

Clark, W. A.V. 1987. "Urban Restructuring from a Demographic Perspective." *Economic Geography* 63 (April): 103–125.

Fainstein, Susan S., Ian Gordon, and Michael Harloe. 1992. *Divided Cities: New York and London in the Contemporary World.* Cambridge: Blackwell.

Frey, William. 1985. "Mover Destination Selectivity and the Changing Suburbanization of Metropolitan Whites and Blacks." *Demography* 22 (May): 223–243.

Hamnett, Chris. 1994. "Social Polarization in Global Cities: Theory and Evidence." *Urban Studies* 31 (April) : 401–425.

Hill, Edward, and Harold Wolman. 1997a. "Accounting for the Change in Income Disparities between US Central Cities and Their Suburbs from 1980 to 1990." *Urban Studies* 34 (January): 43–60.

———. 1997b. "City Suburban Income Disparities and Metropolitan Area Employment." *Urban Affairs Review* 32 (March): 558–582.

MacLachlan, Ian, and Ryo Sawada. 1997. "Measures of Income Inequality and Social Polarization in Canadian Metropolitan Areas." *Canadian Geographer* 41 (Winter): 377–398.

Massey, Douglas. 1996. "The Age of Extremes: Concentrated Affluence and Poverty in the Twenty-First Century" [with commentaries]. *Demography* 33 (November): 395–412.

McLafferty, Sara, and Valerie Preston. 1996. "Spatial Mismatch and Employment in a Decade of Restructuring." *Professional Geographer* 48 (November): 420–431.

Mollenkopf, John, and Manuel Castells. 1991. *Dual City: Restructuring New York.* New York: Russell Sage.

Nord, Mark. 1996. *Poor People on the Move. County to County Migration and the Spatial Concentration of Poverty.* Washington, D.C.: Economic Research Service.

Sassen, Saskia. 1991. *The Global City: New York, London, Tokyo.* Princeton: Princeton University Press.

Short, John R. 1978. "Residential Mobility." *Progress in Human Geography* 2: 419–447.

Smith, Neil, Betsy Duncan, and Laura Reid. 1994. "From Disinvestment to Reinvestment." In Janet Abu-Lughold (ed.), *From Urban Village to East Village.* Cambridge: Blackwell.

St. John, Craig, Mark Edwards, and Deann Wenk. 1995. "Racial Differences in Intraurban Residential Mobility." *Urban Affairs Review* 30 (May): 705–729.

Stanback, Thomas M. 1991. *The New Suburbanization.* Boulder: Westview.

Van Kempen, Eva T. 1994. "The Dual City and the Poor: Social Polarization, Social Segregation and Life Chances." *Urban Studies* 31 (April): 995–1015.

Wilson, William Julius J. 1987. *The Truly Disadvantaged: The Inner City, the Underclass, and Public Policy.* Chicago: University of Chicago Press.

5

Regional Outcomes of Large-Scale Migration in Postindustrial America

William A.V. Clark

An intense debate is under way about the nature and outcomes of recent large-scale migration to the United States. National findings show that recent immigrants (those who entered in the 1990s) are less skilled, have lower wages, and are more likely to be in poverty than similar waves of immigrants in the preceding three decades. Most national research, however, does not deal with outcomes at the regional level. How are migrants doing in specific regions? Are there variations across the major immigrant states, and what do regional patterns say about future trajectories of the most recent waves of immigrants? The research reported in this chapter focuses on these questions, on changes in wages, education, poverty and dependency levels across five major immigrant states—Arizona, California, Florida, New York, and Texas. Examining regional outcomes is particularly appropriate in the context of a recent case study of New Jersey that suggested positive outcomes and impacts of recent immigration (Espenshade 1997). Are the New Jersey findings general or specific?

Debates about the costs of large-scale immigration, about the effects of immigration on native-born workers and the increasing welfare dependency of new immigrants have coalesced into well-developed positions about the "new immigration" of the late twentieth century and implications for U.S. society in the twenty-first century. On the one hand, there is a strongly held consensus that the United States was built as a nation of immigrants and that continued growth of the U.S. economy is bound up with the continuing flow of immigrants. An ancillary view suggests that the United States must also preserve its heritage as a haven for peoples with fewer opportunities (Kennedy 1996). On the other hand, an equally strongly held consensus argues that the context has changed dramatically from the earlier period of high immigration and that it is now necessary to control, if not limit, the flows of immigrants (Borjas 1995; Bouvier 1991). The chapter is set within the context of this debate and provides an enriched picture of what is happening to immigrants in specific regions.

The large-scale immigration to the United States in the1970s and 1980s is not structurally different from the large-scale immigration of the first two decades of the twentieth century. The flows involve large numbers of migrants, include peoples with a wide variety of ethnic backgrounds, and in the main are of low-skilled and poorly educated migrants. But whereas the scale of the immigration may not be basically different, the social and economic climate of the United States is fundamentally changed, and it is this change in the socioeconomic climate that is critical in interpreting changes in the scale, nature, and outcomes of recent immigration to the United States. Economically, as the data will show, the economic opportunity matrix is substantially different from a century ago, and socially the rise of individual and group rights and expectations, has changed the context within which migration is perceived by both migrants and the host society.

The immediate stimulus for the chapter is the national finding that in relative terms, recent immigrants have fewer skills, are doing less well economically, and are more likely to be dependent than earlier migrants (Borjas 1995). Additional work at the metropolitan level has also shown that recent immigrants are more likely to be in poverty and that there may even be evidence of a rising new immigrant underclass (Clark 1998b). This is not to argue against the view that individual immigrants may be doing better than in the countries of origin or that some will successfully make the same upward trajectory earlier migrants achieved; rather the question is about the relative socioeconomic standing of groups of recent migrants. If new immigrants in particular locations are significantly lower in skills than the native-born population and if their relative position is declining over time, the findings would raise real questions about their long-term success rates.

Data for the United States as a whole show that the gap between native born and immigrants in mean years of education is increasing, that the differential between native-born and immigrant earnings is more negative for immigrants who arrived in the late 1980s than for those who came at earlier intervals, and that more of the recent waves of immigrants are in poverty than those who came in earlier waves (Table 5.1). Whereas the native-born population increased the average years of education from 11.5 in 1970 to 13.2 in 1990, immigrants gained less than a year; as a result, the mean educational attainment of immigrants slipped against that of the native born. Similarly, the relative wages of immigrants slipped over the two-decade period. By 1990, immigrants who entered in the period 1985–1990 were doing almost a third less well than the native-born population. To reiterate, the question for this chapter is, how do these national findings translate to specific regional settings and how do the findings hold up when we disaggregate the results for native-born ethnic and racial composition?

Table 5.1 Skill and Poverty Levels for Natives and Immigrants in the United States, 1970–1990

Group/Variable	1970	1980	1990
Native born			
Mean educational attainment in years	11.5	12.7	13.2
Poverty rate(%)	13.7	12.2	12.4
Percent of households with public assistance	6.0	7.9	7.4
All immigrants			
Mean educational attainment in years	10.7	11.7	11.6
Differential from native born	−0.8	−1.0	−1.6
Percent wage differential from native born	+0.9	−9.2	−15.2
Poverty rate (%)	16.4	15.6	18.1
Percent of household with public assistance	5.9	8.7	9.1
Recent immigrants (<5 years in the United States)			
Mean educational attainment in years	11.1	11.8	11.9
Differential from native born	−0.4	−0.9	−1.3
Percent wage differential from native born	−16.6	−27.6	−31.7
Poverty rate (%)	18.8	28.1	29.8
Percent of households with public assistance	5.5	8.3	8.3

Source: Clark,1998a.

Theoretical Context

The analysis of regional variations in large-scale migration is set within the overarching concept of urban and regional restructuring (Cross 1992). There has been an extensive analysis of the emergence of a postindustrial society, especially in the so-called global cities (Fainstein, Gordon, and Harloe 1992; Sassen 1994). The central ideas are well known. A basic change has occurred in the organization of labor markets in developed Western economies. In the new economies the focus is not on the manufacture of goods, although this still occurs, but rather on the processing and transmission of information. During the 1980s a fundamental restructuring took place from goods production to services production, especially in the information and technology sectors. Whereas jobs in finance, trade, and communication grew, jobs in manufacturing were stable. The changes were even greater in big cities (James 1995). The new entry-level jobs in information processing sectors in general require greater skill levels than the previous entry-level jobs in the industrial sector, and productivity has become more dependent on knowledge and skill. In such a situation, the transformation of the economy has robbed urban areas of their ability to absorb new immigrants. The backbone industries and their union jobs have vanished, and there has been no credible refutation of the finding that the net value of unskilled immigrant labor has decreased and continues to decrease (Borjas 1994).

Along with the decrease in entry-level manufacturing work and the increase in professional-level jobs, there has been a growth in the service sector. The increase in clerical, food services, child care, and other privatized work—which is often temporary or part time—has accounted for much of the growth of women's employment (Law and Wolch 1993). These jobs are not only low-wage jobs; they offer less job security than the entry-level industrial work offered to earlier waves of migrants. Even though earlier migrants may not have been able to enter the union-based steady employment offered by a growing manufacturing industry, their children were able to participate in somewhat secure union-based employment. Now those opportunities, in both the jobs on offer and their long-term security, have changed fundamentally. Union membership is significantly lower than in earlier decades, especially in the new service sectors, and those service sectors are thus far less easily unionized (Wilson 1996).

In the past it was manufacturing jobs that provided entry-level positions for many new migrants or if not for the migrants themselves, for their children. To the extent that entry-level, low-skill positions are no longer available to new waves of immigrants, there will be greater difficulty in replicating the paths of earlier migrants. Some earlier flows of migrants did follow the path of even earlier migrants (Clark and Mueller 1988), but as the old entry-level industrial jobs have been replaced by entry-level jobs in the service sector with less security, we must conclude that the past trajectories may be less readily available, if at all (Waldinger and Bozorgmehr 1996). And it is not just for immigrant workers that the paths of upward mobility have changed. There is evidence that these same jobs have disappeared for native-born minorities and that the changing trajectory of opportunities is a fundamental element of the increasing poverty in the inner cities of large metropolitan areas (Wilson 1996).

In the five regions in this analysis there have clearly been fundamental shifts in the job opportunity structure in the past thirty years (Figure 5.1). In 1960, before the recent waves of immigrants, there were a large number of jobs in manufacturing, but the growth of new jobs has been in professional services. It is not that there has been no growth in manufacturing jobs, but the growth (actual decline in New York and slow growth in California) is far less than the growth in population. For example, the number of manufacturing jobs more than doubled in Arizona between 1960 and 1990, but the population almost tripled in that same period. In contrast, most states had significant growth in the professional service sector. The percentage of all jobs in manufacturing held constant as a proportion in Arizona but declined in every other state, whereas the proportion of jobs in professional services increased to more than a fifth of all jobs in every state in the analysis. Thus the change in employment emphasizes decreasing proportions of total employment opportunities in basic low-skill jobs and robust growth in professional jobs. The ultimate outcomes may be in doubt, but there is little question that the job opportunity structure is increasingly polarized between a high-skilled, high education, and professional occupation

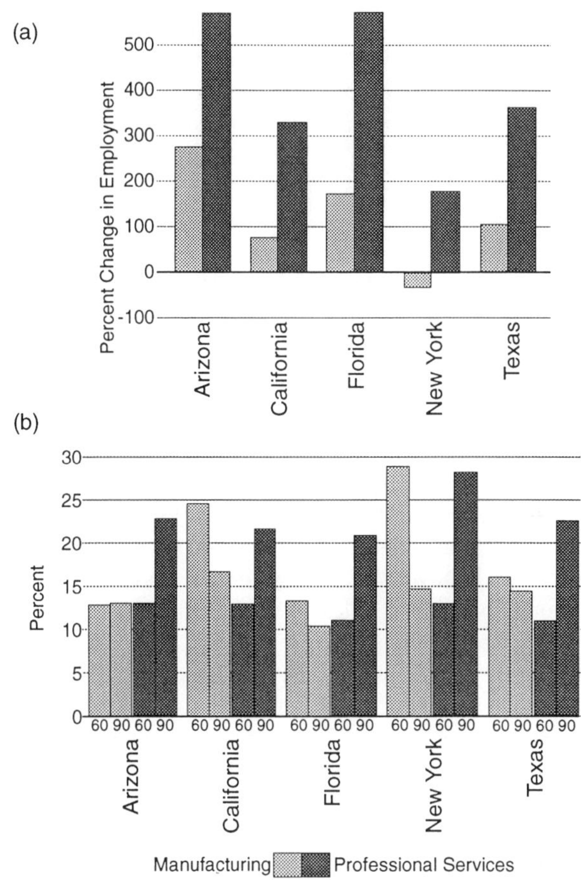

Figure 5.1 (a) Changes in Manufacturing and Professional Employment, 1960–1990; (b) Percentage of Jobs in Manufacturing and the Professions

structure and a low-skilled, nonprofessional occupational group (Hamnett 1994; Clark and McNicholas 1995). It is in this context that immigration impacts are very different from those in an expanding and growing economy.

The changes in the economy as a whole have had more specific effects in particular regions. Overall, the U.S. economy has shifted from about 35 percent in manufacturing in 1960 to about 25 percent in manufacturing in 1990, but the shift has clearly been greater in some regions than others. Thus California has had overall a greater shift to nonmanufacturing jobs but at the same time has had the largest influx of recent migrants. In this way the major regional variations are exacerbating the interaction of large-scale migration and the changing labor market. The significance of changes in regions is that they affect different groups with different intensity. It is increasingly clear that those immigrants with the fewest skills are likely to be the most intensely affected.

The analysis in this chapter examines recent immigrant outcomes in five major entry-point states. I examine changing skill levels, the pattern of earnings over time, and poverty outcomes. The states are compared with the United States as a whole.

Data and Analysis

Data

The data for the analysis are drawn from Public Use Microdata Samples (PUMS) for 1970, 1980, and 1990. For each of these years measures for the native born are compared with all immigrants at those dates and with immigrants who arrived in the preceding five-year period—that is, between 1965 and 1970, between 1975 and 1980, and between 1985 and 1990, respectively. Years of education and earnings are computed for the total workforce between ages 25 and 64. The fraction in poverty and on assistance is computed for households in which the household head is at least 18 years of age.

The five states used in the analysis represent 72 percent of flows between 1985 and 1990 to the United States. The four largest—California, New York, Texas, and Florida—account for 66 percent of those flows. Arizona is also included in the analysis, as the total for California, New York, Florida, Texas, and Arizona accounts for slightly more than 100 percent of the total increase in Aid to Families with Dependent Children in the United States (Clark and Schultz 1997a). In other words, it is a state in which the issues of poverty and dependency are similar to those in the larger immigrant states.

It is important to recognize what I am *not* attempting as well as what I am attempting in this analysis. I am interested in overall outcomes in places. I am not trying to control for age composition and skill levels while measuring earnings. Indeed, immigrants with skills similar to the native born, immigrants who are well trained, are likely to be earning a wage closer to that of the native-born population. Rather, the important focus in this research is on the aggregate outcomes in specific locations of major changes in immigrant composition. How are recent immigrants faring in the states versus the United States as a whole? This is not an unimportant issue as policies on welfare support for low-income and immigrant populations are changed at the federal level.

Analysis and Observations

Skills, as measured by years of education, directly affect the employability of both native born and immigrants and are translated into differential earnings.

The outcomes, in turn, affect both poverty and dependency. The basic data used in the analysis are reproduced in appendix 5.1.

Skill levels, as measured by years of education, increased for all native-born groups. Native-born whites have more years of education than native-born blacks and Hispanics, but all three groups increased their years of education in the twenty-some-year period we are studying (Figure 5.2). In addition, the gap between native-born white and native-born black populations closed, from about two to three years to about one to one and half years. The gap also closed for native-born Hispanics. In contrast, most immigrants lost ground against native-born populations. In some states and for the decade of the 1970s, recent immigrants gained against the native-born population, but in the 1980s the trend was uniformly negative. The rate of loss was greater for both immigrants as a whole and recent immigrants. Obviously, the large recent waves of immigrants are lowering the overall repository of skills in immigrant populations.

The trajectories of earnings follow a path that can be projected from the analysis of skills. In each case earnings are plotted as the percentage wage differential from all native born. Thus, overall, native-born whites have a positive wage differential, and native-born blacks and native-born Hispanics have negative wage differentials, as do immigrants (Figure 5.3). It is the paths of wage differentials over time that are important and revealing. In 1970 immigrants earned the same as or more than native-born Hispanics and blacks. In Florida and New York immigrants earned more than native-born racial and ethnic groups as a whole. By 1990 the picture had reversed. In Arizona, California, Florida, and New York, native-born groups outearned immigrants (although this was not true for the comparison of blacks and all immigrants in Florida). In Texas the native-born groups were well above recent immigrants and were approaching all immigrants.

The most revealing stories with respect to immigrant trajectories are contained in the graphs for New York and California. In California in 1970, blacks were substantially below all immigrants in their wage differential from the total native-born population but were well above recent immigrants. By 1980 they had surpassed all immigrants. They had decreased the earnings gap with the native born and by 1990 had a smaller difference than both all immigrants and recent immigrants. Moreover, their trajectory was such that the gap was narrowing, if only marginally, in the 1980s. Some of this change is related to the aging and maturing of the black population, but the trajectories are still important indicators of changing relationships in the labor market. In New York both blacks and native-born Hispanics were at or below immigrant levels, even recent immigrants, in 1970. A steady decrease in the gap between blacks and native-born Hispanics and all native born, and a steady increase in the gap between immigrants and the native born, resulted in blacks and Hispanics reaching parity with the total immigrant population and being well above the recent

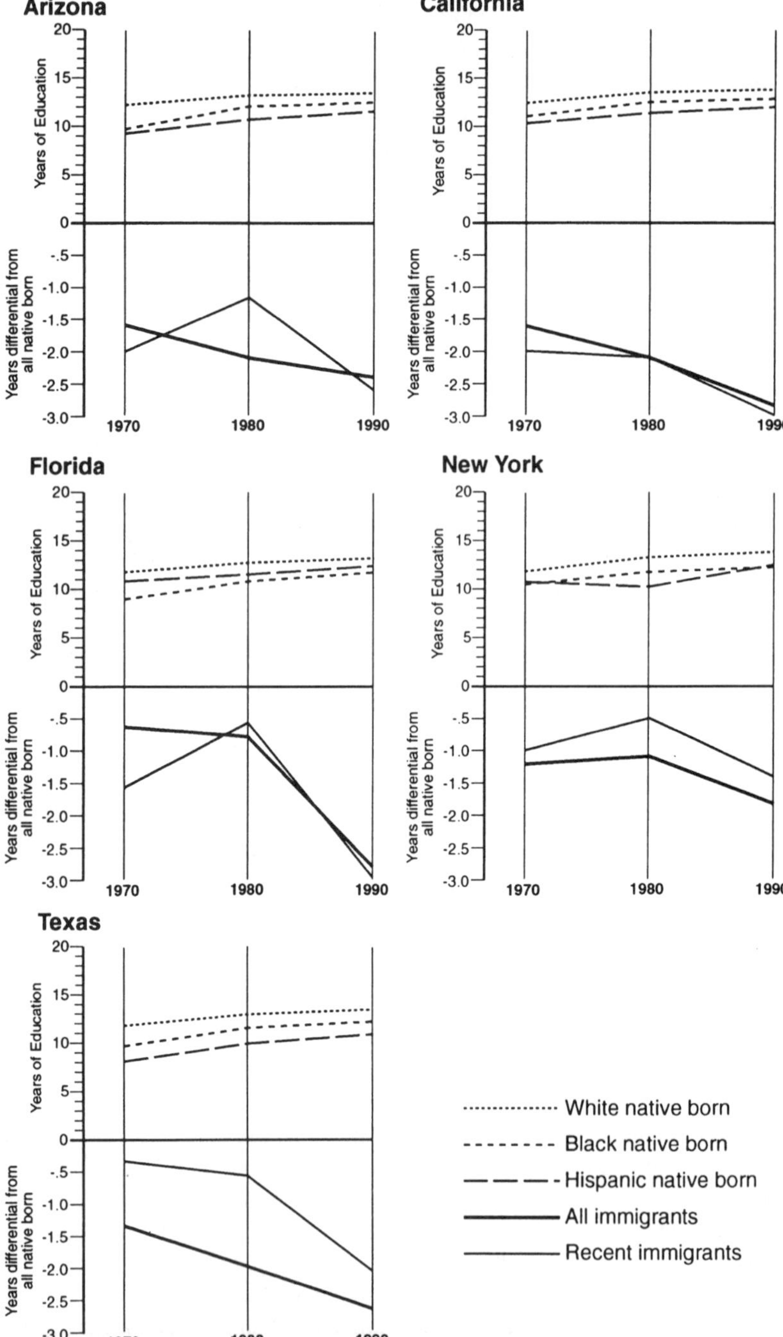

Figure 5.2 Skill Trajectories of Native-Born Groups and Immigrants, 1970–1990

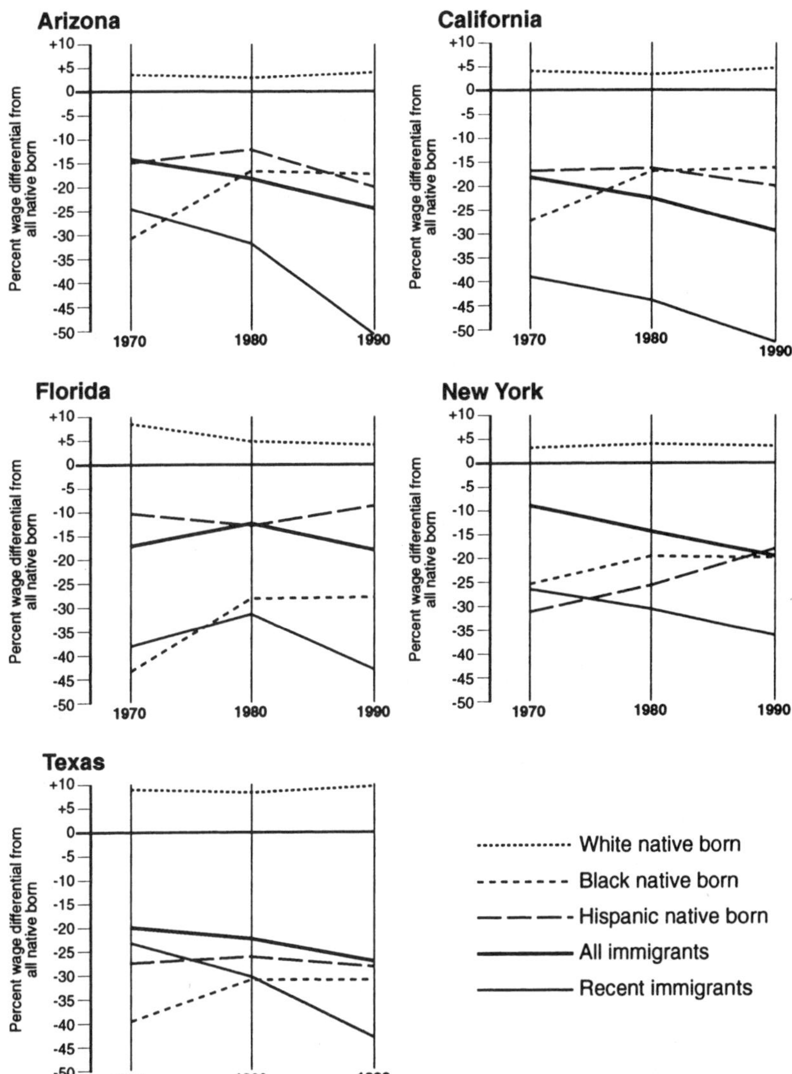

Figure 5.3 Trajectories of Wage Differentials of Native-Born Groups and Immigrants, 1970–1990

immigrant population. The implications are obvious: the success of new immigrants will become increasingly difficult to replicate.

The outcomes of the changes in skill levels and earnings have, by and large, with the exception of New York, decreased poverty for black and Hispanic native-born groups and increased poverty for immigrants (Figure 5.4). The most striking visual outcome is the similarity between the poverty of native-born black and Hispanic groups and that of immigrant groups. All immigrants, that is, immigrants who entered the country at any time in the past several decades, have poverty rates as high or higher in some states as native-born racial and ethnic groups. Clearly, substantial immigrant populations have not been able to translate their new location to much improved economic status. The most striking change is the substantial increase in every state in the proportion in poverty for recent immigrants. The increase varies from as low as 5 percent in Texas to 20 percent in Arizona, where 44 percent of recent immigrants are defined as being in poverty. The rates for all immigrants have increased much less dramatically and in New York have actually decreased.

Dependency is obviously related to poverty and its outcomes. The findings for dependency are less clear-cut than the overall findings for the United States as a whole, and they vary considerably by state and ethnic group (Table 5.2). In general, for the five states studied in this analysis, the white, black, and Hispanic native-born populations have lower dependency ratios as measured by the proportion of households using Aid to Families with Dependent Children and general assistance. Decreases for black households are notable in every state except Florida. Some states had increases in black dependency ratios between 1970 and 1980, but they declined in the following decade. In contrast, ratios for all immigrants were stable or increased slightly. Ratios increased for recent immigrants except for Florida, where the ratio declined rapidly. The ratios are still substantially lower than those for native-born black households, but they are greater than those for native-born whites and are approaching those for native-born Hispanics. These findings are significant given the greater difficulty immigrants have qualifying for aid.

Regional Variations

An examination of wage differentials by region identifies the particular problems of the southern tier of states—California, Arizona, and Texas. Florida has similar problems for recent immigrants (Figure 5.5). California, Arizona, and Texas are similar in their deviations from the U.S. average. California, as expected, has the greatest difference and is more than three times more deviant than New York. Even greater differences are seen for recent immigrant populations. Apart from the obvious reiteration that things are worse in California, there are clearly serious regional implications for im-

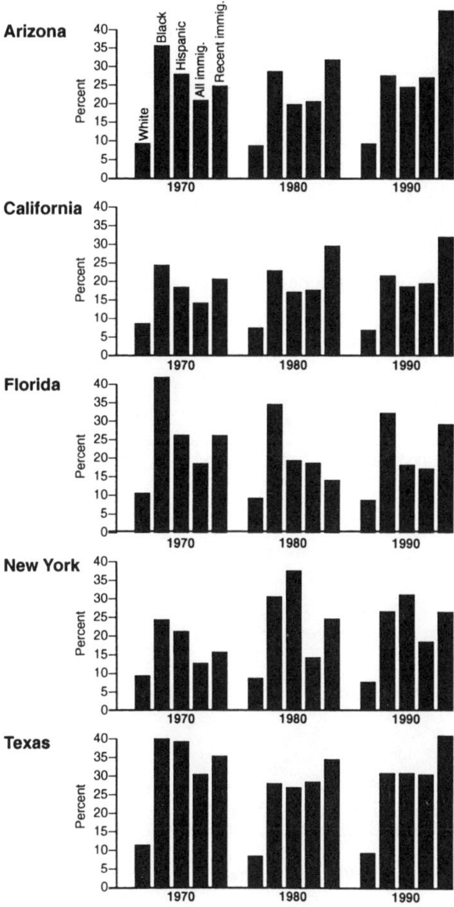

Figure 5.4 Changes in Poverty by Native-Born and Immigrant Status, 1970–1990

migrants. Even adjusted for cost of living the regional disparities are substantial.

The analysis of regional variations is important in the context of changes to the federal support system. It is in these states that the impacts will be the greatest and will, without modification of changes in the welfare devolution, lead to substantial state costs. At least in California, counties are required by law to be a provider of last resort. In such cases county governments will in fact bear the burden of changes set in motion by federal policy or nonpolicy, in the case of migration (Clark and Schultz 1997b).

Table 5.2 Rates of Welfare Use by Race, Ethnicity, and Immigrant Status for Five Entry-Point States, 1970–1990 (%)

	1970	1980	1990
Arizona			
Native-born white, non-Hispanic	1.8	2.1	2.6
Native-born black	18.2	9.8	12.2
Native-born Hispanic	8.4	6.1	7.7
All immigrants	4.8	5.0	4.9
Recent immigrants (arrived in the past 5 years)	0.0	2.0	3.2
California			
Native-born white, non-Hispanic	5.3	5.0	4.5
Native-born black	17.2	18.2	16.9
Native-born Hispanic	9.6	10.3	10.1
All immigrants	7.7	7.3	7.4
Recent immigrants (arrived in the past 5 years)	4.5	6.4	8.3
Florida			
Native-born white, Non-Hispanic	1.9	2.5	2.4
Native-born black	12.8	14.4	14.2
Native-born Hispanic	7.1	5.5	4.3
All immigrants	3.6	5.7	5.0
Recent immigrants (arrived in the past 5 years)	9.6	5.2	2.7
New York			
Native-born white, non-Hispanic	3.8	3.9	3.5
Native-born black	17.8	22.0	17.6
Native-born Hispanic	13.7	30.6	17.7
All immigrants	3.8	6.6	10.8
Recent immigrants (arrived in the past 5 years)	3.1	6.6	7.7
Texas			
Native-born white, non-Hispanic	3.3	2.5	2.6
Native-born black	14.1	11.0	12.0
Native-born Hispanic	7.5	7.8	9.2
All immigrants	6.9	8.1	6.6
Recent immigrants (arrived in the past 5 years)	3.9	3.2	4.0

Source: U.S. Bureau of the Census, PUMS, 1970, 1980, and 1990.

Interactions with Restructuring

There is little doubt that recent immigrants are doing less well than previous immigrants. There are internal and external reasons for these outcomes. Clearly, the composition of recent immigrants is different; they are younger, are less well educated, and have fewer skills. But external reasons are equally important as explanations for the current levels of immigrant performance. It is reasonable to point to restructuring as an explanation for part of the decline in

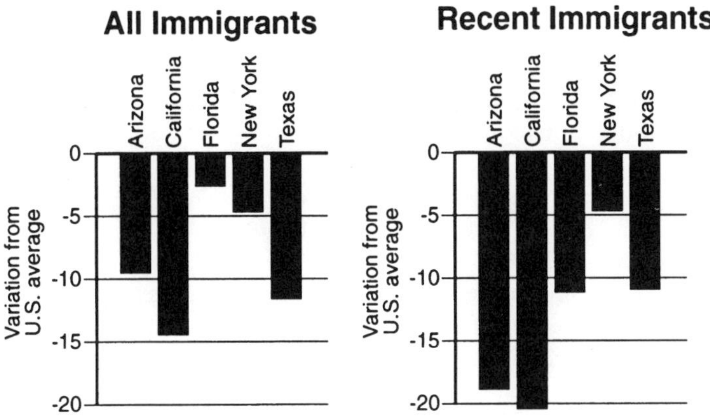

Figure 5.5 Regional Variations of Wage Differentials, 1990

wages and indeed to suggest that the long-run trajectory may have changed fundamentally. But it is also important to recognize that even though manufacturing jobs declined as a proportion of all jobs, apart from New York actual increases occurred in manufacturing jobs; it is simply that the increase in professional service jobs was that much greater. Thus, as others have noted (Edmonston and Passel 1996), we must recognize the impact of the fundamental change in immigration policy. Previous to 1965 the basis for entry was some form of regional quota- or skill-based preference. After the Family Reunification Act of 1965, family connections replaced regional quotas from Europe. The result was a larger influx of children, elderly family members, and migrants who will not contribute to U.S. economic growth. The question for policymakers is, what is the relative proportion of skilled, nonskilled, and family members who should enter the United States?

Restructuring is not independent of global politics, and especially not of recent changes in the trading relationships between the United States and its neighbors. A vigorous debate is under way about the role of free trade agreements such as the North American Free Trade Agreement (NAFTA). Will these agreements stimulate industry in Mexico and provide jobs that will reduce the level of immigration from Mexico to the United States? Or are pressures for noneconomic migration so great that the changes put in place by NAFTA will have little or no effect on the built-up demand for family reunification migration to the southern tier of U.S. states? Although NAFTA is clearly a variable in the interaction between the United States and Mexico, the outcomes are far from clear at this point.

Conclusions and Implications

This chapter has enriched the broad generalization suggested by Borjas (1995) that the optimistic picture of immigrant trajectories suggested by some (Simon 1989) may be misplaced. The chapter also provides support for the caution suggested by Chiswick and Sullivan (1994), who draw attention to the probably localized impacts of large-scale migration. The aggregate data for the United States suggest that immigrants are doing less well and the detailed regional data show that they are doing even less well in particular states, especially California, Arizona, and Texas. The implications of the research reported here are that the newest immigrant waves in these states earn far below even the average migrant to the United States, and because they start out at such a major skill and earnings disadvantage and economic assimilation has always been slow, the new immigrants may never reach parity with the native-born population.

It is particularly revealing that in several of the cases examined in the chapter the new immigrants are performing less well than native-born black and Hispanic populations. Whereas at one time immigrant groups outperformed native-born ethnic groups, this appears to be less true over time. The evidence from this analysis indicates that the policy of family reunification preference over skills, in combination with economic restructuring, is creating state effects that are much more negative than the overall national effects. The evidence implies that new immigrants may even replace the inner-city dependent populations of the past.

We are forced to choose between two competing views of the future path of immigrants to the United States and their attendant implications for states and regions. In one optimistic view the path of these immigrants will eventually follow that of earlier immigrants. This view emphasizes both the value of migrants to the economy and a faith in the ultimate fairness of opening the United States to populations from less favored origins. An alternate and less optimistic view suggests that the increased flow of migrants, although beneficial for the migrants and for at least some employers and even the population as a whole, which benefits from cheaper goods and services, may in the long run create substantial problems for both migrants and the regions in which they are concentrated.

At the same time, the issue of migration is larger than what happens to individuals and even to states. The larger issue is the future pattern of flows from one nation to another. Perhaps 125 million persons are living and working outside their countries of birth, and the number of migrants may be growing faster than the world population. In this context the patterns observed in this analysis are not likely to change in the near future, and even though there is clear evidence of a growing gap between native-born and immigrant groups, that gap is likely to increase rather than decrease. The previously comforting notion that countries could turn the flow of workers off and on to suit employment needs has been changed with the increasing nonemployment flow of family reunification and its implications. Now the debate often turns on the requirements of employers, who say that without a continued flow of workers their businesses will suffer and the economy will not continue to grow. Perhaps a truer interpretation is that adjusting to a decreased flow of inexpensive labor would be costly. The issue this chapter brings to the front is the clear need for local and regional, as well as national agendas to be at the center of discussions of future policies on migration and settlement.

References

Borjas, George J. 1994. "The Economics of Immigration." *Journal of Economic Literature* 32: 1667–1717.

———. 1995. "The Economic Benefits from Immigration." *Journal of Economic Perspectives* 9: 3–22.

Bouvier, Leon. 1991. *Peaceful Invasions: Immigration and Changing America*. Lanham, Md.: Lanham Press.

Chiswick, Barry, and Theresa Sullivan. 1994. "The New Immigrants." In Reynolds Farley (ed.), *The State of the Union: Americas in the 1990s*. New York: Russell Sage Foundation.

Clark, William A.V. 1998a. *The California Cauldron: Immigration and the Fortunes of Local Communities*. New York: Guilford.

———. 1998b. "Mass Migration and Local Outcomes: Is International Migration to the United States Creating a New Urban Underclass?" *Urban Studies* 35: 371–383.

Clark, William A.V., and M. McNicholas. 1995. "Re-examining Economic and Social Polarization in a Multi-ethnic Metropolitan Area: The Case of Los Angeles." *Area* 28: 56–63.

Clark, William A.V., and Milan Mueller. 1988. "Hispanic Relocation and Spatial Assimilation: A Case Study." *Social Science Quarterly* 69: 468–475.

Clark, William A.V., and Freya Schultz. 1997a. "Commentary: The Geographical Impacts of Welfare Reform in the United States." *Environment and Planning A* 29: 762–766.

———. 1997b. "Evaluating the Local Impacts of Recent Migration to California: Realism versus Racism." *Population Research and Policy Review* 16: 475–491.

Cross, Malcolm. 1992. *Racial Minorities and Industrial Change in Europe and North America*. Cambridge: Cambridge University Press.

Edmonston, Barry, and Jeffrey S. Passel (eds.). 1996. *Immigration and Ethnicity: The Integration of Americas Newest Arrivals*. Washington, D.C.: Urban Institute.

Espenshade, Thomas (ed.). 1997. *Keys to Successful Immigration: Implications of the New Jersey Experience*. Washington D.C.: Urban Institute.

Fainstein, Susan S., Ian Gordon, and Michael Harloe. 1992. *Divided Cities*. Oxford: Basil Blackwell.

Hamnett, Chris. 1994. "Social Polarization in Global Cities: Theory and Evidence." *Urban Studies* 31: 401–424.

James, Franklin. 1995. "Urban Economies: Trends, Forces and Implications for the President's National Urban Policy." *Cityscape* 1: 67–123.

Kennedy, David. 1996. "Can We Still Afford to Be a Nation of Immigrants?" *Atlantic Monthly* 278: 52–68.

Law, Robin, and Jennifer Wolch. 1993. "Social Reproduction in the City: Restructuring in Time and Space." In Paul Knox (ed.), *The Restless Urban Landscape*. Englewood Cliffs, N.J.: Prentice-Hall.

Sassen, Saskia. 1994. *Cities in a World Economy*. London: Pine Forge.

Simon, Julian. 1989. *The Economic Consequences of Immigration*. Cambridge: Basil Blackwell.

Waldinger, Roger, and Mehdi Bozorgmehr. 1996. *Ethnic Los Angeles*. New York: Sage.

Wilson, William Julius. 1996. *When Work Disappears*. Boston: Harvard University Press.

Appendix 5.1 Regional Variation in Education, Earnings, and Poverty for Five States, 1970–1990

1990	Arizona	California	Florida	New York	Texas
Native born					
Years education	13.1	13.6	13.0	13.5	12.9
% in poverty	14.5	10.3	11.7	12.3	12.2
Native-born white					
Years education	13.5	13.9	13.2	13.7	13.4
Difference/native born	0.4	0.3	0.2	0.2	0.5
% wage difference	4.6	4.5	4.0	3.3	9.4
% in poverty	9.4	6.7	8.0	7.1	9.3
Native-born black					
Years education	12.6	12.9	11.7	12.3	12.2
Difference/native born	−0.5	−0.7	−1.3	−1.2	−0.7
% wage difference	−17.6	−16.6	−27.8	−20.1	−24.5
% in poverty	27.4	21.3	32.1	26.1	30.5
Native-born Hispanic					
Years education	11.6	12.0	12.4	12.4	10.9
Difference/native born	−1.5	−1.6	−0.6	−1.1	−2.0
% wage difference	−20.3	−20.3	−8.9	−18.1	−28.1
% in poverty	24.8	18.6	18.0	33.1	30.5
All immigrants					
Years education	10.7	10.8	11.8	11.7	9.9
Difference/native born	−2.4	−2.8	−1.2	−1.8	−3.0
% wage differenc	−24.4	−29.5	−17.9	−19.9	−27.3
% in poverty	27.2	19.3	17.0	18.1	30.1
Recent immigrants					
Years education	10.5	10.6	11.5	12.1	10.5
Difference/native born	−2.6	−3.0	−1.5	−1.4	−2.4
% wage difference	−50.4	−52.2	−43.2	−36.4	−43.0
% in poverty	44.9	31.6	29.1	26.2	40.6
1980	**Arizona**	**California**	**Florida**	**New York**	**Texas**
Native born					
Years education	12.9	13.3	12.5	12.8	12.5
% in poverty	12.9	10.4	13.3	13.3	13.9
Native-born white					
Years education	13.3	13.6	12.8	13.2	13.0
Difference/native born	0.4	0.3	0.3	0.4	0.5
% wage difference	3.3	3.8	4.8	4.1	8.4
% in poverty	8.8	7.5	9.1	8.0	8.0
Native-born black					
Years education	12.1	12.6	10.9	11.7	11.6
Difference/native born	−0.8	−0.7	−1.6	−1.1	−0.9
% wage difference	−16.9	−17.0	−28.0	−19.8	−26.2
% in poverty	28.1	22.9	34.8	30.3	27.7

(Cont.)

Appendix 5.1 *(Cont.)*

Native-born Hispanic					
Years education	10.9	11.6	11.5	10.2	10.0
Difference/native born	−2.0	−1.7	−1.0	−2.6	−2.5
% wage difference	−12.6	−16.5	−12.9	−25.9	−26.1
% in poverty	19.9	17.2	19.4	37.6	26.4
All immigrants					
Years education	10.8	11.3	11.7	11.7	10.2
Difference/native born	−2.1	−2.0	−0.8	−1.1	−2.3
% wage difference	−17.9	−22.6	−12.8	−14.7	−22.7
% in poverty	20.7	17.6	18.6	14.3	28.2
Recent immigrants					
Years education	11.7	11.2	11.9	12.3	10.6
Difference/native born	−1.2	−2.1	−0.6	−0.5	−0.9
% wage difference	−31.7	−43.6	−32.0	−31.4	−30.8
% in poverty	32.0	29.4	15.6	24.8	34.8

1970	Arizona	California	Florida	New York	Texas
Native born					
Years education	11.8	12.3	11.4	11.7	11.2
% in poverty	15.4	10.8	16.5	11.0	18.6
Native-born white					
Years education	12.3	12.5	11.8	11.9	11.8
Difference/native born	0.5	0.2	0.4	0.2	0.6
% wage difference	3.9	4.0	8.6	3.2	9.0
% in poverty	9.9	8.7	11.3	9.1	11.4
Native-born black					
Years education	9.9	11.1	9.0	10.4	9.8
Difference/native born	−1.9	−1.2	−2.4	−1.3	−1.4
% wage difference	−31.2	−27.7	−43.4	−25.8	−39.8
% in poverty	35.8	24.3	41.9	24.2	39.8
Native-born Hispanic					
Years education	9.3	10.4	10.9	10.7	8.1
Difference/native born	−2.5	−1.9	−1.5	−1.0	−3.1
% wage difference	−15.0	−17.2	−10.9	−31.7	−27.4
% in poverty	27.7	18.1	26.3	21.3	39.0
All immigrants					
Years education	10.2	10.8	10.7	10.5	9.5
Difference/native born	−1.6	−1.5	−0.7	−1.2	−1.7
% wage difference	−14.6	−18.3	−17.2	−9.1	−20.3
% in poverty	21.3	14.3	18.8	12.9	30.8
Recent immigrants					
Years education	10.8	10.7	9.8	10.7	10.5
Difference/native born	−2.0	−1.6	−1.6	−1.0	−0.7
% wage difference	4.0	−38.5	−38.3	−26.5	−23.1
% in poverty	24.9	20.9	26.1	15.9	35.5

6

Restructuring Incentives for U.S. Immigration

Thomas J. Espenshade, Jessica L. Baraka, and Gregory A. Huber

There are two broad purposes to U.S. immigration policy. One is to preserve opportunities for legal immigrants, refugees, and asylees to settle in the United States to rejoin family members, put high-end labor market skills to better use, or escape political persecution. The second is to control the number of illegal immigrants living in the country by reducing incentives for undocumented migration, guarding U.S. borders more diligently, and encouraging or requiring illegal residents to depart. These purposes are consistent with the views of those who argue that the United States should close the back door to illegal immigration in order to keep open the front door to legal immigrants and refugees. And it is these views that prevailed in Washington in 1996 when the U.S. Congress decided against limiting both legal and illegal immigration, choosing instead to address undocumented migration and leave legal immigration policy intact.

But immigration policies do not always work the way they are intended (Cornelius, Martin, and Hollifield 1994). Temporary guest worker programs in Europe created large pools of permanent residents who proved difficult to repatriate. Terminating the Bracero program changed the legal composition of the immigrant flow in the 1960s but did not stop the influx of Mexican agricultural workers. The 1986 Immigration Reform and Control Act (IRCA) succeeded only temporarily in reducing the number of undocumented migrants crossing the Mexico–U.S. border (Espenshade 1990). And the Special Agricultural Worker program that was part of IRCA and that provided amnesty, temporary legal resident status, and work authorization to farmworkers in perishable crop agriculture created incentives for hundreds of thousands more illegal immigrants to enter the United States in search of legal permanent residence (Bean, Vernez, and Keely 1989).

Major changes in noncitizen eligibility for welfare and in U.S. immigration policy are contained in two pieces of federal legislation signed into law during August and September 1996. The first, the Personal Responsibility and Work Opportunity Reconciliation Act of 1996, reforms the entitlement policy for poor families and imposes new limits on alien access to welfare and other social services. The second, the Illegal Immigration Reform and Immigrant Responsibility Act of 1996, strengthens efforts to combat illegal immigration and creates higher standards of financial self-sufficiency for the admission of sponsored legal immigrants.

How are patterns of U.S. immigration likely to be affected by welfare and immigration reform? Will they be modified at all and, if so, in ways that are consistent with overall directions in immigration policy? The immigration reform bill intends to reduce illegal immigration. But the two laws do not deliberately change legal immigration or the number of refugee or asylee entrants. Nor do they alter the broad criteria for obtaining a lawful permanent resident visa, including the priority current immigration policy gives to family reunification goals. Nevertheless, the new laws may still influence the relative attractiveness of U.S. immigration and the ability of immigrants to enter the country.

We suggest that the combined effects of the 1996 immigration and welfare reforms will produce unintended, and possibly undesirable, consequences. The acts represent congressional failure to consider how individuals and institutions are likely to react in the face of new policies. Policies that reconfigure an existing set of incentives induce adaptive behaviors by affected persons. These adaptive and reactive behaviors have the potential to undo, or at least mitigate, the intended effects of policy changes. In some instances, they can lead to outcomes the opposite of those that were intended. We will argue that the 1996 reform measures, instead of preserving legal immigration and discouraging illegal immigration, are more likely to *reduce* legal immigration and *expand* incentives for illegal immigration.

The remainder of the chapter is organized into five sections. The first two describe the main features of the welfare and immigration reform acts, respectively. The next two examine the behavioral implications of the new policy measures, first for legal immigration and then for undocumented migration. The final section summarizes our main conclusions.

The Welfare Reform Act

The Personal Responsibility and Work Opportunity Reconciliation Act of 1996 (Welfare Reform Act, or WRA) was signed into law by President Clinton on August 22, 1996. The law is a massive overhaul of U.S. welfare policy that eliminates the entitlement "right" of support for poor families and requires that able-bodied persons who receive government assistance must work. Specifically, the WRA abolishes the Aid to Families with Dependent Children (AFDC) entitlement program, first established in 1935, and replaces it with a state-implemented program designed to provide short-term cash assistance to poor families (National Conference of State Legislatures 1996). The law also reforms such federally funded programs as Food Stamps, Supplemental Security Income, child care, and child support and reduces the size of the Social Services Block Grant. Combined federal, state, and local government expenditures on the four major programs affected by welfare reform (Supplemental Security Income, Food Stamps, AFDC, and Medicaid) totaled $230 billion in fiscal year (FY) 1995. By comparison, total federal spending equaled $1,519 billion in FY 1995.

Changes in Immigrant Eligibility for Social Services

Prior to the enactment of the 1996 welfare reform bill, U.S. citizens, legal immigrants, and refugees were eligible for means-tested public benefit programs on more or less the same terms, and illegal immigrants were intentionally excluded. The WRA introduces significant changes in immigrant eligibility for social services by creating a four-tier system. The broadest eligibility is reserved for U.S. citizens; next come refugees and asylees (hereafter "refugees"); newly limited access is imposed on legal immigrants; and illegal immigrants remain ineligible for almost all social programs. Some programs distinguish between legal immigrants who were in the United States on August 22, 1996, and those who came later. Aliens who become naturalized U.S. citizens are eligible to receive benefits on the same terms as all other citizens, although benefits for citizens have also been circumscribed.

Under the old welfare system, refugees were eligible for both federal and joint federal–state benefit programs from the time they entered the country. Under the new system they retain their eligibility for federal means-tested programs except for Supplemental Security Income (SSI) and Food Stamps.[1] They are eligible for SSI and food stamps only during their first five years in the United States. For joint federal–state programs such as Temporary Assistance for Needy Families (TANF) and Medicaid, refugees remain eligible for their first five years and afterward at a state's discretion.[2]

Legal immigrants are noncitizens who have permanent U.S. resident status and work authorization. Prior to the 1996 WRA, legal immigrants were eligible for means-tested public benefit programs from the time they became permanent residents, although "deeming"—considering, or deeming, a sponsor's income to be available to an immigrant when determining the immigrant's eligibility for a means-tested public benefit program—usually applied to sponsored immigrants.[3]

Under the WRA, legal immigrants who were in the country on August 22,

1996, are in general no longer eligible for food stamps. The WRA had also denied SSI benefits to current legal immigrants, but those benefits were restored by the balanced budget accords of 1997. New legal immigrants are permanently disqualified for food stamps and SSI and are ineligible for other federal benefits for their first five years in the United States. For jointly administered federal–state programs, current legal immigrants retain eligibility at state discretion. New immigrants, with some exceptions, are ineligible for these programs for their first five years in this country and may be covered after that at state discretion. In brief, most federal benefit cuts affect new legal immigrants who arrived in the United States after August 1996. Earlier immigrants have been exempted, with the exception of the current ban on food stamps.

Eligibility rules for illegal immigrants were hardly affected by the welfare reform legislation. Illegal immigrants are generally ineligible for all federal and state social programs. The major exceptions include public schooling (guaranteed by the U.S. Supreme Court in the 1982 case *Plyler v. Doe,* 457 U.S.C. 202 [1982]), emergency medical assistance, school lunches, child nutrition programs, public health assistance for immunizations and communicable diseases, and preschool education programs.

Affidavits of Support

In addition to revising eligibility for social services, the WRA reforms the use of affidavits of support, previously considered unenforceable because several courts had ruled that support affidavits were not legally binding (U.S. General Accounting Office 1995). Under the WRA, however, affidavits for future immigrants are legally enforceable against the sponsor, either by the immigrant or by any government agency that provides a means-tested social service, until the immigrant becomes a U.S. citizen or has performed ten years of qualifying work. Moreover, the individual who petitions for an immigrant to come to the United States must also be the financial sponsor, whereas in the past any U.S. citizen or permanent resident could present an affidavit of support.

Projected Cost Savings

As a result of reductions in noncitizen social service access and programmatic spending resulting from the WRA, approximately 500,000 noncitizen AFDC recipients were expected to lose eligibility in 1996–1997, representing a caseload reduction of 35 percent (Social Security Administration 1997). Whereas most of those becoming ineligible are legal immigrants, some of the approximately 200,000 refugee recipients are no longer eligible if they have been in the United States for more than five years. Similarly, all of the approximately 1 million immigrants receiving food stamps are expected to lose their benefits. The total cost savings to the federal government from reduced eligibility for immigrants is estimated at $10–15 billion for the six-year period between 1997 and 2002, approximately 30 percent of the projected $43 billion savings from the entire welfare reform bill (Congressional Budget Office 1996; U.S. General Accounting Office 1995).

The Immigration Reform Act

The FY 1997 Omnibus Consolidated Appropriations Act was signed into law by President Clinton on September 30, 1996. This measure incorporates the Illegal Immigration Reform and Immigrant Responsibility Act of 1996 (Immigration Reform Act or IRA). Although parts of the Immigration Reform Act affect legal immigrants, the majority of the new law is devoted to illegal immigrants. We examine these reforms under three headings: (1) those that affect legal immigrants and refugees, (2) those designed to restrict entry of illegal immigrants, and (3) those directed at illegal aliens who are already in the interior of the United States.

Reforms Affecting Legal Immigrants and Refugees

The Immigration Reform Act reiterates the Welfare Reform Act's delegation of discretionary authority to the states to distinguish among citizens, legal immigrants, and refugees. In addition, individuals who sponsor family members under the family reunification segment of current immigration law are now required to have an income at least 125 percent of the federal poverty level, whereas previously there were no income requirements for sponsors.

Restricting Illegal Entry

The IRA significantly increases resources to prevent illegal entry across the U.S.–Mexico border. For example, it directs the attorney general to augment the number of Border Patrol agents by 5,000 by the year 2001. This change, if fully implemented, would almost double the number of agents now patrolling the southwest border. The IRA also allows an increase of 1,500 persons in Immigration and Naturalization Service (INS) support personnel. Furthermore, the legislation directs the INS to forward deploy Border Patrol agents "to provide a uniform and visible deterrent to illegal entry on a continuing basis," so long as the law enforcement capabilities and functions currently performed at interior Border Patrol stations are not compromised. The IRA strengthens the ability of the attorney general to request available resources from other federal agencies, including fixed-wing aircraft, helicopters, night vision equipment, and four-wheel-drive vehicles. In addition to the expansion in personnel and equipment, the IRA provides $12 million for the construction of a triple fence along the Mexican border, starting at the Pacific Ocean and extending 14 miles inland. General provisions are also included for the construction of better roads and barriers in the border area.

The IRA stiffens civil and criminal penalties for illegal entry and for assisting illegal entry. Every illegal entrant will be fined $50 to $250 for an initial offense, and the amount is doubled for repeat offenses. Civil and criminal penalties are also imposed for using or providing false documents. Finally, the IRA extends the coverage of antiracketeering legislation to include alien smuggling for financial gain and authorizes the use of wiretaps for the investigation of alien smuggling and document fraud.

In a move continued in the portion of the legislation devoted to aliens in the interior, the IRA requires that the INS begin phasing in biometric identifiers on all border-crossing cards within eighteen months and specifies that cards without such identifiers will become invalid in 1999.[4] In a related measure, the IRA requires that the INS implement an automated entry-and-exit control system to record all entries and exits by aliens. This would allow the INS to monitor, for instance, individuals who overstay temporary visas.

Enforcement in the Interior

The IRA authorizes several incremental policy changes directed at illegal aliens in the interior. First, it expands staff for detecting employment eligibility violations and visa overstayers. By 1999 the number of INS staff available to investigate employment violations is expected to grow by 900, and by 1997 300 more INS employees were authorized to investigate visa overstays.

Second, the new law takes broad steps toward federalizing identification document standards. One provision requires the Social Security Administration to develop a prototype counterfeit-resistant identification card. Another requires that federal agencies accept only birth certificates and state identification cards that incorporate similar anticounterfeit security devices.

Third, the law not only significantly expands existing systems for tracking aliens in the interior but also calls for the development of several new ones. In addition to the entry-exit surveillance system mentioned earlier, the IRA authorizes funds to expand nationwide the trial IDENT program that records the fingerprints of all illegal or criminal aliens arrested in the United States. The IRA also orders the attorney general to create a four-year pilot program to increase employment eligibility verification in at least five of the seven states with the highest illegal alien populations. This includes, but is not limited to, improvements in I-9 form data collection,[5] the use of machine-readable employment verification forms, and a toll-free call-in system through which employers can verify the eligibility of job applicants. This trial program, however, is supposed to be implemented only in states that conform to new standards for identification documents and is to a large degree voluntary.

Behavioral Implications: Legal Immigrants

The latest rounds of welfare and immigration policy reforms create important distinctions among citizens, legal immigrants, and refugees in terms of welfare eligibility. It is now more costly to be a noncitizen in the United States, especially a poor noncitizen, than it was before. Moreover, recent reforms differentiate sharply between current and future immigrants. With the exception of the ban on receiving food stamps, current immigrants have been exempted from across-the-board prohibitions, whereas new immigrants are excluded from receiving public benefits for their first five years in the United States. In short, the WRA and IRA have created incentives for poor noncitizens already living in the United States to become naturalized U.S. citizens to preserve their access to public benefits, and they have erected new barriers against legal entry by poorer would-be immigrants.[6]

Altered Incentives for Legal Immigration

Reforms are likely to affect the migration decisions faced by potential new legal immigrants by altering not only the relative attractiveness of U.S. immigration for would-be immigrants but also the willingness and ability of individuals in the United States to become financial sponsors for poorer legal immigrants.

Demand Considerations

The attraction of immigrating to the United States may be decreased for potential future legal immigrants. First, because new immigrants who stay longer than five years now have a greater incentive to become citizens to preserve their access to social services, immigrants from countries where dual citizenship is not allowed may forgo immigrating if they want to retain citizenship in their home country. Second, individuals who under the old law would have migrated for the purpose of receiving government assistance, or perhaps with the knowledge that such assistance would be available in times of difficulty, may be more cautious about coming to the United States. This effect is difficult to measure, however, because it presumes that immigrants are aware of the complexities of the U.S. welfare system. In either case, welfare reform has made U.S. immigration more costly or less beneficial and therefore less desirable from the standpoint of potential new legal immigrants.[7]

Supply Considerations

Welfare and immigration reforms may also combine to reduce the willingness or ability of current residents to sponsor future legal immigrants. First, potential sponsors who will become financially liable under the new affidavits of support may be more reluctant to sponsor poorer immigrants for fear they could be sued for support. Moreover, individuals living in the United States who previously petitioned for family members to become permanent residents may be less inclined to do so now, even if family members' incomes currently exceed the public-charge threshold. This reasoning may apply especially to U.S. residents' older immigrant parents whose opportunity for government assistance is minimal unless they plan to work until they naturalize, accumulate enough years of work to qualify for Social Security, or perform forty quarters of qualifying work for SSI. Under these circumstances, some current residents may discourage the immigration of family members who might later need to rely on them for support.

Second, faced with higher minimum income standards, fewer U.S.-based households will be able to sponsor new immigrants. Under the new law, individuals who sponsor family members for admission to the United States must have a family income at least 25 percent above the federal poverty level. Research supported by the INS that used almost 2,200 randomly selected statements signed by sponsors of family immigrants in 1994 found that about 30 percent of those sponsors would fail to meet the new income criteria. Other research derived from an examination of 1993 Census Bureau income data showed that 40 percent of immigrant families living in the United States and 26 percent of native households would not make enough to sponsor an immigrant under the new standard. Based on the survey of sponsors, INS officials concluded that approximately half of Mexicans and Salvadorans and one-third of Dominicans and Koreans would fail the new income test (Dugger 1997).

The impact of these supply factors will be to decrease the number of potential sponsors for poorer legal immigrants in the future. When demand and supply factors are considered together, they seem certain to reduce the volume of legal U.S. immigration and to produce an immigrant flow with a somewhat higher average level of income and skill. New potential immigrants, especially those who anticipate that they might have to draw on the U.S. welfare system at some point, are likely to find U.S. immigration less attractive. And those who still want to come to the United States will find it more difficult to locate a financial sponsor if they need one.

Behavioral Implications: Undocumented Migrants

Recent estimates released by the U.S. Immigration and Naturalization Service (1997) indicate that approximately 5 million undocumented migrants were living in the United States in October 1996 and that this total is growing by about 275,000 annually. A majority of the illegal residents (2.9 million, or 59 percent) entered the United States undetected and were unauthorized migrants from the day they arrived. An additional 2.1 million illegal residents, or 41 percent of the total, came to this country as legal temporary migrants and overstayed their visas. These estimates suggest that if the IRA is going to achieve the aims its supporters intended, it will have to be more successful than its predecessors at slowing the entry of illegal immigrants into the United States and accelerating their departure, either voluntarily or involuntarily.

Barriers to Entry

Much of the 1996 Immigration Reform Act focuses on restricting illegal migrant entry at the U.S.–Mexico border. As described earlier, the INS has been authorized to expand the number of Border Patrol agents, to deploy them more efficiently, and to spend more for new capital equipment. At the same time, to the extent that improved border management and more effective enforcement of employer sanctions raise the cost to a would-be undocumented migrant of initiating a trip to the United States, the IRA could also slow illegal entry by discouraging illegal immigration at its source. In assessing the impact of the new law, therefore, several questions must be considered. First, does increased INS expenditure translate into a higher probability of apprehending illegal migrants at the border? Second, do higher apprehension probabilities reduce the number of migrants who enter the United States illegally? Third, do higher apprehension probabilities affect the amount of time undocumented migrants spend working in the United States? And fourth, to what extent do the answers to the previous questions depend on migrant characteristics?

Effects on Apprehension Probabilities

Does increased INS expenditure lead to a higher probability of apprehension at the southwest border? Previous work by Espenshade (1990) has shown that a repeated trials model of undocumented migration can be used to estimate the probability that an undocumented migrant will be apprehended on a given single attempt to cross the U.S.–Mexico border. These estimates, calculated on a month-by-month basis between January 1977 and September 1988, range between 21 percent and 40 percent and have an average value of 32 percent. Important determinants of variation in these apprehension probabilities include the number of undocumented migrants attempting to cross the U.S.–Mexico border, as well as the effort the INS expends in apprehending them (Espenshade and Acevedo 1995). Two key components of the enforcement effort are the number of Border Patrol officer hours devoted to apprehension activities and the quantity of capital equipment (for example, unattended electronic ground sensors, lighting, a variety of imaging devices, and transportation vehicles) the INS has at its disposal. The greater the number of Border Patrol officers the INS uses and the more capital equipment these officers have, the higher the chances that an undocumented migrant will be apprehended.

Because the IRA increases both INS staffing levels and access to capital equipment, we will look more closely at the effects of INS enforcement on apprehension probabilities. During FY 1988, the last year for which aggregate apprehension probabilities had previously been calculated, Border Patrol agents averaged 446,000 hours per month in apprehension duties, and total expenditure on capital equipment in the past year averaged $21.4 million. How would further increases in INS enforcement effort affect apprehension activities? In particular, what would be the consequences for apprehension probabilities, the total number of apprehensions, and the average number of attempts needed for a successful border crossing? Some answers are provided in Table 6.1. Here, alternative levels of the monthly undocumented flow, ranging from 75,000 to 300,000, are also considered. This span is broad enough to encompass more than 90 percent of the monthly estimates shown in Espenshade (1990).[8]

During FY 1988 estimated apprehension rates fluctuated in a range between 0.25 and 0.37 (panel A). This range differs little from the historical record for the 1977–1988 period. Panel B is relevant because the number of apprehensions is recorded in INS enforcement statistics and is customarily interpreted as an indicator of the flow of undocumented migrants into the United States (Espenshade 1995). There is not necessarily a one-to-one correspondence between apprehension statistics and undocumented migration. When INS effort is held constant at 1988 levels, doubling the undocumented flow reduces the odds of capture, so the number of apprehensions increases by a smaller multiple. In other words, undocumented migrants confer positive externalities on

Table 6.1 INS Performance Indicators: 1988, 1996, 2001

	Undocumented Flow (per month)			
Fiscal Year	75,000	150,000	225,000	300,000
A. Probability of Apprehension				
1988	0.370	0.327	0.287	0.251
1996	0.509	0.462	0.416	0.372
2001	0.772	0.737	0.699	0.658
B. Number of Apprehensions Each Month				
1988	44,000	72,900	90,700	100,300
1996	77,800	129,000	160,500	177,500
2001	253,400	420,300	522,800	578,200
C. Average Number of Attempts per Migrant				
1988	1.59	1.49	1.40	1.33
1996	2.04	1.86	1.71	1.59
2001	4.38	3.80	3.32	2.93

each other in the sense that when more of them try to cross the border at any one time, the chances that any given migrant will be apprehended are lowered. A central assumption of the repeated trials model is that undocumented migrants, once they have reached the Mexico–U.S. frontier, will make as many attempts as necessary to cross the border. Panel C shows the average number of attempts per migrant for different levels of unauthorized immigration. A higher probability of apprehension means more attempts are required to enter the United States clandestinely.

The same procedures may be used to evaluate the impacts of INS enforcement levels in FY 1996 and also to anticipate the effects of the IRA in FY 2001, when its provisions are expected to be fully operational. Between FY 1988 and FY 1996, the number of Border Patrol agents deployed along the southern border increased by 66 percent, from 3,184 to 5,281. In addition, capital equipment expenditures rose by 45 percent in constant 1988 dollars. These percentage increases have been applied to FY 1988 Border Patrol enforcement levels to produce the FY 1996 results in Table 6.1. As the monthly flow of undocumented migrants ranges between 75,000 and 300,000, the per attempt probability of apprehension falls from 0.51 to 0.37, the monthly number of total apprehensions increases from 77,800 to 177,500, and the average number of attempted border crossings needed to enter the United States declines from 2.0 to 1.6. These apprehension probabilities are above historical averages from the 1980s but not by much.

During FY 1996 the actual number of Border Patrol apprehensions was 1.55 million, or about 129,000 per month (Office of Management and Budget 1997). Table 6.1 shows that given FY 1996 enforcement figures, the only level of undocumented immigration consistent with that many apprehensions is a monthly gross or one-way flow of 150,000, or 1.8 million undocumented migrants who entered without inspection during the year. This level is somewhat below the estimated average monthly values of 175,000 for the period between January 1977 and October 1986 and 178,000 for the twenty-two-month post-IRCA period beginning December 1986 and ending September 1988 (Espenshade 1990). Migrants in FY 1996 typically faced an apprehension probability of 0.462 per attempt, and they needed an average of 1.86 attempts per migrant to enter the United States.

Similar calculations permit us to estimate the possible effects of the 1996 Immigration Reform Act in the year 2001. The IRA authorizes the attorney general to increase the number of Border Patrol agents by a net amount of 1,000 per year each year until FY 2001, for a total net increase of 5,000. If all of these agents are hired, trained, and assigned to the southern U.S. border, it would bring the total number of Border Patrol agents to 10,281 by 2001, an increase of 95 percent over FY 1996 and a growth of 223 percent compared with FY 1988. In addition, the real value of capital investment expenditures for enforcement purposes grew at an average annual rate of 4.6 percent between FY

1988 and FY 1996. Anticipating how these figures are likely to change in the future is complicated by the fact that they are subject to sharp annual fluctuations. For example, the Office of Management and Budget (1997) has estimated that new equipment expenditures will total $46 million and $24 million in FY 1997 and 1998, respectively. We assume that the average annual growth observed between 1988 and 1996 will continue until FY 2001, resulting in an 82 percent growth in equipment expenditures by 2001 compared with 1988.

Table 6.1 shows that under these assumptions, which might be considered a "best-case scenario" by FY 2001, as monthly values for the undocumented flow range from 75,000 to 300,000, estimated apprehension probabilities fluctuate between 0.77 and 0.66; the total number of monthly apprehensions varies between 253,400 and 578,200; and the average number of border crossings needed to enter the United States runs from 4.4 to 2.9. Even with a modest flow of undocumented migrants of 75,000 per month, this potential FY 2001 level of enforcement activity would generate an unprecedented annual number of apprehensions—in excess of 3 million per year, or approximately twice the FY 1996 volume. It is not known how the Border Patrol would cope with this volume of arrests and detentions, whether apprehension probabilities approaching or even exceeding 70 percent could be attained and then sustained, and whether a level of INS enforcement that meant the typical undocumented migrant would have to try three or four times to cross the border would create sufficient deterrence to encourage some would-be undocumented migrants to remain in their home communities instead of attempting a trip to the United States.

As noted earlier, the estimates in Table 6.1 are constructed on the assumption that every illegal migrant apprehended by the Border Patrol will keep trying until he or she crosses the border undetected. The implicit reasoning is that being apprehended is virtually costless, entailing few financial or psychic penalties (Blejer, Johnson, and Porzecanski 1978). Most migrants who are apprehended accept an offer of voluntary departure and are merely returned by bus to the nearest border area in Mexico, from which they make repeated attempts to enter (Passel, Bean, and Edmonston 1990). It seems reasonable to suppose that after INS effort reaches a sufficiently high level, the repeated trials model will begin to break down as some discouraged migrants turn around and go back after being apprehended many times. No one knows what this level is, although it is unlikely that it has been reached. An additional possibility is that the perception of high capture rates will eventually deter some would-be undocumented migrants from making the trip to the border in the first place.

Before this happens, however, migrants are likely to react to an increase in INS enforcement effort in a variety of other ways. First, as some geographic areas are targeted for more intensive border enforcement, migrants will tend to shift their customary routes of entry to places along the border that are less heavily patrolled. Evidence for this phenomenon already exists in El Paso and south of San Diego in response to INS Operation Hold the Line and Operation

Gatekeeper (Bean et al. 1994). A second possibility includes a further shift in the concentration of trips to *El Norte* away from the winter months toward the late spring and summer when the volume of undocumented migration peaks and when, other things equal, a larger number of unauthorized migrants attempting to negotiate the frontier lowers both the probability of apprehension and the expected number of attempts required to cross. Indeed, a more pronounced seasonality pattern in the undocumented flow might be taken as an initial sign that INS enforcement effort is paying off.

Most observers assume that apprehension is also costless to the Border Patrol in terms of both time and effort. But the increases in Border Patrol officers and in new capital equipment expenditures called for by the IRA would lead to a dramatic rise in annual apprehensions. The Border Patrol has never had to cope with more than 1.8 million apprehensions per year. As Table 6.1 indicates, however, the number of apprehensions by the year 2001 could reach 420,000 per month, or more than 5 million annually, if an average of 150,000 undocumented migrants entered the United States each month. This number of apprehensions could quickly overwhelm the ability of the INS to process all of the detainees.

Moreover, if the INS attempts to levy the fines required by the IRA on each undocumented migrant who is apprehended and, in addition, puts migrants in jail unless and until they are able to pay, the system will soon become clogged to the breaking point. In FY 1996 alone, prior to the imposition of fines for illegal border crossers and when the Border Patrol apprehended more than 1.5 million undocumented migrants, the total number of detention days for illegal migrants exceeded 2.8 million (Office of Management and Budget 1997). Therefore, for a combination of reasons, the estimates in Table 6.1 likely overstate the effectiveness of INS enforcement policy because they assume that neither migrants nor the Border Patrol will adjust its behavior in the face of higher apprehension probabilities. In short, the evidence points to the conclusion that a feedback is operating on the process of apprehension that sets a limit on how high apprehension probabilities can go, regardless of the level of INS enforcement effort.

Effects on the Flow of Undocumented Migrants

A more important question is whether higher apprehension probabilities deter undocumented migrants from entering the country. After all, the aim of expanded border enforcement is not so much to arrest people but rather to reduce the number of illegal immigrants who come into the United States. Stepped-up border enforcement could decrease this flow in two ways. First, some migrants who are caught numerous times at the border may eventually give up and return home. Second, other would-be undocumented migrants may hear of the increased apprehension risks and become sufficiently discouraged to decide against making a trip from their home communities northward to the U.S.–Mexico border.

One telling fact comes from data in the Mexican Community Survey analyzed by Donato, Durand, and Massey (1992). In interviews with Mexicans who had illegally sought work in the United States, respondents were asked the number of border-crossing attempts they had made and the number of times they had been apprehended by the INS while trying to cross. In all cases the number of attempts was equal to the number of apprehensions plus one. Apprehended migrants often wait only a few hours or a day before attempting another border crossing. Being apprehended apparently does not have a deterrent effect on migrants once they are at the border and actively trying to cross. Notably, this was true for migrants in the survey both before and after the implementation of the 1986 IRCA. Increased numbers of Border Patrol officers and higher spending on capital equipment might have raised the number of attempts unauthorized migrants had to make to cross the border, but they did not change the fact that everyone who tried to enter the United States was eventually successful.

At the same time, some undocumented migrants who are planning to travel illegally to the United States may decide not to come after hearing about increased border enforcement. The protests in Mexico City surrounding the passage of IRCA provide strong evidence that potential Mexican illegal immigrants are well informed about changes in U.S. immigration law. Changes in the prices of coyote services might be expected to shed light on this issue. Donato, Durand, and Massey (1992) found that the cost of a border-crossing guide did not change significantly after the implementation of IRCA. This finding is open to several interpretations. It could mean undocumented migrants were not finding it more difficult to cross the border after IRCA and did not have to rely more heavily on coyote services. It could also indicate that some migrants heard about the increased INS expenditures and decided not to try to enter the United States, whereas those who did come may have been more likely than otherwise to use a coyote. Finally, a higher initial price for coyote services might encourage more individuals to offer their services as coyotes, thereby bidding down prices. Because these demand and supply effects would not all work in the same direction, the lack of change in coyote costs does not provide definitive evidence about the relative difficulty of border crossings before and after IRCA.

Espenshade (1994) explored whether U.S. Border Patrol enforcement strategies between 1977 and 1988 actively discouraged undocumented migration at its source, that is, in the communities of Mexico and other countries that send illegal migrants to the United States. He examined the relationship between the size of the undocumented migrant flow and the perceived risks of being apprehended at the border. Two models were compared. One included such familiar determinants of undocumented migration as relative economic conditions between the United States and Mexico, the size of the Mexican young adult population, seasonality factors, and the timing of the 1986 Immigration Reform and

Control Act. An alternative model related the magnitude of undocumented migration to lagged monthly values of estimated apprehension probabilities on the assumption that migrants form expectations about the apprehension risks they will face from the experiences of other recent undocumented migrants. Each model contained some explanatory power by itself. When both sets of predictor variables were combined into a single model, however, the influence of perceived risks of apprehension all but disappeared. These findings suggest that the undocumented flow is largely unaffected by variations in the intensity of Border Patrol enforcement activity and that, prior to 1990 at least, the perception of higher apprehension probabilities did little to discourage illegal immigrants from taking an undocumented trip.

The evidence discussed so far raises serious questions about whether the higher border apprehension probabilities likely to materialize if the IRA is fully implemented will actually discourage illegal immigrants from coming to the United States. In addition, the 1996 Immigration Reform Act contains one feature that may actually significantly expand the incentives, if not the opportunities, for illegal migration. As noted earlier, Mexicans and Salvadorans are the two immigrant groups most adversely affected by the new requirement that sponsors of family-based immigrants must now have a household income at least 125 percent of the federal poverty level. These nationalities also constitute the largest segments of the resident undocumented population in the United States. According to estimates by the U.S. Immigration and Naturalization Service (1997), Mexico accounts for 54 percent and El Salvador for another 7 percent of all illegal immigrants living in the United States. If the higher income requirements effectively block legal routes of entry for many would-be migrants from these countries, there will be strong incentives for individuals to come anyway—albeit now illegally—especially if friends and family are waiting to welcome them on the U.S. side of the border.

Effects on Time Spent in the United States

If past, present, and perhaps even expected future levels of INS border enforcement activity are insufficient to restrain the flow of undocumented migrants into the country, it becomes important to know how increased INS enforcement affects the total amount of time undocumented migrants spend working in the United States. Large segments of the American public are concerned that undocumented migrants provide unfair job competition and depress wages of less-skilled native workers (Espenshade and Hempstead 1996; Espenshade 1997; Espenshade and Belanger 1997).

Does prior apprehension change the future quantity of U.S. work done by undocumented migrants? Research by Kossoudji (1992) indicates that higher apprehension probabilities *increase* the amount of time the successful border crosser spends in the United States on any given trip and *reduce* the time between successive trips. As crossing the border becomes more costly (for example, as more attempts are necessary for a successful crossing), migrants will want to spend longer stretches of time working in the United States to pay for the extra time and effort it took to cross. Hence, to the extent that U.S. policymakers are concerned with the total hours worked and wages earned by undocumented migrants there is some evidence that increased spending for the Border Patrol may actually be working against their goals.

The effect of lengthening undocumented migrant stays may be exacerbated by the provision in the IRA that requires that every undocumented migrant caught while attempting to cross the border must pay a fine ranging between $50 and $250. Because promulgating regulations are still being drafted, it is not yet clear how these fines will be collected. But to the extent this provision is enforced, illegal border crossing will become more costly for undocumented migrants. This will probably have two effects: it will increase the length of stay in the United States of those who cross, and it may prevent some migrants who had planned to cross from attempting a trip in the first place. It is difficult to say which of these effects will dominate. We might expect, however, that only a small number of people planning a U.S. trip would be deterred by the new fines. The average return migrant to Mexico brings back several hundred dollars in savings, and many Mexican out-migrants send weekly or monthly remittances to relatives in Mexico (Lozando-Ascencio and McClellan 1997; Massey and Parrado 1997). The fine could reasonably be offset by an extended stay north of the border.

Role of Migrant Characteristics

We have frequently referred to undocumented Mexican migrants as if they were all virtually the same, but even a cursory look at the data shows that migrants are fairly heterogeneous (Massey and Liang 1989). It is therefore reasonable to ask whether the consequences of the IRA's expanded INS border enforcement will depend selectively upon individual migrant characteristics.

One distinction among Mexican migrants is commuter status. Commuters consist of Mexicans who live in communities near the U.S. border and who cross the border on a daily basis to work in the United States. In the data analyzed by Ranney and Kossoudji (1983), approximately half of all male commuters worked legally in the United States, whereas another 44 percent had valid entry permits but not the legal right to work. Increased border enforcement is unlikely to affect these migrants, who can continue to enter the United States legally. The one portion of the IRA designed to affect commuters concerns the introduction of such biometric markers as fingerprints or palm prints on border-crossing cards. These identifiers are intended to prevent undocumented migrants from using someone else's legal crossing card to enter the country.

Noncommuters form a much larger portion of Mexican return migrants and are far more likely than commuters to be in the United States illegally. Some noncommuters are seasonal workers who typically reside in the United States in the summer months, primarily to do agricultural work. Others include migrants who moved to the United States for a period of several years. Perhaps the most meaningful distinction is between those who travel without other dependents, intending to stay only temporarily, and those who come with their families and intend to stay for longer spells. A family traveling together might have a harder time avoiding Border Patrol agents and might therefore be more discouraged by increased enforcement. On the other hand, if a family is planning on settling in the United States, both its emotional and financial incentives to cross the border may be fairly high, possibly causing its members to be extremely persistent.

Apprehension in the U.S. Interior

The previous discussion casts doubt on the efficacy of decreasing the size of the undocumented population living in the United States by interrupting the process of undocumented migration either at its source or at the U.S.–Mexico border. An alternative strategy is to concentrate on raising the number of involuntary and voluntary departures through improved interior enforcement that includes finding and deporting illegal aliens and enforcing laws that prohibit the hiring of undocumented workers.

What can be said about the prospects that an undocumented migrant will be located and removed from the interior of the United States after entering into undocumented status? After an illegal migrant has successfully eluded the Border Patrol and taken up residence in the United States or has overstayed the permissible duration of his or her temporary visa, the chances of being discovered by the INS are small. Estimates of the size of the undocumented resident alien population in 1993 range between 2.7 and 4.0 million, with the median estimates close to 3.2 million (U.S. Bureau of the Census 1994; U.S. Immigration and Naturalization Service 1994; Fix and Passel 1994). At the same time, the Investigations Unit of the INS, the branch that conducts raids and arrests illegal immigrants in the U.S. interior, reported just 45,500 apprehensions during 1993 (U.S. Immigration and Naturalization Service 1993). These numbers imply that the typical undocumented migrant already established in the United States faces an annual probability of being apprehended of 1 or 2 percent (Espenshade 1994).

In the past several years the INS has broadened its efforts to locate and deport unauthorized migrants living in the U.S. interior. By FY 1996 the number of deportable aliens apprehended by the Investigations Unit reached 94,500 (Office of Management and Budget 1997). At the same time, the INS was reporting that in October 1996 the undocumented immigrant population in the country had reached 5 million (U.S. Immigration and Naturalization Service 1997). Putting these numbers together suggests that the chances that an undocumented migrant will be apprehended after entering the United States are roughly 2 percent annually. In other words, the current risks are not much greater than they were in 1993.

The new immigration law includes provisions to help locate and remove undocumented migrants once they are in the United States. For example, it streamlines the process for deporting illegal or criminal aliens. The IRA also provides for 1,200 more INS employees authorized to investigate employment eligibility violations and visa overstays—a 150 percent increase over the 800 or so INS staff charged with these responsibilities in FY 1996 (Bergeron 1997). But the absolute numbers are still small in relation to the estimated size of the illegal alien population and the number of U.S. employers. And so far the necessary money to hire the extra staff has been authorized but not appropriated.

The IRA creates a pilot program aimed at improving verification of employment eligibility in the handful of states with the largest illegal alien populations. Once fully operational on a national scale, the system should make it easier for employers to spot counterfeit documents and verify the eligibility status of new workers. If new document standards are adopted nationwide and employers are required to check employment eligibility through the new system, this measure would increase deterrence and provide one of the most effective means of reducing the flow of undocumented migrants, both by accelerating voluntary departures and by discouraging would-be undocumented migrants from coming to the United States in the first place. As many unauthorized workers have acknowledged, illegal aliens enter the country because jobs here are better. Effectively barring undocumented migrants from working in the United States would provide a far stronger disincentive to illegal immigration than does increasing the number of Border Patrol agents.

To summarize, the IRA takes small and tentative steps toward improved work site enforcement. Many of these steps are in the experimental or design phase rather than capable of becoming fully operational anytime soon. Ultimately, two elements will be required for employer sanctions to be successful. First, employers must be able to distinguish simply and accurately between those who have a legal right to work in this country and those who do not. This is an area in which improved documents and innovative technologies can help. Second, employers must have an incentive not to hire unauthorized workers. Only more widespread and consistent employer oversight can make this happen. A policy that relies primarily on voluntary compliance, backed up only by token or symbolic enforcement measures, seems destined to be ineffective.

Conclusion

The 1996 Welfare and Immigration Reform Acts will have important, unintended, and possibly undesirable consequences for the incentives confronting potential new immigrants to the United States. U.S. immigration policy has traditionally aimed at keeping an open door for legal immigrants and refugees while attempting to reduce the number of illegal immigrants entering the country. The Welfare Reform Act makes major changes in noncitizen eligibility for welfare by reforming the entitlement policy for poor families and imposing new limits on alien access to social services. The Immigration Reform Act strengthens efforts to control illegal immigration and sets new and higher income requirements for individuals who want to sponsor other family members for permanent residence in the United States. The combined effects of these two reform measures on people's incentives to migrate to the United States will be the opposite of what is intended. The WRA and IRA are likely to reduce levels of legal immigration, especially among poor and low-skilled immigrants, and at the same time to expand incentives for illegal immigration.

Legal immigration levels are likely to be reduced by a combination of demand and supply factors. Potential immigrants who might have been attracted to the United States, believing a generous welfare system would be available to help them in time of financial need, will now find that the economic benefits associated with U.S. immigration are lowered. This change should decrease the demand for permanent resident visas. At the same time, poorer, older, and less-skilled migrants who are unable to demonstrate that they will not become a public charge and who need a financial sponsor before they can migrate to the United States will find that sponsors are harder to locate. Some potential sponsors will be more reluctant to assume the role now that support affidavits are legally enforceable against the sponsor. In addition, the fact that individuals who wish to sponsor family members for permanent U.S. residence must now have family incomes at least 25 percent above federal poverty standards means some potential immigrants will be excluded from obtaining a legal immigrant visa even if they could find sponsors willing to provide financial support. When these demand and supply factors are considered jointly, they seem certain to reduce the volume of future U.S. legal immigration and to produce a legal immigrant stream with a higher average level of skill and income.

On the other hand, the IRA is unlikely to be able to cope effectively with existing demands for illegal entry into the United States and may in fact succeed in creating new incentives for undocumented migration. Some potential legal immigrants who find their path blocked by the IRA requirement that their financial sponsors have to meet higher income standards will attempt to find ways to enter the United States illegally. Migrants from Mexico and El Salvador are likely to be the most affected, not only because the new income tests hit these groups the hardest but also because potential migrants from these countries have the largest communities of family and friends already living as illegal immigrants in the United States. In addition, to the extent that the IRA increases the cost of U.S. migration (either because of fines apprehended migrants now have to pay at the border or because being arrested in the interior has cut short an intended stay), illegal migrants have an incentive to return to the United States more quickly and to stay longer on the next trip to recover the costs of a prior arrest.

Greater INS expenditure for border and interior enforcement purposes will increase apprehension probabilities, but prior evidence indicates a lack of correspondence between the chances of being apprehended and the number of immigrants who attempt illegal entry. Higher apprehension probabilities are but a momentary nuisance to many illegal immigrants who keep on trying to evade the U.S. Border Patrol until they are successful at entering the United States.

If the IRA is fully implemented, apprehension probabilities can be expected to rise to unprecedented levels. Assuming an average monthly flow of undocumented migrants in the neighborhood of 150,000, the IRA would have the effect of raising apprehension probabilities from their FY 1996 range of 0.45–0.50 to somewhere between 0.70 and 0.75 by FY 2001. At the same time, the required average number of attempts before successfully crossing the border would double from roughly 1.9 to 3.8. But it is not clear that such high levels are sustainable. Feedbacks operating on both undocumented migrants and the Border Patrol will cause each to adjust its behavior as capture rates rise. Migrants will have an incentive to modify their customary routes of entry and to come across the border where and when the chances of being located are smaller, and the Border Patrol is likely to find that its productivity will decline because of the extra time and effort required to process the tens of thousands of additional apprehensions. Nevertheless, the repeated trials model may break down at some point, and the higher arrest rates associated with intensified border enforcement may eventually wilt the persistence of even the most determined migrants. No one knows what this point is, but it is doubtful that it has been approached.

Additional personnel, more secure identification documents, and innovative technologies have been proposed as means of expanded enforcement in the interior, directed not only against undocumented migrants who entered without inspection but also against visa overstayers. Many of the proposed technologies are still in the experimental phase. Moreover, even though the INS manpower to investigate employment eligibility violations and visa abusers is authorized to increase to 2.5 times its current levels, the absolute numbers involved are still small in relation to the size of the problem. As long as the enforcement of employer sanctions is left primarily to employers, most undocumented migrants can confidently expect that if they can manage to enter the United States they will be able to stay as long as they wish.

If the trial employment verification program, new identification cards, and the entry-and-exit tracking system are all put in place and become mandatory in every state, these steps will likely go much farther in reducing illegal immigration than will increased border enforcement. In the past, employers have greatly resisted stiffer employment eligibility criteria on the grounds that they impose too great an administrative burden on businesses. As long as Congress is sympathetic to these concerns, truly effective employment verification measures are unlikely to be instituted. If the goal of lawmakers is to deter illegal migration, overcoming obstacles to work site enforcement may be the single biggest challenge.

Notes

This chapter is a revised and condensed version of material in Espenshade, Baraka, and Huber (1997). We thank Deborah Garvey, Cecilia Rouse, and the Migration and Restructuring conference participants for valuable suggestions; Michael Hoefer, Joseph Pearce, Connie Brownlee, Carolyn Johnson, Roger Kramer, Lorraine Lewis, Eyeleen Schmidt, and Denise Walton for supplying data; and Melanie Adams, Maryann Belanger, Emily Niebo, and Tracy Rydel for research and technical assistance. Partial support for this research was provided by a Population Research Center grant from the National Institute of Child Health and Human Development.

1. SSI is a federally administered program that provides cash assistance to elderly, blind, and disabled persons who are economically disadvantaged. The Food Stamp program is administered by the U.S. Department of Agriculture and provides coupons redeemable for food purchases to households that qualify on the basis of family size and income.

2. AFDC is a joint federal–state program administered by the states with shared funding obligations. It provides cash benefits to families that meet financial need standards in amounts determined by states according to federal limits. Low-income female-headed households with children are the principal beneficiaries. AFDC is being replaced by the TANF block grant, which allows states to provide both temporary cash assistance and programs that promote job preparation, work, and marriage. Medicaid is another joint federal–state program administered by the states with shared funding obligations. It provides basic and emergency health care to poor persons who meet need and categorical criteria determined by states within federal guidelines. Emergency medical assistance is available to all individuals who meet income standards but who are not categorically eligible for full Medicaid.

3. Under U.S. immigration law, relatives may petition for a close family member to become an immigrant. If that family member is unable to demonstrate that he or she will not become a public charge and fall dependent on the welfare state, however, he or she needs a financial sponsor. A sponsor is someone who signs a support affidavit agreeing to provide financial assistance to the new immigrant to ensure that the immigrant's income will not fall below 125 percent of the federal poverty line during the period in which the affidavit is in effect. Each year about 10 percent of permanent resident visa applications are denied for failure to demonstrate financial self-sufficiency and for lack of sponsorship (Congressional Budget Office 1995).

4. Border-crossing cards are issued to residents of Mexico who are authorized to cross the border for U.S. visits of a few days' duration. Biometric identifiers include fingerprints and palm prints.

5. The Immigration Reform and Control Act of 1986 requires employers to complete an I-9 form for each new employee. Employees must produce physical evidence (a birth certificate, passport, or both a valid driver's license and a social security card) to demonstrate that they have a legal right to work in the United States.

6. Prior to the passage of the WRA, the debate surrounding welfare reform and the prospect of losing SSI, Medicaid, and Food Stamp eligibility caused many legal immigrants to apply for naturalization. Naturalization applications increased sixfold between 1991 and 1996, when almost 1.3 million applications were received. The numbers also

suggest that most petitions were eventually approved. The INS estimates that an additional 1.0–1.3 million legal immigrants will become citizens each of the subsequent four years. Incentives to naturalize may be somewhat weaker now that Congress has restored SSI benefits for current legal immigrants.

7. Although some authors believe the generosity of the U.S. welfare system toward immigrants has increased the attractiveness of U.S. immigration (see Brimelow 1995, for example), others insist that the data supporting such conclusions are weak, that foreign understanding of U.S. welfare policy is minimal, and that the relative desirability of the United States rests on other factors such as political freedom and economic opportunity (Schuck 1996; Massey and Espinosa 1997). Borjas and Hilton (1996–1997) show that immigrants from countries where past immigrants have received welfare are more likely to receive the same type of welfare (housing assistance in the case of Cuban refugees, for example). Whether this information is transmitted back to potential immigrants before they leave or whether the awareness of the general quality of life in the United States includes some component related to the availability of public support, the evidence in Borjas and Hilton suggests that migrant community networks are important mechanisms for transmitting information about the U.S. welfare system. Other research, however, indicates that poorer immigrants are relatively uninformed about the variety of benefits from the U.S. public sector and that immigrants who need help initially turn to family members for assistance and only later begin to assimilate into welfare (Borjas 1994).

8. Estimates in Table 6.1 are based on regression results contained in Model 5 of Table 3 in Espenshade and Acevedo (1995) and on Espenshade's (1990) repeated trials models of undocumented immigration.

References

Bean, Frank D., Roland Chanove, Robert G. Cushing, Rodolfo de la Garza, Gary Freeman, Charles W. Haynes, and David Spener. 1994. *Illegal Mexican Migration and the United States/Mexico Border: The Effects of Operation Hold-the-Line on El Paso/Juarez.* University of Texas, Population Research Center, July 15. Prepared for the U.S. Commission on Immigration Reform.

Bean, Frank D., Georges Vernez, and Charles B. Keely. 1989. *Opening and Closing the Doors: Evaluating Immigration Reform and Control.* Washington, D.C.: Urban Institute.

Bergeron, Russell. 1997. Personal communication, Office of Public Information, U.S. Immigration and Naturalization Service, Washington, D.C., July 7.

Blejer, Mario I., Harry G. Johnson, and Arturo C. Porzecanski. 1978. "An Analysis of the Economic Determinants of Legal and Illegal Mexican Migration to the United States." In Julian L. Simon (ed.), *Research in Population Economics: An Annual Compilation of Research,* Volume I. Greenwich, Ct.: JAI.

Borjas, George J. 1994. "The Economics of Immigration." *Journal of Economic Literature* (December), 32, 4: 1667–1717.

Borjas, George J., and Lynette Hilton. 1996–1997. "Immigrants and Welfare: Evidence from the Survey of Income and Program Participation." *Focus* (University of Wisconsin—Madison, Institute for Research on Poverty) (Fall-Winter), 18, 2: 47–49.

Brimelow, Peter. 1995. *Alien Nation: Common Sense about America's Immigration Disaster*. New York: Random House.

Congressional Budget Office. 1995. *Immigration and Welfare Reform*. CBO Papers, February. Washington, D.C.: U.S. Government Printing Office.

———. 1996. *Reducing the Deficit: Spending and Revenue Options*. Report to the Senate and House Committees on the Budget, August. Washington, D.C.: U.S. Government Printing Office.

Cornelius, Wayne A., Philip L. Martin, and James F. Hollifield. 1994. "Introduction: The Ambivalent Quest for Immigration Control." In Wayne A. Cornelius, Philip L. Martin, and James F. Hollifield (eds.), *Controlling Immigration: A Global Perspective*. Stanford, Calif.: Stanford University Press.

Donato, Katharine M., Jorge Durand, and Douglas S. Massey. 1992. "Stemming the Tide? Assessing the Deterrent Effects of the Immigration Reform and Control Act." *Demography* (May) 29, 2: 139–157.

Dugger, Celia W. 1997. "Immigrant Study Finds Many below New Income Limit." *New York Times,* March 16, p. 1.

Espenshade, Thomas J. 1990. "Undocumented Migration to the United States: Evidence from a Repeated Trials Model." In Frank D. Bean, Barry Edmonston, and Jeffrey S. Passel (eds.), *Undocumented Migration to the United States: IRCA and the Experience of the 1980s*. Washington, D.C.: Urban Institute.

———. 1994. "Does the Threat of Border Apprehension Deter Undocumented U.S. Immigration?" *Population and Development Review* (December), 20, 4: 871–892.

———. 1995. "Using INS Border Apprehension Data to Measure the Flow of Undocumented Migrants Crossing the U.S.-Mexico Frontier." *International Migration Review* (Summer), 29, 2: 545–565.

———. 1997. "Taking the Pulse of Public Opinion toward Immigrants." In Thomas J. Espenshade (ed.), *Keys to Successful Immigration: Implications of the New Jersey Experience*. Washington, D.C.: Urban Institute.

Espenshade, Thomas J., and Dolores Acevedo. 1995. "Migrant Cohort Size, Enforcement Effort, and the Apprehension of Undocumented Aliens." *Population Research and Policy Review* (June), 14, 2: 145–172.

Espenshade, Thomas J., Jessica L. Baraka, and Gregory A. Huber. 1997. "Implications of the 1996 Welfare and Immigration Reform Acts for U.S. Immigration." *Population and Development Review* 23, 4: 769–801.

Espenshade, Thomas J., and Maryann Belanger. 1997. "U.S. Public Perceptions and Reactions to Mexican Migration." In Frank D. Bean, Rodolfo O. de la Garza, Bryan R. Roberts, and Sidney Weintraub (eds.), *At the Crossroads: Mexican Migration and U.S. Policy*. New York: Rowman and Littlefield .

Espenshade, Thomas J., and Katherine Hempstead. 1996. "Contemporary American Attitudes toward U.S. Immigration." *International Migration Review* (Summer), 30, 2: 535–570.

Fix, Michael, and Jeffrey S. Passel. 1994. *Immigration and Immigrants: Setting the Record Straight*. Washington, D.C.: Urban Institute.

Kossoudji, Sherrie A. 1992. "Playing Cat and Mouse at the U.S.–Mexican Border." *Demography* (May), 29, 2: 159–180.

Lozando-Ascencio, Fernando, and Judi L. McClellan. 1997. "Immigration, Settlement in the United States, and Remittances: Evidence from the Mexican Case." Paper presented at the Annual Meetings of the Population Association of America, Washington, D.C., March 27–29.

Massey, Douglas S., and Kristin E. Espinosa. 1997. "What's Driving Mexico–U.S. Migration? A Theoretical, Empirical, and Policy Analysis." *American Journal of Sociology* (January), 102, 4: 939–999.

Massey, Douglas S., and Zai Liang. 1989. "The Long-Term Consequences of a Temporary Worker Program: The U.S.–Bracero Experience." *Population Research and Policy Review* (September), 8, 3: 199–226.

Massey, Douglas S., and Emilio A. Parrado. 1997. "International Migration and Business Formation in Mexico." Paper presented at the Annual Meetings of the Population Association of America, Washington, D.C., March 27–29.

National Conference of State Legislatures. 1996. "Analysis of the Personal Responsibility and Work Opportunity Reconciliation Act of 1996." Washington, D.C. (http://www.ncsl.org/statefed/hr3734.htm).

Office of Management and Budget. 1997. *Budget of the United States Government: Fiscal Year 1998, Appendix*. Washington, D.C.: U.S. Government Printing Office.

Passel, Jeffrey S., Frank D. Bean, and Barry Edmonston. 1990. "Undocumented Migration since IRCA: An Overall Assessment." In Frank D. Bean, Barry Edmonston, and Jeffrey Passel (eds.), *Undocumented Migration to the United States: IRCA and the Experience of the 1980s*. Washington, D.C.: Urban Institute.

Ranney, Susan, and Sherrie A. Kossoudji. 1983. "Profiles of Temporary Mexican Labor Migrants to the United States." *Population and Development Review* (September), 9, 3: 475–493.

Schuck, Peter H. 1996. "Alien Rumination." *Yale Law Journal* (May), 105: 1963–2012.

Social Security Administration. 1997. "Estimates of the Number of Noncitizens Currently Receiving SSI Benefits Who Are Likely to Be Ineligible under Welfare Reform, by State." Office of Legislation and Congressional Affairs, March 20, Washington, D.C.: U.S. Government Printing Office.

U.S. Bureau of the Census. 1994. *Estimated Number and Percent Distribution of the Undocumented Population by State: 1993*. Population Division, Population Analysis and Evaluation Staff. Washington, D.C.: U.S. Government Printing Office.

U.S. General Accounting Office. 1995. *Welfare Reform: Implications of Proposals on Legal Immigrants' Benefits*. GAO/HEHS-95–58, February. Washington, D.C.: U.S. Government Printing Office.

U.S. Immigration and Naturalization Service. 1993. *Statistical Yearbook of the Immigration and Naturalization Service: 1992*, no. M-367, October. Washington, D.C.: U.S. Government Printing Office.

———. 1994. *Estimates of the Resident Illegal Alien Population: October 1992*. Statistics Division. Washington, D.C.: U.S. Government Printing Office.

———. 1997. "Estimates of the Unauthorized Immigrant Population Residing in the United States: October 1996," *Backgrounder* (January), Office of Policy and Planning, Washington, D.C.: U.S. Government Printing Office.

SECTION II

MIGRATION AND DEMOGRAPHIC RESTRUCTURING

The chapters in this section address migration and demographic restructuring, specifically the restructuring of population age composition and ethnic restructuring. Relative to national changes, the regional and local variations of demographic restructuring are less well known, yet they have profound implications for the future size and composition of populations at various scales. These chapters examine the geographic intersection of migration and demographic restructuring and highlight the recursive nature of the relationships. Figure B summarizes how the various chapters fit into the broad scheme of the book.

The first three chapters deal with three pressing aspects of population change facing the nation yet differentially impacting local economies: the aging of the population, the baby-boom cohort, and differential fertility. Moore and McGuinness get at the heart of the components of population aging at the local level by distinguishing aging in place from the internal migration of elders. The authors conduct their case study in Ontario, yet similar pressures and challenges face U.S. communities as well. This theme is continued in the chapter by Rogerson, who follows the changing geography of the baby-boom cohort as it moves through the life course and assesses implications for future migration trends. Both of these chapters highlight the impacts of demographic restructuring and migration on changes in service provision and family relations. The interconnections between migration and demographic restructuring present significant challenges to public policy initiatives. Waldorf's chapter is a theoretical analysis of the impact of immigrant fertility on population size and composition. Given general declines in fertility levels, the fertility behavior of recent immigrants is likely to have important implications for future population growth and migration. Waldorf provides a potent analytical structure for understanding the impact of differential fertility rates on local populations.

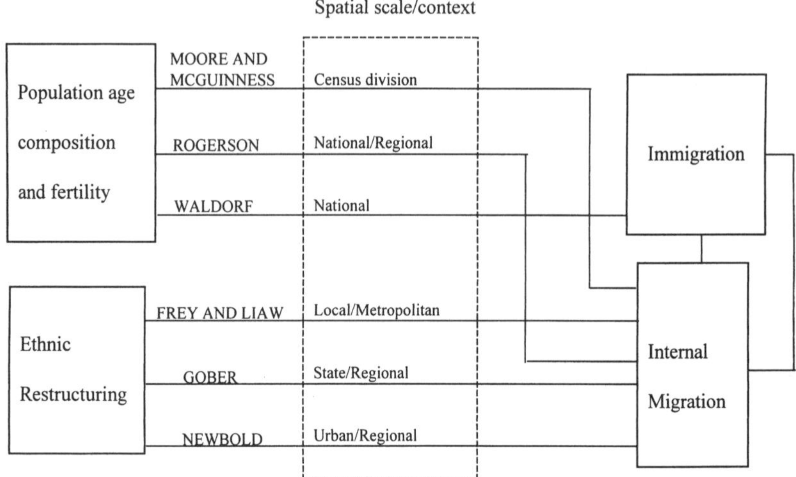

Figure B Demographic Restructuring and Migration: Location of Individual Contributions

A fundamental connection between demographic restructuring and migration is the internal migration of the foreign-born population. The next three chapters examine various assimilation hypotheses: geographic assimilation, behavioral assimilation, and structural assimilation. The extent to which ethnic restructuring will become universal is in large part dependent on the internal migration patterns of recent immigrants. The chapter by Frey and Liaw examines the internal migration of foreign-born Latinos and Asians, the largest groups of immigrants in recent decades, at the metropolitan level. Gober examines settlement dynamics of the foreign born at the state level, with particular emphasis on twelve distinct origin groups. Gober expands the metropolitan focus of Frey's analysis to the state level by asking whether recent patterns of internal migration of the foreign born in the United States have served to reinforce or dissipate their geographic concentration. Newbold examines the evolution of immigrant settlement patterns at the regional scale. When examined over time and space, he finds distinct differences among intended, initial, and established settlement patterns of the foreign born. Although the scale of analysis varies, these chapters share common themes: they all confront questions of geographic concentration and assimilation of the foreign born.

Throughout this section, the chapters call into question the long-term impacts of population redistribution and make a significant contribution to understanding the interconnections of immigration, internal migration, and the demographic restructuring of the nation.

7

Geographic Dimensions of Aging

Eric G. Moore and Donald L. McGuinness

The impacts of an aging population play an increasing role in social and economic policy in many developed countries as the overall rate of population growth declines, fertility falls to below replacement levels, and life expectancy continues to improve. Although the major focus has been on the macrolevel effects of increasing proportions of elderly at the national level—particularly in regard to implications for health care, pensions, and Social Security—increasing attention is being given to the geographic consequences of aging (Rogers 1992; Rogerson 1996; Moore, Rosenberg, and McGuinness 1997). The concentration of the elderly does not unfold in a uniform manner with the consequence that different jurisdictions face both different demands for local goods and services based on their age profiles and different prospects for future growth in these demands. If we are at all concerned with issues of equity in the accessibility of the elderly to a range of social services, it is important that we understand both the demographic and socioeconomic processes that underlie the changing landscape of population aging.

Population aging refers specifically to the relative size and attributes of the elderly in the population as a whole. Whereas trends in population aging clearly reflect temporal shifts in the experiences of elderly individuals, they are sensitive to changes in all segments of the population, young and old. Conventional wisdom has focused on age 65 as the significant dividing line between young and old, largely because of its traditional and institutionalized links to separation from the labor force and initiation of a range of social benefits. The proportion of the population over 65 is the most common measure of population aging (McDaniel 1986) and is used extensively in this chapter. No necessary transition in the life of an individual occurs at that age, however, and the great majority of individuals over 65 clearly consider themselves active, healthy, and contributing to the larger society (Stone and Fletcher 1986). The most significant changes in the likelihood of experiencing major health problems, loss of independence, and institutionalization tend to occur much later and increase sharply over age 80 (Figure 7.1). We therefore also give attention to the variation in conditions and behaviors by age for those over 65.

The major focus of this chapter is on the geographic dimensions of aging and the demographic processes that underlie them, with the empirical focus on the Canadian experience in the latter part of the 1980s. The proportion of the population over 65 varies considerably among census divisions across the country (Figure 7.2). The fundamental question we address is how this distribution changed in the five-year period from 1986 to 1991 and the way in which those changes relate to the demographic and socioeconomic attributes of small areas. Where appropriate, we compare the Canadian experience with research in the United States where many demographic forces are behaving in a similar way to those in Canada.

It is recognized that there are several ways in which the proportion of the population over 65 changes in any given geographic area. Given that we are concerned with the *proportion* of the population that is elderly, this measure must be sensitive to changes that occur both to the segments of the population over 65 and to those under 65. Forces that act on each of these population segments produce changes *within* the geographic area arising from local fertility, aging and mortality, and changes derived from external flows of in-migrants and out-migrants of different ages. Although some variation in terminology is found in the literature, there would appear to be a convergence on the concept of *aging in place* as referring to the processes of change that accrue within a given area and of *net migration* as the summation of changes arising from external flows. Here we focus specifically on the relative roles of aging in place and net migration in population aging at different scales. The role of scale is significant since age-differentiated local flows that contribute to net migration effects for small areas become absorbed into the aging-in-place component at larger scales.

McCarthy (1983) examined the structure of migrant flows of both the young and the old in changing the concentration of the elderly population at the county level in the United States. He identified three main processes by which migration contributes to the changing concentration of the elderly: *accumulation,* where the elderly are left behind by the out-migration of younger individuals; *recomposition,* where younger individuals leave and older ones arrive; and *congregation,* where older individuals arrive at a faster rate than younger ones. These processes, however, are overlain on the effects of aging in place, which, as Morrison (1992) argues, are becoming progressively more important in population aging. In this chapter, we expand on McCarthy's work to combine the structure of his migration scenarios with aging in place to produce a classification of aging scenarios.

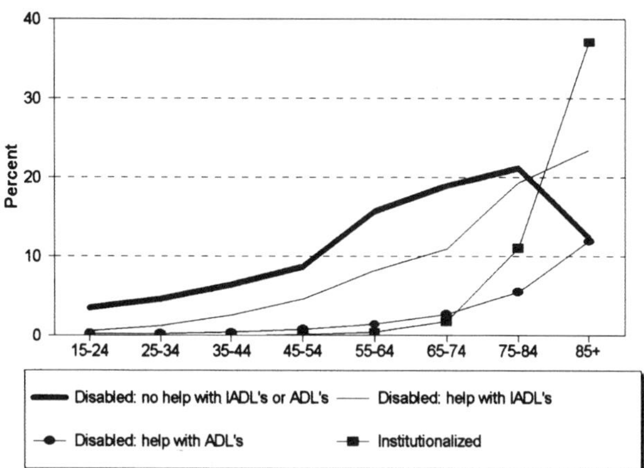

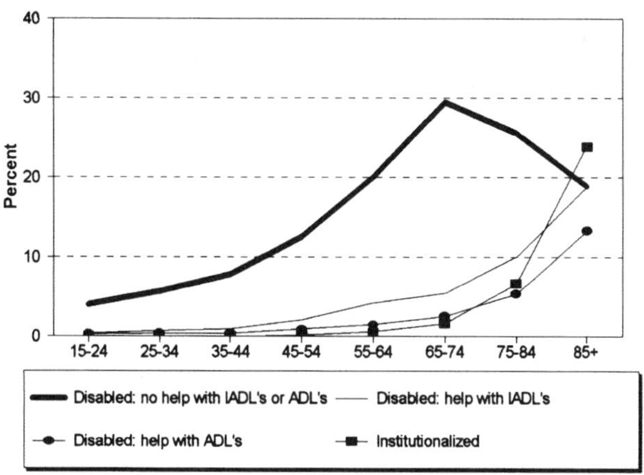

Source: Health and Activity Limitation Survey, 1986.

Figure 7.1 Distribution of Disability/Support by Age and Gender, 1986

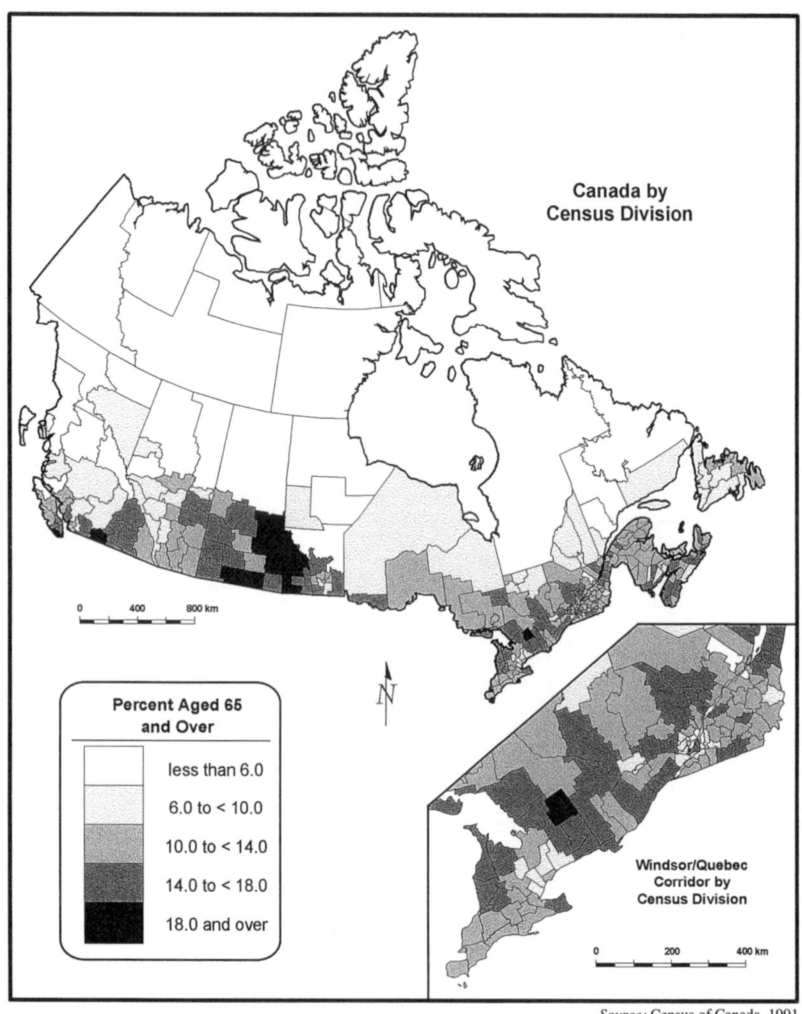

Source: Census of Canada, 1991.

Figure 7.2 Percent of Population Aged 65 and Over by Census Division, 1981

In a recent exploration of these ideas, Rogerson (1996) examined the role of four elements of population aging at the state level in the United States: natural increase of the elderly, natural increase of the nonelderly, net migration of the elderly, and net migration of the nonelderly. Rogerson shows convincingly that a substantial geographic variation exists in the relative importance of these four components, although he also confirmed Morrison's (1992) insight regarding the relative importance of aging in place (the net effects of the two natural increase components) relative to net migration. He argues that there is a tendency for overall geographic variation in the proportion of those over 65 to decline; those areas with the highest concentrations of elderly (namely, the Northern Plains states) are experiencing significantly slower growth than the Rocky Mountain areas where continued out-migration of the young dominates, whereas aging in place is particularly strong in the South and in the Sunbelt states. The emphasis in Rogerson's work is on the macrolevel demographic restructuring of the population generated by the movement, both past and present, of the baby-boom cohort from the Northeast and Midwest to the South and West (Frey 1992; Plane and Rogerson 1991); these migration patterns of today strongly influence the patterns of natural increase in the elderly in the future.

The demographic analyses provided by Rogers and Woodward (1988) and by Rogerson (1996) raise the question of the links between economic restructuring and the demographic changes they report. Clearly, the relocation of the baby-boom cohort is reflective of shifts in the locus of economic opportunity during the postwar period. To the extent that the migration patterns of the nonelderly are both sensitive to changes in employment conditions and influence rates of population aging, we should be able to identify linkages between changes in local economic conditions and population aging. In this chapter, we pursue this issue and go beyond the representation of components of population aging within an accounting framework. The characteristics of the origins and destinations of younger and older migrants have received much attention in the research literature. In particular, communities with more active and growing local economies are particularly attractive to younger migrants (Shaw 1985), whereas those communities with declining economic opportunities are likely to see younger populations depart at a faster rate than older individuals. Sustained over longer periods, these processes produce shifts in the age structure of local communities and would lead us to expect that both the structure and processes of population aging would be intimately linked to the economic geography of the national landscape.

The next section develops a formal accounting of the processes of population aging. The components of aging are then derived for Canada at the provincial and local (county) levels for 1986–1991. Augmented aging scenarios are constructed for the counties, and the relations between structure and processes of aging at the county level and their socioeconomic characteristics are assessed.

Population Aging: Concepts and Measures

The most thorough treatments of accounting for changes in the proportion of the population over 65 are provided by Rogers and Woodward (1988) and Rogerson (1996). They focus explicitly on the relation between aging in place and migration in changing this proportion. We follow the general structure of their argument in this chapter. Population aging is defined as the change in the proportion of the population of an area that is over 65. The following notation is used.

$P_{65+}(0)$, $P_{65+}(1)$ are the number of people aged 65 and over at times 0, 1, respectively.
$P_{<65}(0)$, $P_{<65}(1)$ are the number under 65.
$P_{tot}(0)$, $P_{tot}(0)$ is the total population.
$f_{65}(0)$, $f_{65}(1)$ are the proportions of the population aged 65 and over, where

$$f_{65}(0) = P_{65+}(0) / P_{tot}(0) \qquad (1)$$

Measures of Population Aging

The basic measure of change is defined by the ratio of the proportion of the population over 65 at two different times

$$C_{65} = f_{65}(1) / f_{65}(0) \qquad (2)$$

We can also focus on the change in the elderly population itself and define a growth rate

$$g_{65} = P_{65+}(1) / P_{65+}(0) - 1 \qquad (3)$$

If the time interval from 0–1 is the normal intercensal period of five years (in Canada), then

$$g^*_{65} = (P_{65+}(1) / P_{65+}(0))^{1/5} - 1 \qquad (4)$$

where g^*_{65} is the annualized growth rate of the population over 65. Similar measures can be defined for the total population P_{tot} and the population under 65, $P_{<65.}$

Components of Population Aging

In any area population changes as a function of births and deaths, in-migration, and out-migration. Thus,

$$P_{tot}(1) = P_{tot}(0) + B - D + I - O \qquad (5)$$

where B = births in the interval 0, 1;[1]
D = deaths;
I = in-migrants to the areas in the interval 0, 1; and
O = out-migrants from the area in the interval 0, 1.

If a general concept of *births* to an age group refers to arrivals from the immediately younger age group and *deaths* as passing to the next older age groups, the equation in (5) can be used to define changes in those younger and older than 65.

Thus,

$$P_{65+}(1) = P_{65+}(0) + B_{65} - D_{65} + I_{65} - O_{65} \tag{6}$$

where B_{65} is the number of individuals who become 65 during the interval 0, 1; and

$$P_{<65}(1) = P_{<65}(0) + B_{<65} - D_{<65} + I_{<65} - O_{<65} \tag{7}$$

where $D_{<65}$ is the number who die plus the number who become 65 during the interval 0, 1. In equation (6) we can regard the value $(B_{65} - D_{65})$ as contributing to *aging in place* of the population over 65 (A_{65}) and $(I_{65} - O_{65})$ as defining *net migration* of the population over 65 (N_{65}).

Thus,

$$P_{65+}(1) = P_{65+}(0) + A_{65} + N_{65} \tag{8}$$
$$= P_{65+}(0)\,(1 + a_{65} + n_{65}) \tag{9}$$

where a_{65}, n_{65} are the proportionate changes in the population 65 and over because of aging in place and net migration respectively.

Similarly,

$$P_{<65}(1) = P_{<65}(0)\,(1 + a_{<65} + n_{<65}) \tag{10}$$

Integrating the previous information, it can be shown that:

$$C_{65} = \frac{1 + a_{65} + n_{65}}{f_{65+}(0) * (1 + a_{65} + n_{65}) + (1 - f_{65+}(0)) * (1 + a_{<65} + n_{<65})} \tag{11}$$

It follows directly that C_{65} increases if $(a_{65} + n_{65}) > (a_{<65} + n_{<65})$. Since $a_{65} > a_{<65}$ in the majority of communities and a_{65} is greater than n_{65} virtually everywhere, however, it follows that the overall net migration defined by n_{65} and $n_{<65}$ serves to reinforce or ameliorate the dominant aging-in-place effects. And, in general, C_{65} increases as a_{65} and n_{65} increase and decreases as $a_{<65}$ and $n_{<65}$ increase.

Decomposing C_{65}

It is useful to decompose the ratio of the proportions over 65 at 0 and 1 into the components of change attributable to aging in place and to net migration. Thus,

$$C_{65} = 1 + \alpha + \eta \tag{12}$$

where α is the proportionate change resulting from aging in place; and η is the proportionate change resulting from net migration.

If $S_{65+}(1)$ is the population that survives in the area from 0 to 1 and is over 65 at 1; and $S_{<65}(1)$ is the population that survives from 0 to 1 and includes those born to residents of the areas between 0 and 1 and is under 65 at 1

then

$$C_{65}(S) = \frac{S_{65+}(1)}{S_{tot}(1)} / \frac{P_{65+}(0)}{P_{tot}(1)} = 1 + \alpha \qquad (13)$$

$$\text{then } \alpha = C_{65}(S) - 1 \qquad (14)$$

$$\text{and } \eta = C_{65} - C_{65}(S) \qquad (15)$$

We note that because a_{65} and $a_{<65}$ are defined by the populations at risk who are over or under 65 and α is the contribution of aging in place to aging of the total population, the relation between the parameters is not straightforward.

$$\alpha = \frac{1 + a_{65}}{f_{65}(0)(1 + a_{65}) + (1 - f_{65}(0))(1 + a_{<65})} - 1 \qquad (16)$$

However, it follows directly from (16) that

$$\alpha \lesseqqgtr 0 \text{ as } a_{65} \lesseqqgtr a_{<65}$$

Similarly

$$\eta \lesseqqgtr 0 \text{ as } n_{65} \lesseqqgtr n_{<65}$$

Population Aging in Canada

The national experience establishes a context within which geographical differences are played out. Social values with respect to fertility and reproduction, advances in medical knowledge influencing mortality and morbidity, and controls over immigration have a strong national component that sets the larger stage.

Canada's population has experienced one of the largest growth rates in the developed world since the end of World War II, fueled by the most substantial of the baby booms, which lasted from the late 1940s to the early 1960s (Romaniuc 1994). The total population in 1951 was 14.0 million and reached 27.1 million in 1991. The peak growth rate reached 2.8 percent a year during the height of the baby boom between 1951 and 1956 and declined steadily until the early 1980s when it fell to just under 1.0 percent a year. With a marked increase in immigration levels and the stemming of the free fall in fertility rates at the end of the 1980s, the growth rate increased again to 1.5 percent a year. Over the past thirty years the rate of aging of the Canadian population has been similar to that of the United States, although the greater role of immigration in Canada (proportionately about twice that of the United States) has kept the rate of aging slightly lower than that in the United States.

As in all other developed countries experiencing both declining fertility and declining mortality, the elderly population is growing at a considerably faster rate than the total population. In 1951 the population 65 years and over totaled 1.4 milion and constituted 8.0 percent of the total population. Of the population 65 years of age and over, 149,000 were age 80 and over and comprised 1.1 percent of the population. By 1991 the population aged 65 and over stood at 3.2 million, or 12.0 percent of the total population, and the population over 80 had grown more than fourfold to 657,000, or 2.4 percent of the population. The population over 65 had sustained a growth rate of over 3 percent a year for the entire forty years, whereas for those over 80 growth was close to 4 percent a year. Not only has the Canadian population been aging steadily but the internal composition of the conventionally defined group of elderly "over 65" has changed and contains a progressively higher proportion of "very old" individuals, with a range of important consequences for public policy (Moore, Rosenberg, and McGuinness 1997).

Geography of Aging

The national picture embraces a great deal of geographic diversity in both the distribution and rates of growth of the elderly population. The underpinnings of the differences lie primarily in the regional disparities in economic opportunity, which generate migration flows that are strongly age selective (Shaw 1985; Rogers 1992). The foundations of migration decisionmaking in human capital investment imply much higher propensities to migrate among the young; therefore, in general significant out-migration will increase the rate of aging, whereas substantial in-migration has the opposite effect. There is a secondary effect that receives little attention, and that is the impact of migration decisions on fertility; often the decision by females to leave rural or small-town environments to pursue tertiary education or join the labor force elsewhere is also a decision to forgo earlier marriage and childbearing. Spatially, this results in higher fertility in rural areas and a small effect on reducing the rate of aging, although that effect is offset by the much larger migration effect.

Change in Population Aging at the Provincial and Local Levels

For the country as a whole, the primary influence on population aging has been the long-run decline in fertility and mortality rates (McDaniel 1986). With progressively fewer children born to a female during her childbearing years and proportionately more people surviving to age 80, it is not surprising that the proportion of the population over 65 has risen continuously for the past fifty years. This increase at the national level has been modified only slightly by immigration, which has a tendency to reduce the rate of aging because immigrants are in general younger than the resident population.

For any set of subnational regions, such as provinces or census divisions, not only does the degree of population aging vary considerably between areas but the relative importance of different components of change also tends to shift. Because the likelihood of migrating declines strongly with distance for any origin population, it follows that the smaller the region, the greater the potential role to be played by migration. Thus interprovincial migration plays a role in changing provincial population distributions, and that role is magnified for the much smaller census divisions. For seniors, as for the population in general, the likelihood of moving from a rural census division to an adjacent urban census division is greater than that of moving from one province to another.

Since population change is brought about by births, deaths, and migration, variation in aging is attributable to long-run differences in fertility, mortality, and migration rates. Change is cumulative, so for any five-year intercensal period the rate of population aging is dependent primarily on two demographic influences.

1. The demographic structure of the area at the beginning of the period, which determines the magnitude of *aging in place*—the increase in the proportion of the population over 65 attributable to births and age-specific deaths occurring to the population at the beginning of the period. In a given five-year period, the dominant predictors of the increase in the proportion over 65 are
   - The ratio of the population aged 60–64 to that aged 65–69, which represents the potential for those about to be elderly to increase that segment of the population; if the younger age group is significantly larger it will more than offset the accumulated number of deaths in the elderly population.
   - The proportion of those over 65 who are over 80. This variable defines the shape of the elderly age pyramid—the smaller the ratio, the younger the elderly population and the greater the potential for rapid increase.

   A simple regression for census division data for the period 1986–1991 shows that 73 percent of the variation in aging in place among the population over 65 (the variable a_{65}) is attributable to these two variables.
2. The impact of the demographic structure of migration into and out of the area during the five-year period as defined by the relation between n_{65} and $n_{<65}$ earlier.

In the short run, these two factors are more important than local variations in fertility and mortality rates. In the longer run, however, sustained differences in regional fertility and mortality would produce differences in the aging experience. Higher mortality or fertility rates would tend to slow the aging process. Over longer periods of time it is necessary to take into account the fertility, mortality, and subsequent migration experiences of the migrants themselves (Rees and Wilson 1977; Rogers 1995), which have the potential to change the rate at which local populations age. In a five-year period, however, the marginal effect of these differences is small.

The cumulative nature of population aging means the demographic characteristics of an area at the beginning of an intercensal period reflect a complex history of prior fertility, mortality, and migration experience and may not necessarily be explained by any recent set of events or by current community characteristics. In large part, mortality and fertility effects are macroscale influences that permeate every part of the country. There are also systematic demographic processes that have persisted for many decades, however, that produce geographic variations in the distribution of the elderly. The history of migration within Canada, as in the United States, has seen young adults moving from areas with limited economic opportunity to places where job prospects are more enticing. In general, these moves have been from rural and small-town Canada to bigger towns and cities, and they have occurred at consistently higher rates than for older cohorts whose established social networks and higher job security are associated with significantly lower propensities to migrate (Northcott 1988). A prime consequence of this process has been that many parts of rural Canada, particularly the Prairies and the Atlantic provinces, have experienced significant aging as the older members of the community remain and younger ones depart. In the 1986–1991 period we would still expect that those communities with the most buoyant local economies would continue to attract young in-migrants and experience slower rates of aging.

More recently, the increasing affluence of the elderly, many of whom have significant financial resources at retirement, has led to greater emphasis on high-amenity areas as places to live, particularly those with moderate as opposed to harsh winters (Serow 1987; Northcott 1988). Again, however, selective migration by one group leads to a concentration of others who are less mobile; in this case the less affluent elderly will tend to become concentrated in more disadvantaged origin areas. Finally, within the elderly population the phenomenon of return migration to gain advantages from proximity to family and other services suggests that net flows by the older elderly to less economically and climatically privileged areas would increase and lead to more rapid increases in the population over 80 in many of these areas.

Aging at the Provincial Level

In 1991, 11.7 percent of Canada's population was over 65 and 2.4 percent was over 80. The variation in the proportion of the population over 65 at the provincial level in 1991 is substantial. For both males and females, the Northwest Territories and the Yukon have less than 4 percent of the population in this category. Alberta has just under 8 percent of its male population over 65, whereas Saskatchewan lies at the other end of the spectrum at over 12 percent. The proportion of females over 65 is higher in every province, with Alberta and Saskatchewan again anchoring the distribution, Alberta having 10.3 percent and Saskatchewan 15.7 percent of females over 65.

The differentials tend to reflect the long-run patterns of age-selective migration away from rural and primary resource areas in the Atlantic provinces and the Prairies and toward the regions of economic growth in central Canada and the West. Alberta in particular benefited from the substantial in-migration of younger people in the 1970s, and this is reflected in both low proportions of elderly and low rates of growth of this segment of the population in the 1970s. The trend in the 1980s, however, was for a slow convergence of interprovincial proportions. The highest rates of aging tended to be in provinces with lower proportions over 65 (Quebec, Newfoundland, and Alberta), stressing the importance of the overall aging of larger pre-elderly cohorts. These findings correspond rather closely to the slow convergence of elderly concentration measures at the state level reported by Rogerson (1996).

The role of interprovincial migration is somewhat more complex than that of immigration, which has small but negative effects on the rate of aging in all provinces. The phenomenon of return migration to the place in which one grew up has received some attention in the literature (Newbold 1993), and this is more likely to occur at higher ages, particularly in provinces that have been the origin of strong out-migration streams among those in the labor force years. Superimposed on return migration flows are movements of the elderly to high-amenity regions on retirement, with British Columbia, Ontario, and Prince Edward Island the primary recipients in this regard. The net result is that migration produces differential aging effects across the nation, with the Atlantic provinces and British Columbia the prime recipients of relative gains in elderly populations from these moves. The only major example of consistently higher proportions of elderly among out-migrants than in-migrants is in Quebec, which only serves to ameliorate what is already the highest rate of aging among the provinces.

If we calculate net migration rates by age and sex for the provinces between 1986 and 1991, we see that the patterns for the younger and older ages exhibit important commonalities and differences (Figure 7.3). In Quebec, Ontario, Alberta, and British Columbia, the net effects are in the same direction, whereas they are in the opposite direction for the Atlantic provinces and for females in the eastern Prairies (Saskatchewan and Manitoba), stressing the role played by return migration in these areas (Newbold and Liaw 1990; Newbold 1993). The net migration effects are generally stronger for males, and the positive net migration for males in Prince Edward Island, Nova Scotia, and New Brunswick is particularly noticeable. The higher proportionate effect is attributable to the larger base of low mobility females at older ages in each of these provinces.

We see that the combined patterns of migration outcomes result in fairly different *net* effects of migration (η) on aging (Figure 7.4). Although Ontario and British Columbia receive significant in-flows at all ages, the net effect of migration in both provinces produces significant reductions in the rate of aging. Quebec has a similar experience, although the quantitative effects are much smaller. A significant element in each case is the effect of immigration, which is focused particularly on the three largest metropolitan areas—Toronto, Montreal, and Vancouver—and brings a significant increase in the population under 65 relative to those over 65.

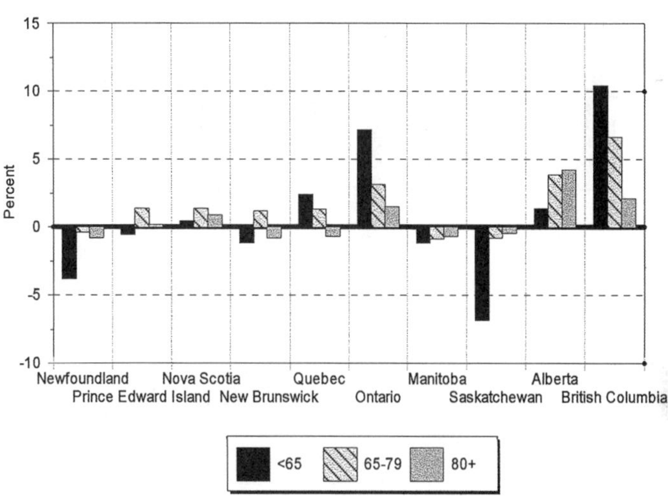

b: MALES

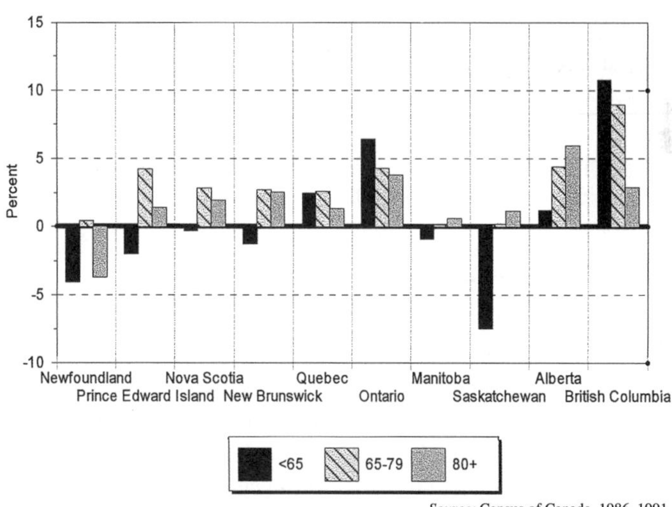

Source: Census of Canada, 1986, 1991.

Figure 7.3 Net Migration by Province, by Elderly Age Groups and Gender, 1986–1991

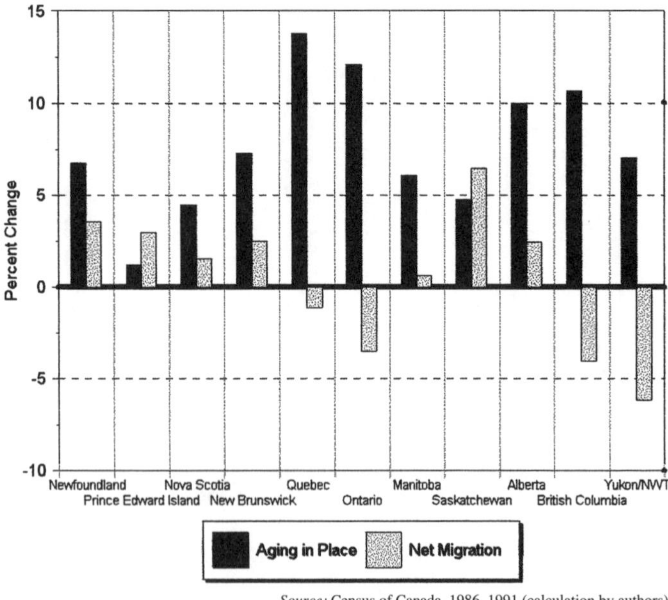

Source: Census of Canada, 1986, 1991 (calculation by authors).

Figure 7.4 Change in Percent over 65 As a Result of Net Migration and Aging in Place, 1986–1991

Patterns of increase caused by aging in place (α) are rather different across provinces (Figure 7.4). The α values are highest in Quebec, Ontario, and British Columbia, where the primary effect of migration is to ameliorate the rate of population aging. Any major shift in the geographic structure of migration and immigration[2] has the potential to shift the rate of aging, particularly in Ontario.

Aging at the Intra-Provincial Level

When we consider the percentages of the population over 65 at the census division level, the variation is even more substantial than at the provincial level. As a percentage of the population in each census division, the elderly made up more than 11.7 percent of the population (the national average) in 56 percent of the census divisions across Canada in 1991 (Figure 7.2). What is striking is the contrast between a *young* northern Canada and an *old* southern Canada. To a large extent, this contrast reflects the differences in the proportion of native peoples living in northern Canada compared with southern Canada and the differences in fertility and mortality patterns of native peoples compared with the nonnative population.[3] The contrast also reflects the tendency of older individuals to move away from areas with harsh climates.

Within southern Canada considerable spatial variation is also seen in the elderly population (Figure 7.2). In Atlantic Canada, parts of Cape Breton and much of Nova Scotia and the census divisions surrounding the Bay of Fundy have relatively large elderly populations (greater than 14.0 percent). In Quebec relatively large elderly populations can be found mainly in the nonmetropolitan census divisions along the St. Lawrence and Ottawa Rivers. In Ontario there are three distinct clusters of census divisions where the proportions of elderly are high: rural eastern Ontario, a wedge of census divisions stretching from Lake Ontario to the north shore of Georgian Bay, and the rural census divisions along Lake Huron and the southern shore of Georgian Bay. On the Prairies there is a growing number of rural census divisions along the border between Manitoba-Saskatchewan and the United States where the elderly population makes up over 18 percent of the population. In British Columbia the census divisions in the southern part of Vancouver Island and the south-central interior, which have become well-known as retirement destinations, appear among those census divisions with relatively large elderly populations.

When we examine values of C_{65}, they also exhibit considerable spatial variability, as is the case in the United States. High values are concentrated in Newfoundland, Quebec, northern Ontario, Saskatchewan, Alberta, and the interior of British Columbia (Figure 7.5). As we noted earlier, the values of C_{65} can be expressed as a function of the constituent rates of aging in place and net migration. The rates of increase in the populations under and over 65 due to aging in place ($a_{<65}$, a_{65+}) have similar general distributions. Although the rates are consistently higher for the over 65 population, the rates tend to be relatively higher for both distributions in northern Quebec, the Prairies, and British Columbia, whereas moderately high values are found in Newfoundland. Strong areas of difference between the two rates arise in southern British Columbia, where the younger population exhibits increases far below average; similar differences exist for central Ontario and the census divisions in the vicinity of Montreal, whereas a contrasting picture arises in Nova Scotia outside Halifax where the growth of the elderly population as a result of natural increase is relatively much higher than that for the younger population.

Turning to the net migration rates $n_{<65}$ and n_{65+}, the two spatial distributions also have some commonalities. Net migration for those under 65 is predominantly one of out-migration from most census divisions, with virtually all of the Prairies, northern Quebec, and the Atlantic provinces outside metropolitan areas experiencing net losses of those under 65. The metropolitan fringes and southern British Columbia experienced net gains during this period, and in general $n_{<65}$ is strongly associated with higher income areas and positive economic growth.

Net migration for the elderly, n_{65+}, also tends to be negative for much of the Prairies and northern Quebec, although often the net losses are much less than those for the younger population. This is similar to the situation depicted in Rogerson (1996) where net migration for the elderly is mostly negative in the

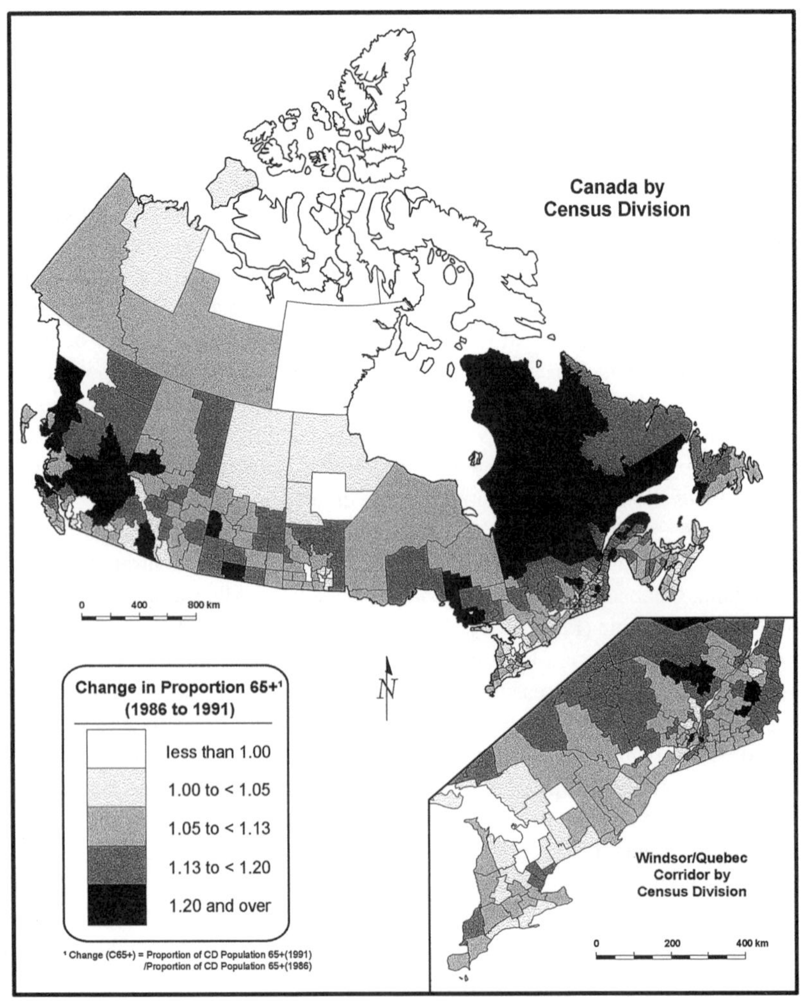

Source: Census of Canada, 1986, 1991

Figure 7.5 Ratio of the Proportion of the Population Aged 65 and Above (C_{65+}), by Census Division, 1986–1991.

Northeast and Midwestern states, although the rates are lower than for those under 65. The main increases are found in central Ontario, the fringes of Montreal, and southern British Columbia.

When we combine these various rates we start to gain a better sense of the components of aging. We first calculate the relative contributions of aging in place (α) and net migration (η) to the increase in population aging between 1986 and 1991. For the country as a whole the value of α is 0.106 (or a 10.6

percent increase in the proportion over 65) and η is -0.013 (a 1.3 percent decrease), which indicates both the magnitude of aging in place and the small negative effect on aging produced by immigration. The values for individual census divisions, however, exhibit broad ranges, although in the majority of cases the aging-in-place component dominates net migration (Figures 7.6, 7.7). The aging-in-place component is a strongly urban phenomenon.

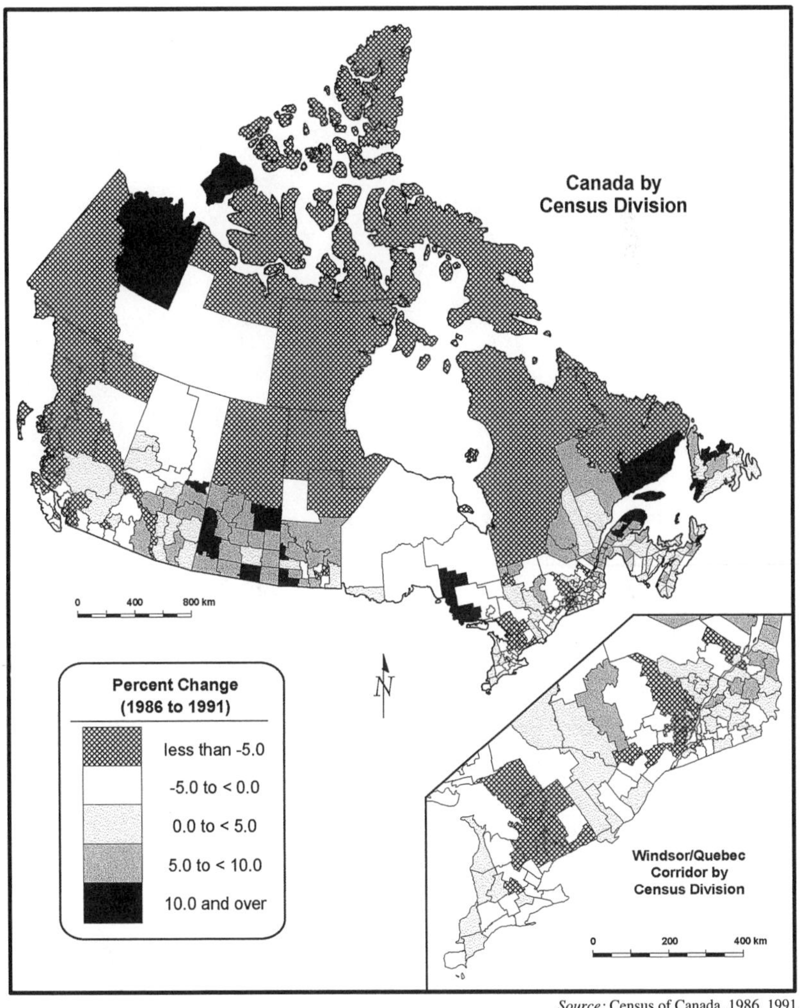

Source: Census of Canada, 1986, 1991.

Figure 7.6 Percent Change in Population Aging As a Result of Net Migration, by Census Division, 1986–1991

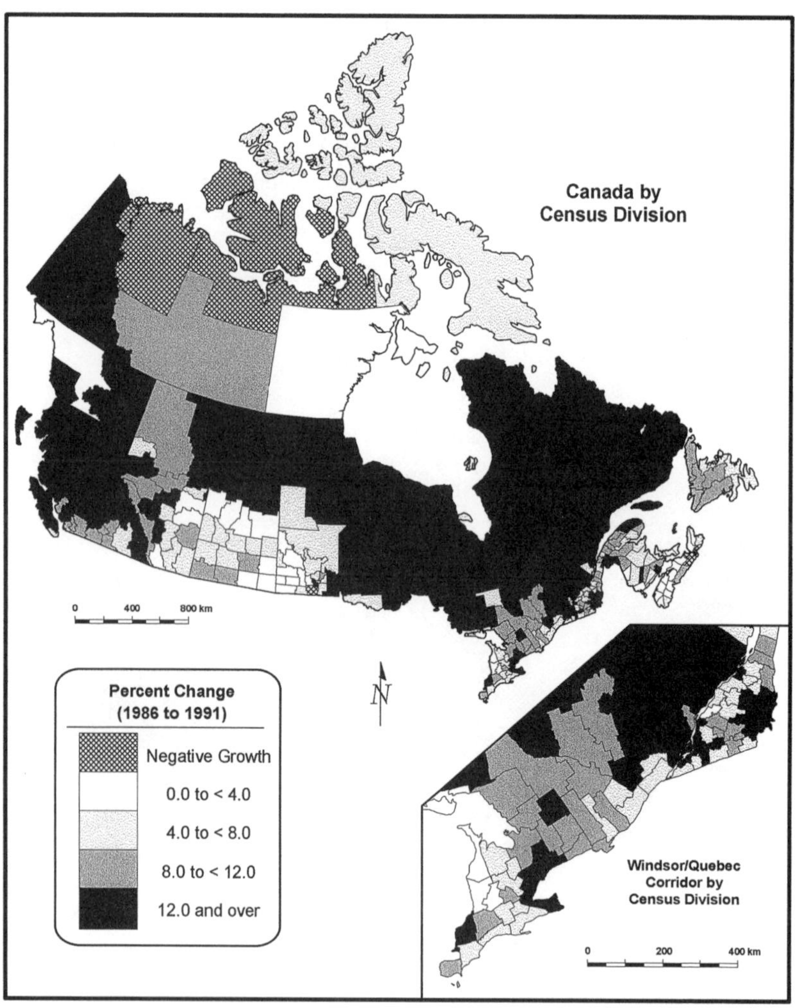

Source: Census of Canada, 1986, 1991.

Figure 7.7 Percent Change in Population Aging As a Result of Aging in Place, by Census Division, 1986–1991

The net migration effects (η) are rather different. Although both $n_{<65}$ and n_{65+} have positive associations with areas with above average income growth, the net effects on aging have the opposite effect and are strongly associated with areas that are less buoyant. This is because the net in-migration of younger individuals to more prosperous areas consistently dominates the inflow of older persons and thereby lowers the rates of population aging. At the same time the net effect of migration on aging is consistently higher in the four other regions relative to British Columbia and the territories, indicating the importance of migration to the latter region of younger people in the labor force years during the late 1980s.

Age Differentials in α and η

At the provincial level, we saw that decomposing α and η by age produced major differences in the magnitudes of effects. A similar set of differences arises when we decompose these measures at the census-division level. Aging-in-place effects for those aged 65–74 are significantly lower in much of the south, most noticeably in the eastern Prairies and Nova Scotia. Higher values are occurring not only in the north but very significantly in the vicinity of metropolitan Toronto and Montreal, where the rates of aging are really beginning to accelerate. For those over age 75,[4] higher values are strongly evident in southern and central British Columbia, as well as in much of Quebec. Much of southern Ontario remains with lower rates but those rates will obviously accelerate in the future.

The net migration effects are also strongly differentiated. They have significant effects on increasing aging for 65- to 74-year-olds in the Prairies, the Gaspé region of eastern Quebec, and rural Newfoundland. For those over 75 the effects are generally weaker in these two regions, but dramatic effects are seen between the negative influences on aging in southern Ontario and Quebec and the positive effects in the north of these two provinces. The overall impact of net migration on aging for those over 75 in British Columbia is the highest of all and is consistent across the province.

The implication of these results is that the overall structure of aging is beginning to shift, with a slowing of the rate of aging in the traditional areas of elderly concentration in the Prairies and the Atlantic provinces, although it continues apace among the very old where the primary burden of care lies. The rate is accelerating in Ontario and Quebec, however, particularly near the major metropolitan areas. In Ontario, if overall patterns of migration among the younger population shift and immigration slows, the rate of aging could increase dramatically.

A Classification of Aging Scenarios

The roles of α and η interact in different ways across the country to produce aging effects, as do the components of η. We can use the joint distribution of these values to produce a classification of aging scenarios. This classification extends the work of McCarthy (1983) and Bekkering (1990); McCarthy focused primarily on the role of migration, whereas Bekkering added an aging-in-place component as a single category. In this classification we distinguish between those areas in which aging in place is dominant although migration is still influential and areas in which migration is dominant in terms of effects on population aging.

Based on the values of α and η and the values of $n_{<65}$ and n_{65+}, nine classes are defined.

1. *Stable:* The total effect of aging in place and migration produces changes of less than 3.5 percent in the proportion of the population that was over 65 between 1986 and 1991, and neither individual effect is larger than 3.5 percent.
2. *Deconcentration:* The combined effects of aging in place and migration produce a decline in population aging ($\alpha + \eta < 0$).

Aging in place dominant

3. *Aging in place—Migration stable or reduces aging:* Net effects of migration are either insignificant or act to reduce the rate of population aging ($\alpha > 3.5$; $\eta \leqq 0$).
4. *Aging in place—Migration produces congregation:* Congregation occurs when both the elderly and nonelderly experience net in-migration but the in-migration rate for the elderly is higher ($\alpha > \eta$; $\eta > 0$; $n_{<65}$, $n_{65+} > 0$,[5] $n_{<65} < n_{65+}$).
5. *Aging in place—Migration produces recomposition:* Recomposition occurs when the elderly are net in-migrants and the nonelderly are net out-migrants ($\alpha > \eta$; $\eta > 0$; $n_{<65}$, < 0, $n_{65+} > 0$, $n_{<65} < n_{65+}$).
6. *Aging in place—Migration produces Accumulation:* Accumulation arises when both elderly and nonelderly experience net out-migration but the out-migration rates are higher for the nonelderly ($\alpha > \eta$; $\eta > 0$; $n_{<65,}$ < 0, $n_{65+} < 0$, $n_{<65} < n_{65+}$).

Migration dominant

7. *Migration produces congregation*: Migration is more important than aging in place and the elderly are gaining at a faster rate than the nonelderly ($\alpha < \eta$; $\eta > 0$; $n_{<65}$, $n_{65+} > 0$, $n_{<65} < n_{65+}$).
8. *Migration produces recomposition:* ($\alpha < \eta$; $\eta > 0$; $n_{<65}$ < 0, $n_{65+} > 0$, $n_{<65} < n_{65+}$).
9. *Migration produces accumulation:* ($\alpha < \eta$; $\eta > 0$; $n_{<65}$, n_{65}, < 0, n_{65+} < 0,n_{65} $< n_{65+}$).

The outcome of this classification shows that the aging scenarios are dominated by aging-in-place processes (Table 7.1). Almost 43 percent of census divisions are experiencing significant aging in place—which is, in fact, ameliorated by migration—whereas 28.2 percent experience both aging in place and in-

Table 7.1 Distribution of Aging Scenarios by Region and Province, 1986–1991

			Aging in Place Dominates				Migration Dominates		
	Stable (1)	Decline in Aging (2)	Migration Reducing Aging (3)	Congregation (4)	Recomposition (5)	Accumulation (6)	Congregation (7)	Recomposition (8)	Accumulation (9)
Regions									
Atlantic	15.2[1]	0.0	15.2	2.2	13.0	19.6	0.0	26.1	8.7
Quebec	0.0	1.0	46.5	11.1	18.2	13.1	0.0	7.1	3
Ontario	4.1	8.2	69.4	10.2	6.1	0.0	2.0	0.0	0.0
Prairies	1.7	6.7	25.0	5.0	5.0	8.3	1.7	30	16.7
B.C./NWT	0.0	19.4	61.1	8.3	5.6	0.0	5.6	0	0
Total	3.4	5.5	42.8	7.9	11.0	9.3	1.4	12.8	5.9
Index of concentration for scenarios[2]									
Atlantic	4.4	0.0	0.4	0.3	1.2	2.1	0.0	2	1.5
Quebec	0.0	0.2	1.1	1.4	1.6	1.4	0.0	0.6	0.5
Ontario	1.2	1.5	1.6	1.3	0.6	0.0	1.5	0	0
Prairies	0.5	1.2	0.6	0.6	0.5	0.9	1.2	2.4	2.8
B.C./NWT	0.0	3.5	1.4	1.1	0.5	0.0	4.0	0	0
Numbers of census divisions by province									
Newfoundland	—	—	2	—	2	3	—	2	1
PEI	1	—	—	—	—	—	—	1	1
Nova Scotia	6	—	1	—	1	1	—	7	2
New Brunswick	—	—	4	1	3	5	—	2	—
Quebec	—	1	46	11	18	13	—	7	3
Ontario	2	4	34	5	3	—	1	—	—
Manitoba	—	4	7	—	—	1	1	7	3
Saskatchewan	—	—	2	—	—	2	—	8	6
Alberta	1	—	6	3	3	2	—	3	1
B.C.	—	4	20	3	2	—	1	—	—
Yukon/NWT	—	3	2	—	—	—	1	—	—
Total	10	16	124	23	32	27	4	37	17

Notes: 1. Percentage of census divisions in Atlantic provinces with "stable" aging scenarios.
2. Percentage of scenario in region/percentage of scenario in nation.

Source: Census of Canada, 1991.

creased aging as a result of migration. Less than 10 percent of areas are either stable or experiencing a decline in aging, whereas 20.1 percent of areas are subject to migration-dominated aging. Among the migration scenarios, recomposition is the most frequent, with accumulation significantly less important than in earlier periods (Bekkering 1990). Congregation is the least important and more often occurs in areas where aging in place is dominant.

The scenarios are far from uniformly distributed geographically (Figures 7.8, 7.9, and Table 7.1, which provides both the percentage distributions by region

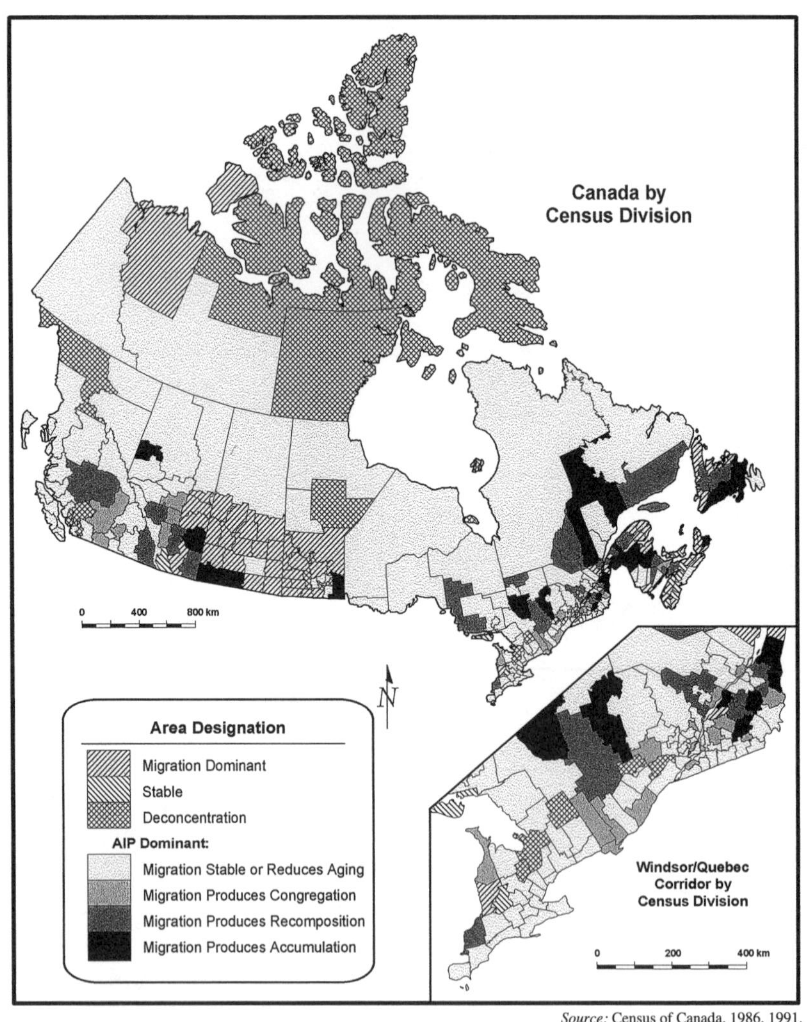

Source: Census of Canada, 1986, 1991.

Figure 7.8 Aging in Place (AIP)-Dominant Areas, 1986–1991

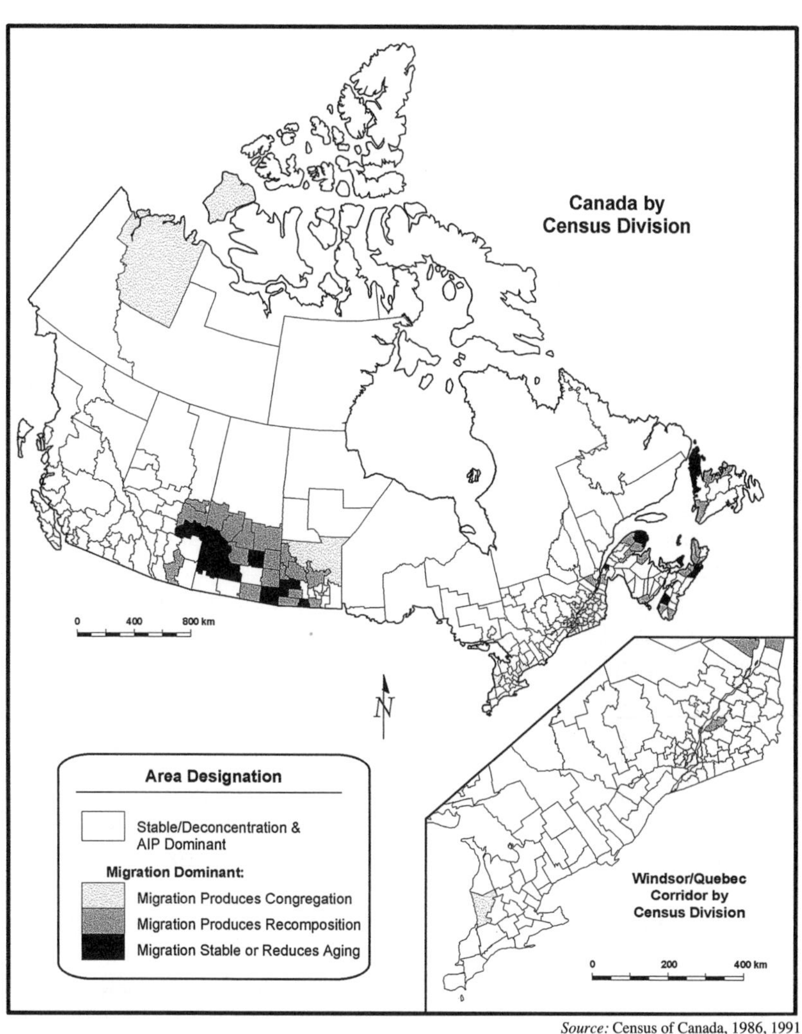

Source: Census of Canada, 1986, 1991

Figure 7.9 Migration-Dominant Areas, 1986–1991

and an index of concentration).[6] Migration-dominated aging areas are much more likely to be found in the Atlantic provinces and the Prairies than elsewhere. Congregation is the exception, but this is associated with net in-migration of the nonelderly and where it occurs is found in British Columbia, Ontario, and the environs of Montreal. Stable areas, with little change induced either by aging in place or by migration are primarily an Atlantic region phenomenon, whereas declines in aging and migration-ameliorated aging are dominant in British Columbia and Ontario.

Socioeconomic Relations to Processes of Aging

The existing knowledge of the processes of population aging suggest that the global aging produced by shifts in fertility and mortality across the country are geographically differentiated by a complex web of additional social, economic, and demographic variables. The dominant message, however, is that we would expect to find a strong association at the local level between population aging and economic disadvantage (Rosenberg and Moore 1990). Communities with more limited local resources can expect to shoulder a disproportionate burden from growth of the elderly population.

The characterization of the structure and change in population aging presented earlier suggests that the various demographic indicators of aging possess multivariate links with selected social, economic, and demographic variables (Table 7.2). In this section the various propositions regarding the links between aging and community profiles are tested with a series of regression analyses. Two types of analysis are pursued; the first relates demographic characteristics in 1991 to socioeconomic characteristics in 1991, and the second relates measures of change between 1986 and 1991 to characteristics in 1986 and to changes in socioeconomic measures between 1986 and 1991. Because of the complexity of the relations underlying aging, these regression analyses are intended to be descriptive rather than explanatory, characterizing the types of communities associated with particular aging scenarios.

As part of these analyses we include regional dummy variables to represent the broad demographic differences among the five main regions (Atlantic provinces, Quebec, Ontario, Prairies, and British Columbia and the territories). In many cases additional regional differentials exist over and above those attributable to the sets of independent variables included in the analyses. The analyses use British Columbia as the reference region, so the coefficients for the other four regions represent the differences between British Columbia and each of those regions after controlling for differences in the other socioeconomic variables.

The proposition behind much of this analysis is that population aging is concentrated in areas that tend to be less economically advantaged. In Table 7.3 the

Table 7.2 Variables Used in Regression Analyses

	Variables Used in Analyses of 1991 Structure	Variables Used in Analyses of Change 1986–1991
Urban variables	% of census division population defined as urban	% of census division population defined as urban
	Metropolitan area (=1 if census metropolitan area, 0 otherwise)	Metropolitan area (=1 if census metropolitan area, 0 otherwise)
Socioeconomic variables	% of census division population who immigrated between 1986 and 1991	% of census division population who immigrated between 1986 and 1991
	% of households falling below low-income cutoff in 1991	% of 15+ population unemployed in 1986
	% of 15+ population unemployed in 1991	% change in average income 1986 to 1991
	Average income in 1991	% change in unemployment rate 1986 to 1991
	Population growth 1986 to 1991	Average income in 1986
	% over 15 with university degree in 1991	% over 15 with university degree in 1986
	% over 15 with less than grade 9	
	% 15 to 24 not in labor force	
Health services environment	Health service employees per thousand population	Health service employees per thousand population
	Physicians per thousand population	Physicians per thousand population
Climate	Mean July temperature	Mean July temperature
	Mean January temperature	Mean January temperature
	Number of hours of sunshine in year	Number of hours of sunshine in year
Regional dummy variables	Atlantic (=1 if census division is in Atlantic provinces, 0 otherwise)	Atlantic
	Quebec	Quebec
	Ontario	Ontario
	Prairies	Prairies
	(Reference category is British Columbia and territories)	
1986 demographic characteristics		% of population who were women aged 20–35 in 1986
		Ratio of (population aged 60–64)/(population aged 65–69) in 1986
		% of population 65+ in 1986
		% of elderly population 80+ in 1986

Table 7.3 Models of Demographic Characteristics in 1991 for Census Divisions

	Percent 65 and over, 1991		Percent 80 and over, 1991		Proportion of Elderly 80 and over, 1991		Sex Ratio 65 and over, 1991	
Independent Variables	Model 1	Model 2	Model 3	Model 4	Model 5	Model 6	Model 7	Model 8
Intercept	24.0374***	26.2728***	5.067***	6.1741***	17.4316***	22.3861***	1.0585***	0.9300***
% urban	−0.0189*	−0.0253**	−0.0041**	−0.0064**	−0.0082	−0.0190*	0.0024***	0.0021***
Metropolitan area	−0.3100	0.2990	−0.0968	0.0704	−0.3001	0.2183	0.0297	0.0321
% immigrants 1986–1991	0.0676	0.3327*	0.0489	0.1281**	0.2503*	0.4777**	0.0000	−0.0128*
% low-income families	−0.0132	−0.1181*	−0.0219	−0.0511***	−0.1343*	−0.1931***	0.0011	0.0062*
% unemployed	−0.3001***	−0.2448***	−0.0770***	−0.0553***	−0.0809	−0.0042	−0.0122***	−0.0100***
Average income	−0.3894***	−0.3827***	−0.0904***	−0.1002***	−0.0777*	−0.1641***	−0.0067***	−0.0040***
Population growth 1986–1991	−0.2934**	−0.3418***	−0.1141***	−0.1421***	−0.3245***	−0.5079***	−0.0007	−0.0034
% with degree	0.1216	0.0503	0.0478*	0.0455*	0.1209	0.2206*	0.0124**	0.0194***
% with less than grade 9	0.1311***	0.0615*	0.0475***	0.0200*	0.2020***	0.0890*	0.0020	0.0049***
% 15–24 not in labor force	−0.0986***	−0.1050***	−0.0286***	−0.0286***	−0.0846***	−0.0746	−0.0003	−0.0005
Health employees per thousand	0.1221***	0.1403***	0.0451***	0.0524***	0.1745***	0.2152***	0.0054***	0.0064***
Physicians per thousand	0.0442	−0.1644	−0.1109	−0.2461**	−0.3799	−1.2537***	0.0025	−0.0087
Mean July temperature	0.0831	0.1344	0.0260	0.0174	0.1263	0.0078	0.0040	0.0157***
Mean January temperature	0.2564***	0.2581***	0.0615***	0.0622***	0.1429***	0.1303*	0.0057***	0.0065***
Number of hours of sunshine	0.3143**	0.2520*	0.0645*	0.0707**	0.0700	0.2305*	0.0028	−0.0086*
Atlantic	−0.0947	—	0.1958	—	2.4101***	—	0.1724***	—
Quebec	−1.6959**	—	−0.4969**	—	−0.6431	—	0.1436***	—
Ontario	1.8834***	—	0.4240**	—	1.4218**	—	0.1449***	—
Prairies	−0.4578	—	0.1213	—	2.7265***	—	0.0253	—
Degrees of freedom	270	274	270	274	270	274	270	274
R-Square	0.7685	0.7182	0.7852	0.7308	0.3947	0.2387	0.7547	0.6862

*** $p < 0.001$
** $p < 0.01$
* $p < 0.05$
Source: Census of Canada, 1991

links between the demographic structure in 1991 and selected variables characterizing local communities are presented in the form of a series of regression models, with and without regional dummy variables. Here the very strong negative association between the concentration of the elderly and measures of economic advantage (average income, rates of recent growth, percentage of households falling below low-income lines, measures of educational attainment, and relative importance of urban as opposed to rural populations in the community) is readily apparent. There is also a significant attraction of older populations to places with warmer winters.

C_{65} is a complex measure in that it is positively associated with more urbanized communities but strongly and negatively associated with high-growth areas (Table 7.4); the latter, particularly in Ontario and near Vancouver and Victoria, attract more than enough younger immigrants to offset growth of the elderly population. Rates of population aging are also strongly associated with prior demographic structures, particularly the relative importance of the 60–64- and 65–69-year-old cohorts in 1986. It is important, however, to note that absolute rates of growth of elderly populations are directly associated with areas of population growth, although they have stronger relationships with suburban areas than with the cores of metropolitan areas for which the coefficient is negative.

Below-average values for $a_{<65}$ tend to reflect areas where women in the childbearing years are a smaller fraction of the local population (Table 7.5). Values are also lower in metropolitan areas where fertility rates tend to be less than in rural areas; $a_{<65}$ tends to be higher in areas with higher levels of unemployment. Higher rates of a_{65+}, on the other hand, are strongly urban related and are also associated with areas with higher average incomes and rates of income increase because the driving force behind the growth of the elderly from direct aging is the shape of the age structure at the beginning of the period. Areas with high ratios of 60–64- to 65–69-year-olds and low proportions of elderly over 80, a situation that characterizes many metropolitan areas, are often associated with high values of a_{65+}.

The variable $n_{<65}$ behaved in a manner consistent with the general migration literature, being strongly associated with higher incomes and positive economic growth. Although n_{65+} also exhibits a general relationship to overall growth areas, the avoidance of metropolitan areas is significant, and there are much stronger associations with climatic variables, indicating the expected attraction of more moderate winters (Table 7.5).

The net effects of aging in place (α) are strongly associated with urban areas and also with above-average incomes. Net migration effects (η) are much more strongly associated with areas with below-average incomes. The expected relations with climatic variables take on major significance only when the demographic variables are removed, as these values are consistently different in Quebec and the Atlantic provinces and are coincident with climatic differences (Table 7.6).

Table 7.4 Models of Growth in Elderly Population for Census Divisions, 1986–1991

	Dependent Variables					
	C(65)		Growth Rate>65, 1986–1991		*C*(80)	
Independent Variables	Model 1	Model 2	Model 3	Model 4	Model 5	Model 6
Intercept	0.8859***	0.8480***	−0.0246*	−0.0350*	1.6054***	1.9331***
% urban	0.0010***	0.0008***	0.0002***	0.0002***	0.0000	0.0000
Metropolitan area	−0.0247*	−0.0255*	−0.0049*	−0.0051*	−0.0224	−0.0228
% immigrants 1986–1991	0.0018	0.0039	0.0003	0.0007	−0.0051	0.0147
% unemployed	0.0069***	0.0043***	0.0013***	0.0008**	0.0158***	0.0105**
% change in income 1986–1991	0.0004	−0.0006	0.0001	−0.0001	−0.0040*	0.0000*
% change in unemployment 1986–1991	−0.0005*	−0.0005**	−0.0001*	−0.0001**	−0.0011	0.0000*
Average income	0.003**	−0.0008	0.0006**	−0.0001	−0.0069*	−0.0100*
Population growth 1986–1991	−0.0221***	−0.0229***	0.0060***	0.0058***	0.0095	−0.0110
% with degree	−0.0063*	−0.0030	−0.0012*	−0.0006	−0.0015	−0.0006
Health employees per thousand	−0.0006	0.0012*	−0.0001	0.0002*	−0.0015	0.0044**
Physicians per thousand	0.0084	0.0062	0.0018	0.0014	0.0331	0.0040
Mean July temperature	0.0027	−0.0006	0.0007	0.0001	0.0141*	0.0110*
Mean January temperature	0.0026**	0.0050***	0.0005***	0.0010***	−0.0026	0.0013
Number of hours of sunshine	0.0000	0.0001***	−0.0000	0.0000***	−0.0003***	−0.0001*
Atlantic	0.0020	0.0478***	0.0015	0.0099***	−0.0349	0.0497
Quebec	0.0689***	0.0750***	0.0134***	0.0145***	0.0087	0.0293
Ontario	0.0368*	0.0584***	0.0073*	0.0112***	0.0460	0.0975**
Prairies	0.0612***	0.0681***	0.0127***	0.0140***	0.1730***	0.2011***
% women aged 20–35	—	−0.0118**	—	−0.0020**	—	−0.0060
Ratio 60–64/65–69	—	0.2801***	—	0.0524***	—	0.1453
% 65 and over, 1986	—	0.0001	—	0.0001	—	0.0048
Proportion of elderly 80 and over	—	−0.0061***	—	−0.0011***	—	−0.0382***
Degrees of freedom	272	268	272	268	272	268
R-Square	0.5616	0.7191	0.6774	0.7899	0.2735	0.5220

*** $p < 0.001$
** $p < 0.01$
* $p < 0.05$
Source: Census of Canada, 1986–1991.

Table 7.5 Models of Migration and Aging in Place for Census Divisions

Dependent Variables	Net Migration under 65 $N(<65)$		Net Migration over 65 $N(65+)$		Aging in Place under 65 $A(<65)$		Aging in Place over 65 $A(65+)$	
Independent Variables	Model 1	Model 2	Model 3	Model 4	Model 5	Model 6	Model 7	Model 8
Intercept	−40.3535***	−38.2926**	−30.5766***	−22.1090	−2.6991	20.4996***	−8.3826	−3.9223
% urban	−0.0197	−0.0440*	0.0160	0.0355	0.0051	−0.0008	0.1053***	.0322*
Metropolitan area	−1.9775	−2.1256	−4.3020*	−4.0066**	−0.4531	−0.1500	−0.0242	−.2219
% immigrants 1986–1991	−0.9667*	−0.4630	0.0660	0.3140	0.0007	0.1145	−0.4288	−.0419
% unemployed	−0.5830***	−0.6475***	−0.0447	0.1960	0.2204***	−0.0189	0.5230***	−.1509
% change in income 1986–1991	0.6721***	0.6739***	0.3026***	0.3274***	0.0039	0.0068	0.1610*	.0194
% change in unemployment 1986–1991	0.0726**	0.0775**	0.0416	0.0399	−0.0105	−0.0176***	−0.0632*	−.0636***
Average income	0.4375**	0.5297**	−0.2959*	0.0704	0.2235***	−0.0922*	1.0249***	.0881
% with degree	1.2801***	0.9753**	0.9056*	0.6911*	−0.0802	−0.1093	−0.8175*	−.4689*
Health employees per thousand	−0.0947	0.0385	0.2163*	0.1648*	−0.0751**	−0.0247	−0.3974***	−.0383
Physicians per thousand	−0.8620	−2.0681*	−1.3076	−1.4300	−0.0373	0.2919	1.6534	1.0520
Mean July temperature	0.6122*	0.6446*	0.2932	0.3874	0.0173	0.0538	0.4572*	.0366
Mean January temperature	0.0666	0.0805	0.3108**	0.1651	0.0177	0.1032***	0.0259	.4795***
Number of hours of sunshine	0.0024	0.0028	0.0103**	0.0070*	−0.0019*	−0.0007	−0.0104**	.0029
Atlantic	−8.1141***	−7.4091***	−0.5219	−1.3434	1.5001**	1.0596**	−3.0343*	3.0543*
Quebec	−3.9941*	−4.1478*	1.3362	2.1842	1.2304**	0.5094	4.4464**	3.9303***
Ontario	−8.1453***	−7.1487***	−0.3117	−0.7291	1.5871**	2.2801***	0.1302	3.9923**
Prairies	−10.3179***	−9.0637***	−2.2158	−1.8177	4.7598***	4.3256***	5.6566**	6.6244***
% women aged 20–35	—	1.5198*	—	0.0742	—	−0.2564**	—	−.6968*
Ratio 60–64/65–69	—	−7.8114*	—	−14.5181**	—	−4.5606***	—	36.7316***
% 65 and over, 1986	—	0.4660	—	0.2251	—	−0.8289***	—	−.4246*
Proportion of elderly 80 and over	—	−1.0372***	—	−0.1890	—	0.1426***	—	−1.0158***
Degrees of freedom	272	268	272	268	272	268	272	268
R-Square	0.5752	0.6249	0.3301	0.3685	0.4483	0.7038	0.5227	0.8006

*** $p < 0.001$
** $p < 0.01$
* $p < 0.05$
Source: Census of Canada, 1986–1991

Table 7.6 Models of Net Effects of Aging in Place and Migration on Population Aging, 1986–1991

	Dependent Variables			
	Net Effects of Aging in Place (a)		Net Effects of Migration (h)	
Independent Variables	Model 1	Model 2	Model 3	Model 4
Intercept	−6.1305	−22.5904**	10.8725	14.1657
% urban	0.0914***	0.0306*	0.0233	0.0614**
Metropolitan area	0.2644	−0.1902	−1.7640	−1.4195
% immigrants 1986–1991	−0.3706	−0.1455	0.9327*	0.6691*
% unemployed	0.2806*	−0.1270	0.5581***	0.8282***
% change in income 1986–1991	0.1395*	0.0106	−0.3632***	−0.3430***
% change in unemployment 1986–1991	−0.0487*	−0.0428**	−0.0266	−0.0317
Average income	0.7515***	0.1686*	−0.6480***	−0.4085**
% with degree	−0.6558*	−0.3087*	−0.4504	−0.3542
Health employees per thousand	−0.2843***	−0.0073	0.2862***	0.1196*
Physicians per thousand	1.4164	0.6148	−0.2623	0.6926
Mean July temperature	0.3886*	−0.0194	−0.3762*	−0.3259
Mean January temperature	−0.0094	0.3278***	0.2280**	0.0892
Number of hours of sunshine	−0.0079**	0.0031*	0.0072**	0.0040
Atlantic	−3.7527*	2.0396*	6.6837***	5.3402***
Quebec	3.0321*	3.1266***	4.9257***	5.7707***
Ontario	−1.4169	1.4230	7.6333***	6.3217***
Prairies	0.7919	1.9840*	7.6362***	6.8523***
% women aged 20–35	—	−0.3976	—	−1.2476**
Ratio 60–64/65–69	—	37.2733***	—	−4.8217
% 65 and over, 1986	—	0.3155*	—	−0.1770
Proportion of elderly 80 and over	—	−1.0017***	—	0.7740***
Degrees of freedom	272	268	272	268
R-Square	0.5175	0.8239	0.5404	0.6052

*** $p < 0.001$
** $p < 0.01$
* $p < 0.05$
Source: Census of Canada, 1986–1991

Socioeconomic Profiles of Aging Scenarios

The average profiles of areas associated with the differing scenarios provide additional insights into the structure of population aging (Table 7.7). Demographically, the stable areas and census divisions dominated by recomposition and accumulation are the oldest both in terms of the proportion over 65 and the relative importance of the very old in the local population. The younger populations are found in those census divisions where aging is declining or migration is ameliorating the aging process, both categories also associated with higher average incomes and high annual growth rates. Areas associated with congregation clearly differentiate themselves from recomposition and accumulation on these economic variables, as well as being much more likely to be urban. Average growth rates are strongly positive in areas with congregation and are negative for the four recomposition and accumulation categories.

The areas of declining aging are sharply differentiated from those with migration-ameliorated aging. The former are primarily nonurban areas with a significant northern component; the latter are dominated by growing areas in Ontario, Quebec, and British Columbia.

The health service variables suggest that the main relationship is between health variables and growth rates of the population. The higher the growth rate, the lower the ratios of health service employees and beds/thousand population. This tends to reinforce the view that smaller places continue to benefit from investments made in earlier periods in relation to a relatively larger population base in smaller urban and rural communities. No great differences are found in the age-standardized rates of disability among the elderly, apart from higher rates in the small number of stable areas.

Conclusion

The primary intent of the research reported here has been to underscore the complexity of the process of population aging for small areas. Population aging is a function of two elements: aging in place and net migration. As Morrison (1992) has noted, aging in place is a critical component of aging that now dominates in most communities, stressing the importance of the existing population structure in determining future patterns of change. Since older people tend to move less, aging in place also increases in relative importance with age and means that future growth of the older elderly at the local level is almost completely determined by the distribution of the younger elderly population. The basic demographic dimensions of aging are similar to those reported by Rogerson (1996) for the United States.

Net migration dominates in certain parts of the country where out-migration of the young is particularly dramatic. Although migration decisions by both the

Table 7.7 Profiles of Aging Scenarios

				Aging in Place Dominates			Migration Dominates		
	Stable	Decline in Aging	Migration Reducing Aging	Congregation	Recomposition	Accumulation	Congregation	Recomposition	Accumulation
	(1)	(2)	(3)	(4)	(5)	(6)	(7)	(8)	(9)
% 65 and over in 1991	14.2[1]	8.8	10.6	12.7	11.8	12.7	10.1	15.1	15.8
% of elderly 80 and over	0.232	0.181	0.191	0.202	0.199	0.197	0.210	0.237	0.230
Sex ratio for elderly	1.33	1.06	1.25	1.39	1.24	1.23	1.06	1.23	1.18
% of area urban	35.3	24.5	58.0	67.5	47.5	41.3	40.2	35.5	29.7
Average income 1991	$37,753	$44,448	$43,703	$41,002	$37,582	$35,456	$40,630	$35,030	$34,598
Annual growth rate 1986–1991	.009	0.033	0.016	0.014	0.000	−0.007	0.033	−.006	−0.013
Mean January temperature	−6.4	−15.2	−10.6	−9.6	−11.4	−11.7	−13.7	−12.4	−13.1
Health services workers/'000	27.9	19.2	24.7	30.2	24.9	24.4	19.7	26.9	24.9
Hospital beds/'000	6.2	2.7	4.9	7.0	5.9	6.1	4.5	7.3	7.0
Disability rate of elderly/'00	26.3	21.9	20.6	19.7	18.3	18.6	24.6	20.2	18.6
C(65)	1.03	0.94	1.10	1.13	1.18	1.16	1.08	1.12	1.13

Note: 1. Unweighted average over census divisions in the "stable" scenario.
Source: Census of Canada, 1991.

young and the elderly are influenced by similar factors and both groups tend to be attracted to the same destinations, with British Columbia's dynamic economy and milder climate proving universally attractive, the net effects of migration for the two groups are very different. Areas with significant out-migration of the younger population tend to greatly increase the rate of population aging in the community, whereas the obverse is true in areas with strong in-migrant flows in the labor force years. Return migration of older populations in the Atlantic provinces and the eastern Prairies also reinforces aging.

The evidence provided in this chapter strongly supports a link between economic restructuring and demographic restructuring, as population aging is very much a function of the economic conditions that underlie differential growth in local economies. The greater burden of rapid aging tends to be borne by communities with fewer economic advantages. Sudden shifts in regional economic performance could produce rapid shifts in the pattern of aging if net migration effects changed from ameliorating aging to reinforcing it.

The demographic dimensions of the Canadian experience seem to mirror those found at the state level in the United States (Rogerson 1996). There is every reason to believe that analyses both at a finer spatial scale and incorporating economic characteristics of local communities would also be similar in the sense that pressures associated with high concentrations of the elderly are also associated with areas of economic disadvantage. From a policy perspective, the most important implication of such a finding is that redistributive mechanisms must be in place for both individual elderly and communities to ensure basic services are available to all, irrespective of economic circumstances.

Notes

This paper is based on research funded by Statistics Canada as part of the Census Analytic Program and by the Social Sciences and Humanities Research Council of Canada, grant no. 410–92–1103. Their support is gratefully acknowledged.

1. A complete accounting would also consider births and deaths to in-migrants and out-migrants (Rogers 1995), but only small errors are introduced by ignoring such multiple events.

2. The net effect of immigration and emigration in the period 1986–1991 was to reduce the rate of population aging by just over 1 percent.

3. Although Canada's native peoples are now well into the demographic transition, as Beaujot (1991) notes, in relative terms native peoples living in remote settlements in northern Canada continue to have higher fertility and mortality rates than the nonnative population of southern Canada.

4. This analysis was undertaken for the population aged 75 and over, as too many small number problems arise when 80 is used as the partition value.

5. The combined effect of net migration for the elderly and nonelderly is greater than 3.5 percent.

6. The index is the ratio of the number of areas with a given scenario to the number that would be expected given identical distributions within each region.

References

Beaujot, Roderic P. 1991. *Population Change in Canada: The Challenges of Policy Adaptation.* Toronto: McClelland and Stewart.

Bekkering, M. 1990. *Patterns of Change in the Spatial Distribution of the Elderly, 1966–1986.* Unpublished M.A. thesis, Department of Geography, Queen's University, Kingston, Ontario.

Frey, William. 1992. "Metropolitan Redistribution of the U.S. Elderly: 1960–70, 1970–80, 1980–90." In Andrei Rogers (ed.), *Elderly Migration and Population Redistribution.* London: Belhaven.

McCarthy, Kevin F. 1983. *The Elderly Population's Changing Spatial Distribution: Patterns of Change since 1960.* Rand Report R–2916–NIA, Santa Monica: Rand Corporation.

McDaniel, Susan A. 1986. *Canada's Aging Population.* Toronto: Butterworths.

Moore, Eric G., M. W. Rosenberg, and Donald McGuinness (1997). *Growing Old in Canada: Demographic and Geographic Perspectives.* Toronto: Nelson and Statistics Canada.

Morrison, Peter A. 1992. "Is 'Aging in Place' a Blueprint for the Future?" Invited address on Major Directions in Population Geography, presented at the Annual Meetings of the Association of American Geographers, San Diego, April.

Newbold, K. Bruce. 1993. *Characterization and Explanation of Primary, Return and Onward Interprovincial Migration: Canada 1976–1986.* Unpublished Ph.D. thesis, Department of Geography, McMaster University, Hamilton, Ontario.

Newbold, K. Bruce, and Kao Lee Liaw. 1990. "Characteristics of Primary, Return, and Onward Inter-provincial Migration in Canada: Overall and Age-Specific Patterns." *Canadian Journal of Regional Science* 13, 1: 17–34.

Northcott, Herbert C. 1988. *Changing Residence: the Geographic Mobility of Elderly Canadians.* Toronto: Butterworths.

Plane, David A., and Peter Rogerson. 1991. "Tracking the Baby Boom, Baby Bust and Baby Boom Echo: Implications of Shifting Age Composition for U.S. Mobility and Migration." *Professional Geographer* 43: 416–430.

Rees, Philip H., and A. G. Wilson. 1977. *Spatial Population Analysis.* London: Edward Arnold.

Rogers, Andrei. 1992. "Elderly Migration and Population Redistribution in the United States." In Andrei Rogers (ed.), *Elderly Migration and Population Redistribution.* London: Belhaven.

———. 1995. *Multiregional Demography: Principles, Methods and Extensions.* New York: John Wiley.

Rogers, Andrei, and Jennifer A. Woodward. 1988. "The Sources of Regional Elderly Population Growth: Migration and Aging-in-Place." *Professional Geographer* 40, 4: 450–459.

Rogerson, Peter A. 1996. "Geographic Perspectives on Elderly Population Growth." *Growth and Change* 27: 75–95.

Romaniuc, A. 1994. "Fertility in Canada: Retrospective and Prospective." In F. Trovato and Carl F. Grindstaff (eds.), *Perspectives on Canada's Population: An Introduction to Concepts and Issues*. Toronto: Oxford University Press.

Rosenberg, M. W., and Eric G. Moore. 1990. "The Elderly, Economic Dependency, and Local Government Revenues and Expenditures." *Environment and Planning C* 8: 149–165.

Serow, Willam J. 1987. "Determinants of Interstate Migration: Differences between Elderly and Non-elderly Movers." *Journal of Gerontology* 42, 1: 5–100.

Shaw, R. Paul. 1985. *Intermetropolitan Migration in Canada: Changing Determinants over Three Decades*. Toronto: NC Press.

Stone, Leroy O., and S. Fletcher. 1986. *The Seniors Boom: Dramatic Increases in Longevity and Prospects for Better Health*. Statistics Canada Catalogue 89–515. Ottawa: Minister of Supply and Services.

8

Geography of the Baby-Boom Cohort

Peter A. Rogerson

So much has been written on the baby-boom generation that the reader may wonder how a niche can be carved out for yet another chapter on the subject. Indeed a decade-and-a-half-old annotated bibliography on the subject (Byerly and Rubin 1985) contains over 700 entries on subjects ranging from Social Security reform to the market for cookies.

Yet little has been written on the baby boom from a geographic perspective. This is surprising given the multifarious spatial aspects of the phenomenon. Illustrative of the many questions demanding a geographic perspective are the following:

- Was the baby boom a spatially uniform event?
- What were the subsequent relocation patterns of baby boomers during the 1970s and 1980s?
- What is the current geographic distribution of baby boomers?
- How much potential mobility is there among cohort members over the next few decades?
- What is the geographic proximity of baby boomers to family members, and what are the potential consequences of that proximity (or lack of proximity) for current and future relationships?

These and related questions have received less attention than have other characteristics of the generation, and they form a primary focus of this chapter that is achieved by organizing the chapter around intergenerational relationships of baby boomers. The cohort's mobility level and migration patterns, taken together with those of their parents and children, have significant implications for the spatial separation of baby boomers from their parents and children. This, in turn, raises important questions and issues associated with caregiving and support.

In addition to a concern with intergenerational relationships and the consequences of mobility and migration patterns, the chapter also addresses related questions associated with measurement. Examples of such questions include

- How many members does the baby-boom echo cohort (defined as children of baby boomers) have, and how old are its members?
- How many parents of baby boomers are still alive, and how will that number change over the next few decades?
- How far do people move, and what is the extent of intergenerational geographic proximity?

These topics will continue to be important well into the twenty-first century. Table 8.1 depicts the annual number of baby-boomer births and, for each annual birth cohort, the number surviving to four points in time, including the present (1996).[1] Over 92 percent of baby boomers are alive today. That figure will drop only slightly to 87.3 percent by 2010. Thereafter, the figure will drop

Table 8.1 Size of the Baby-Boom Cohort over Time

Birth Year	Births	1996	2010	2030	2050
1946	3,288,672	2,923,621	2,572,331	1,137,349	17,155
1947	3,699,940	3,311,952	2,946,177	1,386,918	27,843
1948	3,535,068	3,184,648	2,861,263	1,426,121	37,612
1949	3,559,529	3,225,489	2,924,419	1,537,185	52,587
1950	3,554,149	3,237,960	2,960,408	1,634,699	71,636
1951	3,750,850	3,434,141	3,164,127	1,829,897	101,520
1952	3,846,986	3,537,839	3,282,879	1,982,857	137,675
1953	3,902,120	3,603,465	3,365,798	2,136,422	181,667
1954	4,017,362	3,724,036	3,499,608	2,285,577	239,182
1955	4,047,295	3,764,814	3,557,890	2,404,880	302,783
1956	4,163,090	3,884,883	3,690,657	2,573,846	384,453
1957	4,254,784	3,981,793	3,801,208	2,727,716	476,584
1958	4,203,812	3,944,662	3,782,748	2,786,517	562,142
1959	4,244,796	3,993,152	3,844,882	2,902,140	667,903
1960	4,257,850	4,014,644	3,879,631	2,996,165	777,843
1961	4,268,326	4,033,110	3,909,980	3,085,732	894,297
1962	4,167,362	3,945,261	3,835,595	3,289,184	990,036
1963	4,098,020	3,886,842	3,788,060	3,110,434	1,092,294
1964	4,027,490	3,826,440	3,737,058	3,123,388	1,192,353
Total	74,887,501	69,458,752	65,404,717	44,357,324	8,207,565
% of cohort still alive		92.8	87.3	59.2	11.0
Median Age		40	54	72	90

dramatically—to 59 percent in 2030 and 11 percent by 2050. The last baby boomer will survive until around 2075.

The chapter is organized as follows. The next part focuses on parents of the baby-boom generation, many parents of whom are at or approaching retirement age. This brings to the fore questions involving changes in proximity between baby boomers and their parents, as well as related questions involving care-giving and support. The next section examines the timing and spatial pattern of the birth of the baby boom. Since population change in subnational regions often results primarily from the effects of in- and out-migration, the baby-boom generation has had a significant role in affecting regional change. Then I explore the location and relocation of the baby-boom cohort and analyze past and future migration of the cohort. The next section focuses on the baby-boom echo. The final section provides a discussion of intergenerational geographic proximity, as well as speculation regarding the future.

Parents of the Baby-boom Generation

Although the baby boom is a well-defined cohort, developing a practical definition of the parents of the baby-boom generation is more difficult. In principle, the parents of the baby-boom generation represent a well-defined group—they are the parents of all children born between 1946 and 1964. In practice, the enumeration of that group, so defined, is virtually impossible given the nature of published demographic data. Populations are generally enumerated by such characteristics as age and sex, not by whether they had children born during given time periods.

Yet it is important to find *some* definition since the intergenerational relationships that exist between baby boomers and their parents are of interest. Many parents provide babysitting, day care, and other forms of support to their children. Similarly, baby boomers will increasingly be faced with the question of how to provide support for their aging parents. Here I adopt a somewhat restrictive yet nevertheless useful definition of the parents of the baby-boom generation. The National Center for Health Statistics publishes annual information on births, by birth order. I shall adopt as my definition the set of parents who had first births during the period 1946–1964.

This definition is not all-inclusive since it omits parents who had first births prior to the baby boom and subsequently gave birth to baby-boom children. Unfortunately, there is no way to enumerate the omitted group. There are various ways the size of the omitted group could be estimated, but for my purposes the added effort associated with the estimation is not likely to add much to the interpretation.

Discussion of intergenerational relationships revolves around the relationship between the parents and a specific child. My definition has what may be viewed as the potential benefit of removing any ambiguity regarding *which* child since the definition focuses on parents of those children born during the baby boom who are older than all of their siblings.

Since 21,782,375 baby boomers were first births, this also represents the number of mothers who are parents of baby boomers, using my definition. This figure understates the number of women who had children during the baby-boom years. Furthermore, the women who are omitted will possess an age distribution older than that of the 21,782,375 women who had first births during the baby boom.

Figure 8.1 depicts the 1993 age distribution of the mothers of baby boomers who are first-born children. The figure was constructed using 1990 female survival rates (Social Security Administration 1983) to age the population forward from the time the women first gave birth to 1993.[2] Note the sharp peak in the age distribution of baby boomers' mothers between ages 55 and 65. This cohort is now clearly poised at the brink of retirement. Many potential consequences are being realized, and they will become even more significant over the first decade of the twenty-first century. In many cases retirement of parents may imply extra time available for such activities as babysitting and providing

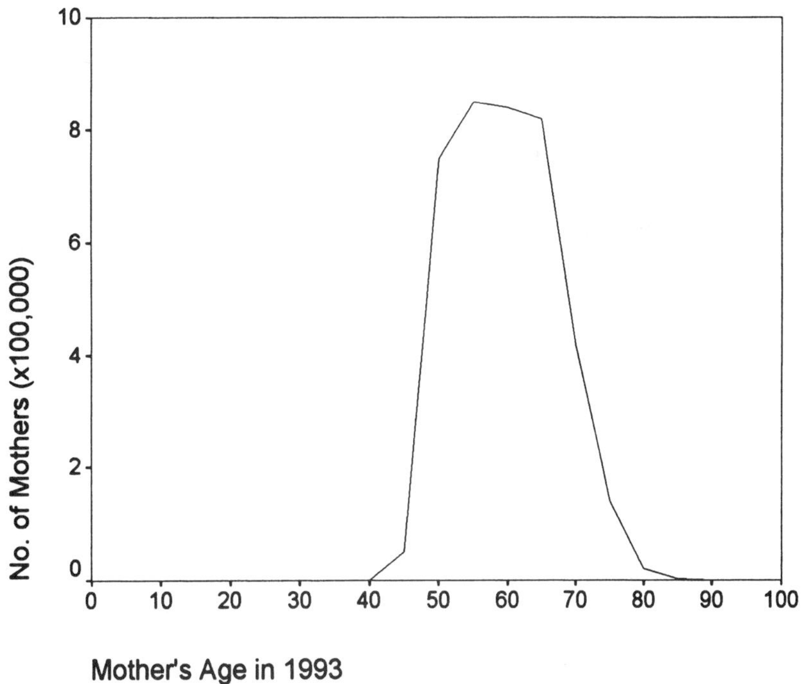

Figure 8.1 Number of Mothers of Baby Boomers, by Age of Mother in 1993

day care for grandchildren. This is especially true in cases where the baby boomer and his or her spouse are both employed, both mother and father of the baby boomer have been in the workforce, and the baby boomer still has young children at home.

The impact of retiring parents on the potential for added contact and support for activities such as day care could be somewhat less significant in cases where either the baby boomer or his or her spouse is already at home caring for the children. One can speculate, however, that the retiring parent willing to care for grandchildren may "free up" baby-boomer parents who are still at home and have chosen not to enter or return to the workplace until now.

For many families the timing of parents' retirement may have come a little too late since, as we will see in the Baby-Boom Echo section, the children of baby boomers are approaching adolescence. For other baby boomers the retirement of their parents may mean a change in the distance by which they are separated from their parents. Litwak and Longino (1987) have argued that there are three stages of elderly migration. In the first stage, following retirement, the elderly individual makes a move often associated with amenities. This may result in increased intergenerational separation as retirees leave long-term residences. Some parents will move farther away to take advantage of, for example, the climate in the southern or southwestern parts of the country. As the parents of baby boomers age further, they will enter Litwak and Longino's second stage, in which moves are made more for health-related reasons and are more likely to be returns to former regions of residence. Members of the baby-boom generation will then become increasingly likely to have their parents move closer to them (see, e.g., Warnes, Howe, and Took 1985; Clark and Wolf 1992; Lin and Rogerson 1995). Indeed, many parents move in with one of their children, and this alone will have implications for housing markets and housing stock over the next few decades. In the final stage, elderly individuals require round-the-clock care and have to move to receive institutionalized care.

Table 8.2 shows the vital status of the parents of baby boomers. Whereas

Table 8.2 Vital Status of Baby Boomers' Parents, 1993–2003

Year	Mother Alive	Father Alive	Father Only Alive	Mother Only Alive	Both Parents Alive	Neither Parent Alive
1993	88.9	76.3	21.1	8.5	67.8	2.6
1998	83.4	67.0	27.5	11.1	55.9	5.5
2003	76.1	55.7	33.7	13.3	42.4	10.6
2008	66.5	43.2	37.8	14.5	28.7	19.0
2013	54.7	30.6	38.0	13.9	16.7	31.4

Note: Entries represent percentage of baby boomers in the given category. In each row, the last four columns sum to 100 percent.
Source: Calculated by author using data from National Center for Health Statistics.

about 56 percent of baby boomers had both parents alive in 1998, that figure will drop to less than one-third by 2013. Whereas the potential effects discussed earlier are merely illustrative and suggestive, a significant point is that the intergenerational relationship between baby boomers and their parents stands poised to change as a result of parents' recent and impending retirements.

Birth of Baby Boomers

Many people believe the term *baby boom* refers to a relatively short period—say, perhaps two or three years—immediately following World War II. During that period the number of marriages and births rose sharply following the return home of soldiers from the war. But the rise in births was in fact sustained for a much longer period, and experts generally agree that 1964 marks the official end of the baby boom.

Those who do recognize that the boom took place over the extended nineteen-year period from 1946 to 1964 often do not appreciate that the height of the boom did not occur at its beginning. The peak of the boom can be measured in different ways, but none of these alternatives implies an early peak. Fertility rates among women of childbearing age peaked in 1957, almost precisely halfway through the period. Even after rates of childbearing began to fall in the late 1950s, the number of births continued to rise since the size of both the population and the female cohort of childbearing age continued to grow. The year 1964 marks the last year during this period in which the number of annual births exceeded 4 million. Interestingly, although *rates* of childbearing have not rebounded since the end of the boom, the number of births in recent years has been almost as great as that during the baby boom.

The reasons suggested for the baby boom have been many and varied. Soldiers returning from the war, pent-up demand for children from during the war years, a small generation of young adults faced with a plethora of labor and housing opportunities, the healthy economy that prevailed during the late 1940s and the 1950s, and the increasing value placed on the notions of family and children (in part fostered by the growing role of television and the media more generally) all played a role in the onset and sustenance of the baby boom.

An extremely important characteristic of the baby boom is that it was *pervasive*. Rindfuss and Sweet (1977: 38) emphasize that analyses of differential contributors to the baby boom should be set within the context that "for virtually every education, racial, and age group examined, fertility rates increased during the 1950s." Jones (1980: 27–28) refers to the "astonishing uniformity within the baby boom" and notes that it was a "mass movement made by millions of families of all races and classes, making millions of individual decisions." This is also the case from a geographic perspective. Plane and Rogerson (1991) argue that the baby boom was essentially a spatially homogeneous event, with no region of the country untouched by its effects.

With the underlying notion that the baby boom was a generally pervasive phenomenon in most respects, I shall now examine in more detail some of the geographic variation that did exist in the unfolding of the generation.

A Geographic Perspective on the Birth of the Baby-Boom Generation

Which regions of the country contributed most to the baby-boom generation? Figure 8.2 shows the baby-boom generation as a proportion of total population in 1960. This figure essentially depicts what may be thought of as the crude birth rate that prevailed during the period 1946–1960. The figure shows that crude birth rates were lowest in the Northeast and the Midwest and highest in the South and in many states in the Rocky Mountain region. As Plane and Rogerson (1991) indicate, this distribution reflects well-known tendencies for urban regions to exhibit lower fertility rates. It also reflects the somewhat older age structure of the Northeast and the Midwest, as well as the higher fertility rates that were characteristic of the South during this period.

Figure 8.3, which shows the spatial pattern of general fertility rates, is more reflective of geographic variation in the rate of childbearing since it standardizes for age structure by using the number of childbearing women instead of the total population in its denominator. The pattern is similar to that in the previous figure, indicating that the map in Figure 8.2 is not too strongly affected by spatial variations in age composition.

The geographic pattern in the *changes* in fertility patterns was different from

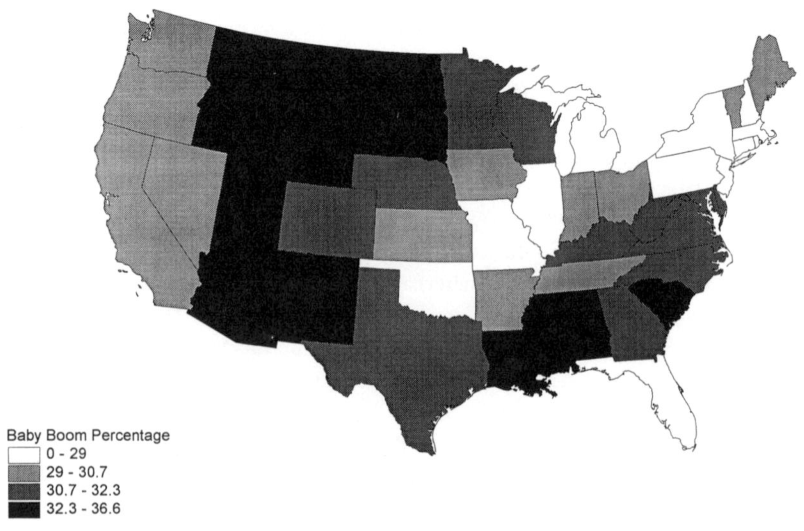

Figure 8.2 Baby-Boom Generation As a Percentage of Total Population, 1960

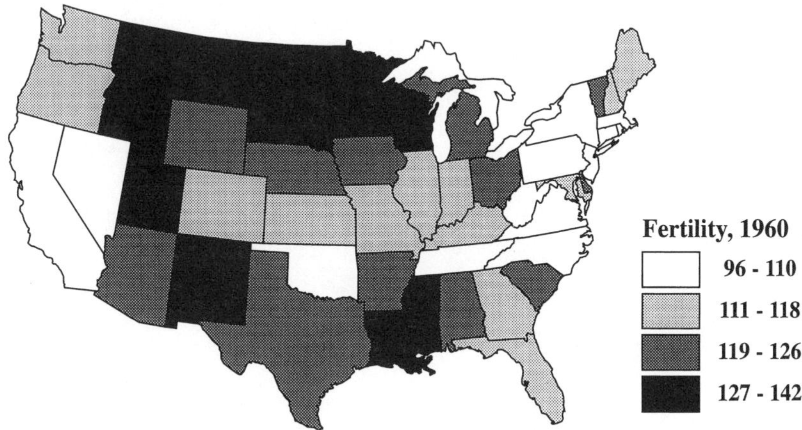

Figure 8.3 General Fertility Rate, 1960

the geographic pattern in the fertility rates themselves. Although urban regions had lower fertility rates than rural regions, the increases in fertility rates were noticeably more pronounced in urban areas. Table 8.3, taken from Rindfuss and Sweet (1977) shows that although both urban and rural areas experienced increases in the rate of childbearing, the increases were greater in urban areas, which is reflected in the narrowing of the urban–rural differential during the

Table 8.3 Percent Change in Age-Specific Fertility Rates of White Women by Education and Rural–Urban Residence, 1945–1957 and 1957–1967

Period and Years of Education	Total Fertility		Fertility 15–29		Fertility 30–44	
	Rural	Urban	Rural	Urban	Rural	Urban
1945–1957						
Total[1]	+ 37	+ 64	+ 60	+ 91	0	+ 22
5–8 years	+ 25	+ 64	+ 38	+ 88	− 3	+ 16
9–11 years	+ 38	+ 67	+ 58	+ 92	− 1	+ 16
12 years	+ 60	+ 76	+ 87	+107	+ 15	+ 26
13+ years	+ 69	+ 55	+109	+ 79	+ 22	+ 25
1957–1967						
Total[1]	− 31	− 31	− 28	− 30	− 40	− 33
5–8 years	− 24	− 14	− 19	− 12	− 37	− 22
9–11 years	− 33	− 33	− 31	− 31	− 38	− 38
12 years	− 30	− 29	− 26	− 27	− 40	− 36
13+ years	− 34	− 32	− 31	− 32	− 40	− 33

Source: Rindfuss and Sweet, 1977: 156.

Note: 1. Includes women with 0–4 years of education.

period 1946–1957. After the peak of the boom the decline was more severe in rural areas, further narrowing the differential. The table also displays the magnitude of these changes by years of education and age of mother. The boom was led by young urban mothers of all educational levels. Participating least in the boom were older women living in rural areas; those with relatively little education experienced declines in fertility during the period 1946–1957. Older women in rural areas experienced the largest declines in the total fertility rate following the peak of the boom.

Location and Relocation of the Baby-Boom Cohort

Current and Previous Location and Relocation Patterns

Figure 8.4 shows where baby boomers are and are not a significant fraction of a county's total population. The pattern is bicoastal, reflective, as we shall see, of recent baby-boomer migration trends. There is an additional area of high concentration in the Rockies, particularly in Colorado. The fraction is lowest in the Midwest, presumably a result of the out-migration of baby boomers to locations nearer the East or West Coast. It is intriguing that places like southern Michigan and central New York do not have lower concentrations of baby boomers, particularly in light of sustained outward migration during the 1970s. Perhaps these are areas of especially high out-migration of retirees or of relatively low mobility, where more baby boomers than average have chosen to age in place.

The highest concentrations of baby boomers in county populations occur in a small number of areas: San Francisco, Seattle, Minneapolis, Denver, Dallas–Fort Worth, Washington, and Atlanta. In these seven metropolitan areas 37.4 percent of the population was composed of baby boomers in 1990, 15 percent higher than the nationwide rate of 32.6 percent. In the remainder of this section, I will take a decade-by-decade look at the changing spatial pattern of baby boomers.

Figure 8.5 shows the ratio of the number of baby boomers in 1970 to the number in 1960. The figure is based on age-disaggregated census population by state. Where the ratio is greater than one, there was a net gain in the absolute size of the cohort; where it is less than one, there was a net loss. Net immigration from abroad is implicitly included; therefore, a state with a net out-migration of baby boomers could still have a ratio of greater than one because of net immigration. Immigration patterns are spatially concentrated in a small number of states. If there were an easy way to adjust for this, we would find that states such as California and New York would have somewhat lower ratios. Mortality is also included implicitly in the ratio, and this exerts a force that causes the ratio to be a bit lower.

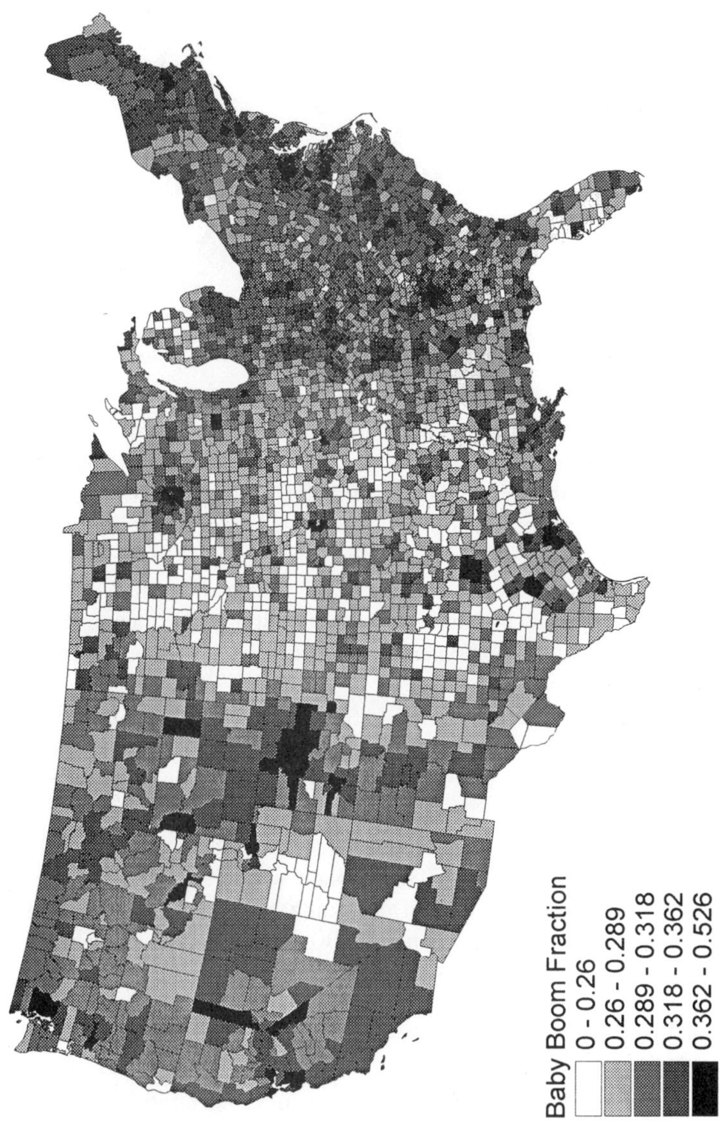

Figure 8.4 Fraction of Population Composed of Baby-Boom Cohort Members

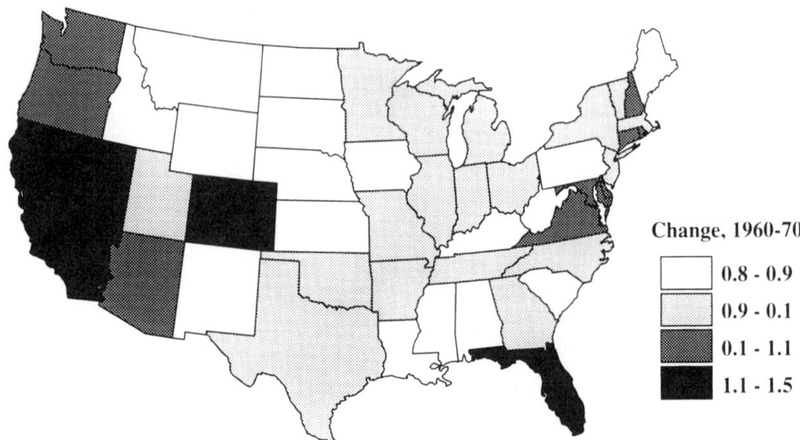

Figure 8.5 Change in Cohort Size, 1960–1970

Figure 8.5 shows that during the 1960s only a small number of states experienced net gains, and they were predominantly in the West. Figure 8.6 shows that during the 1970s the popularity of the West spread to a much larger area; Texas and other parts of the South also experienced net gains. This figure corresponds closely to the Snowbelt-to-Sunbelt images of population change. Growth in the South was not pervasive since states such as Mississippi and Alabama did not experience gains in the size of their baby-boom populations. Finally, New England did not experience the significant net losses felt by other areas of the Northeast.

The pattern of change during the 1980s (Figure 8.7) was in many ways similar to that of the 1970s, although because of the relatively better performance of the Northeast the nationwide pattern of gains in baby-boomer numbers might be described as a bit more bicoastal in nature.

Interestingly, Figures 8.5, 8.6, and 8.7, when compared with Figure 8.3, show that areas where the baby-boom cohort was initially most concentrated (e.g., the Upper Midwest and the Deep South) are those areas that witnessed net declines in baby-boom populations between 1960 and 1990. One might hypothesize that at this scale there has been a decline in the spatial concentration of baby boomers. That is, initial nonuniformities in the spatial distribution of baby boomers have been diminished by subsequent migration, and new concentrations have begun to emerge.

It is interesting to look at the Hoover Index of Concentration to see how the concentration of baby boomers, relative to the remainder of the population, has changed over time. In 1990 the Hoover Index was 5.805, implying that 5.8 percent of the population would have to move to achieve identical spatial distributions of the two groups.

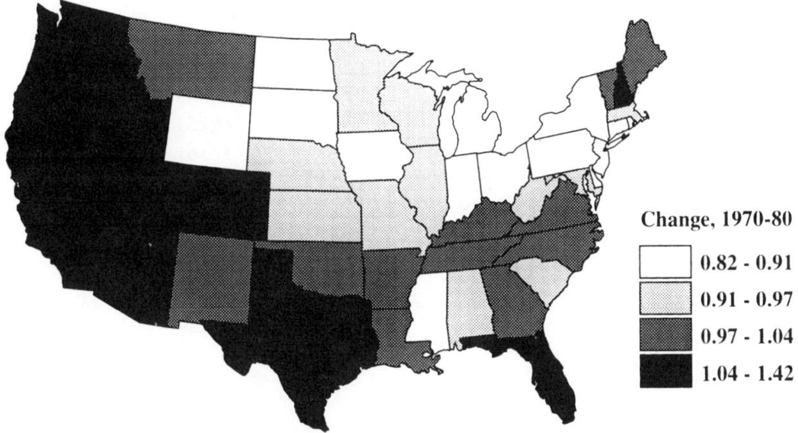

Figure 8.6 Change in Cohort Size, 1970–1980

The effects of the relocations described earlier are summarized, at the scale of the nine census divisions, in Table 8.4. Census divisions witnessing declines in their share of the baby-boom cohort include the Middle Atlantic, the East North Central, the West North Central, and the East South Central. Divisions experiencing gains were the South Atlantic, the Mountain, and the West. The Northeast and the West South Central saw little change.

An important aspect of the cohort's mobility is its level and pattern of

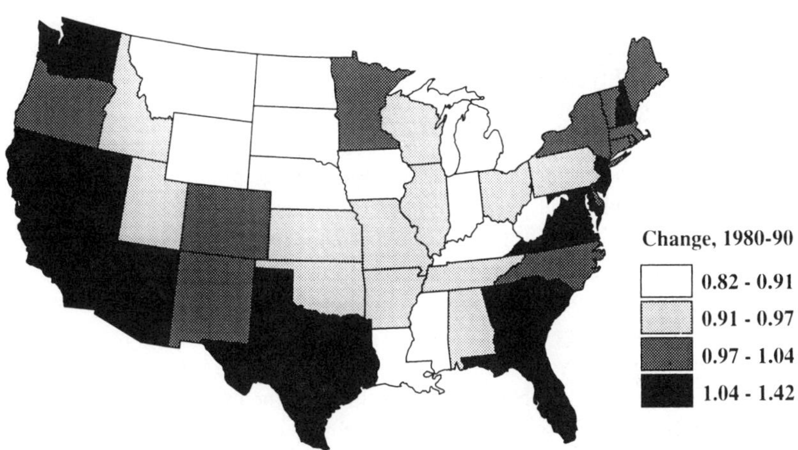

Figure 8.7 Change in Cohort Size, 1980–1990

Table 8.4 Changes in Regional Shares of Baby Boomers, 1960–1990 (%)

Division	1960	1970	1980	1990
Northeast	0.055	0.057	0.054	0.054
Middle Atlantic	0.173	0.171	0.154	0.149
South Atlantic	0.150	0.153	0.161	0.175
East South Central	0.072	0.065	0.064	0.058
West South Central	0.100	0.098	0.107	0.107
East North Central	0.205	0.201	0.184	0.165
West North Central	0.086	0.081	0.075	0.068
Mountain	0.043	0.044	0.053	0.055
West	0.117	0.131	0.148	0.168

mobility relative to other cohorts. By building on the work of Richard Easterlin on the effects of cohort size on various aspects of society, Rogerson (1987) noted that large cohorts of young adults (such as the baby boom) tend to move at relatively low rates. Rogerson provided evidence of the baby-boom cohort's relatively low rates of mobility as the cohort passed through its young adult years in the 1970s. There was also a "delayed mobility" effect, characterized by a later peak in the curve depicting mobility rates by age, during the early 1980s. Plane (1992) noted that such large cohorts have migration patterns characterized by relatively high geographic efficiency (where the net exchange between, for example, states is high relative to the volume of movement). These relationships among cohort size, mobility rates, and migration patterns are summarized and illustrated for the baby-boom cohort by Plane and Rogerson (1991).

Future Mobility of the Cohort

Figure 8.8 summarizes the location of the baby-boom cohort on stylized schedules of fertility, mortality, and mobility. Along with the geographic pattern of population redistribution, the locations on these schedules have had, and will continue to have, an important effect on society. In addition to aging out of their childbearing years and into middle age, baby boomers are also entering age groups traditionally characterized by lower mobility.

How much mobility will the cohort experience in the future? Wilber (1963) describes how life tables concepts can be applied to mobility rate schedules to derive the expected number of moves remaining for individuals of a given age. The use of national age-specific mobility rates, together with the number of baby boomers currently alive at various ages (from Table 8.1), reveals that the cohort has completed approximately two-thirds of the moves individual members will make during the course of their lifetimes. Given a mean of 12 lifetime moves per individual, this implies that approximately $1/3 \times 12 \times 75$ million $= 300$ million residential relocations remain to be made.

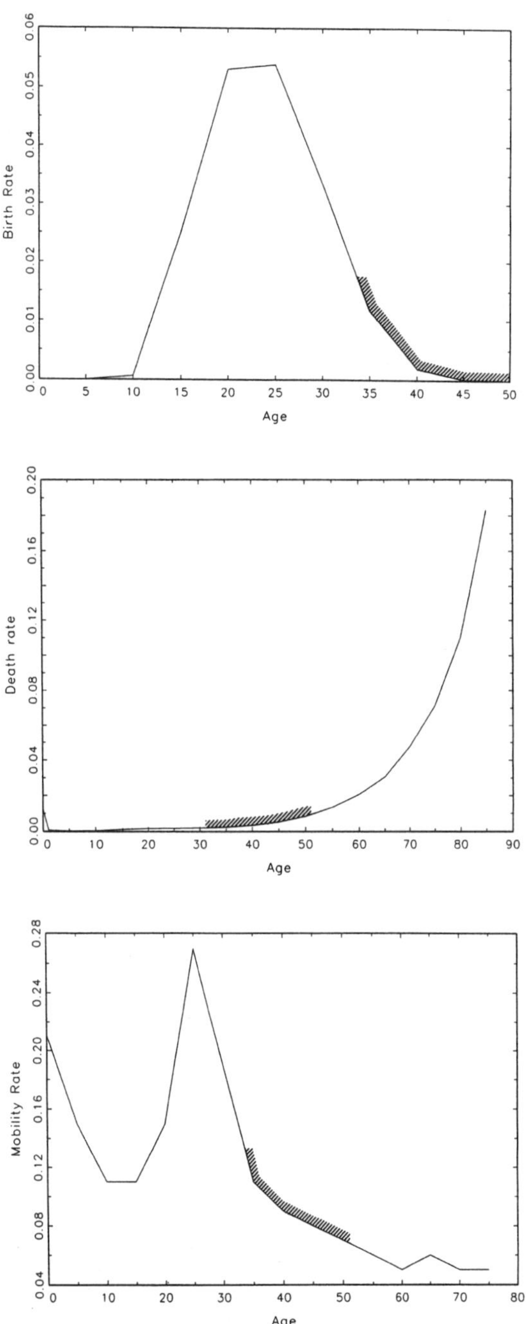

Figure 8.8 Location of the Baby-Boom Cohort on Age Schedules of Fertility, Mortality, and Migration, 1997

Baby-Boom Echo

Figure 8.9 depicts the number of children born to baby-boom members, by year of birth. The figure reveals that the echo reached its peak with births in 1982 and that as of 1988[3] the formation of the echo cohort was still clearly under way. The portion of the curve for subsequent years reflects births that would occur to baby boomers should the age-specific fertility rates prevailing in 1988 continue to hold. The age-specific rates are likely to change but not so drastically that they would dramatically affect the general shape of Figure 8.9. The figure shows that births to baby boomers are dropping off substantially. Through 1988, 61.6 million echo babies had been born. Extrapolating to 2009, when the youngest boomers will end their childbearing, the completed echo cohort will contain about 77.5 million people, which is just slightly larger than the size of the baby boom itself.

Figure 8.10 is the mirror image of the portion of Figure 8.9 between 1960 and 1993, and it reveals the age distribution of the offspring of baby boomers in 1993. The age distribution of echo cohort members grows steadily until reaching its peak at age 12 and then declines just as steadily until about age 22, after which the drop becomes more precipitous.

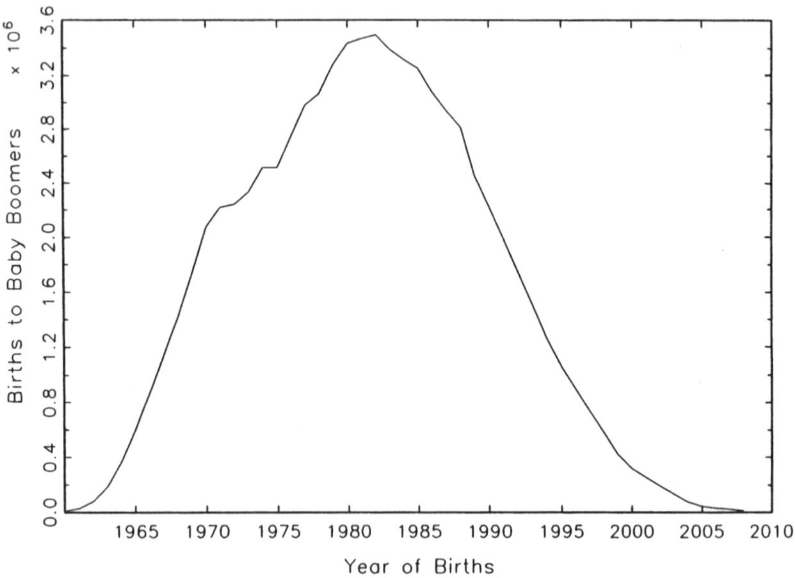

Figure 8.9 Births to Baby Boomers, by Year of Birth.

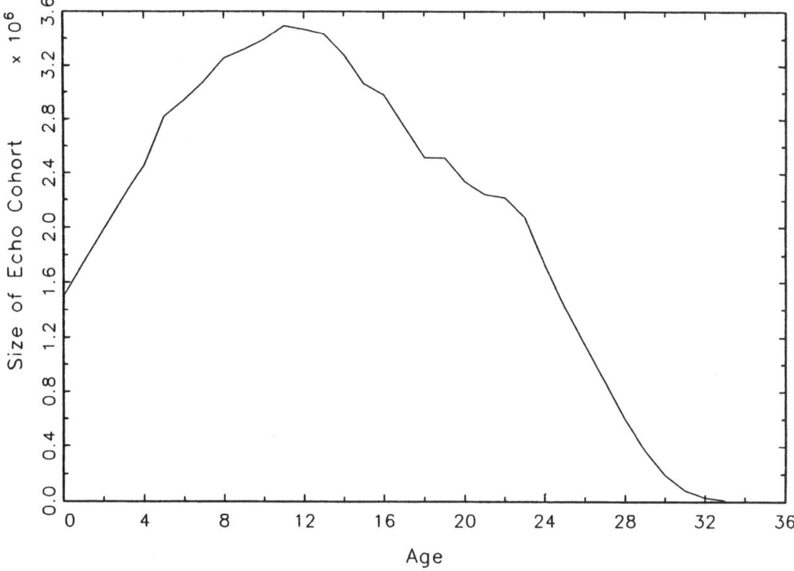

Figure 8.10 Age Distribution of Echo Cohort, 1993.

Implications and Summary

The migration behavior of members of the baby-boom cohort has important consequences for regional economies and in other arenas as well. When coupled with the migration behaviors of both the parents and the children of baby boomers, there are significant consequences for the spatial separation of family members. Although there is a common perception of parents as spatially separated from their adult children by vast distances (see, e.g., Climo 1992), Rogerson, Weng, and Lin (1993) used data from the National Survey of Families and Households to show that the median distance to parents for adults who have left home is only about 25 miles. The misperception originates in part from the people doing the perceiving—usually college-educated thinkers about social and demographic trends. This group is more likely to be spatially distant from parents; Rogerson, Weng, and Lin (1993) found that college-educated adults had a median separation distance of close to 100 miles, whereas those without college educations had a separation distance of only 15 miles.

Thus, despite high annual mobility rates, the majority of baby boomers do not live more than about a half-hour's drive from their parents, because the majority of residential moves are short-distance moves. Rogerson (1990) found that the median distance of residential moves is well under 10 miles and is perhaps no more than 5 to 6 miles. Despite common images of children growing up and leaving home for the other side of the country, most moves are made over short distances, and children in general do not stray far from the nest.

Because baby boomers often live within a short distance of their parents, intergenerational interaction is often not adversely affected. Grandparents can look after grandchildren while baby boomers are at work, and baby boomers can look after the health care and other needs of their parents. But there are interesting subtleties. For example, first-born, college-educated baby boomers live, on average, farther away from their parents than other siblings. Thus younger siblings with less education and income are often left with the caretaking responsibilities associated with aging parents. There are many baby boomers to look after their parents (since their parents had so many children), but there will be relatively fewer echo cohort members to care for their aging baby-boomer parents when the time comes.

Interesting subtleties are also associated with the timing of intergenerational interactions. Although there have been widespread reports about the burdens of the sandwich generation—baby boomers strapped with the simultaneous care of children and parents—the reality is more one of a cohort experiencing an expanded period of caregiving. That is, many baby boomers will begin taking care of their parents after their children have left home and not while their children are still at home. Recall that in 1997 the modal age for mothers of baby boomers is about 67, while the modal age of their children was about 15. The bulk of the caretaking of baby boomers' parents is yet to come, and when that peak does occur many of the boomer cohort's children will have left home.

A true sandwich generation is more likely to emerge when baby boomers retire. Because baby boomers delayed their childbearing it is possible, especially if their children delay marriage and childbearing, that members of the echo cohort will find themselves caught in the middle of the simultaneous caregiving demands characteristic of a sandwich generation.

Other intergenerational effects are brought about by an aging baby-boom population in relatively close geographic contact with parents and children, and many of these effects have impacts for markets in the private sector. Many baby boomers are near the period in their lives where they will have a child old enough to stay at home and watch the younger children if they want to go out at night. Consequently, with the luxury of built-in babysitting (even if parents are in failing health, not geographically proximate, or simply not inclined), we might anticipate a rise in the number of boomers going out to restaurants, movies, and similar activities.

In this chapter, I have examined many of the basic demographic and geographic processes that have guided the evolution of the baby-boom cohort. Much of what has been uncovered in this exercise reinforces what we already knew. In addition, by looking at the cohort from a somewhat different perspective, it has been possible to emphasize important aspects of changes about to take place and to suggest new hypotheses regarding the future of this generation and its relation to other generations.

Notes

This chapter has its origins in work done while I was a Fellow at the Center for Advanced Study in the Behavioral Sciences. I am grateful for the financial support provided by National Science Foundation Grant SES-9022192 to the center and for helpful comments from Kavita Pandit.

1. Because of the difficulties associated with cohort tables and rates, the table is based on period survival rates. The 1970 survival rates were used until 1996, and 1990 survival rates were used for projecting beyond the present. Should mortality rates decline in the future, the numbers of survivors will be higher than the figures in the table. Survival rates for 1970 were used until 1996 because mortality rates are higher during the first year of life than during the young adult years; the use of 1980 or 1990 rates would have underestimated the infant mortality of baby boomers. Rates for 1960 could have been used, but they would have overestimated mortality both during the young adult years and for infants born after 1960. The 1970 rates were therefore used as a compromise. Rates from a slightly earlier or later period would not likely have changed the general picture that emerges.

2. The use of 1990 survival rates results in estimates that are too high of the number of parents since slightly higher mortality rates prevailed during the period between the baby boom and 1993. Survival rates could have been produced by adopting a cohort approach (e.g., using the mortality rates of 17-year-olds in 1946, 18-year-olds in 1947, 19-year-olds in 1948, and so on, to estimate the remaining number of women aged 64 in 1993). It is common, however, to simply use a period definition of mortality to avoid the significant extra burden associated with using separate life tables for each year.

3. The year 1988 is the most recent year for which birth data broken down by age of mother were available from the National Center for Health Statistics when this chapter was written.

References

Byerly, Greg, and Richard E. Rubin. 1985. *The Baby Boom: A Selective Annotated Bibliography*. Lexington, Mass.: D.C. Heath.

Clark, Rebecca, and Douglas Wolf. 1992. Proximity of Children and Elderly Migration. In Andrei Rogers (ed.), *Elderly Migration and Population Redistribution*. London: Belhaven.

Climo, Jacob. 1992. *Distant Parents*. New Brunswick, N.J.: Rutgers University Press.

Jones, Landon Y. 1980. *Great Expectations: America and the Baby Boom Generation*. New York: Conrad, McGann, and Geoghegan.

Lin, Ge, and Peter Rogerson. 1995. "Elderly Parents and the Geographic Availability of Their Adult Children." *Research on Aging* 17: 303–331.

Litwak, Eugene, and Charles F. Longino Jr. 1987. "Migration Patterns among the Elderly: A Developmental Perspective." *Gerontologist* 27: 266–272.

Plane, David. 1992. "Age Composition Change and the Geographical Dynamics of Interregional Migration in the U.S." *Annals of the Association of American Geographers* 82: 283–299.

Plane, David, and Peter Rogerson. 1991. "Tracking the Baby Boom, Baby Bust, and Baby Boom Echo: Implications of Shifting Age Composition for U.S. Mobility and Migration." *Professional Geographer* 43: 416–430.

Rindfuss, Ronald R., and James A. Sweet. 1977. *Postwar Fertility Trends and Differentials in the United States*. New York: Academic.

Rogerson, Peter. 1987. "Changes in U.S. National Mobility Levels." *Professional Geographer* 39: 344–351.

———. 1990. "Buffon's Needle and the Estimation of Migration Distances." *Mathematical Population Studies* 2: 229–238.

Rogerson, Peter, Richard Weng, and Ge Lin. 1993. "The Spatial Separation of Parents and Their Adult Children." *Annals of the Association of American Geographers* 83: 656–671.

Social Security Administration. 1983. *Life Tables for the United States, 1900–2050.* Washington, D.C.: U.S. Department of Health and Human Services.

Warnes, Anthony, D. Howe, and L. Took. 1985. "Intimacy at a Distance under the Microscope." In Alan Butler (ed.), *Ageing: Recent Advances and Creative Responses.* Kent: Croom Helm.

Wilber, George W. 1963. "Migration Expectancy in the United States." *Journal of the American Statistical Association* 58: 444–453.

9

Impacts of Immigrant Fertility on Population Size and Composition

Brigitte Waldorf

Geographers and regional scientists have long recognized the importance of immigration in inducing population change. Direct demographic impacts include not only an increase in population size but, because of the selectivity of immigration, also a change in population composition—namely, a shift in age structure toward a younger mean age of the population and a potentially drastic change in the ethnic and racial composition of the population. Moreover, even if all immigrants were eventually to return to their countries of origin, the number of years spent in the destination country is substantial, thereby strongly affecting the geographic, demographic, social, economic, and political profiles of the host societies.[1]

By and large, however, geographers have ignored the indirect impacts of immigration on population growth—namely, the issue of immigrant fertility. Several aspects are important to understand the impact of immigrant fertility on population change. First, because of the selectivity of immigration, the immigrant population tends to include a disproportionate number of women in their reproductive years. Second, immigrants frequently come from countries with higher fertility than the fertility patterns prevailing in the host society. Third, the immigration experience influences women to adjust their fertility behavior. Thus, if immigrants have substantially higher fertility than the native born and if that higher level persists over an extended time, immigrant fertility will exacerbate the direct impacts of immigration by contributing to an increase in population size, a rejuvenation of the population, and a strengthening of the ethnic and racial diversity of the population. The issue gains added significance as the children of immigrants, the "second generation," often face special problems of assimilation that become evident in education and the labor force (Bürkner 1997; Jensen and Chitose 1994; Fernández-Kelly and Schauffler 1994).

The extent of the indirect, fertility-induced impacts of immigration on population size and composition depends on the gap between the fertility levels of immigrants and of native borns, as well as the persistence of that gap. The literature (Coleman 1995, 1996; De Vita 1996) suggests that immigrant women adjust their fertility levels upon arrival in the destination country, thereby narrowing the gap and lessening the indirect demographic impacts of immigration.

The purposes of this study, therefore, are to investigate adjustments in fertility behavior in response to international migration and to estimate the resulting aggregate population changes. The research focuses on types, speed, and extent of fertility decline among immigrant women subsequent to their relocations across international borders and the resulting aggregate demographic changes. As such, this study significantly advances our understanding by linking international migration and fertility behaviors and by linking insights gained from the microlevel of individual behavioral choices with the aggregate macrolevel outcomes in the population.

Specifically, this chapter provides empirical evidence of immigrants' fertility adjustments, using examples from the United States and Germany; conceptualizes and formalizes the impact of fertility decline on immigrant population size and composition; and simulates the impact of fertility decline under three scenarios. The first assumes no fertility decline subsequent to migration. The second scenario portrays the so-called disruption hypothesis whereby immigrant women lower their fertility immediately following their international move and then return to their initial fertility levels. The third scenario replicates the conditions of the exposure hypothesis, which states that as immigrant women extend their stay abroad, their fertility levels decline and adjust to the low fertility levels of the host societies.

The chapter is organized in five sections. The next section provides some empirical description of fertility levels and adjustments of immigrant women. The section that follows conceptualizes fertility adjustments at the microlevel and the aggregate impact of those adjustments on population change. The Simulations section provides the simulation scenarios, including the mathematical foundations and simulation results. The final section concludes with a summary and future research directions.

Immigrant Fertility in the United States and Germany

During the 1980s and 1990s many Western countries saw a major influx of immigrants. For example, the foreign-born population residing in the United States has grown substantially during recent decades (see chapter 11 in this volume), and in the early 1990s the United States granted immigrant status to approximately 800,000 persons annually (Martin and Widgren 1996). Among the immigrant population in the United States, the sex ratio is balanced on average. Of the 2.17 million immigrants admitted to the United States between 1990 and 1992, 52.8 percent were women (Zlotnik 1995), with variations according to country of origin. For example, women are underrepresented in immigration flows from sub-Saharan Africa but overrepresented among immigrants from Latin America during that time period (Zlotnik 1995).

Most immigrant women are in their reproductive stage; thus they contribute to the natural population increase in the United States. For example, in 1994 foreign-born women made up only 9 percent of women in the United States, yet they had a substantially higher fertility rate than native-born women (De Vita 1996). Foreign-born women had a fertility rate of 93 births per 1,000 women; the equivalent figure for native-born women was only 62 births per 1,000 women. Consequently, 15 percent of babies were born to foreign women.

Not all immigrant women in the United States have higher fertility levels (Bianchi and Spain 1996; Bean and Frisbie 1978). Women from Latin America, however—constituting the largest immigrant group in the 1990s—have traditionally had some of the highest fertility levels. For example, the total fertility rate (TFR) of Hispanic women amounted to 2.7 in 1992 and thus was well above the replacement.[2] In comparison, the TFR of white non-Hispanic women in the United States in 1992 was only 1.9 (O'Hare 1992). Because of the large influx of immigrants from Latin America and their high fertility level, Hispanics are expected to become the largest minority group in the United States (O'Hare 1992).

In Germany immigrant fertility impacts are likely to be even more pronounced than in the United States. The influx of immigrants is proportionately greater, with Germany receiving over 4 million immigrants (*Übersiedler, Aussiedler,*[3] asylum seekers, and other foreigners) between 1988 and 1992 alone (Gieseck, Heilemann, and von Loeffelholz 1995). Moreover, the fertility of German women has reached a very low level. In fact, Germany has been one of the first countries to reach below replacement fertility and sustain it for a long period. The number of births has been, with the exception of a few minor oscillations, steadily declining since 1966. The year 1971 was the last year in which births outnumbered deaths. The resulting population decline in Germany would have been even more pronounced had it not been for the large number of babies born to the foreign population and the low overall mortality of that population, which is a result of its young age structure.[4]

Foreigners, especially those who originated from the southern and southeastern European periphery, have emigrated in large numbers to Germany since the 1960s. At the beginning, most immigrants were male workers who had left their families behind. Since the 1970s, in part as a result of policy changes in Germany, family reunification increased the number of foreign-born women, which, in combination with initially higher fertility levels, increased the number of children born in Germany.

The contribution of foreign babies[5] to Germany's overall population growth cannot be underestimated. For example, whereas in 1960 only 1.2 percent of babies born in Germany were foreign babies, that percentage increased to a maximum of 17.3 percent in 1974. Since then, the percentage of foreign babies has declined somewhat, although it remains high within certain regions, particularly in urban areas. For example, in 1986 foreign babies accounted for 20.7 percent of babies born in (West) Berlin and 15.7 percent of babies born in the city of Hamburg (Statistisches Bundesamt 1986).

Although the absolute numbers of foreign children and their proportions of the total number of children in Germany have important economic and social implications, a more detailed understanding of immigrant fertility in Germany also requires an analysis of aggregate fertility measures for immigrants of different nationalities compared with the fertility trends of (West) German women. The time period between 1975 and 1986 provides a good example of fertility adjustments among immigrant women to Germany (Figure 9.1). During that period Germans had already reached a very low level of fertility, and the TFRs show barely any temporal variation. In contrast, for all foreign nationalities Figure 9.1 displays a rapid decline in TFRs over this time period, although there are important differences across nationalities.

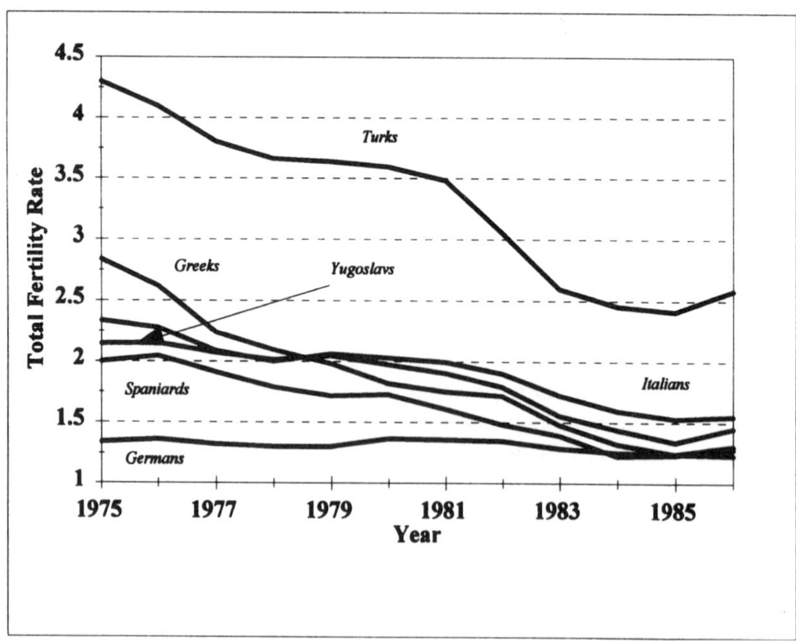

Figure 9.1 Fertility Decline of Foreign Women in Germany

First, Turkish women in Germany have had the highest fertility of all immigrants, although it is substantially lower than the fertility level of women living in Turkey. For example, in 1983 the TFR of Turkish women in Germany was lower than the 1996 TFR in Turkey.[6] Second, compared with all other immigrants, Greek women in Germany experienced the most rapid decline in fertility over the 1975–1986 time period. By 1986 Greek immigrants in Germany had reached the lowest fertility level of all immigrants, even lower than that of German women. Third, Italian women living in Germany have exhibited higher fertility levels than those observed in their home country, and the temporal decline has been moderate. These trends are indicative of a selection effect whereby immigration is more likely to occur among women prone to have higher fertility. This selection effect may stem from the disproportionate number of immigrants from southern Italy, where fertility has traditionally been substantially higher than in the northern, more industrialized, and urban regions of Italy (Coleman 1996). Fourth, Spanish and Yugoslavian women had lower fertility levels than other immigrants in 1975. Consequently, it is not surprising that their fertility decline has not been very pronounced, although their TFR in 1985 also reached the low level of the German fertility rate.

When interpreting this fertility decline among immigrant women in Germany, it should be emphasized that the decline must be attributed in part to the simultaneous decline of the TFR in the respective origin countries. Especially for Turkish women in Germany, however, the decline is much more drastic than could be expected from the fertility decline of Turkish women living in Turkey.

Conceptualization

These examples of immigrant fertility in two developed countries call for a more systematic conceptualization of immigrant women's fertility, its adjustment over time, and the aggregate outcome regarding population size and composition. In this section I introduce conceptual arguments at the microlevel of immigrants' fertility behavior, proceed to the macrolevel aggregate outcomes of immigration and immigrant fertility, and finally link the micro- and macrolevel perspectives.

Microlevel

At the microlevel the migration–fertility link has been examined in the contexts of rural-to-urban migration (e.g., Ritchey 1973; Goldstein 1984; Goldstein and Goldstein 1981; Lee 1992, 1993; Brockerhoff 1994; White, Moreno, and Guo 1995) and international migration (e.g., Friedlander, Eisenbach, and Goldscheider 1980; Ford 1990; Stephen and Bean 1992; Kahn 1994). In both cases the literature puts forward three hypotheses addressing this link: the disruption hypothesis, the selectivity hypothesis, and the adaptation or exposure hypothesis (Figure 9.2).

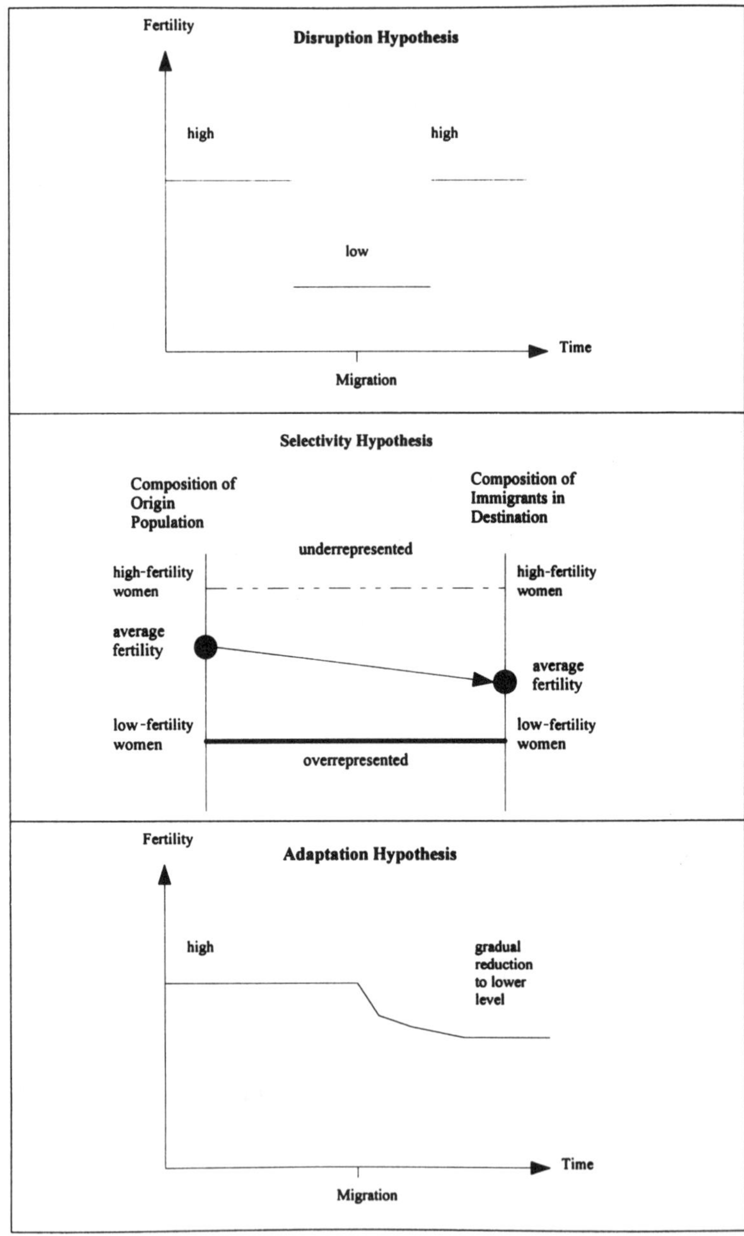

Figure 9.2 Immigration-Induced Fertility Changes

The disruption hypothesis views a move across international borders as a "disorder in the life course" (Rindfuss, Swicegood, and Rosenfeld 1987) that can substantially affect a woman's transition into motherhood, as well as her completed fertility. If an international move disrupts a woman's fertility history, she will have fewer children than expected during the time interval preceding and following the move. Empirical evidence for the validity of the disruption hypothesis is, for example, provided in the analyses of Bean and colleagues (1984), Bean and Stephen (1986), and Stephen and Bean (1992). These studies of women of Mexican origin living in the United States show that disruption effects were particularly strong among young age groups. In their 1987 study they show that the short-term effects of disruption occur near the time of the actual immigration. The long-term effects are manifested in the cumulative fertility, which indicates that Mexican-origin women in the United States never fully recoup their lost fertility.

The selectivity hypothesis states that immigration selects women disposed toward lower fertility. Whereas it is commonly accepted that migration at all spatial levels is a selective process, it is not clear whether it is selective with regard to attributes that significantly influence fertility behavior. Consequently, it is not surprising that the empirical evidence with regard to the selectivity hypothesis is somewhat mixed.

For example, Bray (1984) shows that international migrants from the Dominican Republic are more likely to be composed of the urban middle class than of the rural poor. Thus, since fertility levels vary by socioeconomic status and urban–rural origins, this selectivity in international migration is likely to create differences in fertility levels of immigrants compared with women who do not migrate. In contrast, in her analysis of Puerto Rican migrants to the United States, Ortiz (1986) shows Puerto Rican migrants do not have higher education levels than the Puerto Rican population at large, thereby not constituting a select elite subpopulation. Similarly, Bean and colleagues (1984) argue that the observed fertility patterns among Mexican-origin women are more consistent with the disruption hypothesis than with the effects of selectivity.

The adaptation or exposure hypothesis states that immigrants' fertility behaviors change in response to new economic and social conditions in the destination country, such as rising costs of child rearing, lack of a supporting family network, and increased labor force participation of women. Friedlander and colleagues (1980) analyzed 800 Asian and African Jewish immigrant women in urban areas of Israel. They found that both groups reduced fertility in response to exposure to Israeli society, and that the mechanisms of fertility reduction depended on marital status at the time of immigration and education levels. Women who were married at the time of immigration and less-educated women tended to reduce fertility through stopping (i.e., limiting family size), whereas immigrant women who married after immigration and women with higher levels of education reduced fertility through stopping and spacing (i.e., extending the length of birth intervals). Interestingly, Friedlander and colleagues (1980) cannot show any variation in this regularity by geographic origin.

The adaptation hypothesis is also supported in a study by Bean and Swicegood (1982), who show that the fertility levels of Mexican American women decrease with length of exposure to the United States and rising socioeconomic status. In contrast, Kahn (1994) examines the fertility patterns of immigrants and native borns in the United States during the 1980s. The study reveals a widening fertility gap between natives and immigrants attributed to declining fertility of the native born. The analysis cannot support the hypothesis that immigrants adapt to or assimilate the prevailing fertility behavior in the United States.

Somewhat indistinguishable from adaptation is the concept of fertility decline as an outcome of innovation. The innovation hypothesis (Carlsson 1966) has been formulated in the context of fertility transition and has not been directly applied to immigrants' fertility decline. The hypothesis states that the adoption of fertility control within a population is a manifestation of a new behavior based on new knowledge about fertility control as well as on changes in sociocultural conditions that make fertility control morally acceptable. Although we can assume that immigrant women from all origin countries have at least some knowledge of fertility control,[7] their relocation into the destination country may make fertility control acceptable and accessible for the first time. Empirically and maybe even conceptually, however, it will be difficult to distinguish innovation from adaptation as the cause of immigrant fertility decline.

Macrolevel

At the macrolevel demographers have recently shifted their emphasis toward "open" populations that account for the demographic dynamics resulting from immigration. Immigration counteracts population decline directly through the addition of the immigrants themselves (as long as return migration remains comparatively small) and indirectly if immigrants' fertility levels exceed those of the native population.

Stable population theory has been used to assess the long-run demographic features of an open population experiencing low fertility combined with immigration (Espenshade 1986; Mitra 1990; Feichtinger and Steinmann 1992; Schmertmann 1992). Schmertmann (1992) shows that although fertility increase and immigration are equally effective in preventing population decline, immigration does not halt but may actually foster the aging of low-fertility populations. He shows that increasing fertility is much more effective in rejuvenating the population than is immigration. His numerical examples are based on the crude assumption that immigrants' fertility is either the same or twice as high as that of the native born population. Similarly, the illustrative examples used by Bouvier and colleagues (1997) assume that the fertility levels of immigrants do not differ from those of the native-born population.

Linking Microperspectives and Macroperspectives

So far the literature has not explicitly linked immigrant women's fertility behavior with expected macrolevel demographic changes. Instead, as shown in the previous section, the literature on aggregate changes in population size and composition has included a consideration of immigration yet has only rudimentarily accounted for the underlying behavioral processes of immigrant women's fertility. An understanding of the direct and indirect impacts of immigration on the size and composition of the population in the destination country necessitates a consideration of behavioral fertility processes.

Figure 9.3 portrays the conceptual microlevel and macrolevel linkages among immigration, fertility, and the concomitant demographic change. The linkages are established by explicitly spelling out the relationships between changing demographic rates (behavioral component) and the resulting changes in the population at risk within a demographic-accounting framework. At the microlevel the length of stay abroad (duration) takes on a key role, as it is intimately linked to the disruption and exposure effects outlined earlier. The selectivity effect, especially with respect to attributes affecting fertility (e.g., age, education, and gender composition of the immigrant stream), will affect immi-

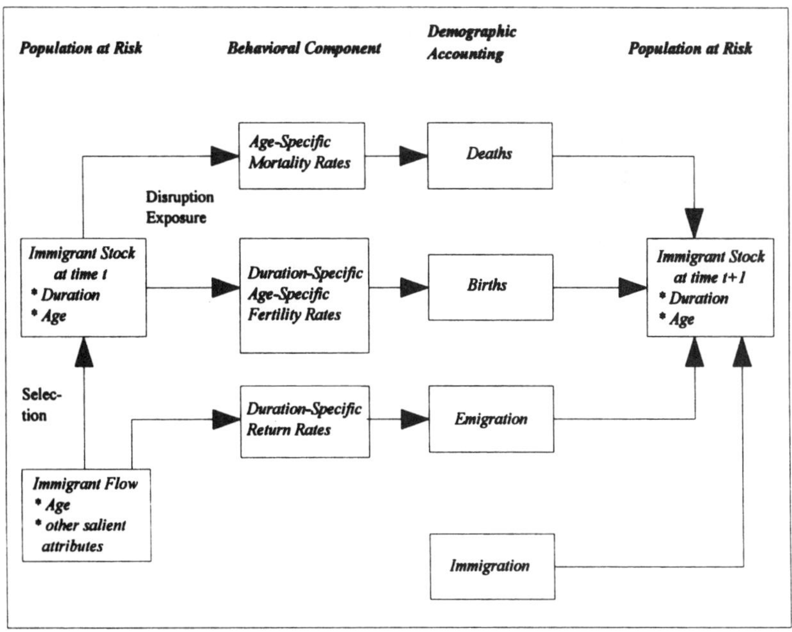

Figure 9.3 Linking Microlevel and Macrolevel Perspectives on Immigrant Fertility

grant fertility rates in the host society. Since the selection effect is primarily an origin-related phenomenon, it will not be addressed in this study.

At the macrolevel fertility-induced population changes must be embedded in the broader context of demographic agents. From a demographic accounting point of view, changes in the size and age composition of the immigrant population occur as a result of fertility, immigration, mortality, and return migration. The fertility component of demographic change (i.e., the number of babies born) depends on age-specific fertility rates, which will change over time (duration) in the presence of disruption and exposure effects. The fertility component also depends on the size and composition of the population at risk (women in their reproductive years), which, in turn, is affected by the composition of immigrant flows, return flows, and age-specific mortality rates. In particular, the size and composition of return flows depend on length-of-stay characteristics of the immigrant population. Thus duration effects will affect not only the population at risk through return migration but also fertility through disruption and exposure effects. This duality of duration effects is at the very core of the mathematical specification of population change that forms the basis of the simulations and is outlined in the next section.

Simulations

A mathematical model is set up in a way that is conducive to simulate the demographic effects of immigrant women's changes in fertility behavior subsequent to their relocation into a foreign country. Toward this end, a number of simplifying conditions are created.

1. The model looks only at immigrant women and baby girls born to immigrant women.
2. The model is based on a temporal scale of one-year units. Choosing one-year units (as opposed to, e.g., five-year increments) is important to tease out the duration effects for both fertility and return migration.
3. Return migration rates vary by length of stay but are independent of age and fertility history.
4. Mortality rates vary by age but are independent of duration.
5. Children are assigned the same length of stay as that of their mothers.
6. All rates are independent of a temporal trend.

The following notation will be used:

x	age
d	length of stay
$P_{xd}(t)$	immigrant population of age x who entered d years ago, at time t

$f_{xd}(t) = f_{xd}$	age-duration-specific fertility rate
$s_x(t) = s_x$	age-specific survival rate
$r_d(t) = r_d$	duration-specific return migration rate

The model expresses the temporal changes in the age-duration cohorts of immigrant women and their baby girls. At time t, the age-duration composition of immigrants can be captured in a matrix of the following form:

	DURATION				
AGE	*0*	*1*	2	3	...
0	$P_{00}(t)$	$P_{01}(t)$	$P_{02}(t)$	$P_{03}(t)$	...
1	$P_{10}(t)$	$P_{11}(t)$	$P_{12}(t)$	$P_{13}(t)$	...
2	$P_{20}(t)$	$P_{21}(t)$	$P_{22}(t)$	$P_{23}(t)$	...
3	$P_{30}(t)$	$P_{31}(t)$	$P_{32}(t)$	$P_{33}(t)$	...

At time $t+1$, the age-duration cohort P_{xd} (t) becomes $P_{x+1,\,d+1}\,(t+1)$, and this transition (along the diagonals) is subject to two attrition processes, return migration and mortality. Thus,

$$P_{x+1,\,d+1}\,(t+1) = P_{xd}\,(t)\,s_x\,(1-r_d) \qquad (1)$$

Equation (1) determines all entries of subsequent age-duration composition except for the first row and the first column. The first row includes babies born to women, disaggregated by duration but not by age of the mother. Thus,

$$P_{0,\,d}\,(t) = \Sigma_x\,P_{xd}\,(t)\,f_{xd} \qquad (2)$$

The first column includes all newcomers during [t,t+1], disaggregated by age and assigned a duration of 0. The number and age composition of newcomers are assumed to be exogenous.[8]

The simulation scenarios are based on additional simplifying assumptions:

7. The number and age composition of newcomers remain constant over time and reflect the typical age composition of immigrant flows—that is, a predominance of migrants in their mid-twenties. There are no migrants younger than 15 and older than 40 years of age.
8. Consistent with observed patterns (Waldorf and Esparza 1991), return migration rates decline with increasing duration of stay.
9. One-year survival rates are age specific and follow typical age-specific survival patterns—increasing survival rates during early childhood, followed by decreasing survival rates.
10. Age-specific fertility rates increase rapidly up to age 25 and decrease at a lower rate thereafter.

The simulations differ with regard to the assumptions governing the duration dependency of fertility rates. The first scenario (SIM1) is the "no-adjustment" scenario in which age-specific fertility rates remain constant with increasing duration of stay. Thus,

SIM1: $f_{xd}(t) = f_x \qquad \forall\, t, x, d$

The second scenario (SIM2) replicates the conditions of a disruption effect. During the first year (i.e. [0,1)) fertility rates drop by 50 percent and during the second year (i.e., [1,2)) fertility rates drop by 30 percent. In all subsequent years fertility rates return to the original (high) levels.

SIM2:

$$f_{xd}(t) = f_x \qquad \forall\, t, x, \text{ and } d > 2$$
$$f_{x0}(t) = 0.5 f_x$$
$$f_{x0}(\mathrm{t}) = 0.7 f_x$$

The third scenario captures the exposure hypothesis, and age-specific fertility rates drop by 10 percent for the first eight years and then remain constant at a level just below replacement.

SIM3: $f_{xd} = 0.9 f_{x(d-1)}$ for $d \leq 8$ and $f_{xd} = f_{x8}$ for $d > 8$

All simulations are run through the beginning of the sixteenth time period—when the babies born abroad during the time interval [0,1) enter their reproductive age. Moreover, each scenario is evaluated under a "high-return" and a "low-return" assumption. The high-return assumption sets return migration probabilities during the first year at 50 percent, during the second year at 30 percent, during the third year at 20 percent, and at 10 percent in all subsequent years. The equivalent figures under the low-return assumption are 30 percent, 20 percent, 10 percent, and 5 percent. The results of the simulations are evaluated with respect to the changing size and age composition of the immigrant population, with a particular emphasis on the number of newborn babies. The simulations do not speak to the relative contribution of immigration and immigrant fertility to overall population change. It is argued that in the short run (15 years) the absolute size more than the proportional size of the immigrant population influences contributions to and demands on the host society, especially if the native-born population grows very little or even declines.

In each simulation, 7,450 immigrant women are entering annually. As shown in Table 9.1, because of variations in fertility rates substantial temporal differences are seen in the size of the immigrant population across the three scenarios. As expected, immigrant population sizes in the first scenario are greater than under either the disruption or exposure hypothesis at all times. Comparing the population sizes of the second and third scenarios shows that a fertility disruption effect leads to a lower population size than does an exposure effect for the first 10 years. Starting at $t = 10$ the situation is reversed, and the predicted population sizes in the disruption scenario are greater than those under the gradual fertility adjustment scenario. Thus the disruption effect is more influential during the early years of a migration system when the proportion of newcom-

Table 9.1 Immigrant Population Sizes

Time		SIM1	SIM2	SIM3	Differences (%)		
					SIM1 vs SIM2	SIM1 vs SIM3	SIM2 vs SIM3
t=5	H	22,737	21,758	22,408	4.31	1.44	−2.99
	L	32,703	31,304	32,123	4.27	1.77	−2.61
t=10	H	33,082	31,651	31,626	4.33	4.43	0.07
	L	56,490	54,091	53,361	4.24	5.54	1.34
t=15	H	40,199	38,502	37,545	4.22	6.60	2.48
	L	77,789	74,616	71,154	4.07	8.53	4.64

Note: H refers to the high-return assumption; L refers to the low-return assumption.

ers affected by the disruption effect is large. As the migration system matures and the composition of immigrants with respect to their length of stay becomes more balanced, the exposure effect of fertility reduction more strongly influences population sizes.

Table 9.1 also shows that the return migration component strongly influences the relative importance of the two fertility adjustment behaviors for the overall growth of the population. The disruption effects are slightly stronger under the high-return assumption than under the low-return assumption. For example, compared with SIM1 the population size at t = 15 under the disruption effect is 4.22 percent lower under the high-return assumption but only 4.07 percent lower under the low-return assumption. In contrast, the low-return assumption exacerbates fertility reduction because of exposure effects. For example, compared with SIM1, the population size in SIM3 at t = 15 is 6.6 percent smaller under the high-return rate but 8.5 percent under the low-return assumption.

Table 9.2 displays the number of children born under each scenario for both the high- and low-return migration assumptions. As expected, given duration-independent age-specific fertility rates (SIM1), the number of babies born each year exceeds the numbers under both the disruption and exposure scenarios, and the differences are fairly substantial. Particularly noteworthy is again that the disruption effect, although assumed to exist only for the first two years, has a "lingering effect" that—compared with the exposure scenario—leads to fewer babies born for the first 9 years when the migration system has not yet matured.

The variations in population sizes are also caused by the return migration behavior of the mothers, who are expected to be joined by their young children. For example, although during the fifth time period only 1,190 babies were born under the disruption scenario and 1,365 under the exposure scenario, many of these newborns will eventually return since they were born to mothers who have not stayed abroad for an extended time and thus are subject to high return

Table 9.2 Number of Newborn Babies

Time Interval		SIM1	SIM2	SIM3	Differences (%) SIM1 vs SIM2	SIM1 vs SIM3	SIM2 vs SIM3
[5,6)	H	1,588	1,190	1,365	25.07	14.04	−14.7
	L	2,243	1,808	1,847	19.39	17.65	−2.15
[10,11)	H	1,972	1,574	1,554	20.18	21.19	1.27
	L	3,134	2,699	2,285	13.88	27.09	18.24
[15,16)	H	2,103	1,704	1,617	18.97	23.58	5.11
	L	3,530	3,094	2,474	12.35	29.9	20.04

Note: H refers to the high-return assumption; L refers to the low-return assumption.

migration rates. The simulations show that lower return rates exacerbate the population size differences between the two fertility adjustment scenarios (SIM2 and SIM3) during the first years.

The age pyramid is broadest under the first scenario of no fertility adjustments and least broad under the conditions of the exposure hypothesis. Particularly insightful are the differences in the cohort size of 14-year-olds since they will be entering their reproductive age and thus will contribute to variations in the numbers of babies born in subsequent time periods.

Table 9.3 shows that the number of girls about to enter their reproductive span is minimized under the disruption hypothesis and maximized under the scenario of duration-independent fertility rates. The differences are fairly substantial and will have a major impact on the growth of the immigrant population by significantly increasing or decreasing the population at risk of giving birth. Similar significant differences are expected once the younger age cohorts (< 14) enter their reproductive span, although the exposure scenario will result in the comparatively smallest number of girls entering the reproductive stage. Interestingly, the return migration rates only influence the absolute number of girls about to enter their reproductive age and do not significantly affect the relative disparities among the three scenarios.

Table 9.3 Cohort Size of 14-Year-Olds at Time $t=15$

	SIM1	SIM2	SIM3	Differences (%) SIM1 vs SIM2	SIM1 vs SIM3	SIM2 vs SIM3
H	101	60	96	40.6	4.96	−60.0
L	339	203	323	40.1	4.72	−59.1

Note: H refers to the high-return assumption; L refers to the low-return assumption.

Conclusion

This study is based on the premise that immigrant fertility is an important agent in inducing demographic changes, especially in developed countries that experienced a drastic decline in fertility, reaching below replacement levels within a very short period. The potential for economic, social, and demographic consequences of persistent below replacement fertility is well known (McNicholl 1986). Among the demographic consequences are population decline, as well as the aging of the population (Coale 1986). Immigration and immigrant fertility can be seen as partially alleviating these problems. At the same time, large numbers of immigrant children force a society to define or redefine its outlook on immigration and potentially create a host of new problems if immigrant children are at risk of being economically and socially marginalized.

In this chapter the contribution of immigrant fertility to the overall growth of the immigrant population is captured conceptually by linking behavioral processes of fertility adjustments to the aggregate macrolevel demographic changes. Analytically, the influence of the fertility component is simulated in three scenarios that portray variations in the duration dependency of immigrants' age-specific fertility rates—the no-adjustment scenario, the disruption effect, and the exposure effect. Duration or length of stay abroad takes on a significant role because it affects not only fertility rates but also return migration rates, a second component influencing demographic changes of the immigrant population.

This dual duration effect creates an interesting dynamic, and the simulations help to illuminate the characteristics of that dynamic. First, the no-adjustment scenario yields the largest population size. Second, in the short run the disruption effect is more influential in reducing immigrant population size than the exposure effect. Third, in the medium to long run the exposure effect yields the smallest fertility component and population size. Finally, in an immigration system with low return migration the demographic differences resulting from disruption as opposed to exposure effects are much stronger than in an immigration system characterized by high return migration rates.

The scenarios rely on a variety of simplifying assumptions that should be relaxed in subsequent research. Of particular importance is allowing for variations in return migrations as a function of a woman's fertility history. That is, are women with children more or less likely to return than childless women? Another avenue of expansion refers to the question of whether immigrant flows depend on women's fertility abroad. Having children while residing in a foreign country may be interpreted as a manifestation of expanding the role of immigration from being primarily economically motivated to implementing social networks. This expanded role is likely to significantly influence the number and characteristics of new immigrants entering the country and thus to affect fertility-induced growth of the immigrant stock (Waldorf 1996).

Finally, immigrant fertility-induced demographic consequences are even more pronounced at regional and urban scales. Since immigrants do not distribute evenly in the destination country (see chapters 5, 10, and 11 in this volume), it is expected that immigrant fertility potentially produces pockets of population growth even in countries of below replacement fertility.

Notes

1. Bouvier and colleagues (1997), for example, estimated that 100,000 immigrants aged 15 at the time of entry will spend nearly 5 million person-years even if they all return at retirement age. Using more realistic assumptions concerning immigrants' return migration behavior, this estimate drops to lower figures ranging from 0.5 to 3.0 million person-years (Waldorf 1999).

2. Given low levels of mortality in more developed countries, the replacement fertility level is just below a total fertility rate (TFR) of 2.1. If the TFR remains below the replacement level for an extended time, the population will eventually decline. The total fertility rate is defined as the number of children a woman is expected to have at the end of her reproductive span given the prevailing age-specific fertility rates and given that she survives her childbearing years. Unless otherwise noted, TFRs will always refer to period rather than cohort fertility.

3. *Übersiedler* are former citizens of the German Democratic Republic who settled in the Federal Republic of Germany before unification. *Aussiedler* are ethnic Germans who have left their Eastern European home countries to settle permanently in the Federal Republic of Germany.

4. For example, in 1986 the crude death rate for the foreign population amounted to only 1.7 deaths per 1,000 persons, whereas the equivalent figure for the on average much older German population was more than seven times higher (12.3 per 1,000).

5. Prior to 1975, children born in Germany did not receive German citizenship under one of the following conditions: (1) both parents were foreigners, (2) the father was a foreigner but the mother was German, (3) the mother was unmarried and had a foreign nationality. In 1975 the second condition was dropped, so a child born to a German mother and a father of foreign nationality also receives German citizenship. In the remainder of this chapter I refer to babies who do not receive German citizenship as "foreign babies" or "foreign children."

6. The TFR of Turkish women in Germany reached 2.6 in 1983. The TFR of Turkish women in Turkey was 2.7 in 1996.

7. The 1976 World Fertility Survey indicates that women in general have knowledge of and a positive attitude toward fertility control. Yet they differ with respect to the practice of fertility control.

8. This is a simplifying assumption since the size and composition of the immigrant inflow have been shown to depend on the size and composition of the immigrant stock (i.e., $P_{xd}(t)$) (see, e.g., Waldorf 1996).

References

Bean, Frank D., Ruth M. Cullen, Elizabeth H. Stephen, and C. Gray Swicegood. 1984. "Generational Differences in Fertility among Mexican Americans: Implications for Assessing the Effects of Immigration." *Social Science Quarterly* 65: 573–582.

Bean, Frank D., and W. Parker Frisbie. 1978. *The Demography of Ethnic and Racial Groups*. New York: Academic.

Bean, Frank D., and Elizabeth H. Stephen. 1986. "The Effect of Disruption on the Fertility of Immigrant Mexican Women in the United States." Paper presented at the 1986 Meetings of the American Sociological Association, New York, August.

Bean, Frank D., and C. Gray Swicegood. 1982. "Generation, Female Education and Mexican American Fertility." *Social Science Quarterly* 63: 131–144.

Bianchi, Suzanne M., and Daphne Spain. 1996. "Women, Work, and Family in America." *Population Bulletin* 52, 3. Washington, D.C.: Population Reference Bureau.

Bouvier, Leon, Dudley J. Poston, and Nanbin B. Zhai. 1997. "Population Growth Impacts of Zero Net International Migration." *International Migration Review* 31: 294–311.

Bray, David. 1984. "Economic Development: The Middle Class and International Migration in the Dominican Republic." *International Migration Review* 18: 217–236.

Brockerhoff, Martin. 1994. "Impact of Migration on Fertility in Sub-Saharan Africa." *Social Biology* 41: 19–44.

Bürkner, Hans-Joachim. 1997. "Jugendliche Arbeitsmigranten in Deutschland." *Geographische Rundschau* 49: 423–427.

Carlsson, Gosta. 1966. "The Decline of Fertility: Innovation or Adjustment Process." *Population Studies* 20, 2: 149–174.

Coale, Ansley. 1986. "Demographic Effects of Below-Replacement Fertility and Their Social Implications." *Population and Development Review,* Supplement to Vol. 12: 203–215.

Coleman, David A. 1995. "International Migration: Demographic and Socioeconomic Consequences in the United Kingdom and Europe." *International Migration Review* 29: 155–206.

———. 1996. "New Patterns and Trends in European Fertility: International and Sub-National Comparisons." In David Coleman (ed.), *Europe's Population in the 1990s.* New York: Oxford University Press.

De Vita, Carol J. 1996. "The United States at Mid-Decade." *Population Bulletin* 56, 4. Washington, D.C.: Population Reference Bureau.

Espenshade, Thomas J. 1986. "Population Dynamics with Immigration and Low Fertility." *Population and Development Review,* Supplement to Vol. 12: 248–261.

Feichtinger, Gustav, and Gunter Steinmann. 1992. "Immigration into a Population with Fertility below Replacement Level—The Case of Germany." *Population Studies* 46: 275–284.

Fernández-Kelly, M. Patricia, and Richard Schauffler. 1994. "Divided Fates: Immigrant Children in a Restructured U.S. Economy." *International Migration Review* 28: 662–689.

Ford, Kathleen. 1990. "Duration of Residence in the United States and the Fertility of U.S. Immigrants." *International Migration Review* 24: 34–69.

Friedlander, Dov, Zvi Eisenbach, and Calvin Goldscheider. 1980. "Family Size Limitation and Birth Spacing: The Fertility Transition of African and Asian Immigrants in Israel." *Population and Development Review* 6: 581–593.

Gieseck, Arne, Ullrich Heilemann, and Hans Dietrich von Loeffelholz. 1995. "Economic Implications of Migration into the Federal Republic of Germany, 1988–1992." *International Migration Review* 29: 693–709.

Goldstein, Sidney. 1984. "Interrelations between Migration and Fertility: Their Significance for Urbanization in Malaysia." *Habitat International* 8: 93–103.

Goldstein, Sidney, and Alice Goldstein. 1981. "The Impact of Migration on Fertility: An 'Own Children' Analysis for Thailand." *Population Studies* 35: 265–284.

Jensen, Leif, and Yoshimi Chitose. 1994. "Today's Second Generation: Evidence from the 1990 U.S. Census." *International Migration Review* 28: 714–735.

Kahn, Joan R. 1994. "Immigrant and Native Fertility during the 1980s: Adaptation and Expectation for the Future." *International Migration Review* 28: 501–519.

Lee, Bun Song. 1992. "The Influence of Rural-Urban Migration on Migrant's Fertility Behavior in Cameroon." *International Migration Review* 26: 1416–1447.

———. 1993. "The Influence of Rural-Urban Migration on Migrants' Fertility in Korea, Mexico and Cameroon." *Population Research and Policy Review* 12: 3–26.

Martin, Philip, and Jonas Widgren. 1996. "International Migration: A Global Challenge." *Population Bulletin* 51, 1. Washington, D.C.: Population Reference Bureau.

McNicholl, Geoffrey. 1986. "Economic Growth with Below-Replacement Fertility." *Population and Development Review,* Supplement to Vol. 12: 217–238.

Mitra, S. 1990. "Immigration, below Replacement Fertility, and Long-Term National Population Trends." *Demography* 27: 121–129.

O'Hare, William P. 1992. "America's Minorities—The Demographics of Diversity." *Population Bulletin* 47, 4. Washington, D.C.: Population Reference Bureau.

Ortiz, Vilma. 1986. "Changes in the Characteristics of Puerto Rican Migrants from 1955 to 1980." *International Migration Review* 20: 612–628.

Rindfuss, Ronald R., C. Gray Swicegood, and Rachel A. Rosenfeld. 1987. "Disorder in the Life Course: How Common and Does It Matter?" *American Sociological Review* 52: 785–801.

Ritchey, P. Neal. 1973. "Effects of Marital Status on the Fertility of Rural-Urban and Urban-Rural Migrants." *Rural Sociology* 38: 26–35.

Schmertmann, Carl P. 1992. "Immigrants' Ages and the Structure of Stationary Populations with Below-Replacement Fertility." *Demography* 29: 595–611.

Statistisches Bundesamt. 1986. *Bevölkerung und Erwerbstätigkeit* (Fachserie 1, Reihe 1: Gebiet und Bevölkerung). Stuttgart: W. Kohlhammer Verlag.

Stephen, Elizabeth H., and Frank D. Bean. 1992. "Assimilation, Disruption, and the Fertility of Mexican-Origin Women in the United States." *International Migration Review* 26: 67–88.

Waldorf, Brigitte. 1996. "The Internal Dynamic of International Migration Systems." *Environment and Planning A* 28: 631–650.

———. 1998. "A Three-Dimensional Life Table Approach to Immigrants' Sojourns Abroad." *Papers in Regional Science.*

Waldorf, Brigitte, and Adrian Esparza, 1991. "A Parametric Failure Time Model of International Return Migration." *Papers in Regional Science: The Journal of the Regional Science Association International* 70: 419–438.

White, Michael, Lorenzo Moreno, and Shenyang Guo. 1995. "The Interrelation of Fertility and Geographic Mobility in Peru: A Hazard Model Analysis." *International Migration Review* 29: 492–514.

Zlotnik, Hania. 1995. "The South-to-North Migration of Women." *International Migration Review* 29: 229–254.

10

Internal Migration of Foreign-Born Latinos and Asians: Are They Assimilating Geographically?

William H. Frey and Kao-Lee Liaw

Changes in U.S. immigration laws since 1965, along with economic forces, have led to sharp rises in the numbers of the nation's Latino and Asian populations (Edmonston and Passel 1994; Martin and Midgley 1994). These gains have not been dispersed evenly across the national landscape but rather are confined to a handful of U.S. states and metropolitan areas. In fact, the focused geographic concentration of Latinos and Asians *within* the United States, along with the existing concentration of blacks and the new redistribution of whites arising from high-immigration metropolitan areas, suggests that an increasing "demographic Balkanization" of the U.S. population may be emerging across broad regions of the country (Frey 1995b, 1995c).

The focused growth of the new minority populations is heavily driven by the tendency of new immigrants to locate in familiar port-of-entry areas. Although the gulf does appear to be widening between large, growing multiethnic metropolitan areas on the one hand and predominantly white (or white and black) regions of the country on the other, a scenario of long-term, persisting geographic racial divisions rests on an important assumption. This scenario assumes that these new immigrant minorities will not disperse more widely with increasing exposure to the United States and as they assimilate socioeconomically. Earlier studies suggest that the internal migration patterns of Latinos and Asians are highly channelized, following same-race and ethnic networks and social ties (Bean and Tienda 1987; McHugh 1989; Pedraza and Rumbaut 1996). Specific research on secondary migration among new immigrant minorities, from the

1980 census, suggests that broader dispersal did not occur (Bartel 1989; Bartel and Koch 1991). This and other evidence for legalized aliens from administrative records (Neuman and Tienda 1994) suggests that the overall impact of secondary migration on reducing Latino and Asian concentrations has been small.

The present analysis examines 1990 census migration data to determine whether more recent internal migration patterns of Latinos and Asians portend a dispersion of these groups away from the traditional port-of-entry areas. The chapter addresses the following questions: (1) Are U.S.-born Latinos and Asians more likely to disperse than their foreign-born counterparts? (2) Are the more educated members of these groups more likely to disperse than those with high school education or less? If the dispersal of these groups is associated with their general assimilation, we would anticipate more dispersed redistribution to occur with native-born residents and those with some college or greater education. It would be especially telling if more educated Latinos and Asians were not dispersing in light of trends that show that the labor force quality of recent immigrants, relative to natives, is declining (Borjas 1994).

To evaluate these questions we examine metropolitan- and state-level migration statistics for Latinos and Asians over the 1985–1990 period based on tabulations of the "residence 5 years ago" question in the 1990 census. The analysis results will be presented in three parts. The first two sections present descriptive findings that reveal the extent to which nativity and education attainment are associated with the greater dispersal of Latinos and Asians. The next section presents a multivariate analysis of metropolitan-area determinants to assess the extent to which a metropolitan area's racial composition becomes less important as a "push" or "pull" among native-born and more educated Latino and Asian residents. The final section evaluates the overall distributional impact of recent immigration and internal migration patterns for these groups in the Los Angeles metropolitan region.

The results of our analysis suggest that although *some* dispersal is found among U.S.-born Latinos and Asians, high levels of racial concentration across regions and metropolitan areas are likely to continue because the magnitude of immigration tends to overwhelm the smaller dispersal effects of U.S.-born and longer-term resident members of these groups. This is illustrated by recent changes in population for the Los Angeles metropolitan area in the concluding section.

Internal Migration of Foreign- and U.S.-Born Residents

To what extent are foreign- and U.S.-born residents likely to relocate out of traditional port-of-entry metropolitan areas? And what are the greatest destination metros for each group? These questions will be answered for Latino and Asian populations based on 1985–1990 migration patterns. Relevant data appear in Tables 10.1 and 10.2 and (for states) Figures 10.1 and 10.2.

Table 10.1 Immigration and Internal Migration Components of 1985–1990 Change for Metro Areas with Largest Latino and Asian Populations

		Migration Components			Rates per 100, 1990 Population		
			Net Internal Migration			Net Internal Migration	
	1990 Population	Immigration (from Abroad)	Foreign Born[1]	U.S. Born	Immigration from Abroad[2]	Foreign Born[3]	U.S. Born[4]
Latino							
Los Angeles	4,779,118	520,653	−22,840	−30,810	12.5	−1.0	−1.7
New York	2,774,937	269,141	−79,129	−68,859	11.0	−5.1	−7.6
Miami	1,061,846	144,692	38,570	9,700	14.6	4.8	5.2
San Francisco	970,403	86,222	−4,910	−19,395	10.2	−1.3	−4.1
Chicago	893,422	72,719	−6,331	−10,838	9.4	−1.5	−3.1
Houston	772,295	50,433	−5,736	−1,557	7.5	−1.9	−0.4
San Antonio	620,290	12,548	−1,565	−2,113	2.3	−1.8	−0.5
Dallas	518,917	34,662	1,397	10,874	7.8	0.7	4.3
San Diego	510,781	54,704	7,258	12,453	12.3	3.3	5.6
Asian							
Los Angeles	1,339,048	219,652	29,845	1,959	17.7	3.2	0.6
San Francisco	926,961	137,006	9,230	1,115	16.0	1.5	0.4
New York	871,999	190,512	−11,404	−6,632	23.7	−1.7	−5.1
Honolulu	526,459	26,869	−5,604	−9,994	5.5	−4.4	−2.7
Chicago	256,050	44,823	−9,664	−3,862	19.0	−5.3	−7.2
Washington, D.C.	202,437	43,481	3,660	194	23.3	2.4	0.6
San Diego	198,311	31,274	3,821	2,534	17.1	3.0	4.7
Seattle	164,286	26,817	1,952	2,038	17.7	1.9	4.3

Notes: 1. Foreign born includes Puerto Rico.
2. Per 1990 population aged 5 and above of group.
3. Per 1990 foreign-born population aged 5 and above of group.
4. Per 1990 U.S.-born population aged 5 and above of group.

Table 10.2 Metro Areas with Greatest Gains and Losses, 1985–1990, of Foreign-Born and U.S.-Born Net Internal Migration: Latinos and Asians

Latinos				Asians			
Foreign Born		U.S. Born		Foreign Born		U.S. Born	
A. Greatest Gains from Net Internal Migration 1985–1990							
Miami	38,570	San Diego	12,453	Los Angeles	29,845	Sacramento	4,148
Orlando	12,951	Dallas	10,874	San Francisco	9,230	San Diego	2,534
Tampa	7,522	Orlando	10,750	Sacramento	7,055	Seattle	2,038
San Diego	7,258	Miami	9,700	Boston	4,031	Los Angeles	1,959
Washington, D.C.	7,019	Las Vegas	9,231	San Diego	3,821	Las Vegas	1,602
Las Vegas	6,985	Sacramento	8,470	Washington, D.C.	3,660	Atlanta	1,353
West Palm Beach	5,951	Phoenix	8,017	Atlanta	3,407	Boston	1,333
Atlanta	4,835	Modesto	7,030	Orlando	2,823	San Francisco	1,115
Phoenix	3,110	Tampa	6,241	Modesto	2,128	Orlando	1,019
Modesto	3,042	Seattle	5,743	Fresno	2,095	Modesto	939
B. Greatest Losses from Net Internal Migration 1985–1990							
New York	−79,129	New York	−68,859	New York	−11,404	Honolulu	−9,994
Los Angeles	−22,840	Los Angeles	−30,810	Chicago	−9,664	New York	−6,632
Chicago	−6,331	San Francisco	−19,395	Houston	−6,972	Chicago	−3,862
Houston	−5,736	Chicago	−10,838	Honolulu	−5,604	Houston-Galveston	−2,283
Fresno	−5,055	Brownsville, Texas	−6,938	New Orleans	−3,417	Denver	−939
San Francisco	−4,910	El Paso	−6,663	Oklahoma City	−1,999	New Orleans	−919
Brownsville, Texas	−4,037	McAllen, Texas	−6,591	Denver	−1,995	Cleveland	−548
New Orleans	−3,610	Corpus Christi	−6,267	Salt Lake City	−1,840	Kansas City	−483
McAllen, Texas	−2,834	New Orleans	−2,920	Minn.–St. Paul	−1,319	Oklahoma City	−427
San Antonio	−1,565	San Antonio	−2,113	St. Louis	−1,283	Bakersfield, Calif.	−367

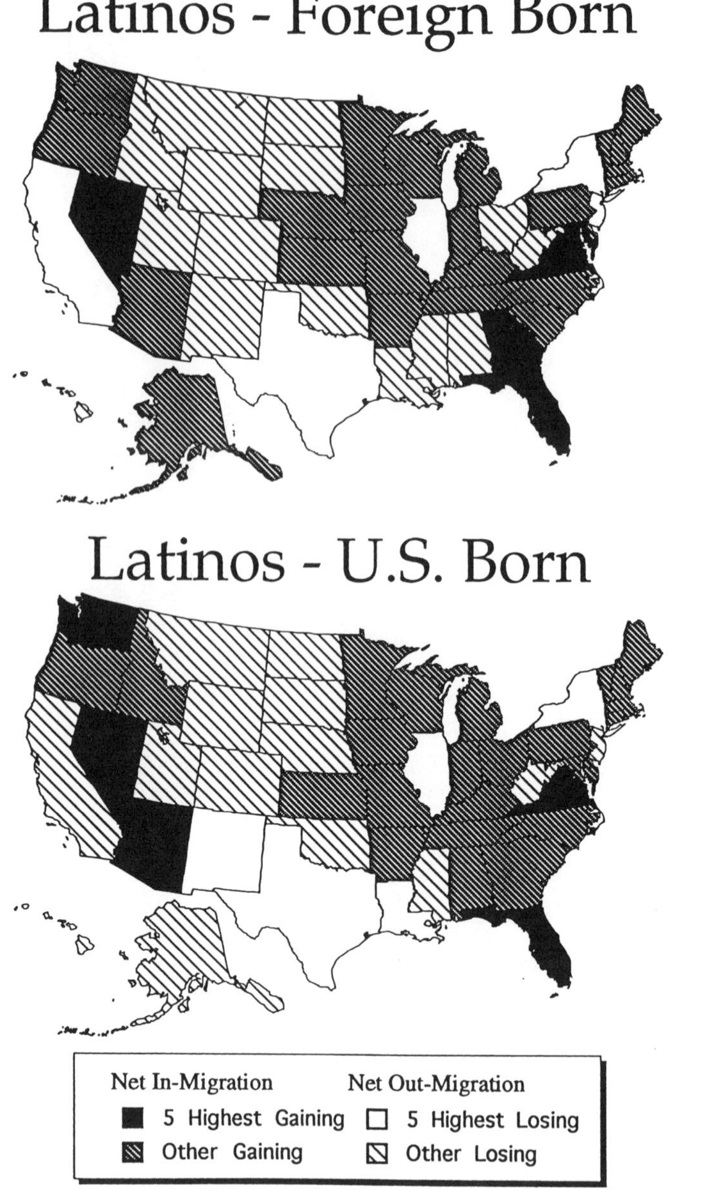

Source: Authors' analysis of special 1990 census migration tabulations.

Figure 10.1 Latino Net Internal Migration for U.S. States, 1985–1990

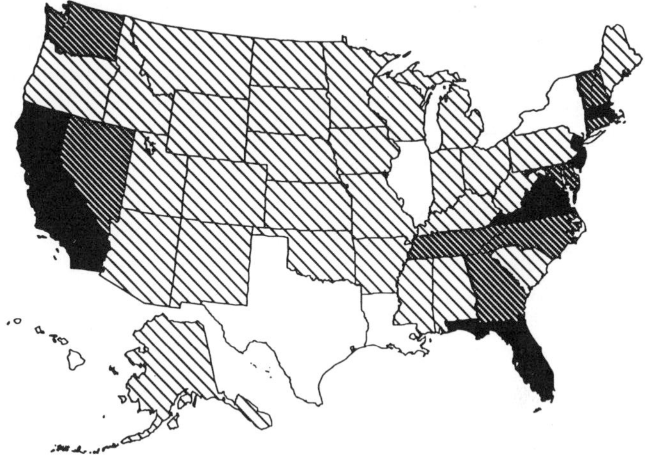

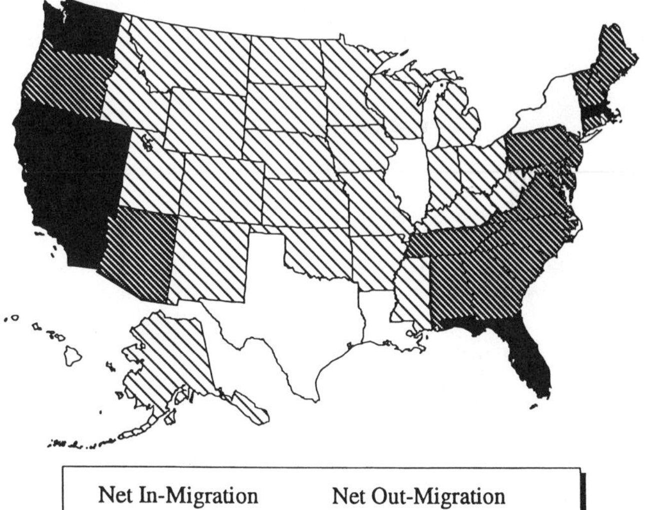

Source: Authors' analysis of special 1990 census migration tabulations.

Figure 10.2 Asian Net Internal Migration for U.S. States, 1985–1990

The 1990 census showed that nine metropolitan areas housed 58 percent of the nation's total Latino population. Listed in Table 10.1 (upper panel), their 1990 Latino populations ranged from 4.8 million for Los Angeles to slightly more than 0.5 million for San Diego. Furthermore, each of these metropolitan areas can be classed as a "high-immigration metropolitan area" in the sense that immigration plays a dominant role in contributing to metropolitan area-wide demographic gains (Frey 1995b). This is clearly the case for Latino populations for these areas, led by Los Angeles where immigrant Latinos over the 1985–1990 period accounted for 12.5 percent of the metropolitan area's 1990 Latino population.

This being the case, to what extent are the internal migration patterns for Latinos in these areas contributing to a dispersal of their members from the high-immigration metro areas? The evidence presented here indicates that some dispersal is occurring in six of these areas. It is most pronounced in the most traditional port-of-entry areas and among U.S.-born Latinos. The latter observation is based on a comparison of rates which shows that the net out-migration of U.S.-born Latinos is greater than for foreign-born Latinos in Los Angeles, New York, San Francisco, and Chicago. Miami, Dallas, and San Diego differ from the general pattern in that they incurred a net *in-migration* of Latino foreign- and U.S.-born residents over the period. Miami has been a traditional magnet for East Coast Latinos, especially Cubans and Puerto Ricans and especially those from New York City. (Note: In this analysis Puerto Ricans who were born in Puerto Rico are considered to be "foreign born.") San Diego during the late 1980s was unique in the sense that it drew large numbers of both immigrants and internal migrants from other parts of the country (Frey 1995a, 1995b). Many in-migrant Latinos may be out-migrants from nearby Los Angeles.

The data in the lower portion of Table 10.1 permit similar analysis for Asians. The eight metropolitan areas shown in the table account for 62 percent of the nation's 1990 Asian population. Except for Honolulu, which houses a substantial native-born Asian population, recent immigration contributed substantially to the Asian populations of these areas. Yet in contrast to Latinos, recent internal migration of Asians in the United States further concentrated them into five of the eight areas shown in the table. This is the case for each of the West Coast metro areas, as well as Washington, D.C. Only New York, Chicago, and Honolulu show a new out-migration of internal Asian migrants. Moreover, foreign-born rather than U.S.-born Asians are contributing most to this concentration in Los Angeles, San Francisco, and Washington, D.C. Certainly, the recent Asian immigration exerts a strong impact on this trend.

Because both Latino and Asian U.S.-born migrants were the most likely to leave (or the least likely to stay) in traditional ports of entry, will they likely differ in their overall migration patterns across U.S. metropolitan areas? To aid in assessing this question, the lists in Table 10.2 show areas with greatest net migration gains and losses separately for foreign-born and U.S.-born Latinos and Asians. Focusing first on Latinos, the port-of-entry metro of Miami clearly dominates as the main net migration destination for foreign-born Latinos, with a net gain of 38,500 over the 1985–1990 period. The remainder of the largest gainers of foreign-born Latinos tend to be metro areas in close proximity to traditional ports of entry (e.g., Orlando, Tampa, and West Palm Beach in proximity to Miami; Phoenix, San Diego, Modesto, and Las Vegas in proximity to Los Angeles and San Francisco). Two areas that do not fit this description are Washington, D.C., and Atlanta, for migration directed to these areas may be more than spillover from high-immigration areas. Rather, it is directed more to opportunities available in these fast-growing labor markets.

Metro areas showing greatest gains for U.S.-born Latinos are not dominated by Miami. They include the metro areas with significant Latino populations, San Diego and Dallas, along with Miami. Again, areas in close proximity to traditional ports of entry are included on this list. Population gains among U.S.-born Latinos are more pervasive than those for the foreign born. Among the 280 metropolitan areas included in this study, 195 showed net gains of U.S.-born Latinos, whereas only 157 gained from migration of the foreign born. Greatest out-migration metros for both groups of Latinos do not differ substantially and include port-of-entry metros—New York, Los Angeles, Chicago, and San Francisco. (The state patterns, displayed in Figure 10.1, show this to be the case as well.)

The greatest net migration gainers for Asians also differ somewhat between foreign-born and U.S.-born Asian residents. Just as foreign-born Latinos gravitated in large numbers to Miami, foreign-born Asians were drawn to Los Angeles. Other areas that rank high in attracting foreign-born Asians are those with significant existing Asian populations (e.g., San Francisco, Boston, San Diego, Washington, D.C.), spillover areas near larger Asian concentrations (e.g., Sacramento, Modesto, Fresno), and areas with fast-growing economies that do not have especially large Asian populations (e.g., Atlanta).

Areas gaining in the U.S.-born Asian population are distinct primarily because the list is not dominated by gains to Los Angeles and San Francisco. Rather, the distribution of U.S.-born migrants is much more dispersed. One hundred and fifty-three metro areas gained U.S.-born internal migrants, compared with only 108 for foreign-born internal migrants. As with Latinos, foreign-born and U.S.-born Asians showed greatest losses for a similar group of metro areas (see Table 10.2). This is also the case with states (see Figure 10.2).

This section has shown that there is some internal migration away from large port-of-entry areas, primarily among Latinos who are U.S. born. Asians, for the most part, have not contributed to further concentration as a result of their internal migration patterns, although this is less the case among the U.S. born. The fact that there is noticeable net out-migration from traditional concentrations of Latinos and that the U.S. born are the least likely Asian residents to concentrate suggests that a gradual spatial assimilation of these groups may be in the offing. The net internal migration numbers (either in or out) observed for Latinos and Asians in the areas considered here, however, are dwarfed by the immigration gains that are likely to continue. Moreover, there is the question of whether the internal out-migration of new immigrant groups represents a response to pulls toward more assimilated residents or pushes resulting from the economic competition among new immigrants to these areas.

Selective Internal Migration by Educational Attainment

The question just raised can be answered in part by the analyses in this section. That is, if the new out-migration of Latinos and some Asians from traditional port-of-entry areas is a positive response to economic opportunities elsewhere, the response should be stronger for the most skilled and educated residents of the two groups (Long 1988). If, on the other hand, new immigrants strongly compete for a limited number of employment opportunities, the out-migration response might be higher for the less skilled, less educated segments of these populations. If the latter is the case, it would be consistent with the recent out-migration of whites from these high-immigration areas (Frey 1995a, 1995b). We address these questions first by looking at the education selectivity associated with net migration of foreign-born and U.S.-born Latinos and Asians from the metropolitan areas introduced earlier. Relevant data are shown in Table 10.3 and Figures 10.3 and 10.4.

Contrary to patterns consistent with a pull migration response, the education selectivity of Latinos—both native born and U.S. born—shows an accentuated net *in-migration* for college graduates. This is consistent with previous analyses of the white population for high-immigration metropolitan areas (Frey 1995b). The interpretation given there is that many of these areas have dual economies in which the best educated whites (and presumably Latinos, Asians, and blacks) will not be in as much direct competition as the predominantly low-skilled immigrants for employment opportunities, housing, and social services (Waldinger 1989; Mollenkopf and Castells 1991). Although this cannot be verified here, the selectivity patterns of Latinos show the greatest out-migration from these areas for persons with less than college education—often high school graduates.

Although Asian internal migration for these areas tends to be positive, college graduates also show accentuated net in-migration. When migration is a net positive flow, upward selectivity on educational attainment is consistent with positive opportunities at these destination areas. Still, there are instances of a net internal out-migration of Asians; the pattern is similar to that for Latinos. This finding suggests that there is a push, perhaps exerted by immigrant competition, and it is consistent with a spillover into nearby metropolitan areas.

Table 10.3 Rates of Net Internal Migration by Educational Attainment, 1985–1990, for Total, Foreign-Born, and U.S.-Born Latinos and Asians

	Foreign Born				U.S. Born			
	Less than High School	High School	Some College	College Graduate	Less than High School	High School	Some College	College Graduate
Latinos								
Los Angeles	−1.2	−1.5	−1.3	−0.1	−1.3	−1.5	−1.8	1.2
New York	−4.7	−5.7	−6.8	−5.0	−5.9	−6.6	−7.4	−4.9
Miami	5.3	5.5	5.0	4.9	3.8	8.2	5.4	5.5
San Francisco	−1.9	−1.7	−2.0	2.6	−5.8	−4.1	−4.1	0.5
Chicago	−1.5	−2.1	−3.3	−2.6	−3.0	−1.1	−2.1	−1.3
Houston	−2.2	−1.9	−4.6	0.7	0.4	0.1	0.3	3.4
San Antonio	−1.2	−4.5	1.5	2.6	−0.4	−0.4	0.0	−0.4
Dallas	−0.5	2.3	2.4	3.2	1.0	4.7	8.5	12.2
San Diego	2.7	4.5	3.8	7.2	3.2	0.9	4.5	4.7
Asians								
Los Angeles	4.4	2.1	2.6	4.0	−1.4	−1.2	−1.6	1.0
San Francisco	1.1	0.4	0.5	3.6	−2.3	0.2	−1.1	2.6
New York	−2.3	−1.7	−2.4	0.1	−5.1	−3.2	−3.1	0.9
Honolulu	−1.5	−2.9	−6.1	−5.4	−1.0	−1.5	−2.6	−2.1
Chicago	−4.8	−5.5	−4.2	−4.7	−9.1	−6.5	−3.1	−2.3
Washington, D.C.	−0.3	0.7	2.1	6.3	−5.3	−0.9	−0.2	11.1
San Diego	0.6	2.2	2.8	4.4	−3.2	2.0	4.5	11.1
Seattle	0.7	2.3	2.7	3.5	5.2	3.1	5.2	4.3

Note: Population aged 25 and above in 1990.

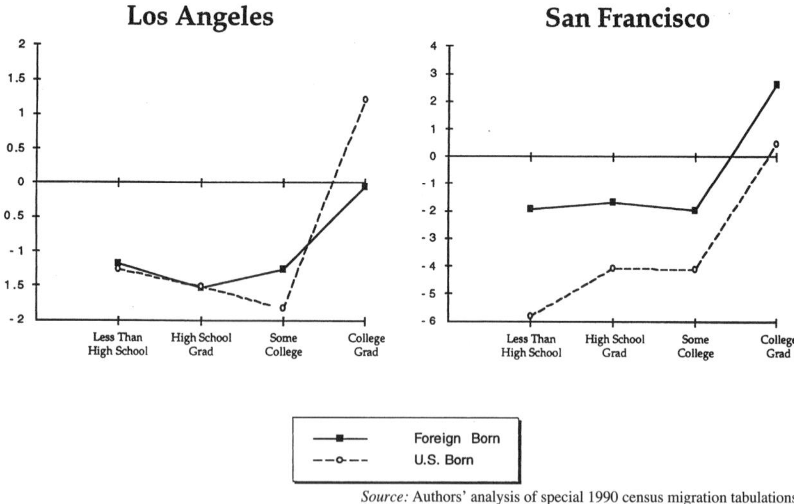

Source: Authors' analysis of special 1990 census migration tabulations.

Figure 10.3 Latino Net Internal Migration by Education, 1985–1990

To address the latter suggestion further, we evaluate separately metropolitan areas that show the greatest gains for both college graduate internal migrants and those with high school education or less. (See Table 10.4 for this comparison of metropolitan areas.) A comparison of the greatest gainers for Latino internal migrants by education and by foreign or U.S. birth reveals a surprising

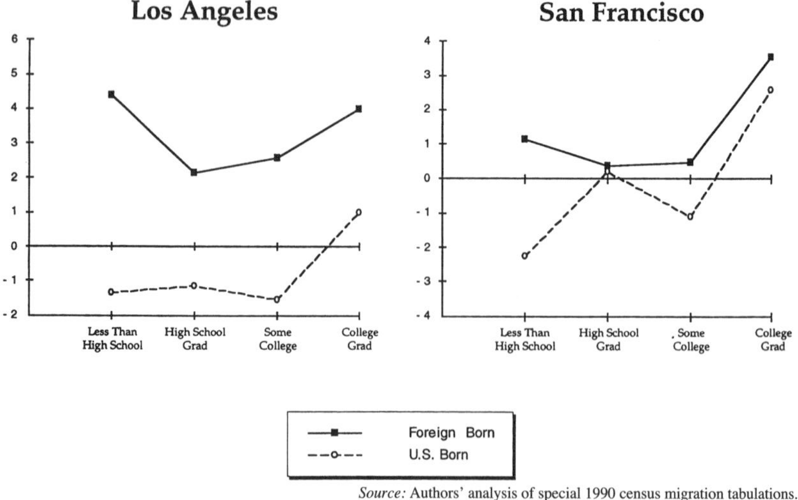

Source: Authors' analysis of special 1990 census migration tabulations.

Figure 10.4 Asian Net Internal Migration by Education, 1985–1990

Table 10.4 Metro Areas with Greatest Net Migration Gains, 1985–1990, for Latinos and Asians by Education and Nativity

Latinos

		College Graduate				High School or Less			
Total		Foreign Born		U.S. Born		Foreign Born		U.S. Born	
Miami	5,059	Miami	4,515	Dallas	1,652	Miami	23,259	Las Vegas	3,015
Washington, D.C.	1,959	Orlando	1,031	Washington, D.C.	1,109	Orlando	7,060	Modesto	2,011
Dallas	1,916	Washington, D.C.	850	Los Angeles	844	Las Vegas	4,210	Dallas	1,885
Orlando	1,567	San Diego	803	Atlanta	689	Tampa	4,107	Orlando	1,828
San Diego	1,361	San Francisco	679	Seattle	564	Washington, D.C.	3,524	Sacramento	1,692
Atlanta	1,235	Tampa	637	San Diego	558	San Diego	3,434	Stockton, Calif.	1,669
Tampa	982	West Palm Beach	613	Miami	544	West Palm Beach	2,928	Tampa	1,633
San Francisco	827	Atlanta	546	Orlando	536	Atlanta	2,481	Miami	1,478
Los Angeles	800	Phoenix	317	Houston	524	Modesto	2,092	Phoenix	1,178
Phoenix	780	Dallas	264	Phoenix	463	Tucson	1,716	San Diego	1,034

Asians

		College Graduate				High School or Less			
Total		Foreign Born		U.S. Born		Foreign Born		U.S. Born	
Los Angeles	10,651	Los Angeles	10,136	San Francisco	1,235	Los Angeles	9,003	Las Vegas	587
San Francisco	6,832	San Francisco	5,597	Washington, D.C.	654	Sacramento	1,969	Sacramento	405
Washington, D.C.	4,117	Washington, D.C.	3,463	San Diego	602	San Francisco	1,668	Seattle	243
San Diego	1,765	San Diego	1,163	Los Angeles	515	Atlanta	1,103	Orlando	154
Atlanta	1,210	Atlanta	1,005	Seattle	376	Stockton, Calif.	990	Modesto	118
Seattle	1,144	Dallas	947	Sacramento	243	Modesto	948	Stockton, Calif.	96
Dallas	1,102	Orlando	859	Atlanta	205	Fresno	933	Newport News	91
Sacramento	1,044	Sacramento	801	Orlando	164	Orlando	886	Atlanta	88
Orlando	1,023	Seattle	768	Dallas	155	Las Vegas	796	Jacksonville	74
Tampa	593	Tampa	586	Phoenix	150	Philadelphia	678	Portland	60

Note: Population aged 25 and above in 1990.

finding: the U.S. born played a more important role in distinguishing magnets for internal migrants than did educational attainment. This is clear when examining the most prominent destination of the groups shown. Miami is the dominant net migration gainer for foreign-born Latinos, both college graduates and those with high school or less education. A good deal of overlap is seen among the other large gainers for both population groups—many with large existing Latino populations or areas we have characterized as spillover metros. In contrast, main destinations for U.S.-born Latino college graduates tended to be national employment magnets for professionals—including Dallas, Washington, Los Angeles, Atlanta, and Seattle. This list, in fact, overlaps strongly with the list of greatest metro gainers who are college graduate whites. In contrast, U.S.-born Latinos with high school education or less tended to locate more exclusively in spillover areas, suggesting that their migration was a response to pushes from nearby high-immigrant areas.

For Asians, lists of largest-gaining metro areas overlap considerably for each group shown in Table 10.4. Nonetheless, a difference is again seen between foreign-born and U.S.-born net migration patterns that cuts across educational attainment. That is, foreign-born college graduate Asians, as well as foreign-born Asians with less education, show the highest net migration gains for Los Angeles. This is not the case for U.S.-born Asians, whose gains are more evenly distributed among different high-opportunity metropolitan areas. For U.S.-born Asians with high school education or less, major destinations do not include Los Angeles or San Francisco, but rather a variety of spillover areas, as well as Seattle.

This review of education selectivity patterns that accompany the recent net internal migration of Latinos and Asians is not consistent with the spatial assimilation picture suggested earlier. Internal migration that relocates these groups away from traditional ports of entry appears to be push rather than pull oriented. In fact, most of these metros are attracting net in-migration of college graduate Latino and Asian residents from other parts of the United States. Out-migration is most evident among less skilled Latino and Asian residents, who opted for nearby spillover metro areas. The only evidence of spatial assimilation appears to be occurring among relatively small numbers of college graduate U.S.-born Latinos and Asians whose primary destinations are consistent with those of college graduate whites.

Metro-Area Influences

To further identify the distinctiveness of the migration processes for more assimilated and less assimilated minorities, we examine the most important metropolitan-area attributes of each group's migration. To do so we undertake separate multivariate regression analyses for selected population subgroups, shown in Table 10.5. Separate analyses are conducted for foreign-born and U.S.-born Latinos and Asians, for Latinos and Asians who are college educated and those with high school education or less, and for blacks and whites in these two education categories.

Metropolitan attributes include a geographic region classification (dummy variables are the Northeast, Midwest, South Atlantic, Mountain, and Pacific divisions, with parts of the South not included in the South Atlantic division representing the omitted category), four variables reflecting the metropolitan area's economic structure (unemployment rate in 1988, per capita income in 1988, percentage of change in manufacturing employment in the period 1982–1987, and percentage of males engaged in professional and managerial employment based on the 1990 census), and the log of the metropolitan area's population size in 1985.

Particular attention is given to two additional variables: percentage of the metropolitan population composed of the given minority group (Latino, Asian, black, or white) and the volume of immigration to the metropolitan area over the 1985–1990 period. If a minority group (especially a new immigrant minority group) is deconcentrating, we would anticipate a negative relationship between that group's percentage of the metropolitan population and the net migration level for that group (the dependent variable). Further, if recent immigrants are exerting a competitive effect on members of that minority group, we would expect a negative relationship between immigration to the metropolitan area and a group's net migration level.

The findings in Table 10.5 show mixed results with respect to expectations about dispersed redistribution, a competitive effect of immigrants. That is, we find the expected negative effect between the group's percentage of the metropolitan population and the net migration level for all Asian groups but a *positive* effect for all Latino groups. Relationships are more complicated when viewed in connection with the immigration effects shown in the table. That is, the expected negative or competitive impact of immigration on net migration is found for all Latino groups (as well as all white and black groups), but the effect is positive for the net migration of Asian groups except for U.S.-born Asians.

Hence, it appears as if Latino net out-migration patterns are a response to recent immigration levels rather than to a desire to deconcentrate in areas with large percentages of Latinos. For Asians, however, there is a tendency to relocate to areas with high levels of immigration, but, controlling for that, there is a desire to relocate away from areas with high percentages of Asians. (A positive relationship for immigration does not hold for U.S.-born Asians, however.) Although this finding is admittedly not amenable to straightforward interpretation, it appears as if recent internal migration of Latinos is the most responsive to the negative impacts of immigration in the areas discussed earlier. Also U.S.-born Latinos do not show the positive relationship with group percentage of metropolitan population shown for the other Latino groups.

Table 10.5 Net Internal Migration, 1985–1990, for Population Groups across U.S. Metro Areas Regressed on Metro-Area Attributes (standardized regression coefficients)

	Persons Aged 5 and Above				Persons Aged 25 and Above							
	Latinos		Asians		Latinos		Asians		Blacks		Whites	
Metro Attributes[1]	Foreign Born	U.S. Born	Foreign Born	U.S. Born	HS	COLL	HS	COLL	HS	COLL	HS	COLL
Region[2]												
Northeast	−0.09	−0.09	−0.10	−0.10	−0.07	−0.19	−0.07	−0.19	−0.16	−0.19	−0.15*	−0.33*
Midwest	0.01	−0.10	−0.15	0.21*	−0.00	−0.03	−0.13	−0.16	−0.10	−0.13	−0.14*	−0.19*
South Atlantic	0.21*	0.06	−0.05	−0.06	0.19*	0.26*	−0.04	−0.01	0.10	0.21*	0.09	0.14
Mountain	0.14	0.16*	0.29*	0.41*	0.14	0.17	0.31*	0.23*	0.14	0.02	0.15	0.24
Pacific	0.07	0.06	−0.08	−0.06	0.08	0.05	−0.06	−0.06	−0.01	−0.06	0.05	−0.01
Unemployment	−0.18	−0.11	−0.20	−0.13	−0.15	−0.20	−0.18	−0.16	−0.13	0.03	−0.12*	−11.00
Income	0.16	0.08	0.03	0.06	0.14	0.22*	0.04	0.12	−0.01	0.17	0.03	0.22*
Mfg. Growth	−0.01	0.10	0.18	0.23*	0.01	−0.05	0.22*	0.06	0.03	0.11	0.12*	−0.11
% upper white collar	−0.13	−0.06	−0.05	−0.01	−0.14	−0.19*	−0.17	0.04	−0.00	0.07	−0.17*	0.22*
Group % of metro pop.	0.23*	0.01	−0.24*	−0.80*	0.18*	0.23*	−0.35*	−0.22*	−0.05	−0.06	0.08	0.06
Immigration	−0.84*	0.98*	0.42*	−0.25*	−0.90*	−0.53*	0.29*	0.64*	−0.74*	−0.29*	−0.76*	−0.44*
Pop Size (log)	0.23*	0.27*	−0.09	0.09	0.23*	0.31*	−0.04	−12.00	0.08	0.23*	−0.03	0.31*
R-square	0.50	0.70	0.36	0.63	0.59	0.27	0.32	0.55	0.50	0.21	0.75	0.36
N	115	115	91	91	115	115	91	91	126	126	126	126

Notes: 1. Metropolitan areas with 1990 total populations exceeding 250,000 and group populations exceeding 5,000. Equations for whites include same metro areas as equations for blacks.

2. Omitted category includes the remainder of the South region (other than South Atlantic).

* Significant at 0.1 level.

For whites and blacks the impact of group percentage on internal migration patterns is negligible, and there is no strong tendency either to concentrate or deconcentrate. Moreover, whites and blacks at each educational level are negatively responsive to recent immigration, whereas the response is strongest among those with high school or less education. Clearly, immigration exerts a significant impact on internal migration for a number of groups.

The remaining metropolitan-area attributes tend to show expected relationships with each of the groups analyzed. That is, unemployment is generally negative related to net migration, whereas income is generally positively related. Area migration appears positively related to increases in manufacturing growth, especially for U.S.-born Asians, Asians with high school or less education, and whites with high school or less education. A somewhat inexplicable finding among the economic and occupation variables is the negative relationship between the percentage of upper-level white-collar workers in an area and the net migration of some groups.

In sum, the results of these equations are not consistent with the view that the internal migration patterns of Latinos and Asians are becoming more dispersed with increasing residence in the United States and greater educational attainment. Rather than confirm an assimilation-based deconcentration of these groups, evidence points to the competitive effects of recent immigrants to traditional port-of-entry metropolitan areas.

Impact on the Los Angeles Metro Area

This chapter has investigated the extent to which recent internal migration patterns of Latinos and Asians may lead to their wider dispersal away from traditional port-of-entry metropolitan areas. The results are hardly consistent with this view. The net out-migration of Latinos is the most accentuated among U.S.-born Latinos with lower skills, possibly in reaction to competition with recent immigrants for lower-level jobs (Borjas 1994; Frey 1995a). Among Asians a net internal migration continues into metro areas with the greatest Asian populations (New York, Honolulu, and Chicago are exceptions), although this tendency is not as strong for U.S.-born Asians.

Nonetheless, the magnitudes of these internal migration patterns are relatively small in relation to the larger numbers of Latino and Asian immigrants who continue to focus on traditional port-of-entry metropolitan areas. Table 10.6 displays the relative impact of immigration and internal migration contributions for each race and minority group in the Los Angeles metropolitan area. These data make plain that, overall, the metro area's migration components are individuals with less than college education. A major impact exerted by internal migration is a positive impact associated primarily with college graduate whites, blacks, and foreign-born Asians. Further, the greatest internal out-migration contribu-

Table 10.6 Immigration and Internal Migration Components of 1985–1990 Change by Race, Latino Status, and Educational Attainment, Los Angeles Metro Area

		Educational Attainment[1]			
	1990 Population[2]	Less than High School	High School Graduate	Some College	College Graduate
Hispanics					
Immigration	520,653	152,992	27,836	21,910	14,794
Internal migration	−53,650	−16,009	−6,177	−6,279	800
Total	467,003	136,983	21,659	15,631	15,594
Asians					
Immigration	219,652	34,769	26,144	29,533	50,646
Internal migration	31,804	6,460	2,020	3,707	10,651
Total	251,456	41,229	28,164	33,240	61,297
Blacks					
Immigration	16,925	2,258	2,798	3,679	1,603
Internal migration	−11,731	−3,172	−3,546	−2,829	3,997
Total	5,194	−914	−748	850	5,600
Whites					
Immigration	140,136	20,268	20,407	24,673	31,561
Internal migration	−136,158	−38,108	−53,232	−57,220	31,550
Total	3,978	−17,840	−32,825	−32,547	63,111
Total					
Immigration	899,007	210,287	77,185	79,795	98,604
Internal migration	−174,673	−50,829	−60,935	−62,621	46,998
Total[3]	724,334	159,458	16,250	17,174	145,602

Notes: 1. Aged 25 and above in 1990.
2. Aged 5 and above in 1990.
3. Total is not exactly equivalent to the four race and Latino groups because of some overlap of Latinos with Asians and blacks and the omission of other race groups.

tions are made by whites with less than a college education and Hispanics with less than a high school education. The overall result of these patterns, should these migration contributions persist, would be an increasingly foreign-born population comprised primarily of the new immigrant minorities that will be especially dominant for persons with less than a high school education. The growth of the college graduate population will be more balanced between immigration and internal migration and will include significant numbers of whites, Asians, and blacks.

The long-term dispersal of immigrants to the United States has been a continuing theme in U.S. history. The results shown in this chapter, however, are in concert with earlier results of the 1980 census. Such a dispersal of new immigrant minorities will not occur quickly. This could well lead to a continued "demographic Balkanization" over broad regions of the country.

Another perspective can be gained by examining the dispersal of the current foreign-born population who immigrated at different times. For this we compiled 1995 statistics from the U.S. Census Bureau's Current Population Survey, which establishes the high concentration of both long-term and recent immigrants in the ten "High-Immigration Metros" (Frey 1995a). Figure 10.5 indicates that this concentration remains relatively strong for native-born Latinos, native-born Asians, and foreign-born populations of all race-ethnic groups who arrived in different five-year intervals since 1965. Indeed, whereas less than

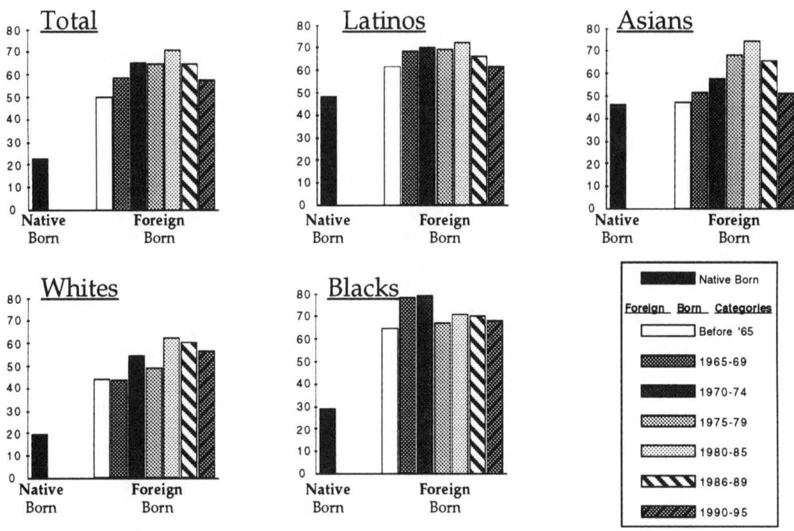

Source: Authors' analysis of 1995 Current Population Survey

Figure 10.5 Percentage Resident in Ten High-Immigration Metros, by Nativity, Foreign-Born Year of Arrival, and Race-Ethnicity

half of 1995 native-born Latinos and Asians are located in combined High-Immigration Metros, over 50 percent of Asians in all recent immigrant cohorts and well over 60 percent of Latinos in those cohorts reside in the High-Immigration Metros. This pattern is relatively pervasive among recent immigrants with different social and demographic characteristics and suggests a continuing concentration of recent foreign born in selected metropolitan areas.

References

Bartel, Ann P. 1989. "Where Do the New Immigrants Live?" *Journal of Labor Economics* 7, 4: 371–391.

Bartel, Ann P., and Marianne J. Koch. 1991. "Internal Migration of U.S. Immigrants." In J. M. Abowd and R. B. Freeman (eds.), *Immigration, Trade and the Labor Market*. Chicago: University of Chicago Press.

Bean, Frank D., and Marta Tienda. 1987. *The Hispanic Population of the United States*. A 1980 Census Monograph. New York: Russell Sage.

Borjas, George J. 1994. "The Economics of Immigration." *Journal of Economic Literature* 32 (December): 1667–1717.

Edmonston, Barry, and Jeffrey S. Passel. 1994. *Immigration and Ethnicity*. Washington, D.C.: Urban Institute.

Frey, William H. 1995a. "Immigration and Internal Migration 'Flight': A California Case Study." *Population and Environment* 16, 4: 353–375.

———. 1995b. "Immigration and Internal Migration Flight: Toward a New Demographic Balkanization." *Urban Studies* 32: 353–375.

———. 1995c. "The New Geography of U.S. Population Shifts: Trends Toward Balkanization." In Reynolds Farley (ed.), *The State of the Union: Social Trends*. New York: Russell Sage.

Long, Larry. 1988. *Migration and Residential Mobility in the United States*. New York: Russell Sage.

Martin, Philip, and Elizabeth Midgley. 1994. "Immigration to the United States: Journey to an Uncertain Destination." *Population Bulletin,* 49, 2. Washington, D.C.: Population Reference Bureau.

McHugh, Kevin E. 1989. "Hispanic Migration and Population Redistribution in the United States." *Professional Geographer* 41, 4: 429–439.

Mollenkopf, John H., and Manuel Castells (eds.). 1991. *Dual City: Restructuring New York*. New York: Russell Sage.

Neuman, Kristen E., and Marta Tienda. 1994. "The Settlement and Secondary Migration Patterns of Legalized Immigrants: Insights from Administrative Records." In Barry Edmonston, and Jeffrey S. Passell (eds.), *Immigration and Ethnicity*. Washington, D.C.: Urban Institute.

Pedraza, Silvia, and Ruben G. Rumbaut. 1996. *Origins and Destinies,* Belmont, Calif.: Wadsworth.

Waldinger, Roger. 1989. "Immigration and Urban Change." *Annual Review of Sociology* 15: 211–232.

11

Settlement Dynamics and Internal Migration of the U.S. Foreign-Born Population

Patricia Gober

The foreign-born population has grown in absolute terms and as a relative share of the total U.S. population. In 1996 the foreign born comprised 8.7 percent of the population, up from 7.9 percent in 1990, 6.2 percent in 1980, and only 4.8 percent as recently as 1970. Reform of restrictive immigration laws in 1965 abolished the quota system of allocating immigrants according to national origins and gave preference to family members of citizens and legal residents and to those with skills in demand in the United States. The result was a marked increase in the number of immigrants and a shift in source areas away from European countries toward developing nations in Latin America, Asia, and the Caribbean. In the 1980 census the percentage of foreign born living in the United States increased for the first time since 1910.

Also significant is the striking geographic concentration of the foreign-born population. In 1990 California contained 49.9 percent of the foreign-born Vietnamese population, 52.8 percent of foreign-born Filipinos, 57.6 percent of Mexicans, and 60.3 percent of Salvadorans. More than two-thirds (67.5 percent) of foreign-born Cubans lived in Florida. New York state was home to 43.9 percent of Jamaicans and 69.6 percent of Dominicans (U.S. Bureau of the Census 1990). Frey (1995, 1996a, 1996b) argues that the concentrating forces of immigration have led to a demographic balkanization of the nation along ethnic and racial lines. He predicts that areas affected by immigration will become increasingly multicultural, young, and more bifurcated with respect to race and class. Areas outside immigration orbits will be far less multicultural and more homogeneous in their social and economic makeup.

In chapter 10 of this volume, Frey and Liaw acknowledge that the balkanization thesis assumes that internal migration will not substantially disperse the foreign-born population. Using data from the 1990 census, they go on to show that although there has been some deconcentration of Latinos away from port-of-entry cities and states, immigrants remain highly concentrated.

This chapter assesses the balkanization thesis using evidence of settlement patterns and internal migration of the foreign-born population from the 1990 census. Three sets of questions are posed: (1) How concentrated are the foreign born, and did they become more or less concentrated between 1985 and 1990; (2) are the size, efficiency, and pattern of major migration streams consistent with the balkanization thesis; and (3) did individual foreign-born residents move toward greater or lesser concentrations of coethnics? Separate analyses are performed for 12 groups of foreign born, defined by place of birth.

Geographic Concentration of Immigrants

The geographic concentration of newcomers has strong precedence in U.S. history. In the late eighteenth century Benjamin Franklin worried that there were so many German immigrants in Pennsylvania that the State Assembly would need interpreters (U.S. Immigration and Naturalization Service 1991). In the early twentieth century immigrants were highly concentrated along nationality lines in cities of the Northeast. Ward (1971) reported that the public was alarmed over the concentration of immigrants from southern and eastern Europe in northeastern industrial cities where they scarcely encountered the society and institutions of native-born Americans. The popular perception was that assimilation into U.S. society of immigrants who arrived from northwestern Europe before 1880 was facilitated by their widespread distribution and their settlement on the land as well as in cities. Although this argument ignored the effects of length of residence in the new country on the distribution of immigrants and obscured major differences in the locational characteristics of individual groups, it profoundly influenced national immigration policy during the first half of the twentieth century.

Many of the same arguments about the geographic concentration of the foreign born resonate today, as immigrant communities serve as powerful magnets for newcomers to the United States. Classical assimilation theory posits that immigrants initially concentrate in immigrant enclaves but later disperse as their human capital increases and they shift their reference group from other immigrants to the total population (Dunlevy 1980). Human capital allows immigrants to function independent of the support system provided by the enclave.

Much has been written more recently about how immigrant communities function in the early adjustment process of new immigrants. Immigrant communities help members locate housing and jobs (Gurak and Caces 1992). Many immigrants find work in businesses owned by coethnics. Others establish their own small businesses, providing goods and services to immigrant niche markets (Waldinger, Ward, and Aldrich 1985; Zhou and Logan 1989). Social lives also revolve around the family and social clubs formed by fellow immigrants (Kritz and Nogle 1994).

The tendency to form immigrant enclaves is reinforced by current immigration policy, which gives priority to family reunification. Immigration to the United States from foreign countries thus occurs in chains that link family and friends to common destinations, particularly for lower-skilled immigrants who are especially dependent on family members for help in finding work and establishing a new social life (Massey et al. 1994).

Previous migration research has addressed the relationship between residence in ethnic and immigrant enclaves and whether or not someone moves. Using the 1980 Public Use Microdata Samples (PUMS) to investigate 1975 to 1980 migration, Kritz and Nogle (1994) found that, controlling for personal characteristics and economic conditions, living in a state with a high nativity concentration significantly reduced the odds of moving. Comparing initial with subsequent resettlement patterns of recently legalized immigrants, Neuman and Tienda (1994) also found that nativity concentration deters migration. Newbold (1996) came to a similar conclusion using in- and out-migration rates of Canadian provinces. Low out-migration rates of the foreign born from Ontario and British Columbia suggest that large immigrant concentrations in Toronto and Vancouver act as a drag on the propensity of immigrants to out-migrate.

Most research on the geography of internal migration has been at the aggregate scale and has concluded that migration reinforces the concentration of immigrants (Belanger and Rogers 1993; Frey 1995, 1996a, 1996b). At the individual scale, Bartel (1989) showed that more highly educated migrants are more likely than those at the lower end of the educational ladder to move to cities that have smaller shares of the relevant ethnic population than the cities they left. This finding is consistent with the notion that as immigrants gain human capital they become more geographically assimilated into U.S. society.

This study investigates the geographic concentration and migration behavior of the U.S. foreign-born population disaggregated into 12 nativity groups by country of origin. The chapter has three parts. Part 1 shows levels of and changes in geographic concentration of immigrants between 1985 and 1990 at the state level and asks about the effects of duration of residence in the United States and human capital in influencing levels of concentration. Part 2 identifies the major migration streams for each of the 12 groups. Part 3 examines, at the individual scale, the direction of migration—toward greater or lesser nativity concentrations.

Data

Data are from the 5 percent PUMS files of the 1990 Census of Population and Housing. The PUMS files allow an examination of the origins and destinations of foreign-born migrants by their place of birth. Included in the study are the 12 largest nativity groups (Mexico, Philippines, China, Cuba, India, Vietnam, El Salvador, Canada, Korea, Germany, Dominican Republic, and Jamaica) in 1996 (U.S. Bureau of the Census 1996). They are not the 12 largest nativity groups in the 1990 PUMS files because some groups were greatly overrepresented and others were greatly underrepresented in 1990 to 1996 immigration to the United States. The 12 groups together represented 53 percent of the foreign-born population in 1990.

Children of American citizens born overseas and those born in Puerto Rico, Guam, and outlying areas are deleted from the analysis. Also excluded are immigrants who came to stay in the United States after 1985 to establish a reasonable at-risk population on which to base 1985 to 1990 migration estimates and rates.

Looking only at persons over 25 years of age in 1990, PUMS data reveal substantial variation across nativity groups with respect to interstate migration rates and demographic characteristics (Table 11.1). The lowest migration rates are among Mexicans and Salvadorans, probably a function of low levels of human capital as evidenced by low levels of education, naturalization, and English competence. Germans and Canadians also have fairly low migration rates,

Table 11.1 Interstate Migration Rates and Demographic Characteristics of Foreign-Born Population

Nativity Group	Number of Cases	Migration Rate	Mean Age	Citizen (%)	Entered Pre-1970 (%)	Speaks English Well (%)	High School Graduate (%)
Mexico	114,074	3.9	41.9	30.1	33.8	52.4	23.4
Germany	31,690	7.9	56.4	78.0	89.6	98.5	75.1
Canada	31,036	8.2	57.4	61.7	83.9	98.9	70.9
Cuba	30,817	7.2	52.0	55.6	63.6	58.6	54.1
Philippines	27,824	8.1	46.7	71.5	27.8	93.5	82.0
China	15,662	6.8	53.1	64.9	39.6	55.5	58.4
Korea	14,306	13.2	43.6	57.9	13.6	72.1	79.7
Vietnam	12,821	10.6	39.6	59.3	2.2	68.0	62.9
India	12,043	14.5	43.1	50.7	17.8	93.3	89.3
El Salvador	10,247	5.1	38.2	22.6	9.9	54.6	35.9
Jamaica	8,419	12.0	45.7	50.9	32.1	99.6	69.1
Dominican Republic	8,019	8.4	42.4	37.0	34.4	53.7	42.5

but in their cases low mobility is better explained by their older ages than by poor human capital. Typical German- and Canadian-born immigrants are in their mid- to late 50s, ages at which the odds of moving are low.

The highest interstate migration rates are among Indians and Koreans, who are young, well educated, and recent arrivals. In chapter 12 of this volume, Newbold finds the highest migration rates are among the most recent arrivals, suggesting that a fine-tuning or settling-in process is at work among new immigrants to the United States. Slightly lower migration rates are found among Jamaicans, who are young and native English speakers but with a longer history of settlement and lower levels of education. Paradoxically, Filipinos are young, very highly educated, and relatively recent arrivals, but they have moderate to low migration rates. A complete explanation of the variation in migration rates and their causes is outside the scope of this chapter. What is clear is that the foreign born are not a monolithic group but a set of individual subgroups with extraordinarily different demographic characteristics and mobility experiences. Even subgroups from the same region are fairly disparate. Consider the cases of Cubans who are older, have long duration of residence, and have low migration rates; Jamaicans who are young, recent arrivals with relatively high interstate migration rates; and Dominicans who are young, recent arrivals but with low migration rates. These unique experiences would be lost in any Caribbean-wide grouping of foreign born.

In addition to the PUMS files, the 1990 Subject Summary Tape File (SSTF-1) on the foreign-born population in the United States was used to calculate nativity concentrations at the state level. This report contains the state of residence for members of each of the 12 nativity groups by year of entry into the United States.

Results

Part 1: Dynamics of Immigrant Settlement

The tendency for immigrants to settle near coethnics is revealed by indexes of dissimilarity at the state level in 1985 and 1990 (Table 11.2). A dissimilarity index measures the proportion of a particular group that must relocate for complete integration to occur. For example, an index of 40 means that 40 percent of the group must move to achieve a population distribution identical to nongroup members. To arrive at the index for 1985, I subtracted immigrants who entered the United States between 1985 and 1990 from the foreign-born totals and then reallocated internal migrants estimated from the 1990 PUMS files. Individual weights in the PUMS files were used to expand the sample to estimates of the total number of in-migrants and out-migrants from each state.

Vast differences in levels of concentration separate the 12 nativity groups. In

Table 11.2 Indexes of Dissimilarity, 1985 and 1990

Nativity Group	Dissimilarity Index 1985	Dissimilarity Index 1990	Highest Percentage	Concentration State
Mexico	68.3	65.8	57.6	California
Germany	20.5	17.7	14.6	California
Cuba	66.7	68.1	67.5	Florida
Canada	35.3	35.3	20.2	California
Philippines	53.5	52.4	52.8	California
China	51.5	48.0	39.9	California
Korea	38.4	38.6	35.2	California
Vietnam	44.6	44.5	49.9	California
India	29.9	30.5	18.6	California
El Salvador	60.1	58.2	60.3	California
Jamaica	64.1	63.6	43.9	New York
Dominican Republic	76.3	75.8	69.6	New York

both 1985 and 1990 the most concentrated groups were Dominicans, Mexicans, Cubans, Jamaicans, and Salvadorans. With the exception of the Cubans, these groups were young; with the exception of the Jamaicans, they had low levels of education and poor English-speaking competency. At the other end of the spectrum Germans and Canadians, with long histories of residence in the United States and high levels of human capital, were geographically assimilated into the U.S. population. Also well integrated were several "new" immigrant groups, including the young, highly mobile, and positively selected Indians and Koreans. Immigrants from the Philippines, China, and Vietnam were in the middle—more concentrated than the "old" immigrant groups and the highly educated Indians and Koreans but less concentrated than the Latin American groups.

Human capital, in the form of education, exerts a moderate to strong effect on the concentrating tendencies of the 12 nativity groups (Figure 11.1). Education provides immigrants with greater information about a wider range of destinations and renders them more sensitive to general labor market conditions and less responsive to the "friends and neighbors effect." Highly educated groups like Indians, Filipinos, and Koreans are dispersed, whereas poorly educated groups like Mexicans, Salvadorans, and Dominicans are highly concentrated. The fact that Germans and Canadians are even more integrated than expected on the basis of their high educational profile speaks to their long tenure in the United States. Almost 90 percent of foreign-born Germans and 84 percent of foreign-born Canadians entered the United States prior to 1970.

Contrary to the conventional wisdom that immigrants are becoming more concentrated, four of the five most highly concentrated groups showed small reductions in their dissimilarity indexes between 1985 and 1990 (Table 11.2).

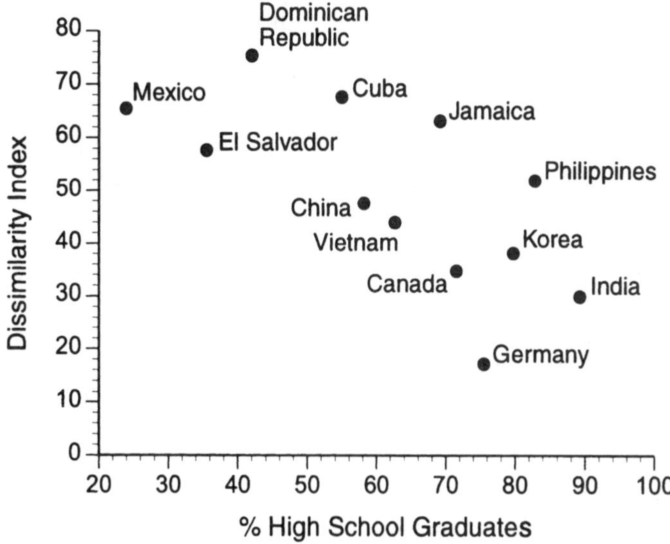

Figure 11.1 Index of Dissimilarity by Levels of Education for 12 Nativity Groups

The index for Mexican-born immigrants fell from 68.3 in 1985 to 65.8 in 1990, largely because Texas failed to attract proportional shares of immigrants from Mexico and Mexican-born domestic migrants. There was also a small reduction in the levels of concentration for Salvadorans, Jamaicans, and Dominicans. Their primary magnet states (California for Salvadorans and New York for Jamaicans and Dominicans) lost proportionality in terms of both domestic migrants and immigrants from abroad. Salvadorans also moved away from their secondary node of settlement in Texas, but Dominicans and Jamaicans moved toward new secondary cores in Florida. Among the highly concentrated nativity groups, Cubans alone experienced greater concentration at the state level.

Thus it is an oversimplification to argue that the foreign-born population is geographically concentrated and becoming more so. Some groups are and others are not. Educational status goes a long way in explaining differences across groups, but the relationship is not perfect. Other factors such as refugee status, length of tenure in the United States, and economic and social conditions in main settlement cores also come into play.

Part 2: Migration Streams

Part 1 established that the settlement systems of nativity groups vary markedly. Part 2 now looks at the internal migration flows that link the major nodes within that system. Only the 10 largest migration streams between 1985 and 1990 are examined because even for groups as large as the 12 chosen here the 51 × 51 state-to-state migrant flow matrix has many empty cells and many with very small numbers. The 10 largest streams capture a small proportion of all interstate migrants for the more dispersed groups but a high proportion for the more concentrated groups (Table 11.3). Over half of Cuban, Jamaican, and Dominican interstate migrants moved in the 10 largest of the 2,550 possible interstate migration streams.

Six of the 10 largest streams of Mexican migrants interconnected the three largest concentrations of the Mexican-born population in California (containing 57.6 percent of Mexicans in 1990), Texas (21.2 percent), and Illinois (6.9 percent). These streams were highly inefficient in the sense that movement between states was self-compensating and little population redistribution occurred (Figure 11.2a). More efficient streams sent migrants from California to neighboring states and from Texas to new growth areas in Florida and Georgia. Between 1985 and 1990 the Mexican-born population grew from 4,000 to 20,000 in Georgia and from 29,000 to 55,000 in Florida.

The internal flows of Cuban-born migrants were highly focused on the single destination of Florida, were highly efficient, and were huge (Figure 11.2b). The Cuban connection between New Jersey and Florida, involving more than 10,000 persons, was the single largest flow of the 12 nativity groups—larger, in fact, than any of the Mexican streams, even though Mexicans were almost four times more numerous than Cubans. Florida clearly has emerged as the overwhelmingly dominant magnet state for Cubans migrants.

The strong concentrating tendencies of Cubans are consistent with Boswell's characterization of Dade County (metropolitan Miami) as a surrogate homeland

Table 11.3 Characteristics of 10 Largest Migration Streams, by Nativity Group

Nativity Group	10 Streams as % of All Domestic Flows	Efficiency of 10 Streams	Migration to Largest State and % of All Flows	
Mexico	36.1	26.5	35.8	California
Germany	15.4	62.2	10.7	California
Cuba	55.0	58.5	61.2	Florida
Canada	14.8	62.2	12.0	California
Philippines	24.0	42.3	34.3	California
China	22.3	60.3	28.6	California
Korea	19.4	31.0	22.5	California
Vietnam	25.4	66.1	39.3	California
India	17.4	36.8	14.9	California
El Salvador	33.6	51.8	30.5	California
Jamaica	50.4	79.0	12.3	New York
Dominican Republic	50.6	68.1	35.3	New York

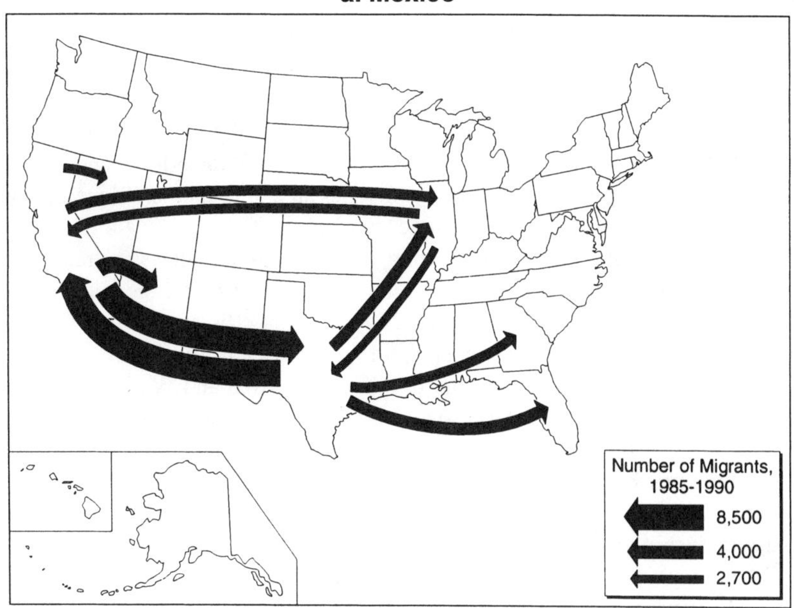

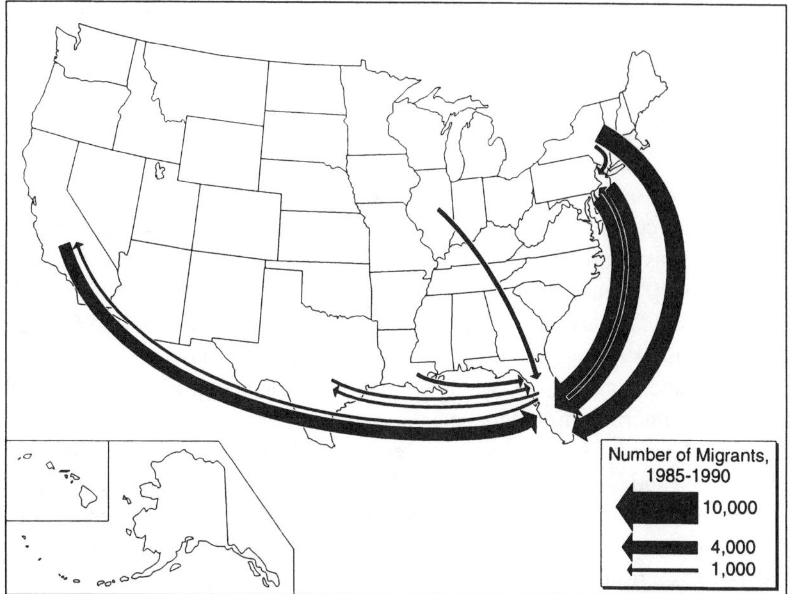

Figure 11.2 Ten Largest Migration Streams for Persons Born in Mexico and Cuba, 1985–1990

for Cuban exiles in the United States. Exiles see themselves as sojourners, not immigrants. Political activity is organized around the overthrow of Castro's regime and the establishment of a new government in Cuba (Boswell 1993). Garcia (1996) argues that a high priority is placed on preserving "Cubanidad," or Cubanness, through exile organizations, an exile media, and an active Cuban arts and intellectual life. This exile mentality and cultural focus has made Florida an unmatchable draw for Cuban migrants—to an extent that is unique among foreign-born groups in the United States today.

The Vietnamese, a second exile group, display a similar but less extreme tendency to concentrate (Figure 11.3a). Like the Cuban streams, the Vietnamese migration streams between 1985 and 1990 were very efficient and overwhelmingly focused on a single magnet state, in this case California. Only 2 streams (between California and Texas and between California and Washington) had counterflows of any appreciable size. Mortland and Ledgerwood (1987) and Haines (1988) note that resettlement near other Vietnamese mitigates problems of an unfamiliar language, a change in social environment, and loss of social identity and economic status. Moreover, it allows the reestablishment of all-important kinship relationships.

In contrast to the Cubans and Vietnamese, Dominicans and Jamaicans moved away from, rather than toward, their main settlement core in New York (Figures 11.3b and 11.4a). By far their most favored destination was Florida. Florida has a relatively long history of Jamaican settlement dating from the 1960s, when temporary farmworkers were brought to the state under contract with sugar growers (Allen and Turner 1988), but settlement of Dominicans is smaller and more recent. Both groups also dispersed to satellite enclaves elsewhere in the Northeast: Jamaicans to the Washington, D.C., area and Dominicans to New Jersey, Rhode Island, and Massachusetts.

Migration flows of Salvadorans are more far-flung than any of the previous groups, interconnecting northeastern states, Texas, and California (Figure 11.4b). Consistent with the decline in the Salvadoran dissimilarity index noted earlier, 6 of 10 streams took migrants away from either Texas or California, the two main foci for Salvadoran settlement in the United States. Virginia emerged during the late1980s as the new growth area for Salvadorans.

Indians and Koreans, the two most positively selected groups of new immigrants, had internal migration systems organized around the urban Northeast (New York and Jersey for Koreans; New York, New Jersey, and Pennsylvania for Indians) and California (Figure 11.5). Although both groups have generally dispersed spatial patterns of settlement, they showed a tendency to consolidate in California. California gained 6,000 Indians and 8,600 Koreans between 1985 and 1990 as a result of domestic migration.

Immigrants from the Philippines and China have similar-looking migration streams, in part because many Filipino-born migrants are of Chinese ancestry (Figure 11.6). Two of the largest migration streams interconnect California, the

a. Vietnam

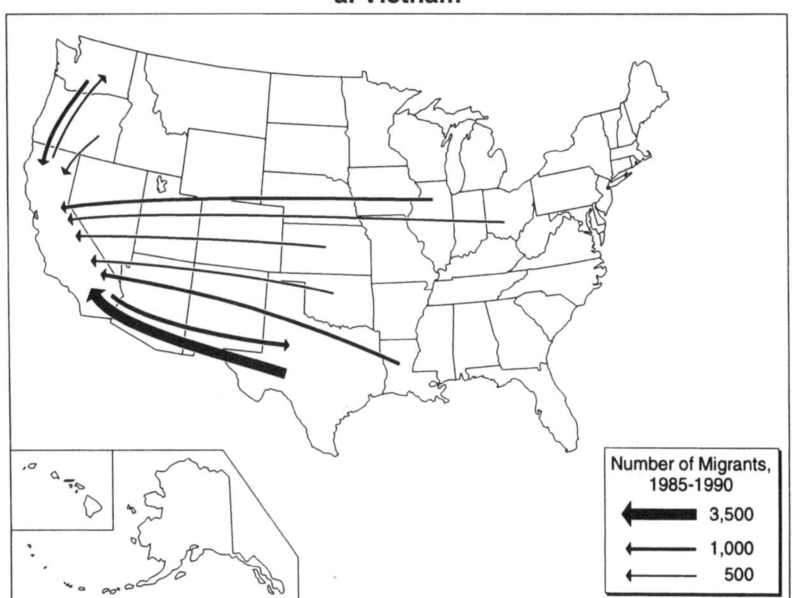

b. Dominican Republic

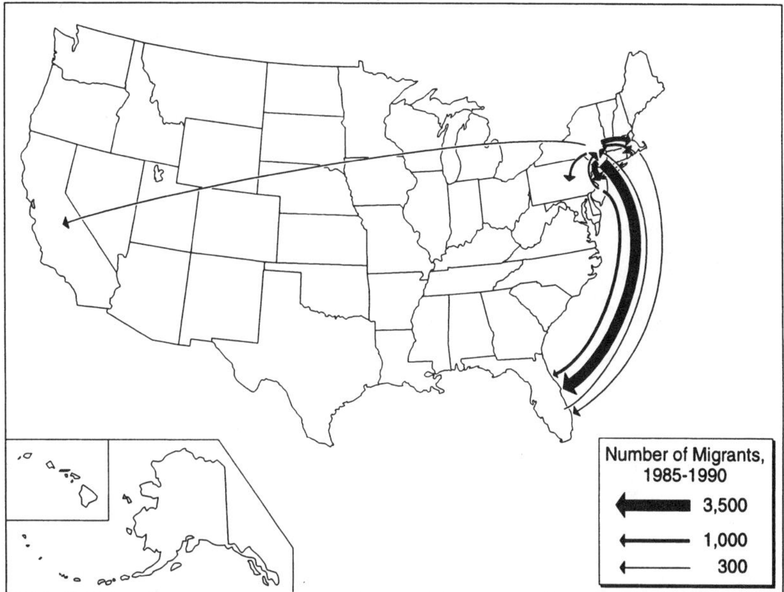

Figure 11.3 Ten Largest Migration Streams for Persons Born in Vietnam and the Dominican Republic, 1985–1990

a. Jamaica

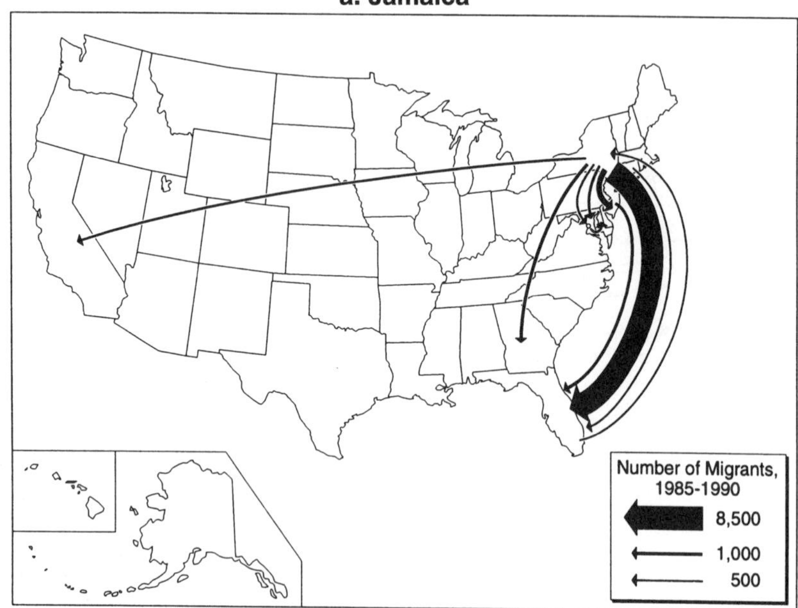

b. El Salvador

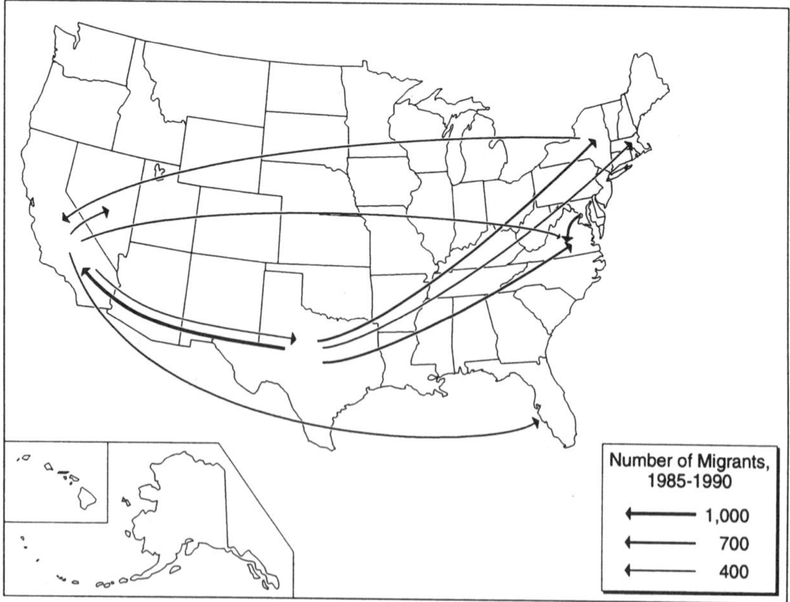

Figure 11.4 Ten Largest Migration Streams for Persons Born in Jamaica and El Salvador, 1985–1990

a. India

b. Korea

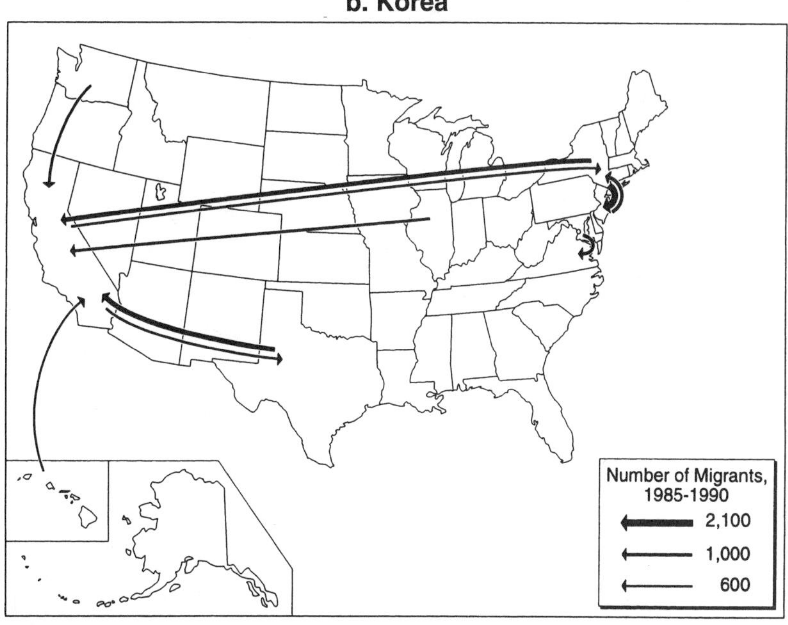

Figure 11.5 Ten Largest Migration Streams for Persons Born in India and Korea, 1985–1990

a. Philippines

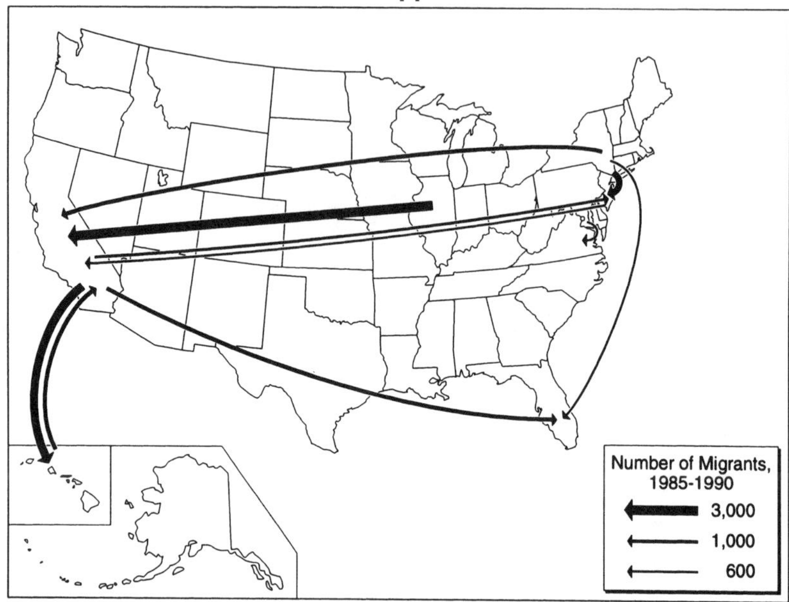

b. China

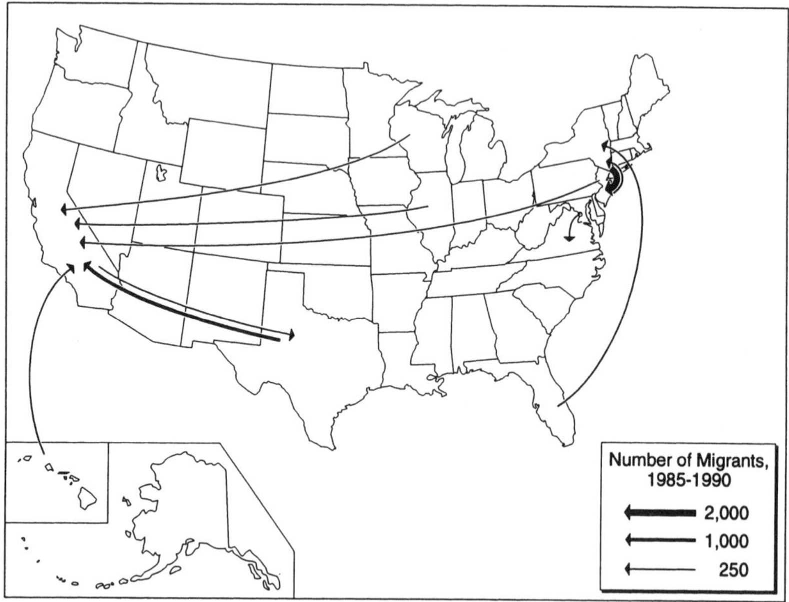

Figure 11.6 Ten Largest Migration Streams for Persons Born in the Philippines and China, 1985–1990

state with the largest Filipino population, with Hawaii, the earliest site of Filipino settlement in the United States. California was the destination for 4 of the 10 largest Filipino streams and 5 of the 10 largest Chinese steams, but several large flows were leaving California as well. The Chinese were perhaps the only national subgroup in which the New York–Florida link was in New York's favor.

Flows of German-born and Canadian-born migrants befit their long tenure in the United States, high levels of human capital, and generally dispersed spatial distribution (Figure 11.7). Given the older average ages of both groups, the Florida-bound movements undoubtedly represent retirement migration. Canadians, like native-born U.S. residents, moved away from California to nearby western states.

Examination of these maps reveals different migration patterns among the 12 nativity groups. Some groups, like the Cubans and Vietnamese, reinforced a single dominant immigrant concentration. Others, like the Jamaicans and Dominicans, moved away from a single-centered model of settlement and formed secondary centers in Florida and tertiary cores elsewhere around the Northeast. Still others, like Mexicans, started new centers of settlement away from their traditional foci of settlement in California, Texas, and Illinois. Major flows of Jamaicans, Dominicans, Vietnamese, Canadians, Germans, and Chinese were highly efficient, resulting in considerable redistribution, whereas other groups, like Mexicans, Indians, and Koreans, moved in inefficient streams.

Part 3: Direction of Migration

The focus in Part 3 is on individual migrants and the direction of their internal movement relative to existing nativity concentration. Each of the 12 nativity groups was recoded for the level of its concentrations in both 1985 and 1990. Levels for 1990 were based on the census summary file of the foreign born (U.S. Bureau of the Census 1990). Counts for each group were divided by states' populations to arrive at a nativity concentration. The 1985 levels were attained by subtracting immigration that occurred between 1985 and 1990 and reallocating 1985–1990 internal migration flows using estimates from 1990 PUMS files. The change in nativity concentration for each foreign-born migrant was the difference between the 1990 and 1985 figures. A positive difference means the person moved to a state with a higher concentration of coethnics; a negative difference signals a move to a lower concentration.

Three distinct groups emerged from this analysis (Table 11.4). Group 1 was led by the refugee groups of Cubans and Vietnamese, among whom almost three-quarters moved to states with higher nativity concentrations. They were followed by Koreans, Indians, and Chinese, whose settlement patterns were initially fairly dispersed but whose internal migration behavior led to greater concentrations. Group 2 included Canadians and Germans, whose long history of settlement in the United States rendered them largely indifferent to existing

a. Germany

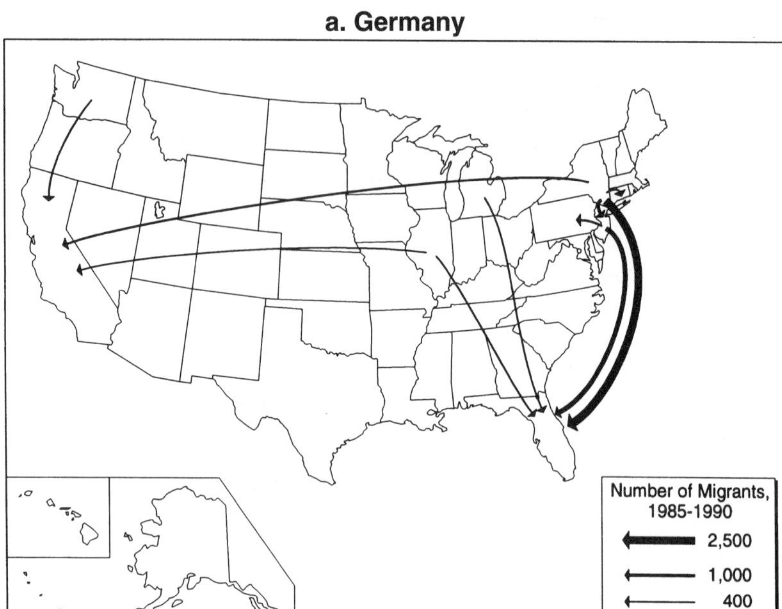

b. Canada

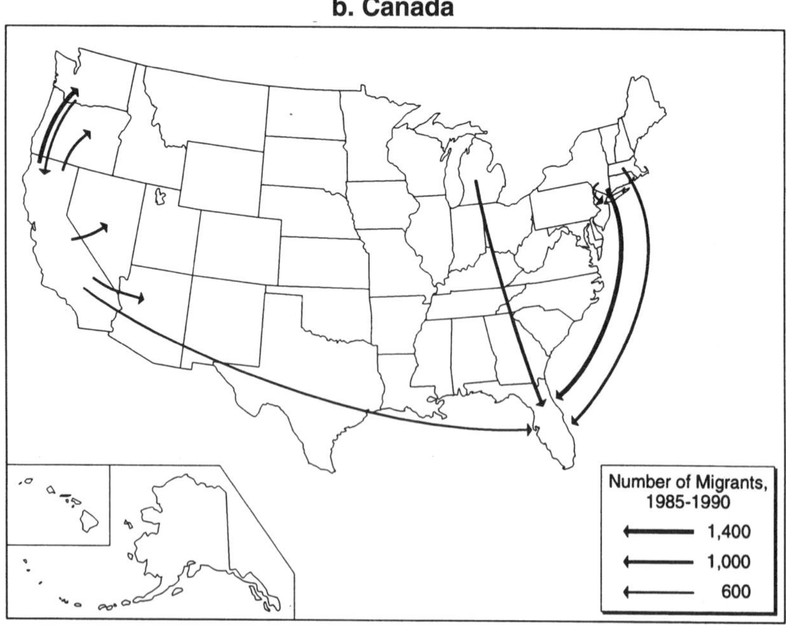

Figure 11.7 Ten Largest Migration Streams for Persons Born in Germany and Canada, 1985–1990

Table 11.4 Migrants Moving to Greater Nativity Concentrations (%)

Nativity Group	Number of migrants	Moving to Greater Concentrations (%)
Cuba	2,218	74.4
Vietnam	1,362	73.6
Korea	1,884	67.3
India	1,750	66.3
China	1,058	59.4
Philippines	2,254	56.6
Canada	2,555	56.3
Germany	2,519	49.9
El Salvador	519	47.6
Mexico	4,412	43.9
Jamaica	1,010	35.2
Dominican Republic	673	26.3

immigrant concentrations. The same was true for Filipinos, who also have a long history of settlement, even though the majority of foreign-born Filipinos are relatively recent arrivals.

Group 3, consisting of Dominican, Jamaican, Mexican, and Salvadoran migrants, moved away from concentrations of coethnics. All four groups were highly concentrated, but their internal migration worked to break down nativity concentrations and to disperse the population. These findings are consistent with Neuman and Tienda's (1994) study of secondary migration among undocumented aliens whose status was legalized under the provisions of the 1986 Immigration Reform and Control Act. They found that Mexican and Salvadoran movers were less residentially concentrated than nonmovers.

Conclusion

The first conclusion of this study is that immigrant groups differ markedly in levels of geographic concentration as a result of differing length of residence in the United States, differing circumstances under which they migrated, and widely varying levels of education and other forms of human capital. The fact that some "new" immigrants are not particularly concentrated and that other, highly concentrated groups seem to be dispersing is inconsistent with the image of a demographically balkanized America. If secondary migration leads to greater residential dispersion, the social impacts of immigration will, in the long term, be less acute than they are now.

Any conclusions about demographic balkanization must be accompanied by a caveat about the scale of analysis. This study investigated geographic concentration, assimilation, and migration at the state scale. A finding that a group is well integrated at the state scale does not necessarily mean that it is integrated at the metropolitan or neighborhood scale. A group may be highly segregated into ethnic neighborhoods or apartment complexes but highly integrated across states. The demographic balkanization thesis, as articulated by Frey, can be argued at both the state and metropolitan scales. The results of this study inform on the state-level balkanization argument.

A second conclusion is that the internal migration streams of the foreign born differ dramatically in size, efficiency, and direction. There is no typical pattern of efficient or inefficient streams, movement toward or away from immigrant concentrations, or focus on a single core or multiple cores. Thus we need to be extremely cautious when referring to the migration patterns of the foreign born. Subgroups of the foreign born are at least as different from one another as the foreign born are from the native born. Their geographic and migration experiences have been conditioned by their differing timing of entry, circumstances of entry, information about alternative destinations, human capital, and conditions at the initial destination (see chapter 12, this volume). Instead of looking for overarching theories of immigrant residential adaption, we may need to look for explanations and policies specific to particular groups in particular settings at particular times in their settlement histories.

References

Allen, James P., and Eugene J. Turner. 1988. *We the People: An Atlas of America's Ethnic Diversity*. New York: Macmillan.

Bartel, Ann P. 1989. "Where Do the New U.S. Immigrants Live?" *Journal of Labor Economics* 7, 4: 371–391.

Belanger, Alain, and Andrei Rogers. 1993. "The Internal Migration and Spatial Redistribution of the Foreign-Born Population in the United States: 1965–70 and 1975–80." *International Migration Review* 26, 4: 1342–1369.

Boswell, Thomas D. 1993. "The Cuban-American Homeland in Miami." *Journal of Cultural Geography* 13: 133–48.

Dunlevy, James A. 1980. "Twentieth Century European Immigration to the U.S.: Intended versus Lifetime Settlement Patterns." *Economic Development and Cultural Change* 13: 79–90.

Frey, William H. 1995. "Immigration, Domestic Migration, and Demographic Balkanization in America: New Evidence for the 1990s." *Population and Development Review*. 22, 4: 741–763.

———. 1996a. "Immigration and Internal Migration 'Flight' from U.S. Metropolitan Areas: Toward a New Demographic Balkanisation." *Urban Studies* 32, 4–5: 733–757.

———. 1996b. "Immigrant and Native Migrant Magnets." *American Demographics* 18, 11: 37–53.

Garcia, Maria C. 1996. *Havana USA: Cuban Exiles and Cuban Americans in South Florida, 1959–1994*. Berkeley: University of California Press.

Gurak, Douglas T., and Fe Caces. 1992. "Migration Networks and the Shaping of Migration Systems." In Mary M. Kritz, Lin L. Lim, and Hania Zlotnick (eds.), *International Migration Systems: A Global Approach*. Oxford: Clarendon.

Haines, David W. 1988. "Kinship in Vietnamese Refugee Resettlement: A Review of the U.S. Experience." *Journal of Comparative Family Studies* 19: 1–16.

Kritz, Mary M., and June M. Nogle. 1994. "Nativity Concentration and Internal Migration among the Foreign-Born." *Demography* 31, 3: 509–524.

Massey, Douglas S., Joaquin Arango, Graeme Hugo, Ali Kouaouci, Adela Pellegrino, and J. Edward Taylor. 1994. "An Evaluation of International Migration Theory: The North American Case." *Population and Development Review* 20, 2: 699–751.

Mortland, Carol A., and Judy Ledgerwood. 1987. "Secondary Migration among Southeast Asian Refugees in the United States." *Urban Anthropology* 16, 3–4: 291–326.

Neuman, Kristin E., and Marta Tienda. 1994. "The Settlement and Secondary Migration Patterns of Legalized Immigrants: Insight from Administrative Records." In Barry Edmonston and Jeffrey Passel (eds.), *Immigration and Ethnicity: The Integration of America's Newest Immigrants*. Lanham, Md.: Urban Institute.

Newbold, K. Bruce. 1996. "Internal Migration of the Foreign-Born in Canada." *International Migration Review* 30, 3: 728–747.

U.S. Bureau of the Census.1990. "The Foreign-Born Population in the United States." CD–DEC90–SSTF–01, Subject Summary Tape Files. Washington, D.C.: U.S. Bureau of the Census.

———. 1996. "Population by Country of Birth, Citizenship, and Year of Entry." *Current Population Survey,* March. Washington, D.C.: U.S. Bureau of the Census.

U.S. Immigration and Naturalization Service. 1991. *An Immigrant Nation: United States Regulation of Immigration, 1798–1991*. Washington, D.C.: U.S. Government Printing Office.

Waldinger, Roger, Robin Ward, and Howard Aldrich. 1985. "Ethnic Business and Occupational Mobility in Advanced Societies." *Sociology* 19, 3: 586–597.

Ward, David. 1971. *Cities and Immigrants*. New York: Oxford University Press.

Zhou, Min, and John R. Logan. 1989. "Returns on Human Capital in Ethnic Enclaves: New York City's Chinatown." *American Sociological Review* 54: 809–820.

12

Evolutionary Immigrant Settlement Patterns: Concepts and Evidence

K. Bruce Newbold

One of the dominant themes in current migration research is the role of immigration in restructuring the demographic profile of the United States (see chapters 5, 6, and 9, this volume). Whereas such questions can and must be set within the context of economic restructuring and a changing political environment, the large number of annual arrivals continues to raise important questions regarding the geography of their settlement patterns, distribution, and adjustment within U.S. society (see chapters 10 and 11, this volume). Such issues are especially relevant in the period immediately following arrival, when the likelihood of a subsequent migration is the highest and settlement choice is adjusted or fine-tuned. Recent studies that analyze the population distribution of the foreign born within the United States demonstrate that economic factors and cultural–ethnic effects are important in explaining observed settlement patterns (see, e.g., Bartel 1989; Bartel and Koch 1991; Belanger and Rogers 1993; Kritz and Nogle 1994), but they represent a cross-sectional (stock) picture of the settlement system only. Ultimately, such studies tell us relatively little of how the settlement system evolved, where it evolved from, or the reasons and processes through which it evolved.

In reality, the demographic restructuring of the population is not a one-time event related to immigrant arrival. The distribution of the immigrant population reflects a settlement system that has evolved over the years and does not necessarily reflect the conditions faced by immigrants or their stated intentions at the time of arrival. Instead, it represents an ongoing process through which the settlement pattern is restructured in response to changes in economic conditions, shifting government policies, new information on alternative locations, employment opportunities, housing and cultural effects (among other factors). As a result, only limited distinctions with respect to settlement patterns or choices can be made among recent and earlier arrivals, those who settled after a series of moves, and those who did not move at all after arrival.

What is missing from the literature is an evaluation of how the foreign-born settlement system evolves. This chapter seeks to extend the understanding of immigrant adjustment within the United States by exploring the temporal settlement patterns of immigrant groups, along with reasons for their spatial adjustment. The temporal dimension adds an important additional component to the analysis of the immigrant settlement system, focusing on how the settlement pattern evolves and is structured over time. Although the emphasis is on both macrolevel and microlevel features of the foreign-born migration system, that is not an implicit acceptance of assimilation theory and its attendant problems (Desbarats 1985; Hirschman 1982; Portes and Zhou 1994). Instead, this chapter asks what spatial adjustments the foreign born have made and what conditions (i.e., political, social, and economic) motivate their decisions within the context of segmented assimilation (Portes and Zhou 1994).

The first part of the chapter introduces three proposed settlement patterns: the intended settlement pattern (the destination reported to Immigration and Naturalization Service at the time of entry), the initial settlement pattern (where immigrants first settle after arrival), and the established settlement pattern (the pattern that evolves after a period of residency in the United States). Throughout, immigrants can be either legal immigrants or refugees, and distinctions between the two groups are made as needed. Evidence drawn from the existing literature and the 1990 census supporting these distinctions is presented in the second section. These examples serve to illustrate, not prove, the existence of an evolutionary settlement system. A proper analysis of linkages among immigration, migration, and settlement patterns requires the collection of data beyond the scope of this chapter and is saved for future research. Such analysis also requires appropriate conceptual and theoretical foundations. The third part of this chapter therefore presents three alternative hypotheses linking the immigrant-migrant-settlement system based on existing migration and immigration theory. The concluding section offers suggestions for future research in this area.

Defining Evolutionary Settlement Systems

The settlement system of the immigrant population is not static but instead reflects complex processes that evolve over time as immigrants respond to evolving pressures and opportunities within both the immigrant group and larger society. As ethnic communities grow and mature, they are often absorbed into the larger community and are not necessarily permanent. Yet complete dispersion may take a generation or more to achieve, depending on factors such as the degree of isolation experienced by the immigrant community, the in-migration of earlier immigrants belonging to the same ethnic group, and the continued arrival of new immigrants who reinforce the existing community. Even when ethnic communities reject or are denied assimilation into larger society, they may relocate but retain their coherence as they outgrow older communities, acquire space, or contain newly affluent members who can afford or compete for housing elsewhere (Alba and Logan 1991; Portes 1994).

Of interest in this chapter are the scale, direction, and magnitude of adjustments made to the immigrant settlement system immediately after arrival and the reasons these adjustments occur. In the following discussion three settlement patterns are conceptualized: the *intended* settlement choice, the *initial* settlement choice, and the *established* settlement choice pattern. Each of these three choice patterns may work at a variety of spatial scales. Although conceptually separate, the proposed settlement patterns are not mutually exclusive, nor is a strict temporal order assumed. Instead, individuals may pass directly from the intended to the established pattern, or the intended pattern may become the established pattern. Further, different groups defined by period of arrival and ethnic identity (among other factors) are likely to display comparatively different settlement systems. Indeed, the literature points to differential evolution rates and settlement patterns across (and within) immigrant and ethnic groups. Chapters 10 and 11 in this volume discuss migration and dispersion tendencies among immigrants, concluding that immigrant groups differ significantly in their concentration, migration patterns, and reasons for migration. Similarly, other studies (e.g., Dunlevy 1980; Gorrie 1991; Frey 1996) have found that earlier waves of immigrants have moved into suburbs and across the country, suggesting greater social and economic acceptance by the existing population, time since arrival, or the existence of other factors aiding spatial adjustment.

Intended, Initial, and Established Settlement Patterns

The intended settlement pattern reflects the stated destination at time of entry and is revealed by annual immigration statistics made available by the Immigration and Naturalization Service (INS). For new arrivals the choice of settlement location is frequently made before arrival and is a function of known information and chain migration, typically occurring within a highly constrained sociocultural context (Castles and Miller 1993; Massey et al. 1994; Pedraza and Rumbaut 1996; Piore 1979). Gateway states such as New York, Texas, California, and Illinois and major metropolitan centers such as New York City, Chicago, Los Angeles, and Miami absorb many of the new immigrant arrivals (Frey 1996) while providing a familiar cultural, social, and economic environment. This is especially true for low-skilled immigrants who are more dependent on their families and friends to link them to local employment networks and offset the risks associated with immigration.

Whereas legal entry to the United States provides access to a preferred location and makes a secondary migration less likely, immigrants cannot know with certainty what the destination (or the future) holds. Instead, the intended destination may represent only a provisional, temporary destination. New information and other effects (i.e., social, cultural, economic) (Dunlevy 1980; Forbes 1985; Roberts 1995) may quickly result in the choice of a new, initial location that satisfies needs and preferences. Although the initial and intended patterns are likely to be highly correlated since new immigrants are likely to be risk adverse, using known contacts and information to make the settlement choice, ascertaining the degree of differentiation between the intended and initial settlement choices is difficult. In testing the accuracy of data gathered by the government on the intended destination as an indicator of the state of residence in 1990, however, Isserman and Kort (1988) noted that a large proportion did in fact settle in their intended destination.

Among refugees the intended settlement location may not be realized at all, and divergence between the intended and initial settlement patterns may be greater. Although the United States does not explicitly pursue national policies of (legal) immigrant settlement, it has pursued *refugee* settlement programs. Such programs, which have included the Cuban Refugee Relocation Program and the Inter Agency Task Force on Indochinese Refugees, represented attempts to ensure population dispersal and to prevent the financial burden of adjustment from falling on a few metropolitan areas or states. Various public organizations such as churches, social groups, and families (in conjunction with the government) have also influenced settlement of these and other groups by providing assistance, contacts, and employment opportunities. Although efforts are made to meet stated locational preferences (i.e., intended settlement location), this is not always the case. Nevertheless, neither legal immigrants nor refugees are bound to their stated (i.e., intended) or assigned (i.e., initial) destination by government legislation. Instead, the economic and social incorporation of immigrants is largely left to market and sociocultural forces along with individual decisions and preferences. In particular, the propensity to relocate may be heightened among refugees with few or no place ties where they were settled, as the "pull" of family or jobs did not serve as a counterpressure to relocate.

The established settlement pattern is revealed after a period of residency in the adopted country. With knowledge of other opportunities, a poor intended or initial settlement choice can be corrected, allowing earlier arrivals to respond to economic, social, and political conditions by making their own migration and settlement decisions (Moore and Rosenberg 1995). Dunlevy (1980), for instance, noted that the ultimate destination pattern of immigrants arriving at the turn of the twentieth century was more dispersed than the pattern indicated in the announced intentions of the immigrants. Although likely to vary from group to group, the established settlement pattern should evolve rather quickly after arrival (Forbes 1985), as duration of residence effects and the accumulation of location-specific capital decrease the likelihood of a subsequent migration (DaVanzo 1978). Similarly, the duration of the established pattern is uncertain and is also likely to vary across contexts, but it is assumed to be temporally stable over the medium to long term.

Evidence of Evolutionary Immigrant Settlement Systems

Evidence from the 1990 Census

Linked to historical patterns, immigration has long exerted strong impacts on a handful of destinations (Frey 1995, 1996). New York has been the point of entry for generations of immigrants, whereas centers such as Los Angeles have more recently been the point of entry for Pacific Rim nationalities. Other metropolitan areas such as Chicago, San Francisco, and Miami are also home to many foreign born.

But knowledge of the proportional share of a group in a metropolitan area or state does not really suggest the evolutionary patterns inherent within the system. When compared over successive periods, for instance, population shares may show relatively little change, clouded by changes in the distribution of the native-born population, continued immigration, and internal migration by the foreign born. At the same time, careful analysis of the 1990 census (5 percent Public Use Microdata Samples) (U.S. Bureau of the Census 1991) provides support for the evolutionary system. Specifically, by examining the geographic distribution of immigrants and their migration rates with respect to period of arrival, systematic changes in their settlement patterns can be observed.

The sample used in the following analysis includes all foreign born aged 5 and over in 1990, with measures computed at both the state and metropolitan scales. The sample excludes individuals originating in Puerto Rico and other U.S. protectorates and the institutionalized.[1] Adjustments to the settlement pattern are assumed to be made by legal immigrants or refugees. At the metropolitan level, the analysis was restricted to those residing in the twenty-five largest metropolitan areas in 1990 (representing approximately 71 percent of the foreign-born population in the United States). Eighteen separate national origin groups were identified, and remaining immigrants were grouped into "rest of Europe," "rest of Asia," "rest of Americas," and "rest of World."[2]

Table 12.1 shows the geographic distribution (G) of immigrants in their 1990 place of residence (state or metropolitan area) by period of immigration and country of origin, where G is defined as (Haggett, Cliff, and Frey 1977)

$$G = [\Sigma f_j] / 100 \tag{1}$$

and f_j is the deviation between the group's share in region j and the total population in region j and only positive deviations are summed. Values of G close

Table 12.1 Geographic Distribution (*G*) of Foreign Born by Major Origin Area, Arrival Cohort, and Place of Residence, Age 5+

A. By 1990 Metropolitan Area of Residence

	Arrival Cohort							
	1985–1990	1980–1984	1975–1979	1970–1974	1965–1969	1960–1964	1950–1959	Pre-1950
Germany	0.14	0.19	0.21	0.15	0.14	0.13	0.13	0.28
Italy	0.29	0.33	0.40	0.48	0.47	0.44	0.43	0.41
Poland	0.49	0.41	0.48	0.46	0.48	0.44	0.39	0.43
U.K.	0.25	0.19	0.15	0.17	0.23	0.22	0.21	0.25
USSR	0.35	0.38	0.37	0.42	0.40	0.35	0.30	0.32
Rest of Europe	0.21	0.22	0.20	0.23	0.19	0.21	0.19	0.25
China[1]	0.37	0.41	0.40	0.36	0.39	0.41	0.40	0.41
India	0.26	0.27	0.25	0.24	0.19	—	—	—
Japan	0.26	0.33	0.33	0.30	0.30	0.35	—	—
Korea	0.32	0.29	0.28	0.28	0.25	0.25	—	—
Philippines	0.42	0.45	0.46	0.39	0.40	0.44	0.50	0.47
Vietnam	0.42	0.47	0.49	0.39	—	—	—	—
Rest of Asia	0.24	0.29	0.27	0.24	0.24	0.27	0.28	0.29
Canada	0.21	0.22	0.21	0.17	0.25	0.30	0.33	0.32
El Salvador	0.50	0.53	0.57	0.51	0.49	—	—	—
Mexico	0.53	0.55	0.57	0.58	0.57	0.58	0.55	0.53
Cuba	0.78	0.71	0.65	0.63	0.63	0.64	0.63	0.58
Dominican Republic	0.72	0.73	0.73	0.72	0.73	—	—	—
Jamaica	0.60	0.59	0.59	0.58	0.59	0.53	—	—
Columbia	0.52	0.55	0.48	0.51	0.50	0.41	—	—
Rest of Americas	0.44	0.40	0.42	0.44	0.42	0.39	0.35	0.33
Rest of World	0.28	0.29	0.27	0.29	0.29	0.31	0.22	0.21
Total	0.28	0.31	0.28	0.29	0.29	0.29	0.19	0.23

B. By 1990 State of Residence

	Arrival Cohort							
	1985–1990	1980–1984	1975–1979	1970–1974	1965–1969	1960–1964	1950–1959	Pre-1950
Germany	0.18	0.19	0.21	0.14	0.15	0.16	0.15	0.30
Italy	0.33	0.35	0.39	0.52	0.51	0.48	0.47	0.45
Poland	0.52	0.46	0.55	0.53	0.56	0.50	0.43	0.46
U.K.	0.32	0.26	0.26	0.23	0.26	0.26	0.28	0.32
USSR	0.50	0.51	0.51	0.54	0.53	0.45	0.36	0.39
Rest of Europe	0.28	0.30	0.29	0.28	0.28	0.28	0.26	0.28
China[1]	0.39	0.49	0.49	0.45	0.47	0.49	0.50	0.49
India	0.29	0.34	0.32	0.31	0.26	—	—	—
Japan	0.30	0.35	0.32	0.30	0.28	0.31	—	—
Korea	0.36	0.38	0.35	0.36	0.31	0.27	—	—

(Cont.)

Table 12.1 Geographic Distribution (*G*) of Foreign Born by Major Origin Area, Arrival Cohort, and Place of Residence, Age 5+ (*Cont.*)

	Arrival Cohort							
	1985–1990	1980–1984	1975–1979	1970–1974	1965–1969	1960–1964	1950–1959	Pre-1950
Philippines	0.50	0.53	0.52	0.48	0.49	0.49	0.51	0.59
Vietnam	0.45	0.48	0.46	0.35	—	—	—	—
Rest of Asia	0.31	0.34	0.31	0.32	0.33	0.34	0.34	0.35
Canada	0.26	0.31	0.28	0.25	0.31	0.35	0.36	0.39
El Salvador	0.56	0.59	0.60	0.60	0.58	—	—	—
Mexico	0.62	0.64	0.66	0.67	0.68	0.68	0.66	0.65
Cuba	0.80	0.72	0.66	0.68	0.67	0.66	0.65	0.60
Dominican Republic	0.76	0.77	0.75	0.75	0.75	—	—	—
Jamaica	0.65	0.64	0.63	0.63	0.65	0.59	—	—
Columbia	0.53	0.56	0.50	0.53	0.52	0.48	—	—
Rest of Americas	0.49	0.51	0.48	0.49	0.48	0.46	0.40	0.39
Rest of World	0.34	0.36	0.34	0.34	0.35	0.33	0.27	0.31
Total	0.34	0.39	0.36	0.36	0.35	0.33	0.25	0.29

Notes: 1. Includes Taiwan and Hong Kong origins.
— = NA.

to 1 indicate that the immigrant population is localized relative to the overall population, and values close to zero indicate the foreign-born population is dispersed throughout the overall population.

The decrease in the overall *G* value from 0.28 to 0.23 at the metropolitan level and from 0.34 to 0.29 at the state level indicates moderate but not necessarily monotonic dispersion with increasing duration of residence in the United States. With respect to place of birth, Europeans and Canadians were generally the least concentrated, whereas immigrants from Asia, Central America, and South America were more concentrated at both the metropolitan and state levels. Two exceptions were the Italians and Poles, who remained concentrated even among the oldest arrival cohorts. Dominicans were the most spatially concentrated group, with *G* values greater than 0.70 regardless of period of arrival.

Restricting the sample to those who arrived in the United States prior to 1985, state and metropolitan migration rates provide alternative indicators of an evolving settlement system.[3] With an interstate migration rate of 9.2 percent, the foreign born were slightly (but significantly) more likely to make an interstate migration than were native-born Americans (9.1 percent) (Newbold 1997). Among the most recent arrivals (i.e., those arriving between 1982 and 1984 and reporting a 1985 state of residence), interstate migration rates were even higher (14.0 percent). Similarly, the overall intermetropolitan migration rate was 6.3 percent among pre-1985 arrivals and was 8.8 percent among the most recently arrived. In comparison, the native-born intermetropolitan migration rate was 8.6 percent. Consequently, the high mobility among the foreign born in general and particularly among the most recent arrivals suggests that the intended settlement pattern created at the time of immigration would be short-lived. In other words, the settlement pattern is more diverse and dynamic than what can be observed at the time of the census.

Table 12.2 shows migration rates for specific age groups by period of arrival. If, as expected, the foreign born are more likely to migrate in the period immediately after arrival, migration rates should be higher for recent arrivals as compared with earlier arrival cohorts for each age group. Indeed, this is largely confirmed. At both the state and metropolitan levels, the most recent arrivals (those arriving between 1980 and 1984) were more likely to migrate than their like-aged counterparts who arrived earlier. This pattern was observed even among the elderly. For example, 1980 to 1984 arrivals aged 70 and over had an interstate migration rate of 7.1 percent. Those arriving between 1975 and 1979 had a migration rate of 5.5 percent, and pre-1950 arrivals had a migration rate of just 4.2 percent. At the metropolitan scale, arrivals between 1980 and 1984

Table 12.2 Migration Rates by Age in 1990 and Arrival Cohort (%)

	Arrival Cohort						
Age in 1990	1980–1984	1975–1979	1970–1974	1965–1969	1960–1964	1950–1959	Pre-1950
A. Metropolitan Area[1]							
30–34	9.2	6.9	—[2]	—	—	—	—
35–39	7.9	6.7	5.8	—	—	—	—
40–45	7.1	5.7	4.7	4.9	—	—	—
45–49	5.9	4.1	4.4	4.3	4.0	—	—
50–54	5.6	4.0	3.8	3.7	4.0	3.8	—
55–59	4.7	3.7	3.3	4.4	3.6	3.5	3.9
60–64	4.5	3.7	4.1	4.4	4.6	4.8	4.9
65–69	4.4	3.6	4.3	6.0	6.1	5.1	5.8
70+	4.5	3.6	3.3	4.6	3.9	4.3	3.6
B. State							
30–34	14.9	10.6	—	—	—	—	—
35–39	12.6	10.4	8.3	—	—	—	—
40–45	10.5	9.0	7.5	7.1	—	—	—
45–49	9.2	7.0	6.3	6.0	5.7	—	—
50–54	8.2	6.5	5.4	5.1	5.4	4.8	—
55–59	7.0	5.6	4.8	5.3	4.9	4.5	5.5
60–64	7.2	5.4	5.2	4.6	5.0	5.5	5.7
65–69	7.6	5.3	5.4	6.9	5.9	5.6	6.2
70+	7.1	5.5	5.0	5.3	4.3	4.8	4.2

Notes: 1. Based on 25 largest metropolitan areas.
— = NA.

(aged 70+) had a migration rate of 4.5 percent, whereas their counterparts who arrived before 1950 had a migration rate of only 3.6 percent. Similarly, migration rates declined with increasing duration of residence (expressed by arrival cohort) across other age groups, providing further evidence of potentially strong redistributional tendencies within the foreign-born population.

Foreign-Born Settlement Patterns: Specific Examples

The previous analysis still provides only a cross-sectional picture of the immigrant population (stock) and fails to provide insight into the dynamic evolution of the immigrant settlement system (flows). More specific examples of the evolutionary nature of the immigrant settlement system can be found within the existing literature. For example, Walker and Hannan (1989) examined immigrant settlement patterns based on yearly immigration statistics. Their findings noted that immigrants from traditional source countries tended to deconcentrate as the influence of family and friends decreased over the study period. Conversely, more recent immigrants from nontraditional source countries concentrated in ethnic communities and displayed differing responses to economic influences across ethnic groups. The authors concluded that the settlement process was "a complex immigration process of several stages" and that "static results should not be compared at a single point in time for groups that may be at different stages of an immigration process" (Walker and Hannan 1989: 181).

Similarly, Allen and Turner (1996) noted variations in population concentration by arrival cohort among immigrants residing in Los Angeles. The percentage of recent arrivals (those arriving between 1987 and 1990) residing in zones of ethnic concentration was nearly twice that of pre-1970 arrivals, confirming the expectation that settlement is initially concentrated but disperses with increasing duration of residence and further adjustment within U.S. society. Further disaggregation of immigrant groups found that higher-income immigrants tended to be more dispersed. Those more likely to settle in ethnically concentrated areas frequently had poorer English-language abilities, lower educational attainment, lower rates of naturalization, and lower income levels.

More specific evidence of evolutionary settlement systems can be found among particular ethnic groups. First, no sizable Vietnamese community existed within the United States prior to 1975. With the end of the Vietnam War, the settlement of Vietnamese refugees in the United States was supervised by a special Interagency Task Force. On the assumption that a dispersed settlement pattern would speed adaptation, priority was given to the geographic dispersion of Vietnamese (Desbarats 1985, 1986), resulting in a distribution that closely resembled that of the U.S. population. Despite the efforts of the task force and other groups, approximately 45 percent of the Indochinese refugees who arrived in the United States in 1975 resided in a different state by 1980 (Baker and North 1984). This correlates closely with the approximately 50 percent of refugees who were settled by the task force in a state other than their state of choice (i.e., intended destination). Further analysis showed that preferred settlement locations included urban areas, areas with milder climates, and areas for which refugees had prior information. Proximity to family or national groups was not a factor since there were few Vietnamese in the United States at the time of their arrival. On the other hand, secondary migration occurred quickly after arrival and resulted in an increasingly concentrated Indochinese population, largely propelled by the desire to reside within a familiar cultural community. As roots and place ties were established with increasing duration of residence, migration rates declined.

The long-term survival of Chinatowns in many North American cities provides an example of established settlement patterns. Historically, Chinatowns were the product of discrimination and self-protection from the external community. Whereas immigration continues into traditional Chinatowns, new arrivals are typically poorly educated and skilled. In contrast, the better-educated and higher-income groups (both new arrivals and existing community members) have more recently been attracted to suburban locations. Recent movement into suburbia points not only to changing preferences for newer homes and communities and social mobility but also to the importance of social and cultural ties in maintaining and creating spatially concentrated communities. Similarly, the movement suggests that ethnic communities are no longer restricted to highly centralized, older parts of cities (Alba and Logan 1991; Gorrie 1991; Allen and Turner 1996). Their evolving settlement system may also be a result of metropolitan deconcentration, transportation developments that encourage suburban locations, and long-term migration chains. If, for example, earlier immigrants had already dispersed out of traditional ethnic areas, new arrivals would follow (Allen and Turner 1996).

Miami's Cuban population provides a third and final example that illustrates an established settlement pattern similar to the intended pattern despite relocation attempts by the government. Upon arrival, Cuban refugees placed themselves in Miami (their intended settlement). The large-scale immigration to south Florida prompted the government to initiate the Cuban Refugee Program, designed to lessen south Florida's service provision burden. The program was initiated in 1961, and more than 150,000 Cubans had been relocated from Miami by 1967. The better educated, the better skilled, and those with some knowledge of English were especially targeted by the government (Boswell and Curtis 1984). By the 1970s, however, large numbers of Cubans were returning to south Florida (and to Miami in particular). Most returnees cited the desire to live near friends, family, and coethnics, along with the south Florida climate, as reasons for returning. Although economic effects and job opportunities were rarely mentioned (Bean and Tienda 1987), large numbers of those returning to south Florida were poverty migrants and poorly educated, suggesting their need to access Miami's Cuban community (McHugh, Miyares, and Skop 1997). Further evidence from the 1980 and 1990 censuses has shown a continued movement back to Miami and that Cubans have become even more highly concentrated than before (Perez 1992; McHugh, Miyares, and Skop 1997). The large Cuban community in Miami and Dade County can now be defined as an established settlement pattern.

The complexities of the immigrant settlement system are evident, but care must be taken when comparing results across groups that may be at different stages in the immigration-migration-settlement process. Despite available evidence, it is still uncertain exactly how this process evolves, what its stages are, or if some generalizable theory can be extracted. Duration of residence effects, age, ethnic–national ties, changing personal preferences, and economic conditions (among other effects) are all likely to influence the relocation decision. Clearly, the settlement system should be conceptualized as a complex process through which individuals, households, and groups adapt to opportunities or difficulties over space and time. In addition, more appropriate questions should include the motivations for long-term group cohesion and settlement patterns, along with the reasons for spatial relocation. This means that the settlement system should be viewed through appropriate theoretical lenses.

Theoretical Considerations

Theories of immigrant adaptation and assimilation provide the framework to evaluate the settlement patterns of the foreign born. Classical assimilation theory (e.g., Park 1928; Gordon 1964) stressed the relationship between the geographic distribution of an immigrant group and its integration into the host society. Immigrants were assumed to concentrate and settle in immigrant communities upon arrival but move to other areas as social capital increased or other opportunities were presented. Because social interaction was assumed to depend on physical proximity, an immigrant distribution similar to the overall population would reduce interaction between group members and increase interaction between the immigrant group and the native-born population. On the other hand, if the immigrant group was spatially isolated, the assimilation process would be slow. Velocity of absorption could also vary with language, religion, and race, but the steps and end result were essentially the same: it was expected that all groups would eventually assimilate into mainstream society and that the degree of spatial assimilation was therefore a barometer of a group's overall assimilation into mainstream society. Even institutionally complete ethnic communities (such as the Jewish community on the Lower East Side of Manhattan or the Japanese community in Los Angeles, which existed during the first decades of the twentieth century but are now gone) rarely last longer than one or two generations (Portes 1995).

More recent experience has shown that assimilation does not necessarily or automatically lead to similarity and equality with mainstream culture; nor is this necessarily the only outcome (Portes and Böröcz 1989; Portes 1994; Portes and

Zhou 1994). Instead, assimilation is "segmented" and dependent on issues such as race, degree of discrimination, the economy, and the presence of a preexisting ethnic community. Although assimilation *may* lead to integration with mainstream society, integration may also occur in the reverse direction: into the underclass (i.e., the values and norms of the inner city). In other words, the settlement options available to the immigrant may be spatially bounded by socially constructed barriers. Constraints may be imposed by the ethnic community itself (particularly if it perceives itself as oppressed or threatened) or through government policies, economic conditions, social acceptance by the larger community, or the individual (Portes 1995). Assimilation may also represent a combination of economic advancement and preservation of the immigrant community.

Instead of directly confronting assimilation theory, the spatial adjustments made by immigrants and the conditions (i.e., political, social, ethnic, and economic) motivating these decisions are of interest in this chapter. Regardless of population concentration or dispersion, hypotheses describing the evolution of immigration settlement patterns are missing or inadequately articulated and tested within the literature. As such, the literature needs to address not just *why* the foreign born move but *how* their settlement pattern evolves. Acknowledging that different groups (i.e., defined along ethnic, national, personal, or period of arrival lines) may follow different settlement trajectories, immigrant-migrant-settlement path linkages can be examined through three conceptual frameworks. Each framework represents extensions of existing migration and immigration theory and includes the *selectivity hypothesis,* the *adaption-exposure hypothesis,* and the *ethnic effects hypothesis*. The hypotheses do not necessarily imply that immigrant settlement patterns will become more dispersed (concentrated) with time; nor are they mutually exclusive. Instead, they represent an attempt to provide a more robust and empirically testable theoretical foundation for subsequent research.

Selectivity Hypothesis

The selectivity hypothesis argues that secondary migration after arrival in the United States results from the migration experience along with other personal factors such as age, level of education, and sex (DaVanzo 1978; Nogle 1994; Trovato and Halli 1983, 1990). Such sociodemographic factors are hypothesized to influence the migration of the foreign born in much the same way as the native-born population. Migration is seen as the outcome of individual-level processes rather than of a group or social process; as individuals acquire human capital and improve their ability to interact within society, the likelihood of migration increases.

The well-established positive association between education and internal migration, for example (Greenwood 1975; Long 1988), reflects a greater willingness on the part of the better educated to take risks and to gather and process information on competing destinations. Bartel (1989) found that better-educated immigrants had higher rates of migration and that their movement resulted in increased geographic dispersion, although dispersionary tendencies among the foreign-born population as a whole were absent. Immigrants who are successful may be predisposed to move again, further improving their circumstances. Those who are unsuccessful may emigrate or stay.

Although it is widely accepted that migration and immigration are selective processes at all spatial scales, a large proportion of foreign born are poorly educated and skilled in comparison with the native-born population (Frey 1995) and may therefore be less likely to make a secondary migration. Since they are not positively selective in the classical sense (Myrdal 1957), the intended settlement pattern may closely resemble the established pattern. For refugees in particular, level of education is unlikely to make a difference in migration propensities. Given language barriers and the tendency for even better-educated newcomers to take entry-level positions, education would not reduce the costs associated with migration (Forbes 1985).

Adaption-Exposure Hypothesis

The adaption-exposure hypothesis suggests that the settlement system is shaped by individual, societal, and economic conditions in the origin and potential settlement areas. Differences in personal attributes (e.g., level of education) along with differences in labor market participation, employment, and skill qualifications will result in different settlement patterns. Once discrepancies in sociodemographic and socioeconomic effects disappear or are minimized, differences in settlement patterns and population distribution will also disappear.

As new arrivals, immigrants may be more dissatisfied with their employment opportunities, be more prone to periods of unemployment, and have shallower ties to their region of first settlement and may therefore migrate for new opportunities (Forbes 1985; Neuman and Tienda 1994; Nogle 1994). The literature supports the idea that the foreign born migrate for similar reasons as the native born. In an analysis of the internal migration of the foreign born in Canada, Newbold (1996) found that the foreign born were attracted to destinations with high employment growth and high income levels. Whereas immigrants responded to the national labor market and amenities, distance decreased interaction across space. Personal attributes such as age, education, and sex also influenced the migration of the foreign born but in a way that was similar to the overall Canadian population. Because of the similarities with respect to reasons for migration of foreign-born and native-born Canadians, the results suggested that differences in migration were largely the result of individual characteristics and less of ethnicity per se.

An additional dimension along which adaptation varies is the host society. Economic, political, and legal constraints imposed by the larger community organize or limit opportunities for new arrivals within mainstream society (Portes and Zhou 1994; Portes 1995). Portes (1995) identified three levels of reception–

government policy, civic society, and public opinion—that reflect the constraints influencing the incorporation of some ethnic groups. Government policy may run the continuum from complete acceptance to active opposition. Initial settlement patterns have been in part determined by government policies that have encouraged the dispersal of refugee populations and family reunification. Likewise, civic and public acceptance of immigrants may run from fanfare to indifference to opposition. Immigrants from northwestern Europe have typically met with the least resistance, whereas ethnically or racially distinct groups have often faced greater opposition.

Public opinion toward arrivals and the presence of ethnic communities will also affect the speed of spatial adaptation. Immigrants belonging to groups too small in number to create distinct communities are more likely to find themselves dispersed throughout the larger population. Other arrivals may join or create ethnic communities, thereby providing employment, protection, and economic mobility not available to others. Faced with prejudice or poverty conditions, immigrants may be less likely to migrate and disperse. Participation in ethnic–national communities may similarly limit socioeconomic and spatial mobility and opportunities within larger society. Segregation may also be voluntary as immigrants choose to live in ethnic neighborhoods to maintain linguistic or cultural ties (Howenstine 1996). Research in the 1970s, for example, showed that Hispanic segregation was mostly voluntary, determined by residential succession and spatial assimilation (Massey 1985; Bean and Tienda 1987). Over time, processes of succession and consolidation produced segregated residential districts with the advantages of opportunities for employment and political representation and greater cultural, linguistic and religious expression. Ultimately, immigrants must be viewed not simply as individuals but also as members of groups who participate in broader social structures that affect their spatial behavior and consequently the evolution of their settlement system.

Ethnic Effects Hypothesis

Of the three hypothesized linkages among immigration, migration, and settlement, the ethnic effects hypothesis has (implicitly) received the greatest attention in the literature. Essentially, the ethnic effects hypothesis argues that ethnicity has an independent effect on the settlement pattern of immigrants. Although the foreign born respond to economic attractions similarly to the native-born population (Bartel and Koch 1991; Newbold 1996), the role of ethnic effects and social networks may weaken the influence of those factors in the migration and settlement decision. Ethnicity has been hypothesized to encourage (or discourage) migration through the strength of ties to family and friends (Lansing and Mueller 1973; Ritchey 1976; Tienda and Wilson 1992; Roberts 1995), social ties to community and kin (Massey et al. 1987; Massey and España

1987; Uhlenburg 1973), historical inertia and temporal ties (Dunlevy 1980; Frey 1995; Roberts 1995), assistance in employment and housing (Boswell and Curtis 1984; Massey et al. 1987; Tienda and Wilson 1992), and community size (Moore and Rosenberg 1995).

As part of the migration process, sociocultural and socioethnic networks connect origins and destinations. Decisions to migrate are made by the individual but within the collective context of family or community, thus reflecting dimensions that have an independent effect on migration. Immigrant settlement begins with the arrival of so-called pioneers (Piore 1979). Because of the risk associated with immigration, pioneers are positively self-selective, having strong incentives to gather information on alternative destinations before immigrating and increasing the likelihood of success in their new environment. Newcomers are also more likely to locate where incomes are high and employment is available. As the ethnic community is established, new potential immigrants can reduce their search for alternative locations given the presence of an established community. Later arrivals may select and remain within the ethnic community despite changing economic conditions rather than search for potentially more rewarding locations. Instead, nonpecuniary considerations such as the role of the ethnic community may become important in the settlement decision.

Once again, the literature supports the importance and role of ethnicity in the settlement choice. Immigrants entering the United States through states or cities that are traditional ports of entry for fellow nationals (i.e., their intended or initial settlement) have been observed to be less likely to make a secondary migration (Neuman and Tienda 1994). Social networks most likely account for the strong retention power observed in these gateway areas. Ethnic groups characterized by a dense network of social and economic ties do not sponsor outmigration but deter it by providing opportunities within the communities (Kobrin and Goldsheider 1978; Kobrin and Speare 1983; Trovato and Halli 1990; Baker and North 1984; Piore 1979).

Settlement and ethnicity patterns may also reflect transnationalism (Massey et al. 1994; Massey, Goldring, and Durand 1994) and the temporal basis of ethnic identity (Roberts 1995). First, the transnationalism literature provides evidence of the importance and maintenance of ethnic networks. While settling and incorporating themselves into the economic and political institutions where they reside, individuals may also be engaged in maintaining ties to the countries from which they emigrated. Socialization, education, and business may be transacted across international space. The prospect of a future return migration to the country of birth decreases the likelihood of long-term commitments to the host country, suggesting that further adjustments to the settlement system are unlikely. Unfortunately, the census (and other data files) assumes that individuals reside permanently in the United States and have cut their ties to their countries of birth.

Second, ethnic groups such as Cubans or Jews who adhere to long-term group goals and see themselves as long-term exiles will be more willing to make commitments in terms of property acquisition, business ventures, or investments in the local community. As refugees' hopes for returning to Cuba have come and gone, Miami has been transformed into a "homeland" among exiles (Boswell 1993). Alternatively, group members who do not sustain their goals or group identity over the long term and who are not augmented by new arrivals will be more likely to make a secondary migration. The lower the degree of societal assimilation, the lower the propensity to move away from ethnic communities and the shorter the distance moved should relocation occur.

Despite the acknowledgment that ethnicity is important in the migration decision, what ethnicity actually represents and how it relates to nationality is uncertain and debatable. Included within the measure may be historical effects and temporal identification, kinship ties, assimilation norms (encouraging or discouraging migration), social and cultural organization, psychological effects, and community investment. Most agree that an ethnic group has shared cultural characteristics, identifiable history, structural attributes, and physical and other behaviors (Roseman, Laux, and Thieme 1996), yet its role varies across contexts and has a social value that shapes migration decisions (Neuman and Tienda 1994). Conversely, little agreement exists on whether ethnicity is an intervening variable filtering other effects or an independent effect. In their analysis of interprovincial migration of the foreign born in Canada, Trovato and Halli (1990) noted that ethnicity was relatively unimportant compared with factors such as age and education (confirming the selectivity hypothesis). They also noted that language was more relevant in explaining migration propensities, but since language and ethnicity are closely related the ethnic effects hypothesis may still be valid. If ethnicity does exert an independent effect on the settlement pattern of immigrants, the efficacy of ethnic effects may be derived only through the application of multivariate models or detailed survey methods.

Conclusion

This chapter has synthesized available research regarding the settlement pattern of U.S. immigrants. Throughout, I have argued that the analysis of the internal migration and evolutionary settlement patterns of the foreign born must be considered a dynamic, ongoing process, influenced by period effects, the host society (economic and social acceptance), immigration policy, duration of residence, and ethnicity effects, among other factors. High levels of mobility in the period immediately following migration and changing geographic concentration among other, more specific examples drawn from the existing literature reinforce this need.

As part of the need to look at an evolutionary settlement system, this chapter has introduced or focused on a number of concepts. First, distinctions were made among intended, initial, and established settlement patterns. Three alternative theories were proposed as possible links in the immigration-migration-settlement system. Drawing upon and extending existing migration and immigration theory, these theories present avenues of change and motivations for spatial adjustments among immigrant groups. The selectivity hypothesis argues that subsequent migrations after arrival in the United States are likely a result of the migration experience along with other personal factors such as age, level of education, and sex. The adaption-exposure hypothesis suggests that the settlement system evolves in response to economic and social conditions in the origin and potential settlement areas and as the foreign born become aware of new opportunities that could improve their lot in life. Finally, the ethnic effects hypothesis argues that ethnicity may have an independent effect on the settlement pattern of immigrants and that changes (or lack thereof) in foreign-born settlement patterns after arrival are result of ethnicity.

Immigration has affected (and will continue to affect) the restructuring of U.S. society through internal migration of the foreign born and native born alike and the accompanying economic, demographic, political, and social changes. But will the settlement system evolve as suggested? What is the time frame involved? Which proposed theory best explains the process, or is it some combination of all three that varies across immigrant groups, time of arrival, type of reception, and overall economic conditions?

Further research is needed to answer these and other questions. If the evolution of the settlement pattern is a consequence of a combination of factors, deriving a generalizable theory of adjustment to the settlement pattern of immigrants and the reasons for those adjustments may be impossible. When looking at examples, we tend to try to seek generalizations. At the same time, we must be aware of and sensitive to variations that exist from place to place, in timing, between immigrant groups, and within society. Regardless, the previous discussion raises important questions and issues that need to be resolved before further research can be initiated. They include the need for analysis at a variety of spatial scales; data that allow immigrant groups to be followed over a period of time; differences in and construction of ethnicity, nationality, and ancestry; and complementary methodological approaches. Because of the complexity of the questions at hand, alternative approaches will likely lead to the richest results. Detailed surveys and ethnographic approaches such as those discussed in chapter 14 in this volume may provide greater insight into the decision to relocate, among other issues. Multivariate statistical methods would provide an alternative, complementary picture by enabling the research to control for various effects.

Notes

1. Because illegal immigrants may go unrecorded in the census, some states probably contain larger proportions of foreign born than suggested in the discussion. Such

undercounting minimizes the immigrant presence and may distort the composition of groups. The existing literature suggests that legal and illegal immigrants have somewhat different settlement patterns and propensities to migrate (Neuman and Tienda 1994).

2. Much of the existing literature focuses on ethnic distinctions but either uses national origins as a proxy for ethnic groups or includes both foreign and native born in the analysis. If, however, ethnic concentration influences migration, nativity concentration should have a similar effect (Kritz and Nogle 1994). Although neither ethnicity nor national origin may fully describe or capture a specific group, national origin is focused on to reduce the heterogeneity associated with ethnic origin (Belanger and Rogers 1993).

3. Migration rates are based on the foreign-born population (pre-1985 arrivals) at risk of migration. Intermetropolitan migration rates are based on migration among the twenty-five largest metropolitan areas. Given problems with the period of arrival question in the census (Ellis and Wright 1998), the sample is restricted to immigrants who arrived prior to 1985 and resided in the United States in 1985.

References

Alba, Richard D., and John R. Logan. 1991. "Variations on Two Themes: Racial and Ethnic Patterns in the Attainment of Suburban Residence." *Demography* 28, 3: 431–453.

Allen, James P., and Eugene Turner. 1996. "Spatial Patterns of Immigrant Assimilation." *Professional Geographer* 48, 2: 140–155.

Baker, Reginald P., and David S. North. 1984. *The 1975 Refugees: Their First Five Years in America*. Washington, D.C.: New TransCentury Foundation.

Bartel, Ann P. 1989. "Where Do the New U.S. Immigrants Live?" *Journal of Labor Economics* 7, 4: 371–391.

Bartel, Ann P., and Marianne J. Koch. 1991. "Internal Migration of U.S. Immigrants." In John M. Abowd and Richard B. Freeman (eds.), *Immigration, Trade and the Labor Market*. Chicago: University of Chicago Press.

Bean, Frank D., and Marta Tienda. 1987. *The Hispanic Population of the United States*. New York: Russell Sage.

Belanger, Alain, and Andrei Rogers. 1993. "The Internal Migration and Spatial Redistribution of the Foreign-Born Population in the United States: 1965–70 and 1975–80." *International Migration Review* 26, 4: 1342–1369.

Boswell, Thomas D. 1993. "The Cuban-American Homeland in Miami." *Journal of Cultural Geography* 13: 133–148.

Boswell, Thomas D., and James R. Curtis. 1984. *The Cuban-American Experience: Culture, Images and Perspectives*. Totawa N.J.: Rowman and Allanheld.

Castles, Stephen, and Mark J. Miller. 1993. *The Age of Migration*. New York: Guilford.

DaVanzo, Julie S. 1978. "Does Unemployment Affect Migration? Evidence from Micro Data." *Review of Economics and Statistics* 60, 4: 504–514.

Desbarats, Jacqueline. 1985. "Indochinese Resettlement in the United States." *Annals of the Association of American Geographers* 75, 4: 522–538.

———. 1986. "Ethnic Differences in Adaptation: Sino-Vietnamese Refugees in the United States." *International Migration Review* 20: 405–427.

Dunlevy, James A. 1980. "Nineteenth-Century European Immigration to the United States: Intended versus Lifetime Settlement Patterns." *Economic Development and Cultural Change* 29: 77–90.

Ellis, Mark, and Richard Wright. 1998. "When Immigrants Are Not Migrants: Counting Arrivals of the Foreign-Born Using the U.S. Census." *International Migration Review* 32: 127–144.

Forbes, Susan S. 1985. "Residency Patterns and Secondary Migration of Refugees." *Migration News* 34, 1: 3–18.

Frey, William. 1995. "Immigration and Internal Migration "Flight": A California Case Study." *Population and Environment* 16, 4: 353–375.

———. 1996. "Immigrant and Native Migrant Magnets." *American Demographics* 18, 11: 37–53.

Gordon, Milton, M. 1964. *Assimilation in American Life: The Role of Race, Religion, and National Origins*. New York: Oxford University Press.

Gorrie, Peter. 1991. "Farewell to Chinatown." *Canadian Geographic* 111, 4: 1–28.

Greenwood, Michael J. 1975. "Research on Internal Migration in the United States: A Survey." *Journal of Economic Literature* 13: 397–433.

Haggett, Peter, Andrew Cliff, and Allan Frey. 1977. *Locational Analysis in Human Geography*. New York: Wiley.

Hirschman, Charles. 1982. "Problems and Prospects of Studying Immigration Adaptation from the 1990 Population Census: From General Comparisons to the Process of "Becoming American." *International Migration Review* 28, 4: 690–713.

Howenstine, Erick. 1996. "Ethnic Change and Segregation in Chicago." In Curtis Roseman, Hans-Dieter Laux and Gunter Thieme (eds.), *EthniCity*. Lanham, M.D.: Rowman and Littlefield.

Isserman, Andrew, and John Kort. 1988. *Regional Economic Consequences of U.S. Immigration Policy*. Morgantown, WV: Regional Research Institute, Working Paper 8810.

Kobrin, Frances E., and Calvin Goldscheider. 1978. *The Ethnic Factor in Family Structure and Mobility*. Cambridge, MA: Ballinger.

Kobrin, Frances E., and Alden Speare. 1983. "Outmigration and Ethnic Communities." *International Migration Review* 17, 3: 425–444.

Kritz, Mary M., and June Marie Nogle. 1994. "Nativity Concentration and Internal Migration among the Foreign-born." *Demography* 31, 3: 509–524.

Lansing, John B., and Eva Mueller. 1973. *The Geographic Mobility of Labor*. Ann Arbor: University of Michigan Press.

Long, Larry. 1988. *Migration and Residential Mobility in the United States*. New York: Russell Sage.

Massey, Douglas S. 1985. "Ethnic Residential Segregation: A Theoretical and Empirical Review." *Sociology and Social Research* 69: 315–350.

Massey, Douglas S., S. Rafael Alarcon, Jorge Durand, and Humberto Gonzalez. 1987. *Return to Aztlan: The Social Processes of International Migration from Western Mexico*. Los Angeles: University of California Press.

Massey, Douglas S., Joaquin Arango, Graeme Hugo, Ali Kouaouci, Adelo Pellegrino, and J. Edward Taylor. 1994. "An Evaluation of International Migration Theory: The North American Case." *Population and Development Review* 20, 4: 699–751.

Massey, Douglas S., and Felipe Garcia España. 1987. "The Social Process of International Migration." *Science* 237: 733–738.

Massey, Douglas S., Luis Goldring, and Jorge Durand. 1994. "Continuities in Transnational Migration: An Analysis of Nineteen Mexican Communities." *American Journal of Sociology* 99: 1492–1533.

McHugh, Kevin E., Ines N. Miyares, and Emily H. Skop. 1997. "The Magnetism of Miami: Segmented Paths in Cuban Migration." *Geographical Review* 87, 4: 504–519.

Moore, Eric G., and Mark W. Rosenberg. 1995. "Modeling Migration Flows of Immigrant Groups in Canada." *Environment and Planning A* 27: 699–714.

Myrdal, Gunnar. 1957. *Economic Theory and Underdeveloped Regions*. London: Methuen.

Neuman, Kristin E., and Marta Tienda. 1994. "The Settlement and Secondary Migration Patterns of Legalized Immigrants: Insights from Administrative Records." In Barry Edmonston and Jeffrey S. Passel (eds.), *Immigration and Ethnicity*. Washington, D.C.: The Urban Institute.

Newbold, K. Bruce. 1996. "Internal Migration of the Foreign-Born in Canada." *International Migration Review* 28, 1: 31–48.

———. 1997. "Primary, Return and Onward Migration in the U.S. and Canada: Is There a Difference?" *Papers in Regional Science* 76, 2: 175–198.

Nogle, June Marie. 1994. "Internal Migration for Recent Immigrants to Canada." *International Migration Review* 28, 1: 31–48.

Park, Robert E. 1928. *Race and Culture*. New York: Free Press.

Pedraza, Silvia, and Rubén G. Rumbaut. 1996. *Origins and Destinations: Immigration, Race and Ethnicity in America*. Belmont Calif.: Wadsworth.

Perez, Lisandro. 1992. "Cuban Miami." In Guillermo J. Grenier and Alex Stepic (eds.), *Miami Now! Immigration, Ethnicity and Social Change*. Gainesville: University of Florida Press.

Piore, Michael J. 1979. *Birds of Passage: Migrant Labor and Industrial Societies*. Cambridge: Cambridge University Press.

Portes, Alejandro. 1994. "Introduction: Immigration and Its Aftermath." *International Migration Review* 28, 4: 632–639.

———. 1995. "Economic Sociology and the Sociology of Immigration: A Conceptual Overview." In Alejandro Portes (ed.), *The Economic Sociology of Immigration*. New York: Russell Sage.

Portes, Alejandro, and Józef Böröcz. 1989. "Contemporary Immigration: Theoretical Perspectives on Its Determinants and Modes of Incorporation." *International Migration Review* 23, 3: 606–630.

Portes, Alejandro, and Min Zhou. 1994. "Should Immigrants Assimilate?" *Public Interest* 116: 18–33.

Ritchey, P. Neal. 1976. "Explanations of Migration." *Annual Review of Sociology* 2: 363–404.

Roberts, Bryan R. 1995. "Socially Expected Durations and the Economic Adjustment of Immigrants." In Alejandro Portes (ed.), *The Economic Sociology of Immigration*. New York: Russell Sage.

Roseman, Curtis, Hans-Dieter Laux, and Gunter Thieme. 1996. "Modern EthniCities." In Curtis Roseman, Hans-Dieter Laux, and Gunter Thieme (eds.), *EthniCity*. Lanham, Md.: Rowman and Littlefield.

Tienda, Marta, and Franklin D. Wilson. 1992. "Migration and the Earnings of Hispanic Men." *American Sociological Review* 57: 661–678.

Trovato, Frank, and Shiva S. Halli. 1983. "Ethnicity and Immigration in Canada." *International Migration Review* 17, 2: 245–267.

———. 1990. "Ethnicity and Geographic Mobility." In Shiva S. Halli (ed.), *Ethnic Demography*. Ottawa: Carleton University Press.

Uhlenburg, Peter H. 1973. "Non-economic Determinants of Nonmigration: Sociological Considerations for Migration Theory." *Rural Sociology* 38, 3: 296–311.

U.S. Bureau of the Census. 1991. *Census of Population and Housing, 1990: 5 Percent Public Use Microdata Samples*. Washington, D.C.: U.S. Department of Commerce, Bureau of the Census (producer).

Walker, Robert, and Michael Hannan. 1989. "Dynamic Settlement Processes: The Case of U.S. Immigration." *Professional Geographer* 41, 2: 172–183.

SECTION III

METHODOLOGICAL FRONTIERS IN MIGRATION RESEARCH

Situated within the context of migration and restructuring, the chapters in this section present a variety of innovative methodological alternatives to understanding migration dynamics. They collectively underscore the importance of a longitudinal analysis to understand migration dynamics and population redistribution. The chapters also draw attention to the nature of data needed to unravel the complexity of migration stimuli at various scales.

De Jong provides an overview of a relatively traditional research methodology in migration research, yet a central tenet of his chapter is the importance of life-course analysis and individually specific experiences in migration. He argues that choice processes in migration behavior can benefit from individual migration histories. De Jong emphasizes the importance of individual intentions and behavior in the analysis of migration and presents a theoretical model of migration decisionmaking that incorporates both these aspects.

Watkins provides a creative approach to understanding migration by examining personal narrative life histories. He uses the life course as an important analytical construct, which, together with ethnographic methods, lends insight into how the sources and extent of spatial knowledge influence mobility decisions. His work emphasizes the dynamic and unpredictable aspects of people's lives and brings to the fore the changing ties between people and places over the life course.

Plane explores the utility of analogies from the physical sciences to further our understanding of migration streams. As with the previous chapters, Plane's main thrust is that fruitful avenues of migration research can be achieved by incorporating the dimension of time. He notes that the growing availability of time series data on state-to-state migration flows now makes it possible for migration researchers to depart from conventional cross-sectional approaches. Plane argues that migration studies can benefit by using explicitly longitudinal approaches such as those favored by physical geographers and hydrologists.

These three chapters represent emerging methodologies and changing directions in migration research. They also advance the merits of a geographic perspective to migration and restructuring, for they remind us to be cognizant of the embedded nature of individual choice and the importance of context, as well as the powerful connection between spatial and temporal dynamics. The final chapter in this volume provides an overview of the current state of migration research and promising future directions in the study of migration and restructuring in the United States.

13

Choice Processes in Migration Behavior

Gordon F. De Jong

What will be the driving forces of U.S. internal migration in the twenty-first century? Arguably, the dominant current perspectives on internal migration focus on economic restructuring and population deconcentration. The economic restructuring perspective emphasizes the spatial variation in economic opportunities, which are seen as determinants of migration and employment patterns. From this perspective the causes of population redistribution are found in regional macroeconomic competitiveness (Kasarda 1995; Plane 1989). The deconcentration perspective emphasizes the role of microlevel preference for smaller-size places as a causal factor in population redistribution (Frey 1987, 1995).

Although migration takes many forms—local and distant, temporary and permanent, voluntary and involuntary, national and international—all forms involve individuals and places, micro and macro units. The dominant demographic research tradition has focused on migration as an aggregate phenomenon. But scholars and policymakers have recognized increasingly that to explain aggregate migration patterns it is necessary to understand how individuals and families decide to move and evaluate (or in Wolpert's [1965] terms, attach subjective place utility to) their current location versus other locations. As Willekens (1985) correctly noted, policy measures that attempt to impact population redistribution without understanding the motives and life-cycle events behind migration decisions are bound to fail. The basic proposition of this chapter is that an increasingly diverse set of human values and expectations about regional and size-of-place locations of where those values can best be attained will be major explanations for internal migration patterns of individuals and families in the twenty-first century.

Are there choice theory frameworks and behavioral demography concepts that are useful in articulating a general model of migration decisionmaking?

What does the longitudinal research evidence show about the determinants of individual-level migration intentions and behavior? The objective of this chapter is to explore these issues. The thesis is that the intentions-behavior relationship is fundamental to understanding migration decisionmaking. Placing this relationship in the context of a general model derived from choice theory and the microlevel literature in the discipline of demography is the strategy used to help advance our understanding of why people move.

Although I am aware of the impacts of macroeconomic labor market and national restructuring on employment patterns, this chapter will focus on individual- and family-level factors in the migration decisionmaking process. The logic is that decision processes are the proximate determinants of migration behavior. From this perspective, decision processes mediate the influence of economic restructuring on internal migration patterns. And although models of mobility decisionmaking sometimes distinguish different stages in the decisionmaking process, the focus here will be on the fundamental decision to move or stay—a decision that is common to local and distant, temporary and permanent migration.

Preconditions for Migration Choice Behavior

In what has become a classic statement in the demographic literature, Ansley Coale (1973) identified preconditions for fertility behavior change. The value of specifying preconditions is in defining a threshold of societal change and restructuring that can reliably identify when a behavioral response—for Coale, fertility reduction—will take place. Are there threshold preconditions for migration choice behavior in contemporary societies? Certainly, varying amounts of internal and international world migration behavior today are forced or impelled (Petersen 1958) by war, severe environmental degradation, repressive government policies, race and ethnic discrimination, and similar factors. Indeed, the evidence on current world refugee flows is striking. But much, perhaps even most, internal migration is not stimulated by these factors. The diversity of change and restructuring in which migration takes place suggests the presence of more than one precondition for migration. I suggest three preconditions for migration choice behavior.

First, migration choice must be *cognitively and physically available* to potential decisionmakers. Sell and De Jong (1978) note that some people may not move either because such behavior is not within the calculus of conscious choice or it is not physically possible for them to do so. Although the issue of cognitive availability of alternatives is complex, it can be argued that seldom do circumstances exist in which conscious consideration of alternative living environments is not available. Forced migration presents a different condition in which staying in the current place is not possible for decisionmakers. This represents a range of conditions such as housing being torn down, housing eviction, extreme physical endangerment, enforced labor transfers, and the like. Forced immobility, as through incarceration or legal constraints on place of residence, is seldom a concern in population analysis.

Second, migration must be expected to produce *positive outcomes*. Perceived social and economic opportunities must make migration seem advantageous to potential decisionmakers. Third, sufficient *resources*—money, information, social network contacts—must be available to implement a move.

When all three preconditions are present in the context of social change and restructuring, significant migration would be expected. On the other hand, for subpopulations in which all preconditions are absent, little instrumental migration would be expected, even where structural factors favor migration behavior. These preconditions are thus seen as basic building blocks for understanding migration behavior.

Is Migration Decisionmaking Rational?

A key issue in migration choice behavior concerns the concept of *rationality*. To what extent do research procedures impose an orderly, logical, goal-oriented framework on behavior that may in fact be normatively controlled, emotional, or based on seemingly chance factors? This question can be answered in part by empirical research, especially through longitudinal studies that use a decisionmaking approach for predicting migration behavior compared with other analytic frameworks. Beyond empirical tests it is possible to make some reality-grounded observations about the rationality of migration intentions and behavior.

If extreme situations such as migration forced by war, natural disasters, environmental calamities, and eviction are excluded, migration should be more amenable to a choice behavior analysis than almost any other demographic behavior. Migration is not linked directly to sexual behavior, as is fertility; it is usually less affected by emotional attachments than is nuptiality; and it is under greater volitional control than mortality. Moreover, substantial evidence in conceptual and empirical writings shows that the decision to move is often the result of deliberations over an extended period of time, implying a careful weighing of pros and cons (Roseman 1983; Sell and De Jong 1983). Even the early work of Rossi (1955) discussed a decisionmaking sequence from inclinations to move to intentions to move and then behavior. Such a typology is fully congruent with the idea that most, although certainly not all, migration behavior can be viewed as instrumental to attain certain valued goals. If potential decisionmakers give some consideration to the benefits and costs of an alternative destination or the consequences of moving versus staying, the decisionmaking process is considered to be "rational" and a choice framework to be an appropriate research approach.

Choice Theory

If much of migration is instrumental behavior directed toward maintaining or enhancing the well-being of individuals or families, what social science theories of choice are available to explain this type of goal-directed behavior? Theorists in economics, sociology, and psychology have addressed this issue, and a brief review of selected writings will help to identify common ideas and concepts for examining migration intentions and behavior.

Undoubtedly the best-known and most widely accepted model is the neoclassical microeconomic model of individual choice, which has been applied specifically to migration behavior (Sjaastad 1962; Todaro 1969, 1976; Todaro and Maruszko 1987). From this perspective individual rational actors choose a behavior on the basis of a cost-benefit calculation of an expected positive net financial return from the behavior. For migration, actors choose to move to where they can be most productive given their human capital skills and the costs associated with relocation—travel, job search, maintenance, and language-learning costs. Since costs and benefits vary over time, this theory argues that the net returns have to be estimated over some time horizon of "expected" earnings compared by the decisionmaker to expected earnings in the present and alternative locations. The theory asserts that migration choice stems from differentials in both current wages and employment, whose product determines longer-term expected earnings.

Stark and colleagues (Stark and Bloom 1985; Stark 1991) have argued that migration choice is made not by individuals but by families or households, which act not only to maximize expected income but also to minimize risks associated with market failures. This argument is particularly relevant in developing country contexts where government and private insurance programs are largely absent.

Several features of the microeconomic theory of choice have been criticized by scholars in economics and other social science disciplines. These criticisms include the assumption that individuals can perform complex information processing and that they possess perfect information. Psychologists argue that most individuals are not able to perform the cost-benefit analysis required by microeconomic theory (Alexander and Giesen 1987). Rather, decisions are based on limited information that is reduced to a simple, understandable form. A telling criticism of the microeconomic theory of choice is that the validity of the central cost-benefit calculation proposition is not empirically tested but rather *inferred* from behavioral outcomes. Thus the *process* inherent in the theory is not measured.

A second criticism maintains that the microeconomic theory of choice is overly simplistic. Economists usually examine incentives and behavioral responses and take values and norms as givens. Aaron and colleagues (1994) argue, however, that preferences and values often intervene in the choice process and cannot be viewed as immutable givens as previously assumed in neoclassical microeconomic models. Values and tastes emerge from lessons taught by family, friends, and the community and are not exogenous or independent of decisionmaking. The idea that values can change, combined with the recognition that responses depend on people's values (preferences), emphasizes the importance of considering how values affect choice behavior.

Sociologists' foray into choice theory has been championed by Coleman's (1990) major treatise on rational choice as a basis for general social theory. Building on neoclassical microeconomic theory, one of Coleman's major tasks is to move from the microchoice model of rational, purposive actors exchanging resources to macrolevel explanations of choice behavior embedded in internalized societal norms, the vesting of authority, and the dynamics of collective behavior. One approach to explaining the norms and authority in choice behavior is that they emerge from the simple aggregation of individual rational choice behaviors by persons acting in their own self-interest. Coleman rejects this approach and instead treats normative *systems* as purposively generated and enforced out of self-interest. This analysis of norms emerging out of self-interest and rationality fits with and works better for relations and structures in which voluntary exchange is an institutionalized principle, such as free markets, contractual authority relations, and banking-finance relations.

Difficulties arise in explaining choice behaviors embedded in a complex of values and institutions—the context for much demographic choice behavior. In these situations decisionmakers behave according to norms that endorse and reward such behavior. In this context decisions are often made within the framework of known normative rules, commonly called institutions, and the structure of an institution may be as predictive of behavior as are personal preferences.

For some sociologists rational choice can be a powerful theory of choice behavior *if* contextual factors are allowed to influence the decisionmaking process. Marini (1992) argued that values are one set of contextual factors. For example, an assessment of the impact of values on decisionmaking provides some understanding of how available information is interpreted by individuals. Values also provide insights into the stimuli for decisions and why some decisions appear to be irrational, based on external utility maximization criteria.

A second major contextual factor influencing decisionmaking processes is social networks. According to Pescosolido (1992: 1098), "The rational choice explanation, with economic psychology as the fundamental microdynamic, presents but one useful way of exploring social action and denies what is the most likely contribution of sociology to understanding decision making." Social interaction, she argues, is the basis of social life, and social networks provide the mechanism through which individuals learn about, come to understand, and attempt to address social problems. The emphasis on social networks in decisionmaking shifts the focus from purely individual choice to socially constructed patterns of decisions, especially through consultation with significant others within social networks. In some decision contexts social networks are composed primarily of family members, whereas in others social networks may include friends, coworkers, professional "loose ties," and organizational affiliates.

Within the rational choice tradition in sociology, then, notions of utility maximization, purposive action, and bounded rationality—derived from economic and psychological theory—are overlaid with sociological premises about the importance of interaction, values, and social networks in social life.

Perhaps *the* major psychological statement of intentions and behavior decisionmaking is the Theory of Reasoned Action (Fishbein and Ajzen 1975; Ajzen and Fishbein 1980). In the more than twenty years since it was proposed, the theory has emerged as the dominant theoretical statement in the attitude-behavior literature (Olson 1993). Not only is the theory used to predict behavioral outcomes, but it is also the standard to which new theories are compared. The theory has been used successfully to predict numerous intentions and behaviors in a variety of domains, including smoking, seat belt use, and applying to educational programs (Olson 1993: 131).

The theory states that the best predictor of behavior is the individual's attitude (Aact) toward the behavior, along with social norms (SN)—perceptions of what significant others think about the behavior—that influence the likelihood of performing the behavior. The key determinants of attitudes toward a behavior are the individual's values and expectations about salient consequences of the behavior. The person's evaluative judgments are assumed to be combined through the expectancy-value formulation process (Ajzen and Fishbein 1980). Here Ajzen and Fishbein argued that if the behavior was under "volitional control," intentions derived from this theoretical process would completely predict behavior. Subsequent research, however, has made it clear that some variables have direct effects on behavior that are not mediated by behavioral intentions (Chaiken and Stangor 1987; Ajzen and Madden 1986). The most robust of these direct effects is past behavior.

Since the original Theory of Reasoned Action did not explicitly include a concept of *volitional control* (i.e., situational factors or obstacles that prevent one from performing the behavior), Ajzen (1985) has added *perceived control* along with attitudes and social norms, and called the new model a Theory of Planned Behavior. Perceived control taps the individual's perception of obstacles and constraints that might prevent behavior from occurring even if value-expectancy judgments and social norms supported a response. Thus perceived control can affect behavior both directly and indirectly through intentions. Similar concepts have been suggested to capture the effects of situational contexts and personal constraints on behavior (Bagozzi and Schnedlitz 1985).

From this review of selected choice theories in economics, sociology, and psychology, several common themes emerge. First, theorists in all three disciplines conceptualize decisionmaking in terms of purposive action, reasoned action, or rational choice. Second, writers in all of these traditions identify rational actors who engage in instrumental behavior that enhances (maximizes) the individual's or family's well-being. Third, expectation, based on the perceived consequences of the behavior, is a key concept in decisionmaking. Evaluating these expected consequences involves values in psychological theory, expected (but inferred) monetary costs and benefits in economic theory, and social interaction and exchanges in sociological theory. Finally, several social contexts are identified as having direct and indirect impacts on intentions and behavior-norms, family networks, and personal constraints. These commonalities in theoretical model concepts are important for analyzing migration intentions and behaviors.

General Behavioral Demography Concepts

What important microlevel concepts are most applicable to behavioral migration research? In his essay on "The Agenda of Population Studies," McNicoll (1992) elucidated some basic features of behavioral demography. The outcomes of chief interest for demographers, he noted, are vital events—birth, death, migration, marriage, divorce—or their proximate antecedents. Although this list is brief and clear, the behaviors that precipitate the events are far from simple. They encompass social, economic, cultural, and biological dimensions of society.

Unlike macrodemographic perspectives in which rates are fundamental concepts, in behavioral demography a first major concept is *preferences,* a behavior that is an object of choice of higher valuation or desirability than another. Perhaps the most extensive application of preferences in demography is in fertility research, where family size preferences (ideal or intended number of children) are used to calibrate demand and supply of children models (Bulatao and Lee 1983) and "tastes" are a debated concept in dealing with preference change. The empirical problem of gauging family size preferences is problematic, however, as the way a question is understood and responded to in a survey may bear little relation to the real situation in which childbearing decisions are made.

Processes, a second important concept in behavioral demography, vary with the vital event of interest. In family and household units, an important demographic process is how decisionmaking takes place. Within the calculus of choice context, the assumption is that decisionmaking is a process of assessing the relevant costs and benefits of alternative demographic behaviors. Whether the decision is to maximize the desired outcome for an individual or for the family unit is part of the continuing empirical and conceptual debate. For fertility research, diffusion is an important process in explaining differences across social classes and ethnic groups, as well as between urban and rural areas. Diffusion as a process traces the web of communication that links individuals to other individuals and to the larger society through formal and informal information and persuasion channels.

A third important concept in behavioral demography is *institutions.* Arguably the family is the most salient institutional structure for demographic behavior. Studies of contemporary family change—whether in high-fertility Africa or the low-fertility West, whether in high-mobility developed or low-mobility developing country contexts—are highly relevant to explaining and predicting demographic behavior. Furthermore, family structure and processes are more amenable to demographic formal and statistical modeling than are political, religious, educational, and community institutions that may also affect demographic behaviors.

McNicoll (1992) also argues that *biology* and *culture* are important concepts in behavioral demography. Biology sets bounds on the feasible behavior decisionmakers must take into account. Fertility behavior takes place within observable biological constraints that are integral to the proximate determinants framework. Perhaps deeper issues for behavioral demography are the sociobiological arguments concerning competition, social status hierarchies, survival strategies, mate selection, nurturing, aggression, and so on, and how they may be related to social and economic factors demographers regularly use in constructing behavioral explanations.

Culture, Hammel (1990: 467) noted, "provides social constructions—a transitory and negotiated set of understandings . . . a constantly modified and elaborated system of moral symbols. Culture affects behavioral demography through 'systemness'—the limitations on individual freedom inherent in cultural (and perhaps national) symbols. It also affects behavioral demography through cultural 'processual' qualities that produce unique political agendas as well as delineate social networks, the communication threads that locate and provide meaning for individuals in social space."

Behavioral Migration Concepts

If, as McNicoll (1992) argues, preferences, processes, institutions, culture, and biology are basic concepts for behavioral demography, what specific dimensions of these concepts are uniquely relevant to the study of choice behavior in migration? As shown in Table 13.1, I suggest that the most salient concepts for migration behavior are (1) intentions, (2) values and goals, (3) expectations, (4) satisfactions, (5) family and friend interaction networks, (6) norms, and (7) gender roles.

Migration Intentions

The intention to move or not move is a first-order preference choice concept in migration research. Intentions simply indicate what one has in mind or proposes to do or accomplish. Under the assumption that migration is cognitively and physically available to decisionmakers, migration intentions provide a basic statement of the desirability of a location.

Substantively, an attractive feature of intentions data is that for instrumental moves intentions precede actual migration behavior and thus provide insights into the underlying causes of mobility. Migration intentions may be more proximate to family socialization and household economic context than is migration behavior.

Table 13.1 Key Concepts in Behavioral Demography

General Behavioral Demography Concepts	Specific Behavioral Migration Concepts
Preferences	Intentions Values and goals Satisfactions
Processes	Evaluating expectancies Social interaction
Institutions	Family networks
Culture	Family norms Gender roles
Biology	—

Coming early in the decisionmaking process, the molding of intentions is useful from a policy perspective in providing an understanding of why some policies designed to affect population redistribution work and others do not (Simmons 1986).

What motivates migration intentions and behavior? Unfortunately, motive is one of the more ubiquitous terms in social science (e.g., What is the motivation for this research?). In the migration literature motive ranges from an individual response to "reasons-for-moving" questions to aggregate-level area determinants of migration, such as the unemployment rate, that in some research are used to infer individual-level decisionmaking.

As a concept, motive refers to a stimulus influencing a choice or prompting a person to act in a certain way (De Jong and Fawcett 1981). The focus of the concept is on individuals, not on geographic or political units. Migration stimuli can be of various forms including life-cycle events, such as marriage, divorce, or death of a spouse, as well as goal attainment, such as higher income, a better living environment, or higher social status.

The diversity of possible motives is captured in the literature on reasons for a move (cf. Nam, Serow, and Sly 1990; Serow 1987; De Jong and Fawcett 1981). Such microlevel data are almost always derived from a survey question asking "Why did you move?" Although reason-for-move information is almost universally taken as an indicator of motives for migration, the data have several serious shortcomings.

1. Studies are usually based on interviews with people who have already migrated, so answers given are subject to rationalization of past behavior, simplification because of recall errors, and possible distortion owing to changes over time in the migrant and his or her environment.
2. Since reason-for-move studies are retrospective, there is no basis for predicting behavior or testing such predictions.

3. The concentration on migrants as subjects of research implies a corresponding lack of attention to nonmigrants or potential migrants, thus precluding the analysis of motivational differences between these groups.
4. In the analysis of results, the focus is usually on single motives rather than on the multiple factors that normally enter into any human decision.
5. Economic and job-related motives tend to be dominant; in interpreting such findings there is little recognition of the fact that financial rewards are not necessarily ends in themselves, but are means to satisfy other needs and desires.

The inadequacies of reason-for-move data can be demonstrated best by asking the complementary question, "Why do people *not* move?" If better economic opportunities exist elsewhere, for example, and a vast pool of demographically equivalent potential migrations is found in a given community, what distinguishes the movers from the stayers? Better conceptualization and measurement of motives that stimulate migration intentions and behavior are essential.

Values and Goals

Following the Theory of Reasoned Action (Fishbein and Ajzen 1975), migration motivation can be defined as a function of relevant values and goals and perceived expectations that a behavior will lead to the attainment of those goals (De Jong and Fawcett 1981). Although Rokeach (1973) and others have provided evidence on general societal values, there are relatively few *empirical* studies of migration-related values and goals (cf. SyCip and Fawcett 1988; De Jong, Richter, and Isarabhakdi 1996; De Jong et al. 1995; Heida and Gordijn 1984; Williams and Sofranko 1979; and Sandu and De Jong 1996). From this and related empirical research emerge some important value dimensions, shown in Table 13.2.

Whereas all of these migration-related values and goals have some empirical support in the literature, the list is neither exhaustive nor necessarily mutually exclusive, and their relative strength in developed and developing country settings has not been tested. In this early stage of migration motivation research, however, this list of values and goals provides a set of partially validated concepts for migration intentions and behavior research.

Expectations

Establishing predictive migration motives requires more than just identifying values and goals—*expectations* of goal attainment must also be evaluated. Expectations link an action to its consequence. What is the methodology for evaluating expectations? The theoretical model requires that for each value a corresponding expectancy is obtained. For migration the application of such an approach is especially interesting because expectations can be measured for alternative places. For example, having established that "a high income" is highly

Table 13.2 Values and Goals in Migration Decisionmaking: Some Concepts from Empirical Research

Values	Goals
Income/wealth	Attaining desired income, affiliation, stable income, high standard of living, and employment stability
Comfort	Living in a pleasant, healthful, and socially and morally acceptable community and home environment
Stimulation	Gaining entertainment and educational opportunities and variety in interpersonal relations
Affiliation	Living near family and friends, being with a spouse, and having family and friend support available
Easier lifestyle	Attaining a less strenuous and more peaceful life
Environmental quality	Having clean air and water, scenic landscapes, and low noise and pollution
Health	Preserving or improving one's physical or mental well-being
Functional independence	Attaining or maintaining self-reliance
Political and economic freedom	Having choices in economic and political behaviors

valued by a respondent, the researcher can ask what the chances are for achieving this goal in the community of residence and at several alternative destinations. For each dimension, then, cognitive choices are measured with reference to potential mobility behavior.

The value–expectancy approach to establishing migration motives calls for the measurement of multiple values on the assumption that human behavior is a complex phenomenon motivated by many factors simultaneously. Operationally, both the value and expectations are measures on a scale. The formal procedure calls for summing the products of the scores for each value–expectancy pair; the total score is then considered an index of a behavioral intention. For migration there might be several such scores for each individual, one for the place of current residence, and one for each of several alternative destinations. The highest score would, in effect, represent a propensity to move or to stay. The summed migration intention score is hypothesized to be predictive of future mobility behavior. This type of data can also have policy implications if, for example, it is shown that certain subgroups have different goals or if expectations are not congruent with reality at particular destinations. The value–expectancy approach, then, provides a method for obtaining a subjective evaluation of factors hypothesized to stimulate migration decisionmaking.

Satisfactions

An extensive literature in demography and geography has identified residential satisfactions as important determinants of intentions to move (McHugh, Gober, and Reid 1990; Moore 1986; Landale and Guest 1985; Newman and Duncan 1979; Bach and Smith 1977; Speare 1974). This literature focuses on the evaluation of such place-of-origin characteristics as housing and community quality, community service availability, and neighborhood institutions. Satisfaction measures are an *absolute-level* evaluation of the place of origin, whereas expectation measures are a *relative assessment* of attaining important value and goals in the place of origin compared with an alternative location(s). The distinction between absolute and relative concepts and measurement is fundamental in all sciences, including migration research.

Family and Friend Interaction Networks, Norms, and Gender Roles

The institution of the family falls directly in the migration behavior bailiwick (Harbison 1981; Lauby and Stark 1988; Root and De Jong 1991). Socialization within the family helps to form migration-related intentions and values, and from family interaction emerge norms and migration strategies. Nowhere is the importance of the family more apparent than in comparative studies of male and female migration intentions and behavior (United Nations 1993). The traditional view is that for men intentions to move and migration behavior are motivated by employment and income goals, whereas for women the motives are to create or reunite a family (Pedraza 1991). The dominance in the migration literature of theoretical frameworks stressing neoclassical microeconomic individual choice (Todaro 1976) and the more recent family "new economics of migration" (Stark and Bloom 1985) fits with the traditional male-as-family-provider motive for migration. For women, Grasmuck and Pessar (1991) argue that the changing household political economy and family power relations have resulted in migration intentions and behavior motivated by personal autonomy, freedom, and status gain. The institution of the family, as defined by the norms of each culture, is squarely in the middle of the gender debate in migration decisionmaking.

Framing migration decisionmaking in the family context as the most proximate social structure is restrictive, however, and research shows that it must be expanded to include interaction networks with friends. The family and friend context and social interaction process create spatially diffuse migrant networks that Massey and Garcia Espana (1987) document as salient explanations for migration behavior. They define migrant networks as the sets of interpersonal ties among migrants, nonmigrants, and former migrants that link origin and potential destination areas through friendship, kinship, and shared community relations. Migrant networks can be uniquely cultural—"a transitory and negotiated set of understandings" (Hammel 1990: 467). The form and content of U.S. migrant networks may be rather different from those of Mexican migrant networks.

The way migrant networks help to determine migration behavior is summarized by Massey.

> They link migrants and nonmigrants together in a system of reciprocal obligations and mutual expectations. They develop rapidly because the act of migration itself generates network connections; every new migrant creates a set of friends and relatives with a social tie to someone with valuable migrant experience. Networks bring about the cumulative causation of migration because every new migrant reduces the costs of migration for a set of nonmigrants, thereby inducing some of them to migrate, creating new network ties to the destination area for another set of people, some of whom also are induced to migrate, creating more network ties, and so on. The structural impact of networks acts on the cost side of the cost-benefit calculation to build a strong dynamic momentum into migration. Having a social tie to someone with migrant experience greatly increases the likelihood of labor migration. (Massey 1990: 17)

Whereas the migrant network context for income- and employment-motivated migration would seem most apparent, networks may also affect migration when other motives are involved. Networks provide information not just about jobs but also about environmental quality, lifestyles, entertainment, housing, community living, health care, marriage markets, and other valued goals. For these values, migrant networks may impact not only family and community norms but also migration constraints (e.g., money to move, housing, fear). As noted in the earlier discussion of Pescosolido's work (1992), the social networks emphasis shifts the focus of migration decisionmaking from individual choice to socially constructed patterns. And these networks are not limited to family members and close friends but may include "loose" acquaintances, coworkers, and professional and social associates.

Still, in spite of the salience of migrant networks, not everyone exposed to these networks will actually migrate. Why do potential decisionmakers exposed to the same network contexts engage in different migration behaviors? The answer perhaps lies in differentiating between family and friend networks as a *context for* versus the *cause of* (cumulative cause of) migration intentions and behavior (Massey 1990). Causal factors, I suggest, include values, goals, and expectations as well as migrant networks. In other words, migrant networks are only one aspect of the cumulative cause of migration thesis.

Evaluating a Basic Model of Migration Decisionmaking

Based on the preceding literature review of multidisciplinary choice theory and the behavioral demographic literature, I suggest a general model of migration decisionmaking presented in Figure 13.1. The linchpin relationship in migra-

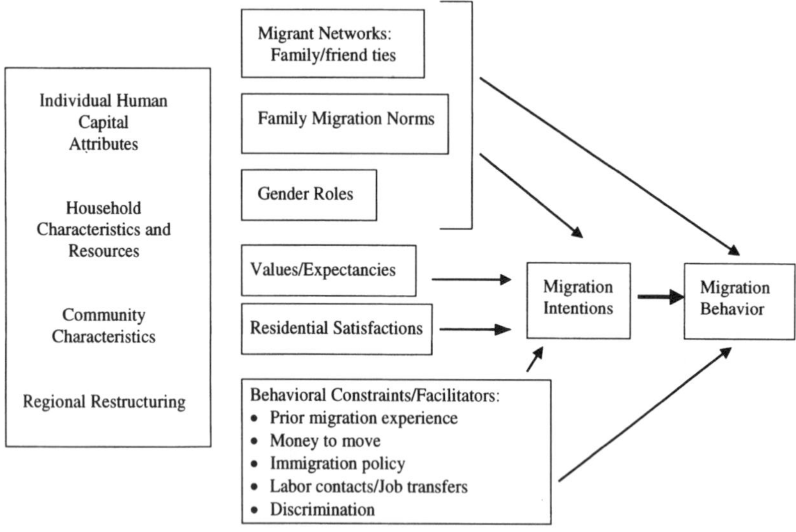

Figure 13.1 General Model of Migration Decisionmaking

tion decisionmaking is the intentions–behavior hypothesis, whereas a second basic set of relationships includes the norms and value–expectancy (of income, affiliation, comfort, and other valued goals) determinants of migration intentions. Following Ajzen and Fishbein (1980), the argument is that this model of migration decisions will provide stronger predictions than models that ignore the values and associated expectations and norms that help to determine migrant motives. Residential satisfactions–dissatisfactions with the origin community either promote or impede initial entry into the migration decisionmaking process. The sociological literature's emphasis on family and friend migrant networks as the "cumulative causation" in choice behavior is another major component of this model. Finally, Ajzen's (1985) concept of "perceived behavioral control" over choice in the form of constraints on and facilitators of the decision process is an important component of outcome behavior. The indicated sets of relationships among these key components, along with the background social, economic, and demographic structure and change contexts, form a basic microlevel model of migration decisionmaking.

What empirical evidence validates this model of migration decisionmaking? The optimal evidence would be from *longitudinal* studies in which most of the previous model determinants of migration intentions and behavior are operationalized and tested in a causal-effect time order and with multivariate statistical analysis strategies. Six selected migration studies meet these criteria; three are from the United States (Landale and Guest 1985; Lee, Oropesa, and Kanan 1994; and McHugh 1984), with one each from Thailand (Fuller, Lightfoot, and Kamnuansilpa 1985), the Philippines (De Jong et al. 1986), and Kenya (Sly and Wrigley 1986).[1] Based on the results from these studies and following the logic of Simmons's (1986) analysis, it is possible to provide a preliminary evaluation of the central arguments of the proposed basic model of migration decisionmaking.

1. How Well Do Migration Intentions Predict Actual Behavior?

Across these six studies there was moderate support for this hypothesis (moderate meaning a standardized regression coefficient, where presented, mostly in the 0.20–0.40 range and with at least 3–4 times more intended movers than intended stayers actually engaging in migration behavior over a specified time frame). In all studies there was statistically significant support for the intentions–behavior relationship even when all other variables in the model were considered. This evidence supports a basic proposition of migration decisionmaking.

Still, there are frequent inconsistencies between intentions and behavior (Gardner et al. 1986). How can this lack of prediction be explained? Differences in the measurement of migration intentions provide one explanation. The ideal measurement would include (1) a consistent concept (i.e., intend, plan, thinking about, expect, want, and so on), (2) a direction to the intention (to move or to stay), (3) a scale of commitment to the intention (i.e., very certain to uncertain), (4) a common time period for a behavior (i.e., one year, two years), and (5) intentions for alternative destinations. Few studies address all of these criteria, and the variation across studies is striking.

A second possible explanation for the imperfect relationship between migration intentions and behavior may be insufficient detail in specifying intentions. One such specification rests on the fact that migration behavior may be the result of a *series of decisions* in which intentions to move change as intervening conditions or events prompt a reconsideration of prior intentions (Sly and Wrigley 1986). Like family size preferences, migration intentions cannot be assumed to be a *once and done,* fixed decision.

Third, constraints and facilitators or migrant networks may intervene in the decision process even though the motives and norms that underlie intentions and behavior may remain essentially the same (McHugh 1984; Yang and Bilsborrow 1993). That is, individuals or households may be inconsistent in their intentions and behaviors because the conditions that prompted the development of intentions to move or stay were altered by intervening events. The importance of intentions in behavioral migration research is not just to mechanically predict behavior but to understand the conditions that prompt the decisionmaking process.

2. Do Migrant Networks and Constraints and Facilitator Factors Determine Migration Behavior in Addition to Migration Intentions?

Across five of the six studies that include measures of these dimensions, the evidence shows that migrant family and friend network indicators have statistically significant but generally moderate to weak (standardized coefficients generally between 0.40 and 0.20 and under 0.20, respectively) direct effects on migration behavior when intentions are considered in the model. Prior migration experience as a facilitator factor has a moderate but mixed direct effect on migration behavior, net the effect of migration intentions. McHugh (1984) also found that anticipated constraints were major factors differentiating stayers from movers. This evidence provides limited support for the basic migration decisionmaking model, which conceptualizes migrant networks as a direct "cumulative cause" and constraint and facilitator factors as perceived controls over migration behavior, in addition to their effects on migration intentions.

3. Do Subjective Values and Expectancies and Social Norms Determine Migration Intentions?

In half of these six studies, subjective "place utility" evaluation of the area of origin is the concept measured rather than values and associated expectancies of attaining these goals in *both* origin and (alternative) destination areas. The findings across the six studies show moderate to very strong (standardized coefficients over 0.40) support for this relationship in the migration decisionmaking model. The failure to differentiate perceptions of place for short-term versus longer-term migrants, however, poses a challenge for the subjective expectations approach to assess the motivations behind migration intentions (McHugh 1984; Simmons 1986). Nevertheless, this empirical evidence confirms the important argument that intentions are at least partially determined by people's perceptions and expectations of migration-related individual and family well-being.

Some theoretical literature suggests that subjective expectations should be the sole determinant of intentions. The studies reviewed do not support this position. As the theoretical model predicts, however, value–expectancy and place utility measures are not directly related to migration behavior but rather are indirectly related through migration intentions.

Three studies tested the hypothesized relationship between social norms and migration intentions. The evidence showed strong statistically significant associations in two studies but a weak relationship in the third, controlling for the effect of other variables in the model.

4. Do Background Social, Economic, and Demographic Factors Directly Determine Migration Intentions and Behavior?

According to the theoretical literature, the influence of these structural and change factors should be mediated through values and expectancies, norms, migrant networks, and constraint–facilitator factors. The evidence across the six studies does not support this proposition. Age, marital status, education, landownership, home ownership, and rural–urban residence were occasionally directly related to migration intentions, although seldom directly related to migration behavior, controlling for the impact of other variables in the model. Although operationalization issues are undoubtedly part of the explanation, these relationships raise broader theoretical questions about the additive and interactive nature of the macrosocial and macroeconomic contexts of individual and family migration decisionmaking. For example, socioeconomic structural and change factors may affect components of the migration decisionmaking model differently for local versus more distant, circular versus more permanent, and survival versus social mobility migration.

Conclusion

This chapter has been based on the thesis that the intention–behavior relationship is fundamental to understand migration decisionmaking. Common features of choice theory in economics, sociology, and psychology were identified and integrated with key concepts in behavioral migration research to propose a basic model of migration decisionmaking. One major proposition of this model is that intentions are the primary determinant of migration behavior, along with family and friend migrant networks and constraining and facilitating (perceived control) factors. A second major proposition of the model is that values and expectations are direct determinants of migration intentions. An evaluation, based on the results of six longitudinal migration intention and behavior studies, showed considerable, albeit not perfect, support for the basic model and its central propositions.

Some important features of the proposed model of migration decisionmaking include motivational stimuli based on *multiple* migration-related values and goals (as opposed to a single goal of maximizing financial returns) and a focus on evaluating place-specific subjective expectations associated with those values and goals for the origin *and* (alternative) destination locations. The salience of family and friend migrant networks is also a prominent feature of the model.

How does this migration decisionmaking model provide a *geographic* perspective on U.S. migration? If, as the literature suggests, migration values and expectations of potential migrants vary not only across population groups but also across spatial locations, demographic restructuring in the twenty-first century will be driven at least in part by changing values. For example, the metropolitan-nonmetropolitan migration stream trade-offs of income versus environment and lifestyle values and expectations have parallels in the interregional elderly migration trade-offs of the stimulations of warm weather retirement communities versus health concerns and affiliation ties with family and friends in home community locations. Likewise, the strong family affiliation values and expectations of prospective immigrants to the United States are a driving force in their residential location choice of a limited number of U.S. immigrant gateway cities. In the context of increasing diversity of U.S. race and ethnic population composition, human capital attributes, and family lifestyles, it can be argued that human values and expectations of where, in terms of region and size of place, those values can be attained will be more, not less, important explanations of internal migration patterns in the twenty-first century.

Notes

Partial support for this research was provided by the Population Research Institute, Pennsylvania State University, which has core support from the National Institute of Child Health and Human Development (grant 1-HD 28263–01) and the Hewlett Foundation.

1. Earlier U.S. and Canadian longitudinal migration studies with research frameworks similar to the ones cited include Bach and Smith 1977; Lee 1978; Michelson 1977; and Speare, Goldstein, and Frey 1975.

References

Aaron, Henry J., Thomas E. Mann, and Timothy Taylor (eds.). 1994. *Values and Public Policy*. Washington, D.C.: Brookings Institution.

Ajzen, Icek. 1985. "From Intentions to Actions: A Theory of Planned Behavior." In J. Kuhl and J. Beckmann (eds.), *Action-Control: From Cognition to Behavior*. Heidelberg: Springer.

Ajzen, Icek, and Martin Fishbein. 1980. *Understanding Attitudes and Predicting Social Behavior*. Englewood Cliffs, N.J.: Prentice-Hall.

Ajzen, Icek, and R. J. Madden. 1986. "Prediction of Goal-Directed Behavior: The Role of Intention, Perceived Control, and Prior Behavior." *Journal of Experimental Social Psychology* 22: 453–474.

Alexander, Jeffrey C., and Bernhard Giesen. 1987. "From Reduction to Linkage: The Long View of the Micro-Macro Link." In J. C. Alexander, B. Giesen, R. Munch, and N. J. Smelser (eds.), *The Micro-Macro Link*. Los Angeles: University of California Press.

Bach, Robert L., and Joel Smith. 1977. "Community Satisfaction, Expectations of Moving, and Migration." *Demography* 14: 147–167.

Bagozzi, R. P., and P. Schnedlitz. 1985. "Social Contingencies in the Attitude Model: A Test of Certain Interaction Hypotheses." *Social Psychology Quarterly* 48: 366–373.

Bulatao, Rodolfo A., and Ronald D. Lee (eds.). 1983. *Determinants of Fertility in Developing Countries*. New York: Academic.

Chaiken, Shelly, and Charles Stangor. 1987. "Attitudes and Attitude Change." *Annual Review of Psychology* 44: 117–154.

Coale, Ansley J. 1973. "The Demographic Transition." In *Proceedings of the IUSSP International Population Conference,* vol. 1, Liege, Belgium.

Coleman, James S. 1990. *Foundations of Social Theory*. Cambridge, M.A.: Harvard University Press.

De Jong, Gordon F., and James T. Fawcett. 1981. "Motivations for Migration: An Assessment and a Value-Expectancy Research Model." In G. F. De Jong and R. W. Gardner (eds.), *Migration Decision Making*. New York: Pergamon.

De Jong, Gordon F., Kerry Richter, and Pimonpan Isarabhakdi. 1996. "Gender, Values, and Intentions to Move in Rural Thailand." *International Migration Review* 30: 748–770.

De Jong, Gordon F., Brenda Davis Root, Robert W. Gardner, James T. Fawcett, and Ricardo G. Abad. 1986. "Migration Intentions and Behavior: Decision Making in a Rural Philippine Province." *Population and Environment* 8: 41–62.

De Jong, Gordon F., Janet M. Wilmoth, Jacqueline L. Angel, and Gretchen T. Cornwell. 1995. "Motives and the Geographic Mobility of Very Old Americans." *Journal of Gerontology: Social Sciences* 50: S395–S404.

Fishbein, Martin, and Icek Ajzen. 1975. *Belief, Attitude, Intention, and Behavior*. New York: Addison-Wesley.

Frey, William H. 1987. "Migration and Depopulation of the Metropolis: Regional Restructuring or Rural Renaissance?" *American Sociological Review* 52: 240–257.

———. 1995. "The New Geography of Population Shifts." In Reynolds Farley (ed.), *State of the Union: America in the 1990s*. Vol. 2. New York: Russell Sage Foundation.

Fuller, Theodore D., Paul Lightfoot, and Peersit Kamnuansilpa. 1985. "Rural-Urban Mobility in Thailand: A Decision Making Approach." *Demography* 22: 565–579.

Gardner, Robert W., Gordon F. De Jong, Fred Arnold, and Benjamine V. Carino. 1986. "The Best-Laid Schemes: An Analysis of Discrepancies between Migration Intentions and Behavior." *Population and Environment* 8: 63–77.

Grasmuck, S., and P. R. Pessar. 1991. *Between Two Islands: Dominican International Migration*. Berkeley: University of California Press.

Hammel, E. A. 1990. "A Theory of Culture for Demography." *Population and Development Review* 16: 455–485.

Harbison, Sarah F. 1981. "Family Structure and Family Strategy in Migration Decision Making." In Gordon F. De Jong and Robert W. Gardner (eds.), *Migration Decision Making*. New York: Pergamon.

Heida, H. R., and H. E. Gordijn. 1984. "Residential Preferences and Inclination to Move." In Henk ter Heide and Frans J. Willekens (eds.), *Demographic Research and Spatial Policy: The Dutch Experience*. New York: Academic.

Kasarda, John D. 1995. "Industrial Restructuring and the Changing Location of Jobs." In Reynolds Farley (ed.), *State of the Union: America in the 1990s*. Vol. 1. New York: Russell Sage.

Landale, Nancy S., and Avery M. Guest. 1985. "Constraints, Satisfactions, and Residential Mobility: Spear's Model Reconsidered." *Demography* 22: 199–220.

Lauby, Jennifer, and Oded Stark. 1988. "Individual Migration As a Family Strategy: Young Women in the Philippines." *Population Studies* 42: 473–486.

Lee, Barrett A. 1978. "Residential Mobility on Skid Row: Disaffiliation, Powerlessness, and Decision Making." *Demography* 15: 285–300.

Lee, Barrett A., R. S. Oropesa, and James W. Kanan. 1994. "Neighborhood Context and Residential Mobility." *Demography* 31: 249–270.

Marini, Margaret Mooney. 1992. "The Role of Models of Purposive Action in Sociology." In J. S. Coleman and T. J. Feraro (eds.), *Rational Choice Theory: Advocacy and Critique*. NewYork: Sage.

Massey, Douglas S. 1990. "Social Structure, Household Strategies, and the Cumulative Causation of Migration." *Population Index* 56: 3–26.

Massey, Douglas S., and Felipe Garcia Espana. 1987. "The Social Process of International Migration." *Science* 237: 733–738.

McHugh, Kevin E. 1984. "Explaining Migration Intentions and Destination Selection." *Professional Geographer* 36: 315–325.

McHugh, Kevin E., Patricia Gober, and Neil Reid. 1990. "Determinants of Short- and Long-Term Mobility Expectations for Home Owners and Renters." *Demography* 27: 81–95.

McNicoll, Geoffrey. 1992. "The Agenda of Population Studies: A Commentary and Complaint." *Population and Development Review* 18: 399–420.

Michelson, William M. 1977. *Environmental Choice, Human Behavior and Residential Satisfaction*. New York: Oxford University Press.

Moore, Eric G. 1986. "Mobility Intentions and Subsequent Relocation." *Urban Geography* 7: 497–514.

Nam, Charles B., William J. Serow, and David F. Sly (eds.). 1990. *International Handbook on Internal Migration* New York: Greenwood.

Newman, S. J., and Greg J. Duncan. 1979. "Residential Problems, Dissatisfaction, and Mobility." *Journal of the American Planning Association* 45: 154–166.

Olson, James M. 1993. "Attitudes and Attitude Change." *Annual Review of Psychology* 44: 117–154.

Pedraza, Silvia. 1991. "Women and Migration: The Social Consequences of Gender." *Annual Review of Sociology* 17: 303–325.

Pescosolido, Bernice A. 1992. "Beyond Rational Choice: The Social Dynamics of How People Seek Help." *American Journal of Sociology* 97: 1096–1138.

Petersen, William. 1958. "A General Typology of Migration." *American Sociological Review* 37: 256–266.

Plane, David A. 1989. "Population Migration and Economic Restructuring in the United States." *International Regional Science Review* 12: 263–280.

Rokeach, Milton. 1973. *The Nature of Human Values*. New York: Free Press.

Root, Brenda Davis, and Gordon F. De Jong. 1991. "Family Migration in a Developing Country." *Population Studies* 45: 221–233.

Roseman, Curtis C. 1983. "A Framework for the Study of Migration Destination Selection." *Population and Environment* 6: 151–165.

Rossi, Peter. 1955. *Why Families Move*. New York: Free Press.

Sandu, Dumitru, and Gordon F. De Jong. 1996. "Migration in Market and Democracy Transition: Migration Intentions and Behavior in Romania." *Population Research and Policy Review:* 15: 437–457.

Sell, Ralph R., and Gordon F. De Jong. 1978. "Toward a Motivational Theory of Migration Decision Making." *Journal of Population* 1: 313–335.

———. 1983. "Deciding Whether to Move: Mobility, Wishful Thinking and Adjustment." *Sociology and Social Research* 67: 146–165.

Serow, William J. 1987. "Why the Elderly Move: Cross-National Comparisons." *Research on Aging* 9: 582–597.

Simmons, Alan B. 1986. "Recent Studies on Place-Utility and Intentions to Migrate: An International Comparison." *Population and Environment* 8: 120–140.

Sjaastad, Larry A. 1962. "The Costs and Returns to Human Migration." *Journal of Political Economy* 70S: 80–93.

Sly, David F., and J. Michael Wrigley. 1986. "Migration Decision Making and Migration Behavior in Rural Kenya." *Population and Environment* 8: 78–97.

Speare, Alden, Jr. 1974. "Residential Satisfaction As an Intervening Variable in Residential Mobility." *Demography* 11: 173–188.

Speare, Alden Jr., Sidney Goldstein, and William H. Frey. 1975. *Residential Mobility, Migration, and Metropolitan Change*. Cambridge: Ballinger.

Stark, Oded. 1991. *The Migration of Labor*. Cambridge: Basil Blackwell.

Stark, Oded, and David E. Bloom. 1985. "The New Economics of Labor Migration." *American Economic Review* 75: 173–178.

SyCip, Lynna-Marie, and James T. Fawcett. 1988. "Expectations, Family Networks, and Emigration." *Philippine Journal of Psychology* 24: 1–20.

Todaro, Michael P. 1969. "A Model of Labor Migration and Urban Unemployment in Less-Developed Countries." *American Economic Review* 59: 138–148.

———. 1976. *Internal Migration in Developing Countries*. Geneva: International Labor Office.

Todaro, Michael P., and Lydia Maruszko. 1987. "Illegal Migration and US Immigration Reform: A Conceptual Framework." *Population and Development Review* 13: 101–114.

United Nations. 1993. *Internal Migration of Women in Developing Countries*. New York: United Nations.

Willekens, Frans. 1985. *Migration and Development: A Micro-Perspective*. Voorburg: Netherlands Interuniversity Demographic Institute. Working Paper No. 62.

Williams, James D., and Andrew J. Sofranko. 1979. "Motivations for the Inmigration Component of Population Turnaround in Nonmetropolitan Areas." *Demography* 16: 239–255.

Wolpert, Julian. 1965. "Behavioral Aspects of the Decision to Move." *Papers and Proceedings of the Regional Science Association* 15: 159–169.

Yang, Xiushi, and Richard E. Bilsborrow. 1993. "Differences in the Determinants of Intentions to Migrate versus Actual Migration." Paper presented at the Annual Meeting of the Population Association of America, Cincinnati, Ohio.

14

Life Course and Spatial Experience: A Personal Narrative Approach in Migration Studies

John F. Watkins

The human life course represents a central influence in mobility behavior. Any survey of the migration literature, for example, reveals a preponderance of studies focused on the labor force or, within the past several decades, the elderly component of the population. These "active adult" and "senescent" periods, along with childhood, have been recognized for centuries as dominant stages in a person's life, and geographic movement has been linked to these stages through the level of ability to contribute to personal and societal well-being. Active adults—especially males—will move more often and longer distances to promote income or gain political or ideological freedom. Children and inactive adults (traditionally women and the elderly) may or may not accompany the active movers through reasons of dependency.

The life course, however, is not so simple, and neither are personal motivations to move. The terminal age of education and the onset of full-time employment or the ages of first marriage, childbearing, and retirement are not fixed and static. And depending on the situation people may move for reasons beyond economic advancement; proximity to relatives or friends, natural and cultural amenities, or previous experience in and preference for special places may all serve as key motivators for a move.

This chapter presents a more detailed inspection of the life course than can normally be found in migration research. One goal is to illustrate how "unimposed" life-course trajectories and transitions play into the migration decision, which means I will be examining the diversity of times, ages, and events that influence individual spatial behavior. This is in contrast to an "imposed" life course in which individuals are slotted in stages defined primarily by an age range and often bounded by selected events such as graduation from school, marriage, or retirement. A second goal is to examine the spatial nature of the life course: the sources and extent of spatial knowledge and how that knowledge is incorporated into mobility decisions.

These goals are achieved through a critical examination of narrative life histories, a form of qualitative research that, although now common in such disciplines as psychology, history, and allied health fields, has been lacking among tools used by migration researchers. Narratives allow for an examination of the interconnections of the many elements of a complex life course. Trajectories of family, education, and work, for example, gain texture and enhanced meaning when considered in unison. Finally, narratives allow the factors of age and life-course stage to be viewed independently, and the notion of age is extended beyond simple chronological time to include social, psychological, and physiological development.

The chapter closes with an assessment of the life-course perspective of migration, with special attention given to the added information that emerges from narrative life histories. Qualitative approaches cannot replace sound empirical analyses in migration studies, yet I hope to demonstrate the benefits of considering individual voices and experiences as we seek to expand our understanding of the migration process.

Life Experience

Life course loosely refers to the ongoing period of growth and development in an individual's life from birth through death (Osgood 1982; Kastenbaum 1987). As compared with life cycle or life span, however, life course implies that maturation progresses through sequential phases that also mark dynamics of broad social and economic behavior. (For a review of how these terms are used in the social sciences, see O'Rand and Krecker 1990).) Children are born into a particular family at a particular time. As they mature they are influenced by a wide array of institutions, starting with the family and eventually including social networks, church, and the workplace.

Indeed, the family has assumed a central position in many life-course studies, a consequence of its recognized importance in the development of the individual (e.g., Germain 1994; Pollak and Wise 1979). Leaving the parental home, marriage, birth of first child, and widowhood are just a few of the events that mark transitions in a person's family life. Life-course perspectives have also been extended to specifically address the dynamics of employment and housing, and in both instances family change maintains a pivotal role of influence (e.g., Duncan 1988; England and Farkas 1986; Kendig 1990; Sweet 1990).

The life-course schedules of my four respondents illustrate the occurrence and sequencing of typical life-course events (Table 14.1). Major life events can be plotted with a high degree of accuracy, and many seem "normally" sequenced in time by age. Residential histories have also been identified, and strong associations appear between moves and certain events involving family, education, and work. Indeed, the information in Table 14.1 coordinates well with existing research on age patterns of migration (Rogers and Castro 1986; Rogers and Watkins 1987) and even with some studies of the life course/life cycle and mobility (Butler, Sabagh, and Van Ardsol 1964; Leslie and Richardson 1961; McHugh, Gober, and Reid 1990; Pickvance 1974; Rossi 1955; Rudel 1987; Speare and Goldscheider 1987; Speare, Goldstein, and Frey 1975; Varady 1983).

Unfortunately, most mobility studies treat the life course as a static phenomenon, a collection of discrete and usually predictable "stages" in which age, housing status, and family composition are used as surrogates for life-course "variables." Life-course and life-cycle research, however, has increasingly recognized diversity in the occurrence, timing, and sequencing of life events (Hogan 1978; Marini 1985; O'Rand 1990). This body of research has also paid increasing attention to historical changes in life-course pathways and cohort aging experiences (Buchmann 1989; Mayer and Müller 1986; Riley 1986; O'Rand 1990), an area in which migration studies have only recently begun to make headway (see, e.g., Plane and Rogerson 1991; and chapter 8, in this volume).

Finally, there is little texture to most existing life-course studies of migration. Individuals are treated basically as faceless soldiers marching unidirectionally toward death; along the way they pass through school and an array of career, family, and housing situations (Glick 1947). These soldiers may move away from their parental home and change their place of residence with job changes and marriage. The need for a larger house with the addition of children inspires a move, and when those children move out a smaller house may be sought. People relocate at retirement and then again to seek assistance when physical health declines. Such an orderly progression of events and consequent moves appears fairly normal, which is part of its appeal in empirical studies of aggregate populations. But migration decisions are rarely so simple (chapter 13, this volume), and many people do not move at all in the face of family or employment changes. In addition, a comprehensive life-course perspective alone, without attention to experiences in and of place, can add little to our understanding of destination selection among movers.

The life course is cumulative. Each day of life brings new experiences and knowledge that add to our growing memories and modify our perceptions of events and situations gone by. These memories and perceptions serve as a first source of information in decisionmaking. The life course is also inherently spatial, and as we move around we acquire and file away information

Table 14.1 Life-Course Event Schedules of Study Respondents

Residential	Family	Education/Work
Charlene		
1930: Birth, Ryerton, SD 1944: Move to Grand Rapids, MN 1948: Move to Chicago, IL 1950: Move within Chicago, IL 1958: Move to Jaysville, IL 1992: Move to Rural Northern MN	1951: Married 1953: First Child Born 1957: Second Child Born 1958: Third Child Born 1971: First Child Moves Out 1977: Third Child Moves Out 1982: Second Child Moves Out 1997: Husband's Death	1948: Completed High School 1948 Began Full-Time Employment 1949: Job Change 1953: Stopped All Employment 1966: Began Full-Time Employment 1991: Retired
Michael		
1927: Birth, Detroit, MI 1931: Move to Detroit, MI 1940: Move to Chicago, IL 1943–45: Military, Return to Chicago 1950: Move within Chicago, IL 1960: Move to Jaysville, IL 1972: Move to Flint, MI 1994: Move to Rural Northern MN	1950: Married 1958: First Child Born 1961: Second Child Born 1976: First Child Moves Out 1978: Second Child Moves Out 1994: Retirement	1943: Exit High School 1945: Began Full-Time Employment 1950: Job Change 1952: Job Change 1972: Job Change
Harriette		
1932: Birth, Railside, IL 1959: Move to Jaysville, IL	1945: Father Dies 1953: Married 1955: First Child Born 1956: Second Child Born 1961: Third Child Born 1975: Second Child Moves Out 1978: First Child Moves Out 1980: Third Child Moves Out	1950: Completed High School 1951: Began Vocation School 1954: Exited Vocation School 1963: Began Part-Time Employment 1964: Job Change 1975: Job Change 1989: Retirement
Junior		
1941: Birth, Rural Northern MN 1957–59: Military, Return to Northern MN 1961: Move to Minneapolis, MN	1962: Married 1964: First Child Born 1966: Second Child Born 1972: Divorce 1986: Remarriage 1972: Job Change	1957: Completed High School 1959: Began Full-Time Employment 1961: Job Change

(Cont.)

Table 14.1 Life-Course Event Schedules of Study Respondents *(Cont.)*

Residential	Family	Education/Work
1962: Move within Minneapolis, MN 1964: Move within Minneapolis, MN 1972: Move to Rural Northern MN 1986: Move within Rural Northern MN 1990: Move within Rural Northern MN		1961: Began Part-Time College 1963: Exit Part-Time College

about and perceptions of the places of our journeys. Finally, the life course is complex; it is an intricate tapestry of many events and states of existence that can be observed and measured and of many more successes, failures, and emotions that remain hidden but that combine to define a person as an individual.

A person's life course is not a sole product of that person; it embraces the influence of family and friends, of societal norms and expectations, and of a structural character that involves economic and political institutions and the built environment (O'Rand 1990). Chronological age, for example, may serve as a social marker for the attainment of certain life goals. The sixteenth birthday is an event of independence marked by obtaining a legal license to drive a car. Age 17 or 18, with graduation from high school, marks another transition to adulthood when adolescents either enter the labor force or move away to college. By the early to mid-20s, a person should be considering marriage, and children should be a part of life in the 30s, as should a stable job. A person in his or her 40s should be a home owner with suitable investments under way for offspring's education and for retirement. The 50s mark a time of independence from children, and the 60s are a time to ponder retirement and begin worrying about the nearing onset of physical decline.

Why are such ages so special? In part it is because of socially determined sequencing of schooling and the emergent economic necessity of attending college. It is also in part a function of political decisions to establish minimum ages for certain activities like voting, driving, marriage, and retirement. Finally, it is a consequence of individuals developing expectations based on "norms" of behavior and achievement that are central to any culture. People who deviate from the norms are often considered aberrant—a 25-year-old who still does not drive, a married couple that decides to remain childless, or someone still working at age 75. There is, in fact, tremendous social pressure to sequence our life events appropriately.

Personal Narratives of Life Experiences

One goal of this chapter is to place a much-needed dynamic into examinations of the life course and migration. Personal life history narratives serve as the basic foundation in achieving this goal. For too long perhaps researchers have examined migration from the outside, gathering numeric data through surveys or census tabulations and drawing inferences about individual action (Halfacree and Boyle 1993; Massey 1990). Few studies exist in which the researcher has moved to the inside to probe explicitly for meaning and explanations of life experiences as they shape personal decisions and mobility behavior (McHugh and Mings 1996; Vandsemb 1995). Life-history narratives allow such an inside view; they offer insights into personal goals and life strategies, into the development of perceptions of place and events, and into the personal interpretation of one's life (Olney 1980; Polkinghorne 1996b).

As employed in this study the narratives take the form of life reviews (Polkinghorne 1996a) in which subjects orally construct retrospective accounts of their entire lives. Four subjects are presented; their narratives were obtained through personal interviews (primary monologue with selective inquiry) that lasted from four and a half hours to twenty two hours each. Some portions of the interviews were recorded and later transcribed. Other portions were not recorded because of inconvenience, a respondent's request, or my own preference. In all cases a journal of detailed notes was maintained that included not only the respondent's words but my own thoughts and interpretations (see, e.g., the methodology described by Western 1992).

The accuracy of narrative information has been questioned. Can people really remember exactly what happened in the past, especially after many decades have passed? Not necessarily. What prevents a person from simply telling a self-serving collection of lies? Nothing, actually. What good, then, are the data that emerge from this type of research? As Polkinghorne (1996a: 95) suggests: "The subject matter of narrative stories is not the 'real' past, but the subject's current retrospective interpretations of past events and actions." Events and situations serve as important motivations in migration decisions, but people do not necessarily respond to strict realities. Instead they filter reality, imposing their own impressions and beliefs through their experience, and then act or react to this filtered reality. It could be argued that narrative data may indeed be a better means of probing for the true motivations that underscore decisions. Certain events and their sequencing in time, however, could be confirmed during the interviews with the help of scrapbooks and photo albums (Gardner 1990), and several respondents also referred to financial records for assistance.

Birth to Having Children

Charlene

"Have you ever seen real Homestead papers?" she asks as we sit drinking coffee on a cold winter evening. In a flash Charlene disappears into her bedroom, emerging a few moments later with a large envelope from which came a visual history of her kin. A Danish Bible of her grandfather's, pictures from long ago showing young Danish couples and places far away, her parents' marriage certificate, baptism records, and Homestead papers, signed by the president's signature forger of the time. Each item had its own story, and each clearly illustrated a certain aspect of Charlene's being.

> My birth was never reported, which wasn't unusual back then. The doctor would come by, deliver a baby, and then head to the next farm and deliver one there. . . . I don't have a real birth certificate. Lucky I was able to find that doctor when I got married, to prove that I was who I am and was born where and when I always knew anyway.
>
> Life was tough when I was small. But don't we all say that? Our farm [outside the small town of Ryerton, South Dakota] was a part of the land first homesteaded by my dad's family. We had no plumbing or gas heat, just the pump in the kitchen, a big wood stove, and the one-seater out back.
>
> My two sisters were a lot older, so I spent most of my time making trouble with my brother, who wasn't that much older. I was a tomboy; I hunted and fished, and I did all the usual farm chores.

Early life experience in the farmlands of eastern South Dakota will not go away. It endured and compounded for the first fourteen years of Charlene's life. She learned to use a shotgun before age 10 and because of the Great Depression learned never to shoot unless she could get "at least two birds with a single shell." She developed a sense of attachment to her Danish ancestry because of the high concentration of Danes in the area. And she developed a deep and genuine love for nature and for northern climates. She did not, however, develop a longing to remain in that particular place.

> My sister had moved to Grand Rapids [northcentral Minnesota] and got married when I was still in grade school. She had her first baby when I was ready to enter high school, and she wanted our mother to come stay with her, to be a sort of nanny because both she [the sister] and her husband worked. Well, Mom couldn't do that! And she didn't. But it was a great chance for me, so Mom let me move in with my sister. I went through high school and graduated in Grand Rapids.

This experience, although brief, opened a door in Charlene's life. She discovered forests and the beauty of countless lakes, for starters, and gained confidence in her ability to strike out on her own and make the most of her situation in place.

I could have gone back to the farm after high school, but I can't say I really wanted to. By then my other sister had moved down to the Big City. A lot of people from these parts were attracted to Chicago. It was growing so fast back then, and there was always work. My sister had taken a roommate who eventually got married and moved out. So there I was again with a great chance. I moved in with her [in Chicago] and started working.

I met Louie [her husband] at a Christmas party in 1950. I was engaged to another boy already, but I had decided to break that off when he came back on leave.

Me and Louie just clicked. We were engaged on Valentine's Day and married in October of 1951. I got along great with his family, even his father. He and Louie never did too well. I think he liked me because I could manage money. Louie could make money disappear so fast and never have anything to show for it. And his sister was so sweet to me.

We had Debbie [first child] in Chicago, and that's when I stopped working. We knew at that time that more would be on the way, and we also knew that we needed to get away from the city even though we couldn't yet afford it. We needed more room, and we wanted more outdoors around us. Louie was used to that city environment, but I found it too confining. But we stayed [in the city] for a while to get more savings under us but mostly because I kept miscarrying. The pregnancies just wouldn't last full term, and it wasn't until four years later that I finally delivered Jim [second child] and we started working on the move. I was almost ready to explode with Donny [third child] when we found our home out in Jaysville.

Harriette

Harriette's experiences brought her to Jaysville in a very different way. She was an infant in Railside, just west of Chicago; she finished high school in Railside, married in Railside, and had her first two children in Railside—all while living in the same house.

My father died early in life . . . a burst appendix of all things. Being an only child, Mother and I sort of took care of each other from then on. She worked, and the couple a few doors away watched me when I wasn't in school.

I studied at the Institute in Chicago after graduating [from high school]. Since the train station was only a few blocks away from home, it was an easy trip to the city. That's where I met Larry [her husband].

When we married Larry moved in with me, and Mother left to get an apartment closer to where she worked. I know that sounds awful, but it was her idea. Much better that way since I had no brothers or sisters, and she could save money by finding a smaller place closer to work.

By this stage in life, Harriette's spatial experience was remarkably limited. Her action space was confined to the general Railside area and to selected points within walking distance of a few stops on the train to Chicago. She had never been on a "real" vacation or even been outside of Illinois. She did not yet drive; with her mother, the train, and eventually Larry, she had never needed to learn. Eventually, however, certain pressures caused Harriette and Larry to consider an alternative place of residence.

> I remember not looking forward to moving, but we didn't have much of a choice. Our second child was up and running, and he just filled up the house. We needed more room, and the old house didn't have that room. And the old house needed a lot of work . . . big work . . . that we couldn't afford along with the taxes.
>
> What really helped was that Jaysville was only a few miles away, we knew the builders, and the price was right . . . only $13,500. We could drive out in twenty minutes and watch them build the house, and it was exciting to watch "our home" take form. And still not too far from Mother.

Early Place Experience: Charlene and Harriette

Harriette would have a third child, and as time progressed Harriette became firmly ensconced in place. Her family's vacations were local (within two hours' drive), brief (less than three days in length), and fairly infrequent (only three trips while the children lived at home). The financial situation was tight, and Harriette's and her husband's work schedules did not allow much time with the children or for vacationing. As a consequence and in addition to her early residential history, Harriette's first-hand experiences with places other than home and her immediate community were limited. This does not suggest, however, that her full place experience was limited. Indeed, Harriette has always been an avid reader, which has allowed her to develop tremendous geographical knowledge and to establish vivid mental depictions of many places.

Charlene's early residential history is far more diverse than Harriette's. And in comparison, she and her husband insisted on making family time a part of life and made conscious efforts to introduce their children to "the big world out there." They made frequent weekend trips to locations throughout northern Illinois and Wisconsin. Each year they planned a camping vacation of one or two weeks to destinations across the country. These comparative family traditions, of contact with children and the nature of vacation travel, would form the basis for later spatial behavior.

Another interesting comparison between Charlene and Harriette is how they perceived their shared community of Jaysville. Harriette has become somewhat inured to the rapid growth of the town and the associated congestion.

> I'm sure the village isn't as safe as it used to be with all these new young people moving in all the time. But we've had sidewalks now for almost fifteen years, there're a lot more streetlights, and the force [police] is pretty good at watching out for us.
>
> But everything is so much closer now! Little shops and restaurants right around the corner, and we even have our own banks and a post office now. But it isn't

> much different where we live. . . . The houses are the same, same trees but bigger, and two of the kids still live close by.

Charlene is a bit more critical in her thoughts of her former place of residence.

> It was getting much too big. We never worried about the kids back when they were small. They could be gone and out of sight for hours, playing in the fields or down by the creek, but there was no place for them to get into trouble. I feel sorry for today's young parents there.
>
> We moved there for the country feel, the knowing that we had some control about what was happening. That really disappeared in a hurry.
>
> And the police force was something else. Just before we moved away, Louie was "pulled over" for not walking on the sidewalk. Well, he had been walking the same street to work every day for seventeen years—same time and same side of the road. Suddenly they wanted to arrest him. Oh well . . . some new guy who didn't know the routine.

They had very different perceptions of the same place. Harriette, with little first-hand experience in other geographical situations, tended to feel more secure and more fixed to Jaysville. Charlotte was far more critical and admitted that she would constantly evaluate and compare the "livability" of most places she visited. She developed strong social ties in Jaysville, which, along with consistency in her children's schooling, maintained a certain level of comfort during her time there. But she always knew she would leave that community given the appropriate circumstances.

Children to Beyond

Michael

Michael spent his younger years in the Detroit area and moved to Chicago at age 13 because of his father's job transfer. Like his father, Michael developed skills as a machinist in high school and the army, and he went to work immediately in the automotive parts industry upon his return from the service. Although he considered himself then to be "a city person by heart and trade," he felt obligated to move to the suburbs after the birth of his first child. He and his wife were not pleased with the city schools and were especially concerned about the increases in crime in their immediate neighborhood. A suburb would remedy those concerns at the cost of a slightly longer commute to work.

The move placed him in Jaysville, next door to Charlene. Over the next eleven years the two families would become close friends. Eventually, however, the automotive parts industry in the Upper Midwest found itself in decline. Michael's job security was in jeopardy, and he and his wife chose to return to Michigan in 1972, to a small machine shop that was prospering in Flint.

> Oh, we would have liked to stay back there [in Jaysville] if we could have. But everything still turned out all right. The kids adjusted fine to the new schools, mostly I guess because they would have been about ready to switch to another school anyway. Maura [his wife], as usual, got right into the new house and into the town. I worked. Good people there.
>
> It's amazing we spent near twenty years there before I retired. I never stayed in one place for so long in my life, and for a while I just kept wondering what might happen next. Nothing did.
>
> Kids grew up and headed for college . . . son's an engineer, and the daughter's in communications now. At first we figured . . . maybe its time to move again. You know, no kids to worry about anymore and that. But my job was solid, and we were both pretty wrapped up in town stuff, so we stayed put.

Michael and his wife were not, however, totally tied to place. They vacationed regularly with their children to destinations in the Upper Midwest, and they remained in frequent contact with their friends from Jaysville, who they would visit as time and money permitted. Indeed, these social connections would play a major role in their later life decisions.

> We would wait all year for those summer trips. At first we all met up there at Bear Lake [in Minnesota, with Charlene and husband and another couple from Jaysville]. Those were great times together . . . peaceful, good company, good fishing. . . . We were all crazy enough to always have fun when we got together. And no kids to worry about. Now we always liked our kids, sure. But this was different. This was for us.
>
> Those trips made it pretty easy to figure out what to do when we retired. A good eight or so years at the cabin each summer, and when Charlene and Louie retired up there we stayed with them on vacation.
>
> The tricky part was finding the right house. Being close by them might have been good, but I think they got the last nice house, and prices in that area went sky high real soon after they got there. It was out of our league.
>
> Ended up finding a nice place right here, about the same distance on the other side of Grand Rapids. Cheaper, I suppose, because we're not right on a lake, and there aren't as many people living in these woods. But it took a few years to get.
>
> At first I really thought that Charlene and Louie was why we moved up here. You know, because we all had so much fun together . . . they're good friends. But it's not that way. No. We see them every couple of weeks or so and on special days. It's the outside here that we like. We even kinda like the winters, too.
>
> You know, the city's been me for so long. It was all I knew. Winters were bad there, sure. And we sure do get colder and snowier up here. But it's a different winter . . . smoother, prettier. People here help you through the winter, and you learn how good it can be . . . how the people can make anything good. I suppose I never knew what the outside was really like. That's why we moved up here.

Junior

My fourth old friend is Junior, a bricklayer turned contractor whose life began in 1941 just a few miles from where Charlene now lives in rural northern Minnesota. His childhood was typical of the area; he learned to fish and hunt at an early age and became habitualized to the actions and behavior necessary to function out-of-doors in the cold northern climes. His childhood was also set in the iron-mining culture of the region. His father operated heavy equipment at a nearby mine, and although his income was low it was consistent because of the war demand for American ore. The "mining community," as spread out as it was acted as a large family for Junior. Other mine children were his brothers and sisters; other workers and their wives were often substitute parents. This close-knit community would gather often to celebrate almost anything, from major holidays to births, birthdays, and baptisms, school graduations and marriages, and deaths.

He remained in the same house with his family until entering the U.S. Navy at age 17. The immediate postwar boom in iron ore had passed, and as Junior left for training in the coastal South several mine closures had already cost the area hundreds of jobs. Employment was therefore hard to come by when he completed his tour of duty and returned home. The local rural economy was in sharp decline, and like so many other longtime residents of the rural North he moved away to find employment.

Junior quickly found a construction job in Minneapolis. Long hours and hard work refined his bricklaying skills, which helped to rapidly increase his income. Within three years of the move, he had met and married his wife and started filling his spare hours with college business classes. By the time his second child was born, he had been promoted to a site management position and felt comfortable with his income and with his new custom-built house on the outskirts of Minneapolis.

> It was all great there for a while . . . the job, the house, the family. I think it really started falling apart about the year after [my second child] was born. I would work from sunup until five o'clock, come home, eat with them, and work on the house until late. Most every day. Weekends, well . . . I worked a lot of Saturdays. Sundays we went to church, and I tried to relax the rest of the day.
>
> I was raised around that kind of work. Us kids didn't see our dads that often, and I guess our moms seemed to manage pretty well back then. My family was poor . . . poor, when I left for the Cities . . . we never had much anyway, and I suddenly found I was doing so much better in the Cities. I just kept at it. I worked, that's what men did. But [my wife then] was a city girl, she lived a city life, and she had those city dreams. We didn't mix. We were like salad dressing; we tried for years to stay together, but eventually the oil and vinegar just came apart.

Junior was suddenly faced with a major life decision. He admits to being confused over his situation; there were two children to account for, and he wanted to maintain contact with them. He had a secure job that would provide for his children, yet he began to understand the fundamental problem causing his dilemma.

> I don't think divorce is ever easy; it shouldn't be easy because it's not the right thing to do. Especially with kids. I couldn't imagine changing the way I worked

back then because I wanted the kids to have enough, to have more; that's what my folks did, what my folks' folks did, and I couldn't see being different. I gave them everything with the divorce . . . house, savings, both cars. I worked for them, and I gave everything to them at the end because it was right.

The problems with that marriage didn't make me think that I was living wrong, just that I was living in the wrong place. Hell, it's almost funny now to think about, but Minneapolis tore us apart. I never felt home there, never really comfortable with those city homes and city shops and city rules and city this and city that. Just no control over who I was; someone else in the mayor's office always saw to that for me. That divorce woke me up, at least enough to get some coffee. I did what I could for the kids and I went home.

Twenty-five years after the divorce, Junior holds no regrets about his decision to return to the rural north-woods. Economically, he started from scratch again with the move. He found construction work that barely paid the bills from month to month and lived in a small old cabin near the ruins of the mine that had once supported his childhood community. He had, however, accumulated enough knowledge and experience from his life in the city to plan an effective strategy for personal renewal.

I made mistakes when I was younger. I had no idea the sort of power that was in the money I made. And I made damn good money! But I never let the money work for me, I never invested it, never turned it into something that could grow. Everyone else I knew did the same damn thing. Stupid.

A big change for me after the divorce was the pressure release. I wasn't being pushed to make more and more, I wasn't fighting anymore to look better and be better than the other guy. I could fish again . . . or just walk back in the woods and think. I slowed down a lot, not really how much I worked but what I did with the paychecks. It took a good ten years to get the foundation pulled together, but then the rest took care of itself. I started my own business just when I saw this area starting to spring back to life, absorbed the place I used to work when the owner retired, and ended up building most of the new houses all these new people wanted.

I work now, sure, and I'll work maybe another five years or so. But [my new wife] and I are happy now. We do a lot of other stuff around here [the rural township] that we like, and that really helps. She runs around all day doing her hospice and church work. A lot of people she helps need something fixed with their house. Mostly older people, and you know they can't do that much anymore, so I spend my spare time fixing them [their houses] up. You know, some of those folks watched after me when I was growing up. They taught me to be the man I am. And it's about time they got their payback.

Life-Course Experience and Migration Decisions

My four old friends exhibit fairly regular life-course trajectories. They attended and completed school according to expected norms of their time, married and had children at ages we would anticipate, worked (or did not work) in temporal accordance with their ages, and retired at an "average expected" age (Kohli and Meyer 1986; Hagestad and Neugarten 1985; Litwak and Longino 1987). They sought and were able to acquire housing to accommodate their families during specific stages of their life courses (Sweet 1990; Kendig 1990). They also appeared to move as a consequence of regular life transitions, including job search and change, marriage, new children, child "launching," and retirement. These trajectories have been well documented in the literature and have served as bases for theoretical development (Rowland 1991; Germain 1994; Fox and Quitt 1980; Cowan and Cowan 1988; Goldscheider, Thornton, and Young-DeMarco 1993; Stern 1991; Pratt and Hanson 1993; Clark and Onaka 1983; Davies and Pickles 1985; Sandefur and Scott 1981; Warnes 1992). What, then, do my old friends have to say that is different?

Cumulative Experience

All of my old friends expressed their lives as oral narratives. They conveyed memories of the past, of specific events, and of their feelings before, during, and following the events. They were sharing, in essence, their experience, the accumulation of which took their entire lives and represented highly varying forms. We all have certain levels of practical experience that come out of our daily routines and the minor and major life-course events in our lives. We also gain experience from education, either formal schooling or our personal quest for knowledge through books, printed and broadcast media, travel, movies, plays, art, and music. Regardless of the source, we all cast our own light on experiences as they emerge. A job change, for example, may be viewed as a source of tension, stress, and fear by one individual, whereas another may see it as welcome mystery, opportunity, relief, or even uncontrollable destiny. We constantly filter "reality" according to existing experience, present context, and personal life goals and aspirations, so that new experiences take on individual meaning and character and old experiences become transformed.

Personal experience is the first source of information used in decisionmaking that influences our life-course trajectories: the types of jobs and careers we assume, if or when we get married and how many children we plan, the nature of housing we seek, how we take care of our health. Experience influences our social interactions, political preferences, and spending habits. And it strongly influences mobility decisions. Experience gives us a frame of options within which to conduct a search for a new destination. Just as important, it supports or discourages risk-taking behavior. Harriette, for example, is not a risk taker; she has little firsthand spatial experience, and the perceived loss of security—which has emerged from place—that would accompany a move is fairly intimidating. My other three old friends have no such trepidation. They have all successfully "survived" numerous moves, and although they recognize the hardships associated with any move, they are more inclined to remain focused on the benefits of a relocation.

Life-Course Complexity

Elements of the human life course are necessarily simplified when addressed in the literature because they are inherently too complex to study adequately in their entirety. The life course, therefore, has been unpacked into representative themes, including family and housing, education and employment, and physiological change associated with biological aging. Certain interactions between life-course themes are commonly recognized, such as the linkage among marriage and children and housing or between physiology and employment. Complexity extends more deeply, however, when we contextualize life-course elements with personal experience. In so doing we can move beyond identification of triggering mechanisms that invoke a move and begin to understand the *conditions* in which the migrant may find her or himself.

Junior's divorce serves as a case in point. Although we would expect divorce to cause a move, we would first be at a loss to determine where Junior might move. Would he stay local to ensure proximity to his children? Would he move back (as he did) to a childhood home—to his place of birth? Furthermore, current economic models and theories would be hard-pressed to explain many of his decisions. He not only moved a long distance from children and from the more favorable employment market of Minneapolis, but he also willingly relinquished considerable capital and material goods to his estranged spouse and children.

Spatial and Place Experience

The human life course is inherently geographic. Few people today are born, age, and die in the same house, and fewer still never venture beyond the walls of their home. Each sojourn we make, either physically or in our minds, introduces new knowledge and perceptions and modifies our existing knowledge and perceptions. Each sojourn adds to our base of experience and thus influences our future.

An individual's life is composed of a collection of discrete places having real or assigned names. Home, neighborhood, community, the road to the store—all serve as places about which we have intimate knowledge and in which we often (but not always) play an active role. Places are "collected" through the life course and become part of our accumulated experience. Space, on the other hand, is the continuous canvas on which we situate known places and search for new places. Space includes the unknown or the little known, the areas for which we have no developed experience from our life actions. Still, we categorize space, assigning characteristics and emotions based on perceptions and experience with often tenuously representative places. Rural is a space, a large city is a space.

Notions of place and space also have trajectories in the personal life course. The collection of discrete places increases from the moment of birth, and space is mapped with these places and is continuously refined and redefined in our perceptions. Place and space experiences are intimately linked to other life-course elements and add to the knowledge base of decisions, and the importance of certain place and space experiences rises and falls throughout life. The mobility behavior of my old friends is really a product of their experiences. The retirement locations chosen by Charlene and Michael, the postdivorce move made by Junior, and the relative immobility of Harriette are all actions motivated by lifelong collections of information that have shaped who these people are and what they prefer. It would be impossible to explain their behavior using such static measures as income or cost-of-living differentials, climate and amenities, or proximity to kin; and life-course events like divorce or retirement appeared only to set migration decisions in motion. Why did Charlene choose to move at retirement and choose to move where she did? Twenty-two hours of interviewing provided only a partial explanation for her actions.

Conclusion

I have presented in this chapter only a small portion of an admittedly incomplete data set, leaving out large sections relating to wage earnings; capital investment in housing; capital transfers with migration; the spatial behavior of parents, children, siblings, and many close friends; and even detailed accounts of the respondent's accumulation of spatial knowledge. This is not the type of foundation upon which traditional studies of migration are based; it illustrates, however, the inherent complexities migration researchers have long had to contend with.

I have presented the stories of my old friends primarily to demonstrate the potential of qualitative methods, especially the narrative approach, for extending our understanding of the migration process. We have made great strides in identifying diversity in migration across age, ethnicity, gender, and residential situation; and as this book shows we have certainly made progress in assessing the impact of migration in the broad restructuring trends now under way. Yet it would seem that we have stagnated in our attempts to make significant progress in developing theories of migration that allow us to explain and understand what we see and engage in. chapter 13 in this book gives us an excellent springboard for probing more deeply into critical mobility decisions. If we maintain a reliance on the collection and analysis of empirical data, however, we may find ourselves unable to surmount a barrier that prevents true understanding; our inquiries and hypotheses will remain restricted by available and measurable data.

Narrative data alone cannot provide definitive answers or firm conclusions. Indeed they are more likely to result in far more questions. This is a good thing, because the questions are likely to be new and unfamiliar and capable of directing research down pathways previously overlooked or ignored. The meaning of place, for example, is one area that requires closer inspection among migration researchers. How do we develop ties to place, and how do elements of physical setting, social networks, and cultural meaning evolve as we experience place over the life course? How durable is spatial memory, and what factors cause us to revise and embellish our memories of place? How do individuals variously react to societal expectations and structural changes in economic and political arenas, and how do they reconcile broader expectations and change with their own goals and strategies throughout life? These are questions that emerged from time spent with my old friends and from only a cursory analysis of their life stories. Addressing these questions will first require more interviews and careful examinations of the interview transcripts. It will also require the eventual infusion of empirical research tools so that answers can be transformed into knowledge accessible to those who must plan for the impacts of a constantly moving population.

References

Buchmann, Marlis. 1989. *The Script of Life in Modern Society: Entry into Adulthood in a Changing World*. Chicago: University of Chicago Press.

Butler, Edgar W., G. Sabagh, and M. D. Van Ardsol Jr. 1964. "Demographic and Social Psychological Factors in Residential Mobility." *Sociology and Social Research* 48: 139–154.

Clark, William A.V., and Jun L. Onaka. 1983. "Life Cycle and Housing Adjustment As Explanations of Residential Mobility." *Urban Studies* 20: 47–57.

Cowan, Philip A., and Carolyn P. Cowan. 1988. "Changes in Marriage during the Transition to Parenthood: Must We Blame the Baby?" In Gerald Y. Michaels and Wendy A. Goldberg (eds.), *The Transition to Parenthood: Current Theory and Research*. Cambridge: Cambridge University Press.

Davies, R. B., and A. R. Pickles. 1985. "A Panel Study of Life-Cycle Effects in Residential Mobility." *Geographical Analysis* 17: 199–216.

Duncan, Greg J. 1988. "The Volatility of Family Income over the Life Course." In Paul B. Baltes, David L. Featherman, and Richard M. Lerner (eds.), *Life-Span Development and Behavior*. Hillsdale, N.J.: Erlbaum.

England, Paula, and George Farkas. 1986. *Household, Employment, and Gender: A Social, Economic, and Demographic View*. New York: Aldine.

Fox, Vivian C., and Martin H. Quitt. 1980. "Stage I: Courtship to Marriage Formation." In Vivian C. Fox and Martin H. Quitt (eds.), *Loving, Parenting and Dying: The Family Life Cycle in England and America, Past and Present*. New York: Psychohistory Press.

Gardner, Sandra. 1990. "Images of Family Life over the Life Course." *Sociological Quarterly* 31: 77–92.

Germain, Carel B. 1994. "Emerging Conceptions of Family Development over the Life Course." *Families in Society: The Journal of Contemporary Human Services* 75: 259–268.

Glick, Paul C. 1947. "The Family Life Cycle." *American Sociological Review* 12: 164–174.

Goldscheider, Frances, Arland Thornton, and Linda Young-DeMarco. 1993. "A Portrait of the Nest-Leaving Process in Early Adulthood." *Demography* 30: 683–699.

Hagestad, G. O., and Bernice L. Neugarten. 1985. "Age and the Life Course." In Robert H. Binstock and Ethel Shana (eds.), *Handbook of Aging and the Social Sciences,* 2d ed. New York: VanNostrand Reinhold.

Halfacree, Keith H., and Paul J. Boyle. 1993. "The Challenge Facing Migration Research: The Case for a Biographical Approach." *Progress in Human Geography* 17: 333–348.

Hogan, Dennis. 1978. "The Variable Order of Events in the Life Course." *American Sociological Review* 43: 573–586.

Kastenbaum, Robert. 1987. "Life-Course." In George L. Maddox (ed.), *The Encyclopedia of Aging*. New York: Springer.

Kendig, Hal L. 1990. "A Life Course Perspective on Housing Attainment." In Dowell Myers (ed.), *Housing Demography: Linking Demographic Structure and Housing Markets*. Madison: University of Wisconsin Press.

Kohli, Martin, and John W. Meyer. 1986. "Social Structure and Social Construction of Life Stages." *Human Development* 29: 145–180.

Leslie, Gerald R., and A. H. Richardson. 1961. "Life-Cycle, Career Pattern and the Decision to Move." *American Sociological Review* 26: 894–901.

Litwak, Eugene, and Charles F. Longino Jr. 1987. "Migration Patterns among the Elderly: A Developmental Perspective." *Gerontologist* 27: 266–272.

Marini, M. M. 1985. "Determinants of the Timing of Adult Role Entry." *Social Science Research* 14: 309–350.

Massey, Douglas S. 1990. "Social Structure, Household Strategies, and the Cumulative Causation of Migration." *Population Index* 56 (Spring): 3–26.

Mayer, Karl U., and Walter Müller. 1986. "The State and the Structure of the Life Course." In Aage Sorensen, Franz E. Weinert, and Lonnie R. Sherrod (eds.), *Human Development and the Life Course: Multidisciplinary Perspectives*. Hillsdale, N.J.: Lawrence Erlbaum.

McHugh, Kevin E., Patricia Gober, and Neil Reid. 1990. "Determinants of Short- and Long-Term Mobility Expectations for Home Owners and Renters." *Demography* 27: 81–95.

McHugh, Kevin E., and Robert C. Mings. 1996. "The Circle of Migration: Attachment to Place in Aging." *Annals of the Association of American Geographers* 86: 530–550.

Olney, James. 1980. "Biography, Autobiography and the Life Course." In Kurt W. Back (ed.), *Life Course, Integrative Theories, and Exemplary Populations*. Boulder: Westview.

O'Rand, Angela M. 1990. "Stratification and the Life Course." In Robert H. Binstock and Linda K. George (eds.), *Handbook of Aging and the Social Sciences*. New York: Academic.

O'Rand, Angela M., and Margaret L. Krecker. 1990. "Concepts of the Life Cycle: Their History, Meanings, and Uses in the Social Sciences." *Annual Review of Sociology* 16: 241–262.

Osgood, Nancy J. 1982. "The Life Cycle Development Approach." In Nancy J. Osgood (ed.), *Life after Work: Retirement, Leisure, Recreation, and the Elderly*. New York: Praeger.

Pickvance, C. G. 1974. "Life Cycle, Housing Tenure, and Residential Mobility: A Path Analytical Approach." *Urban Studies* 11: 171–188.

Plane, David, and Peter Rogerson. 1991. "Tracking the Baby Boom, Baby Bust, and Baby Boom Echo: Implications of Shifting Age Composition for U.S. Mobility and Migration." *Professional Geographer* 43: 416–430.

Polkinghorne, Donald E. 1996a. "Narrative Knowing and the Study of Lives." In James E. Birren, Gary M. Kenyon, Jan-Erik Ruth, Johannes J. F. Schroots, and Torbjorn

Svensson (eds.), *Aging and Biography: Explorations in Adult Development*. New York: Springer.

———. 1996b. "Use of Biography in the Development of Applicable Knowledge." *Aging and Society* 16: 721–745.

Pollak, Otto, and Ellen S. Wise. 1979. *Invitation to Dialogue: Union and Separation in Family Life*. New York: SP Medical and Scientific Books.

Pratt, Geraldine, and Susan Hanson. 1993. "Women and Work across the Life Course: Moving beyond Essentialism." In Cindi Katz and Janice Monk (eds.), *Full Circles: Geographies of Women over the Life Course*. London: Routledge.

Riley, Matilda White. 1986. "The Dynamisms of Life Stages: Roles, People, and Age." *Human Development* 29: 150–156.

Rogers, Andrei, and Luis Castro. 1986. "Migration." In Andrei Rogers and Frans J. Willekens (eds.), *Migration and Settlement: A Multiregional Comparative Study*. Boston: D. Reidel.

Rogers, Andrei, and John F. Watkins. 1987. "General versus Elderly Interstate Migration and Population Redistribution in the United States." *Research on Aging* 9: 483–529.

Rossi, Peter H. 1955. *Why Families Move*. Glencoe, Il.: Free Press.

Rowland, Donald T. 1991. "Family Diversity and the Life Cycle." *Journal of Comparative Family Studies* 22: 1–14.

Rudel, Thomas K. 1987. "Housing Price Inflation, Family Growth and the Move from Rented to Owner Occupied Housing." *Urban Studies* 24: 258–267.

Sandefur, Gary D., and William J. Scott. 1981. "A Dynamic Analysis of Migration: An Assessment of the Effects of Age, Family, and Career Variables." *Demography* 18: 355–368.

Speare, Allen Jr., and Frances Goldscheider. 1987. "Effects of Marital Change on Residential Mobility." *Journal of Marriage and the Family* 49: 455–464.

Speare, Allen Jr., Sidney Goldstein, and William H. Frey. 1975. *Residential Mobility, Migration, and Metropolitan Change*. Cambridge: Ballinger.

Stern, M. J. 1991. "Poverty and the Life-Cycle, 1940–1960." *Journal of Social History* 24: 521–540.

Sweet, James A. 1990. "Changes in the Life-Cycle Composition of the United States Population and the Demand on Housing." In Dowell Myers (ed.), *Housing Demography: Linking Demographic Structure and Housing Markets*. Madison: University of Wisconsin Press.

Vandsemb, Berit H. 1995. "The Place of Narrative in the Study of Third World Migration: The Case of Spontaneous Rural Migration in Sri Lanka." *Professional Geographer* 47: 411–425.

Varady, David P. 1983. "Determinants of Residential Mobility Decisions: The Role of Government Services in Relation to Other Factors." *Journal of the American Planning Association* 49: 184–199.

Warnes, Anthony. 1992. "Migration and the Life Course." In T. Champion and T. Fielding (eds.), *Migration Processes and Patterns*. London: Belhaven.

Western, John. 1992. *A Passage to England: Barbadian Londerners Speak of Home*. Minneapolis: University of Minnesota Press.

15

Time Series Perspectives and Physical Geography Analogies in Migration Research

David A. Plane

Little of the migration research carried out to date in human geography and regional science has taken an explicit *time series* focus (see the discussion of research trends in Greenwood 1975, 1985; Rogerson 1984; Clark 1986; Plane and Rogerson 1991; Greenwood et al. 1991; and Plane and Bitter 1997). Currently, interesting microscale work is examining the *timing* of individual migrant's movement decisions over the life course (see, for instance, Pickles and Davies 1985; Odland and Bailey 1990; Waldorf and Esparza 1994; and Glavac 1995; for macroscale perspectives on life-course effects on mobility and migration patterns, see also Rogerson 1987; Plane and Rogerson 1991; Plane 1993; and Pandit 1997). Typically, however, when we analyze the aggregate geographic patterns of internal population movements in a country, we do so for a single time period or we compare the patterns taking place during two or more past periods. We frequently analyze migration pattern changes from one time period to another, and we sometimes analyze changing levels of *net* migration for specific regions, but only rarely do we examine, over a reasonably long time span, the annual rises and falls in the gross levels of migration flows in each of the origin destination-specific streams of population movement that make up a migration system.

The cross-section focus of much human migration research is in contrast to the research hydrologists and physical geographers engage in when they examine the changing level of flow in hydrologic streams. In migration research since at least the time of Ravenstein (1885), we have adopted the terminology of physical geographic systems (see the discussion of this nomenclature in Tobler 1995), but we have not developed the analogy between migration *streams* and hydrologic streams as much as we might. Curiously, another physical geography analogy has probably been better developed. Tobler in a series of articles (for example, 1976, 1987, 1995) proposes methods for mapping migration flows as if they were similar to wind patterns, ocean currents, or other continuously distributed fields.

In part, the lack of good-quality time series data for U.S. internal migration has hampered our research efforts. Recently, however, consistent annual data generated jointly by the Internal Revenue Service (IRS) and the Bureau of the Census have become available for a fifteen-year time span (from 1980–1981 to 1994–1995) permitting us to explore recent time trends in each of the 2,550 streams of state-to-state population. In this chapter, I examine the IRS–Census data from a time series perspective and propose methods to *gauge* the changing levels of migrant flow in each interstate migration stream.

After briefly describing the construction of my database and displaying sample graphs of adjusted IRS–Bureau of the Census migration time series, I set forth a methodology for *benchmarking* each series to take into account the influence on observed migration flow levels of changes in origin and destination populations over the study period. I then calculate z-scores from the population-benchmarked flows and analyze coefficients of variation calculated for each state-to-state stream of movement over the fifteen-year study period. This analysis highlights the most *volatile* and the most *stable* interstate migration streams. I then use the z-scores to carry out a frequency analysis similar to those used by hydrologists to examine the recurrence intervals of extremal events in rivers and streams. In this fashion it is possible to define numerically the levels of flow that represent *migration floods* (and, similarly, migration *droughts)*. I examine the migration floods (and droughts) that occurred in the United States over the 1980–1981 to 1994–1995 period. Finally, I begin to explore how the time series of the various interstate migration streams are correlated with one another over the study period.

Constructing a Time Series Database from IRS–Census Bureau Migration Estimates

The annual migration data released by the U.S. Internal Revenue Service's Statistics of Income Division provide an excellent source of information on recent population movement patterns in the United States. For this study, data were used that were derived from fifteen annual matches of limited information taken from individual tax returns. Each year programmers at the Census Bureau match the Social Security numbers of tax-return filers and compare the filing addresses for consecutive tax years. If the addresses differ, a move is assumed to have occurred. The number of exemptions claimed on the forms for spouses and dependents—plus that for the filer—can be used to proxy the volume of migration that occurred from one tax year to the next between each state and every other state. (IRS data are also available for many larger county-to-county streams of movement.) Consistent data are now available representing movement for each annual period from 1980–1981 to 1994–1995.

Tax returns are filed by individuals during the first quarter of each year, with many payers waiting until close to the April 15 filing deadline. On average we can assume that returns are filed around April 1, which is also, conveniently, the date of all recent decennial censuses. The patterns of movement recorded in this data source thus correspond roughly to second-quarter (April 1) state populations.

The database for this study consists of 15 annual observations of migration flow levels in the 2,550 streams between all pairs of states (plus the District of Columbia). Additionally, 51 annual "same state" estimates represent the number of nonmovers and intrastate movers disclosed by each match of tax forms. Therefore, my database comprises 2,601 time series for the fifteen-year study period, or a total of 39,015 data values.

The IRS–Bureau of the Census data represent an extremely large sample compared with other migration sources, such as the Current Population Survey's March mobility question or the decennial census (long-form) question on place of previous residence. This permits geographic disaggregation down to the level of individual state-to-state streams of movement. The coverage, however, is not total. There are nonmatches of a proportion of returns filed in consecutive years, and excluded from coverage are nonfilers of income taxes (those with below threshold income levels, as well as "tax cheats") and their dependents. Coverage ratios vary by state; for instance, although about 78 percent of the national population is represented in the 1994–1995 data, at the state level the range is from approximately 73 percent (for the District of Columbia) to 86 percent (for Nebraska).

To compare the migration series somewhat more accurately I use a simple coverage adjustment procedure based on a Markov-transition-probability formula to differentially inflate the destination-specific flows of migrants originating in each state:

$$M_{ijt,t+1}{}^{\text{adj}} = P_{it}{}^{\text{cen.est.}} \, (M_{ijt,t+1}{}^{\text{IRS}} \, / \, P_{it}{}^{\text{IRS}})$$

where:

$\mathrm{M}_{ijt,t+1}{}^{\text{IRS}}$ is the adjusted migration flow from state i to state j for time period $t,t+1$

$P_{it}{}^{cen.est}$ is the April 1 population in year t of state i taken from the decennial census or interpolated from official Bureau of the Census estimates for July 1 of years $t-1$ and t

$M_{ijt,t+1}{}^{\text{IRS}}$ is the unadjusted IRS estimated flow

$P_{it}{}^{\text{IRS}}$ is the April 1 IRS covered population (nonmovers plus out-migrants).

My adjustment procedure is crude in that it assumes that persons in the noncovered population move at the same frequencies and with the same geographic patterns as those listed on tax returns. Nonfilers of income taxes, however, are likely to have lower average incomes (and thus somewhat lower mobility) than tax filers. It would greatly enhance research uses of tax-return migration data if the Bureau of the Census were to develop and carry out a more sophisticated method for coverage adjustment based on matching those data to other migration and place-of-residence data sources. Also lacking from the data is any information on the demographic characteristics of migrants and nonmovers. For the most recent three years as of this writing, however, the IRS has released the aggregate and mean incomes reported on the tax returns represented by each flow (see Nord and Cromartie 1997 for a study of recent income migration at the county level using this new information).

Despite these difficulties, I believe the IRS–Bureau of the Census migration data constitute an excellent source of information with which to track or monitor the changing levels of recent internal population movement in the United States. (see Engels and Healy 1981; and Isserman, Plane, and McMillan 1982 for more information about this data source). Figures 15.1, 15.2, and 15.3 display some of the time series information contained in the data. Figure 15.1 re-

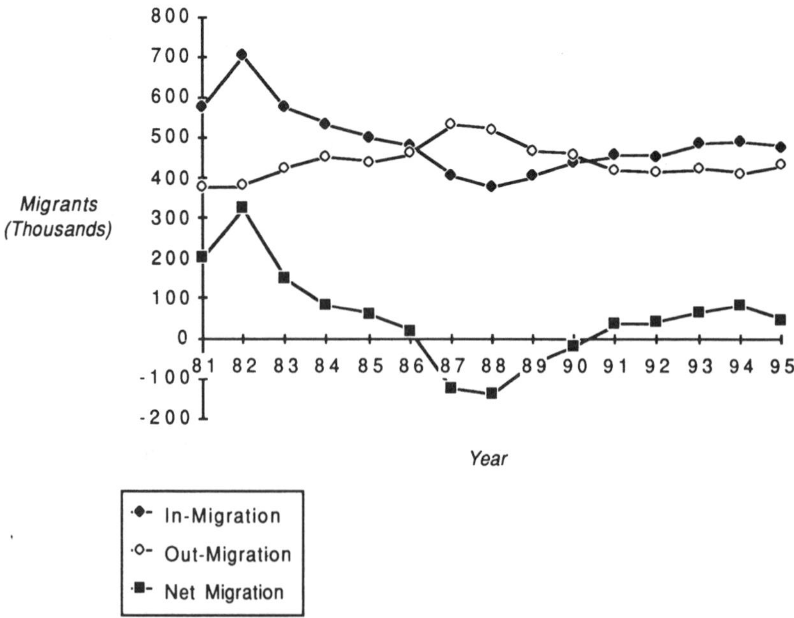

Figure 15.1 Texas Gross and Net Migration, 1980–1981 to 1994–1995

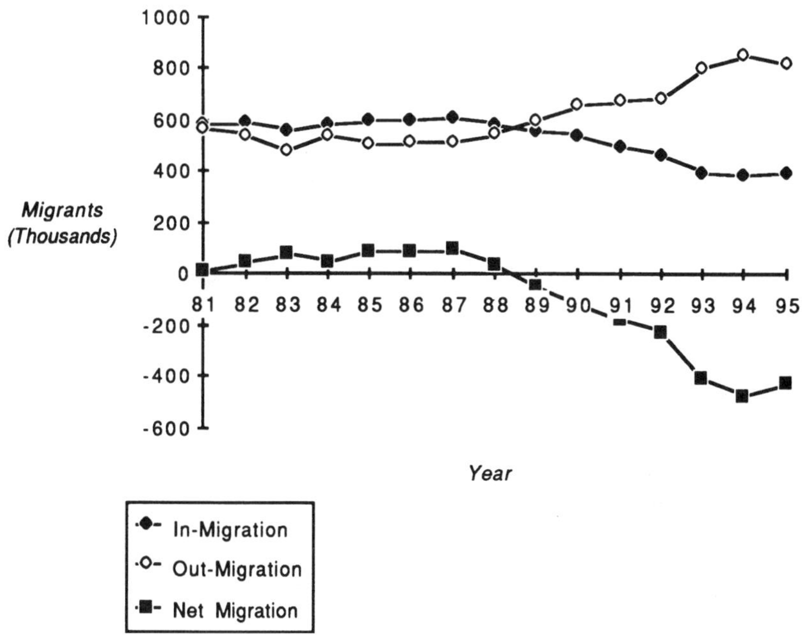

Figure 15.2 California Gross and Net Migration, 1980–1981 to 1994–1995

veals the impacts on Texas migration of the oil boom of the early 1980s, the oil glut of the mid-1980s, and the subsequent recovery period during the first half of the 1990s. Figure 15.2 similarly discloses the dramatic internal migration population losses experienced by California since 1989. These figures illustrate two of the most significant migration trends during the 1980–1995 study period. Figure 15.3 shows the trends in annual migration flow for 2 of the 2,550 interstate streams of movement that were most strongly affected by the early 1990s conjunction of events in California (defense cutbacks, unemployment, exorbitant housing prices, tensions associated with high international immigration, riots, earthquakes, fires, and so forth). The significant recent net out-migration from California to Arizona involves both a substantially higher gross flow from California to Arizona and significantly lessened movement out of Arizona into California.

One additional aspect of Figure 15.3 is the general upslope of both the Arizona-to-California and California-to-Arizona lines. Because both states were experiencing population increases throughout the study period (more recently in California as a result of natural increase and net foreign immigration), there is a structural reason to expect increasing levels of gross population exchange.

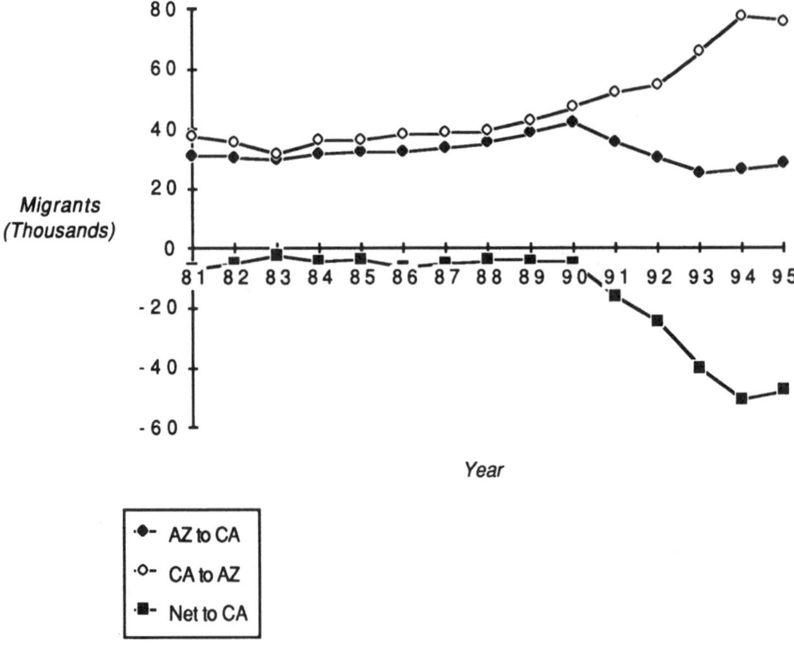

Figure 15.3 Flow Levels in California–Arizona Migration Streams, 1980–1981 to 1994–1995

A Method for Creating Population-Benchmarked Migration Time Series

To gauge the relative significance of any given level of migration flow occurring within one of the many migration streams of the national system, it seems desirable to *benchmark* each series to take into account the influence on observed migration of the changes in populations of origin and destination states during the study period. Consequently, I benchmarked all 2,550 series in my database to April 1, 1990, decennial census "base period" population counts. The concept is similar to inflation-weighting economic series to represent "constant" base year dollars. Thus my unbenchmarked migration estimates are analogous to, for instance, *nominal* income, whereas my benchmarked flows are akin to *real* income.

The procedure I propose for population benchmarking of migration time series is derived from a *spatial interaction* (or gravity model) perspective. It involves first applying both origin and destination state population change factors:

$$\mathrm{M}_{ijt,t+1}{}^{90} = (P_{i,90} / P_{it})\,(P_{j,90} / \mathrm{P}_{jt})\,M_{ijt,t+1}{}^{\mathrm{adj}}$$

This, however, "double weights" total population change taking place throughout the nation, so an additional pro rata adjustment procedure is needed to ensure consistency of benchmarked migration flows with national-scale population change:

$$M_{ijt,t+1}{}^{\text{b-mrkd}} = (P_{us,90} / \mathrm{P}_{us,t})\,(T_t / T_t^{90})\,\mathrm{M}_{ijt,t+1}{}^{90}$$

where:

T_t is the actual total number of migrants throughout the system in time period $t,t+1$ and $T_t{}^{90}$ is the sum of all of the hypothetical migrants in the system after the first step of the benchmarking procedure:

$$T_t^{90} = \Sigma_i\, \Sigma_{j \neq i} \mathrm{M}_{ijt,t+1}{}^{90}$$

The results of this benchmarking procedure in the case of the California and Arizona streams can be seen by comparing Figure 15.4 with Figure 15.3. The pre-1990 period appears as one of remarkable stability: adjusting for the growing populations of both states discloses that the degree of interaction remained almost constant throughout the 1980s.

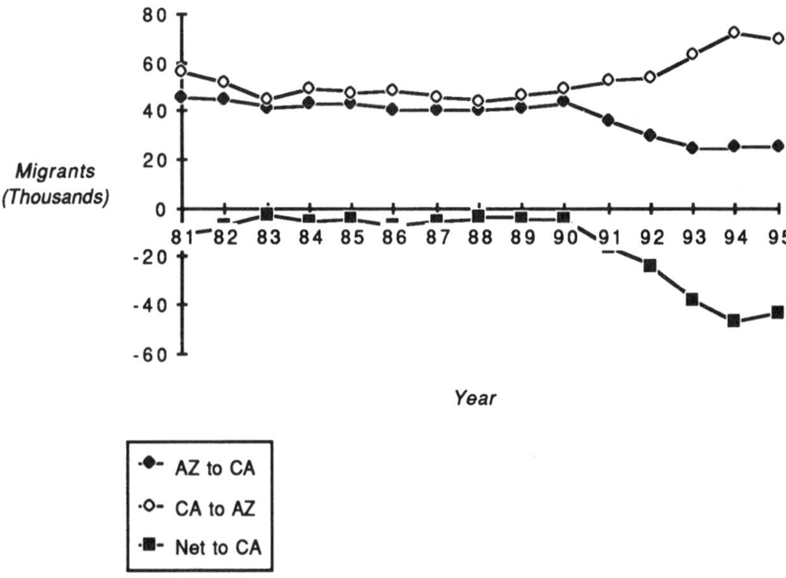

Figure 15.4 Flow Levels in California–Arizona Migration Streams (benchmarked to 1990 populations)

Z-Score and Coefficient of Variation Analysis

To facilitate a frequency analysis of the levels of migration flow across all interstate migration streams I next converted each of the 38,250 (2,550 × 15) benchmarked observations into z-scores:

$$z_{ijt,t+1} = (M_{ijt,t+1}{}^{b\text{-}mrkd} - \bar{M}_{ij}) / S_{ij}$$

where the sample estimates of the mean stream flows (μ) from state i to state j and the standard deviations of these flows (σ) are:

$$\bar{M}_{ij} = \Sigma_{t=80,94} M_{ijt,t+1}{}^{b\text{-}mrkd} / 15$$

$$S_{ij} = \sqrt{(\Sigma_{t=80,94} M_{ijt,t+1}{}^{b\text{-}markd} - \bar{M}_{ij}) / (15-1).}$$

A useful measure of the temporal *volatility* of each of the migration streams over the study period is its *coefficient of variation:*

$$CV_{ij} = S_{ij} / \bar{M}_{ij}.$$

Table 15.1 Most Volatile and Stable Interstate Migration Streams, 1980–1981 to 1994–1995, Based on Coefficients of Variability of Population-Benchmarked Flows

Most Volatile Streams			
Inflows (average CV ≥ 0.200)		*Outflows (average CV ≥ 0.200)*	
Wyoming	0.338	Wyoming	0.230
Oklahoma	0.307	Michigan	0.216
Alaska	0.295	West Virginia	0.211
Louisiana	0.256	Idaho	0.200
Texas	0.255		
California	0.241		
New Hampshire	0.229		
North Dakota	0.228		
Arizona	0.216		
Most Stable Streams			
Inflows (average CV ≤ 0.130)		*Outflows (average CV ≤ 0.140)*	
Alabama	0.102	Florida	0.131
Missouri	0.103	District of Columbia	0.132
District of Columbia	0.106	Virginia	0.132
Illinois	0.107	Georgia	0.136
Kentucky	0.118		
Pennsylvania	0.118		
Ohio	0.120		
Kansas	0.122		
New York	0.122		

I computed CV measures for each of the 2,008 streams having a mean annual benchmarked migration flow of 250 or more migrants. I eliminated the 542 streams with smaller flows from this analysis because sampling variation could result in a spurious picture of their actual variability over the fifteen years of the study period.

Table 15.1 lists the states whose inflow and outflow streams are, on average, the most volatile and those that are the most stable. The group of states having the most variability over the study period in their inflows includes the states most affected by the oil boom-and-bust events of the 1980s, as well as California, whose benchmarked in-migration streams dipped radically during the early 1990s.

The average coefficient of variability across the 2,008 individual interstate migration time series is 0.171. The most stable stream over the 1980–1995 study period was that from Maryland to Virginia ($CV = 0.029$); the most volatile was New York to North Dakota ($CV = 0.720$). Figure 15.5 shows the essentially flat population-benchmarked time series of Maryland-to-Virginia migration flow compared with the time trend for the Nevada-to-Mississippi stream. The flow levels in the latter stream had an extremely high coefficient of variation of 0.665, with the major portion of the variability caused by a migration *flood* event during the 1992–1993 through 1994–1995 period—responding to the time when casino gambling was legalized in Mississippi.

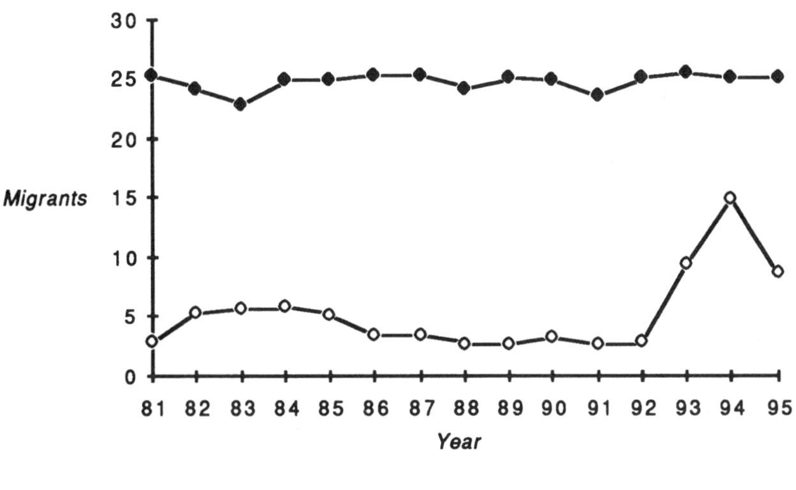

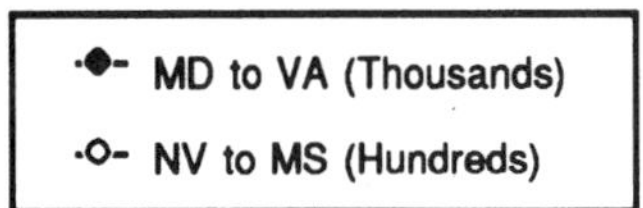

Figure 15.5 Most Stable and Most Volatile Interstate Migration Streams, 1980–1981 to 1994–1995 (benchmarked to 1990 populations)

Frequency Analysis and Definition of Flood Stages for Migration Stream Flow

The Nevada–Mississippi flow levels in the last three years of the study period are atypically high for this period. But how can we more formally define what constitutes the flood stage for a migration stream? Unlike hydrologic streams, migration streams do not have banks they spill over when upstream discharges are unusually high. Although we talk about the *channelization* of migration, we use the term to mean something rather different from what a physical geographer would mean in describing the down-cutting of the sediments or rock strata underlining a river.

We can, however, perform the same kind of frequency analysis widely employed by hydrologists for measuring the recurrence intervals of various peak flows (for basic descriptions see, e.g., Chow 1964; Dunne and Leopold 1978). If a hydrologic event equal to or greater than some magnitude (x) occurs once in T years, its probability $P(X \geq x)$ is equal to 1 in T cases, so the recurrence interval is:

$$T = 1 / P(X \geq x).$$

A variety of probability distributions can be used to estimate recurrence intervals. For instance, if events were to be normally distributed, a "forty-year flood" would correspond to any event with a z-score greater than or equal to +1.96. Frequency

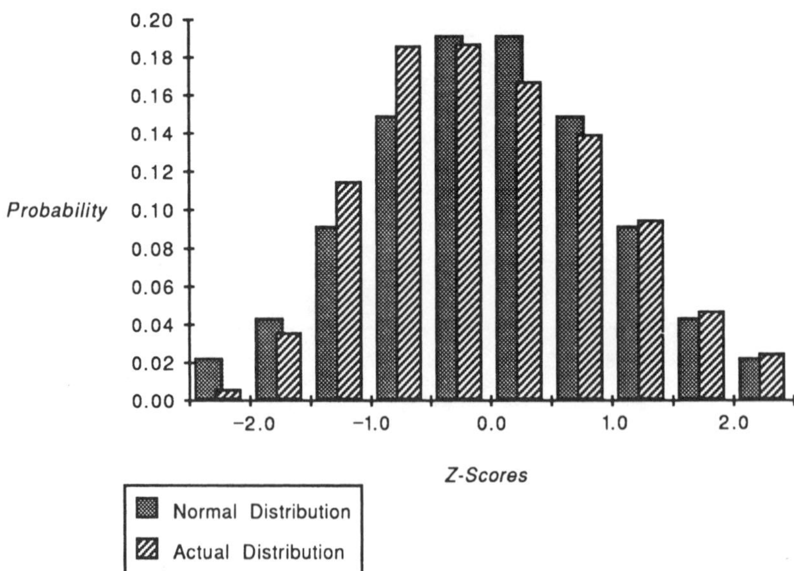

Figure 15.6 Frequency Distribution of Z-Scores for U.S. Interstate Migration Streams

Table 15.2 Frequency Distribution of Z-Scores, 1980–1981 to 1994–1995, U.S. Interstate Migration (benchmarked to 1990 population)

	Normal Distribution	Actual Distribution[1]	
		All Streams	Streams ≥ 250[2]
$P(z < -2.0)$	0.0228	0.0054	0.0058
$P(-2.0 \leq z < -1.5)$	0.0440	0.0361	0.0351
$P(-1.5 \leq z < -1.0)$	0.0919	0.1144	0.1149
$P(-1.0 \leq z < -0.5)$	0.1498	0.1854	0.1876
$P(-0.5 \leq z < 0)$	0.1915	0.1873	0.1844
$P(0 \leq z < 0.5)$	0.1915	0.1669	0.1642
$P(0.5 < z \leq 1.0)$	0.1498	0.1390	0.1420
$P(1.0 < z \leq 1.5)$	0.0919	0.0946	0.0965
$P(1.5 < z \leq 2.0)$	0.0440	0.0465	0.0455
$P(z > 2.0)$	0.0228	0.0245	0.0240

Notes: 1. Probabilities were calculated from 2,550 interstate migration flows over 15 time periods, or $N = 38{,}250$ observations for the "All Streams" column.
2. 2,008 streams having a mean flow of 250 migrants or more were used, in this case $N = 30{,}120$ observations.

distributions of hydrologic events are usually right skewed, however. Consequently, other distributions, such as the Gumbel and Weibull, are frequently used.

What about migration stream flow frequencies? The IRS–Bureau of the Census database gives us a relatively large sample of observations to study this matter, although each of the individual time series is shorter than we would like. Figure 15.6 shows a frequency plot of the pooled z-scores compared with a normal distribution. The observed migration stream flows are somewhat right skewed; however, the right tail of the distribution is fairly closely approximated by the normal distribution. Table 15.2 gives a more precise numerical breakdown by z-score interval and demonstrates that excluding the smaller streams (those with mean flow ≤ 250) makes only a minor difference in the frequency of extreme events.

Because the actual frequency of z-scores greater than or equal to $+2.0$ is 0.0245, we can claim that population-benchmarked flow levels at or above two standard deviations of their mean correspond roughly to forty-year migration floods. When, and in which of the U.S. interstate migration streams, did such forty-year flood events occur?

Floods (and Droughts) in U.S. Interstate Migration Streams, 1980–1981 to 1994–1995

If we exclude the streams having mean annual flows of less than 250 migrants, 722 flood events were recorded over my study period. If we were to similarly define a migration *drought* to have occurred whenever the benchmarked flow in a stream dropped to a z-score level of −2.0 or lower, there were 174 such abnormally low migration events. Note, however, that from a frequency analysis perspective this definition of a migration drought is considerably more stringent than what we adopted for defining a migration "flood"; the corresponding observed recurrence interval is on the order of two-hundred years rather than forty years.

How were interstate migration floods (and droughts) over the 1980 to 1995 time span temporally and spatially distributed? These events did not occur evenly throughout the study period. And certain states experienced many migration floods (and droughts) in their inflows and outflows, whereas other states recorded few or none. Figure 15.7 is a graph of extremal events by year of occurrence, and Tables 15.3, 15.4, and 15.5 list the states having the most streams at flood stage during selected periods. The largest number of streams at flood stage were found during the first two years of the study period, when the south-central part of the nation was experiencing a huge population influx associated with the oil boom. All of the states listed in Table 15.3 were among those experiencing rapid growth brought on by job growth in oil and related sectors. By 1982–1983, however, a large number of streams dried up to drought levels, and during the subsequent 1985–1988 period a number of counterbalancing movements out of the south-central region reached flood stage. Significant numbers of flood events were also registered for the 1992–1993 and 1993–1994 periods, when the net outflow from California was cresting, and for 1994–1995 (see Tables 15.4 and 15.5).

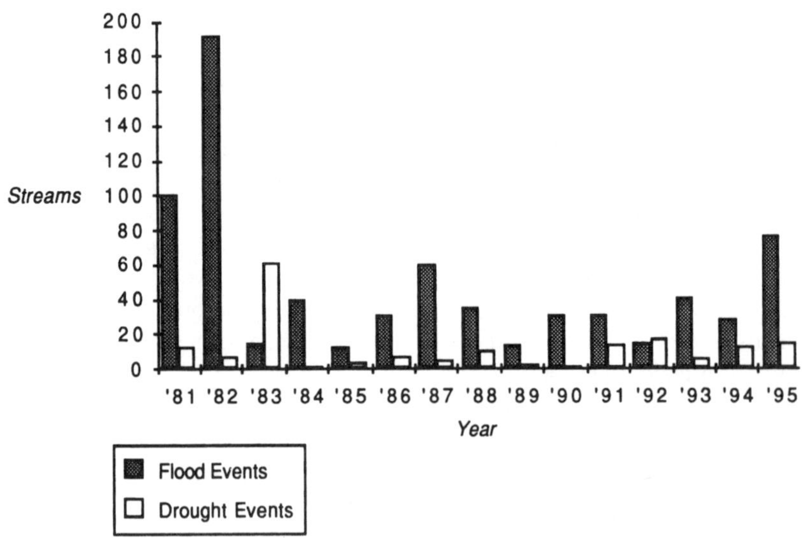

Figure 15.7 Number of Migration Streams at Flood and Drought Stages, 1980–1981 to 1994–1995

Table 15.3 States with Most 1981–1982 Migration Streams at Flood Stage

Number of Streams	Inflows To	From
38	Oklahoma	AL, AK, AZ, AR, CA, CO, FL, GA, ID, IL, IN, IA, KS, KY, LA, MA, MI, MN, MS, MO, MT, NE, NV, NJ, NM, NY, OH, OR, PA, SD, TN, TX, UT, VA, WA, WV, WI, WY
31	Texas	AL, AZ, AR, CT, FL, GA, ID, IL, IN, KY, MD, MA, MI, MO, MT, NV, NJ, NM, NY, NC, OH, OR, PA, RI, SC, TN, VT, WA, WV, WI, WY
20	Louisiana	AL, AR, FL, IL, IN, IA, KS, KY, ME, MD, MI, MS, MO, NY, OH, OR, PA, TN, WV, WI
17	Colorado	AZ, AR, IN, KY, LA, MI, MN, MS, MO, NM, OH, OR, SD, TN, TX, WA, WV
16	Alaska	AZ, AR, CA, FL, IN, KS, MD, MA, AK, MO, MT, NJ, NM, NY, SC, UT
Number of Streams	**Outflows From**	**To**
13	Michigan	AK, AZ, AR, CO, KS, LA, MS, NV, NM, OK, SC, TX, WY, CO, MT, ND, OK, SC, WY
9	Oregon	CO, KS, LA, NV, OK, SC, TX, UT, WY
8	Florida	AK, AR, LA, MS, NV, OK, SC, TX
8	Missouri	AK, CO, KY, LA, NM, OK, TX, WY
7	Indiana	AK, CO, LA, OK, TX, UT, WY

This partial analysis of migration flood events suggests the need to better understand how the rise and fall of flows occurring in any one migration stream are correlated over time with the changing levels of flow in other streams. Certain types of economic and societal changes clearly beget rippling effects throughout the place-to place streams of population movement within a migration system. A structure of interregional linkages and complementarities underlies the response of a migration system to long trends and exogenous "shocks." Ravenstein first set forth ideas like these in his classic 1885 paper. I argue that a migration system could be conceptualized as influenced over time by three types of effects.

First, a certain normal level of interaction takes place among human populations. Ledent (1991) argued for a concept of *natural migration* with a base level of flows consistent with the distribution of population across origin and destination regions. I argue for a somewhat expanded concept that I might term *structural* migration. The distance of potential destinations from the various home regions of persons "at risk" of becoming migrants also imparts some time-invariant regularities. In a previous article (Plane 1984a) I showed that

Table 15.4 States with Most 1993–1994 Migration Streams at Flood Stage

Number of Streams	Outflows From	To
7	California	AK, AZ, DC, IN, KY, KS, NM, TN
4	Virginia	AR, GA, ND, SD
2	Indiana	MT, NE
2	Nevada	MS, MO
2	New York	MO, VT
2	Oregon	MO, TN
Number of Streams	**Inflows To**	**From**
4	Mississippi	MN, NV, NJ, WI
3	Missouri	NV, NY, OR
2	Georgia	CA, VA
2	Kentucky	AR, CA
2	New Mexico	CA, ID
2	South Dakota	VA, IA
2	Tennessee	CA, OR

comparing maps of the actual locations of state population centroids with those drawn by finding the distances that would cause a doubly constrained gravity model to exactly fit a matrix of observed migration flows provides an interesting perspective on the extent to which the current population movements in a nation depart from the flows that would be expected if only *structural* migration were taking place.

A second major effect that may be found in many systems of internal movement are longer-term migration *regimes*. As I argued in Plane (1984b), the long-term history of migration systems seems to be influenced by long waves of historical, societal, and economic events. I contended that there were periods when migration patterns became strongly etched and longer periods—interregnums—when the force of such major events dissipated. Ravenstein's (1885) laws of migration were an attempt to codify the geographic patterns of migration set in motion by the Industrial Revolution. In Plane (1992) I argued that the broadscale (Snowbelt to Sunbelt) migration patterns so strongly evident during the 1970s and early 1980s were a somewhat analogous phenomenon.

Overlaid on top of structural migration patterns and the net population exchanges characteristic of longer-term migration regimes are shorter-term phenomena associated with, for instance, shorter-term economic cycles. Every business cycle has somewhat different underlying causes, with certain sectors of the economy more affected than others. Consequently, they play themselves

Table 15.5 States with the Most 1994–1995 Migration Streams at Flood Stage

Number of Streams	Outflows From	To
11	New York	DE, GA, IA, KS, KY, NC, ND, OH, SC, TN, WV
5	Dist. Columbia	CT, IL, MA, NY, OH
5	Pennsylvania	IL, IA, MO, NE, NC
4	Connecticut	AZ, HI, NC, TN
4	Mississippi	AZ, IA, KY, MO
4	Virginia	AR, GA, IL, TN
4	Washington	GA, IN, MO, SD
Number of Streams	**Inflows To**	**From**
10	Tennessee	CO, CT, DE, KS, ME, NE, NV, NY, OH, VA
7	North Carolina	AK, CO, CT, FL, ME, NY, PA
6	Missouri	MS, NC, ND, PA, UT, WA
5	Iowa	AL, MS, NY, PA, SD,
4	Arizona	CT, MS, NC, RI
4	Georgia	NJ, NY, VA, WA
4	Nebraska	CA, KY, NM, PA

out across space in rather different ways. Milne (1993) explored the impacts of business cycles on the Canadian migration system. Plane and Rogerson (1989) analyzed the impacts of the oil boom and bust and the recession of the early 1980s on U.S. migration patterns (see also McHugh and Gober 1992; Plane 1994). More research, however, is needed.

In the final substantive section of this chapter I begin to examine how the IRS–Bureau of the Census benchmarked migration time series are interrelated. Once again, an analogy with hydrologic, physical geography research may be instructive. Much of the work on flood forecasting involves trying to understand how unusually heavy rainfall events lead to storm surges throughout interconnected stream and river systems, but we know very little about the structural responses of migration systems to flood-triggering events.

Correlations of Benchmarked Migration Time Series: Some Preliminary Results

As a first crack at analyzing the synchronicity of time trends in interstate migration, I decided to examine how the times series are correlated for the 50 migration streams out of California and the 50 migration streams into Arizona.

For each of these two subsets of the overall database, I first computed correlation coefficients for all 1,225 unique pairwise stream comparisons. As we would suspect, it is more common for the pairs of migration streams, out of or into the same state, to be positively than negatively correlated. In the case of out-migration from California I found 856 positive R values and only 369 negative ones. For the Arizona in-migration streams, 978 pairs were positively and only 247 negatively correlated. Of the negative correlations for Arizona, the time trend in the population-benchmarked California in-migration stream was negatively correlated with 31 of the 49 other states' inflows to Arizona.

Table 15.6 lists the largest positive and negative correlations found. The highest positive correlations are all for pairs of contiguous states or states in close proximity to one another. The highest negative correlations for California out-migration are for New England or Mid-Atlantic states paired with western or midwestern ones and for Alaska with Michigan, Delaware, and Pennsylvania. For Arizona in-migration, the time trend for the inflows from California is highly dissimilar to those for inflows coming from many Mountain states, as well as for the states most influenced by the oil boom and bust (such as Louisiana, Oklahoma, Texas). Massachusetts and New Mexico time trends in sending migrants to Arizona differ significantly from the patterns for several other source states.

To explore further the regional patterns of correlations among the time trends, I performed factor analyses on California out-migration and Arizona in-migration subdata sets. In each case six factors were extracted having eigenvalues greater than one. The first six factors for California out-migration accounted for 93.4 percent of overall variance, whereas the first six for Arizona in-migration explained 93.7 percent of variance. In each case the first six factors were retained and a Varimax rotation was performed. The primary loadings on each of the rotated factors are shown in Figures 15.8 and 15.9.

In both the California out-migration and Arizona in-migration cases, the first factor results from the similar time trends in the streams, involving much of the rest of the western United States. This field of states displaying similar trends is somewhat more extensive for California out-migration than for Arizona in-migration. The trends for California outflows to Washington and Oregon differ from those to the rest of the West, as do the trends for Alaska (primary loading, not shown, is a negative one on Factor 2) and Hawaii (which, although not shown, loads uniquely on Factor 6). Many of the Midwest industrial states have their highest loadings on Factor 2, as do Tennessee, North Carolina, and Georgia. The similar time trends in out-migration from California to a group of northeastern Atlantic Seaboard and the New England states is accounted for by Factor 3. Florida loads with the Pacific Northwest states, whereas Wisconsin, with a positive loading, and West Virginia, with a negative one, are represented by Factor 5.

For Arizona the trend for migration into the state from California differs significantly from the trends for the other western states. California inflows load

Table 15.6 Highest Positive and Negative Correlation Coefficients between Benchmarked Time Series of Migration Flow for California Out-Migration and Arizona In-Migration Streams

Out-Migration Streams from California					
0.975	Idaho	Montana	−0.865	Connecticut	Iowa
0.968	Kentucky	Tennessee	−0.832	Alaska	Michigan
0.966	Colorado	Utah	−0.816	Iowa	New Hampshire
0.951	Utah	Wyoming	−0.763	Alaska	Delaware
0.950	Arizona	Colorado	−0.763	Alaska	Pennsylvania
0.949	Montana	South Dakota	−0.741	Connecticut	Idaho
0.948	New Mexico	Utah	−0.739	New Jersey	Oregon
0.947	Arkansas	Kansas	−0.735	New Hampshire	Oregon
0.946	Colorado	Montana	−0.731	Idaho	New Hampshire
0.945	Colorado	New Mexico	−0.730	New Jersey	Washington
0.944	Montana	Utah	−0.729	Connecticut	Illinois
0.944	Arizona	Kansas	−0.711	Connecticut	Montana
0.942	Indiana	Tennessee	−0.708	Connecticut	Oregon
0.941	Idaho	Utah	−0.707	New Hampshire	Washington
0.940	Georgia	Tennessee	−0.701	Iowa	New Jersey
In-Migration Streams to Arizona					
0.990	Iowa	Nebraska	−0.792	California	New Mexico
0.983	Indiana	Ohio	−0.663	California	Louisiana
0.978	Iowa	South Dakota	−0.647	California	Colorado
0.978	Colorado	Utah	−0.623	California	Oklahoma
0.974	Idaho	Nebraska	−0.616	California	Wyoming
0.973	Indiana	Kentucky	−0.613	Massachusetts	North Dakota
0.970	Idaho	South Dakota	−0.612	California	Utah
0.970	Arkansas	Ohio	−0.596	California	North Dakota
0.966	Kentucky	Ohio	−0.590	Massachusetts	New Mexico
0.961	Idaho	Iowa	−0.584	Massachusetts	Oklahoma
0.960	Illinois	Wisconsin	−0.568	California	Texas
0.958	Kansas	Minnesota	−0.562	California	Montana
0.956	Kansas	Wisconsin	−0.548	New Mexico	North Carolina
0.951	Illinois	Missouri	−0.540	California	South Dakota
0.950	Idaho	Wyoming	−0.535	California	Idaho

with those from Hawaii (not shown), southern New England, Maryland, Delaware, and North Carolina on Factor 3. The remaining northeastern states, those in the eastern Midwest, and those in the southeast have their primary loadings on Factor 2. Inflows from Nevada are also significantly different in trend, loading on Factor 4 rather than 1.

Much more work remains to be done to explore the synchronicity of migration time trends across the rest of the nation. It will prove interesting to examine how the geographic patterns of factor loadings based on *time trends* in migration

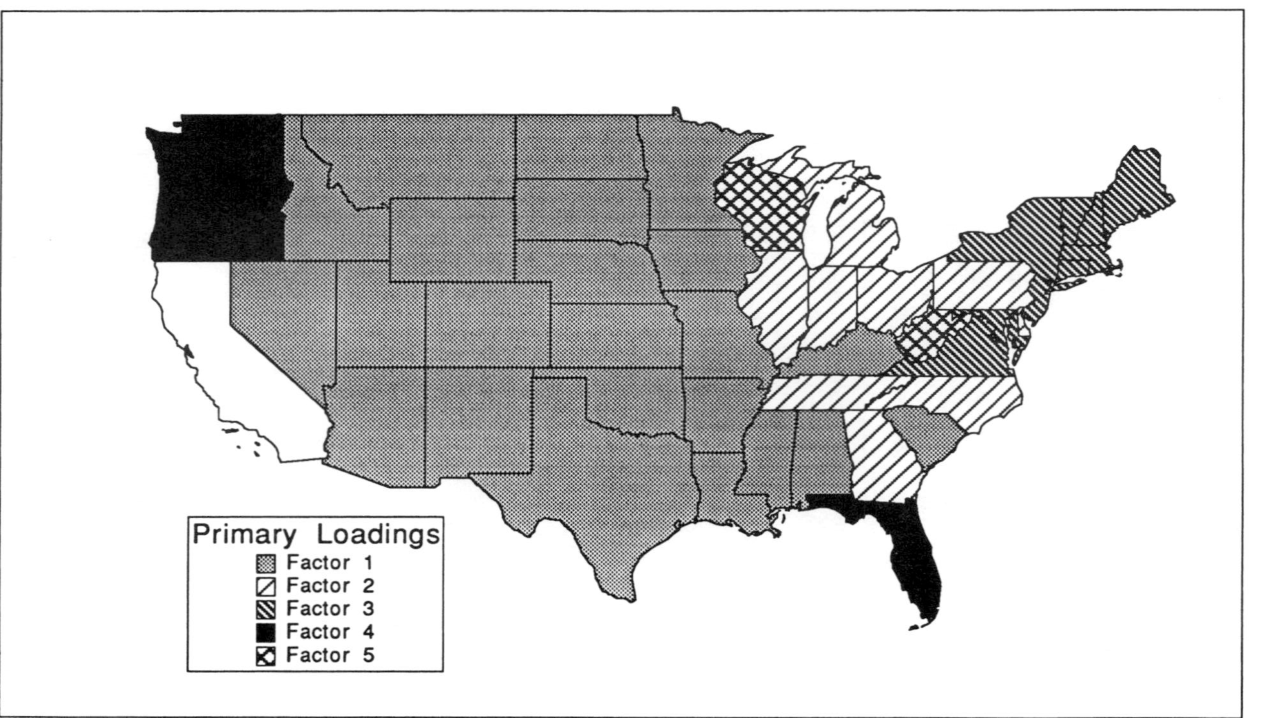

Figure 15.8 Regional Patterns in Time Trends for Out-Migration Streams from California

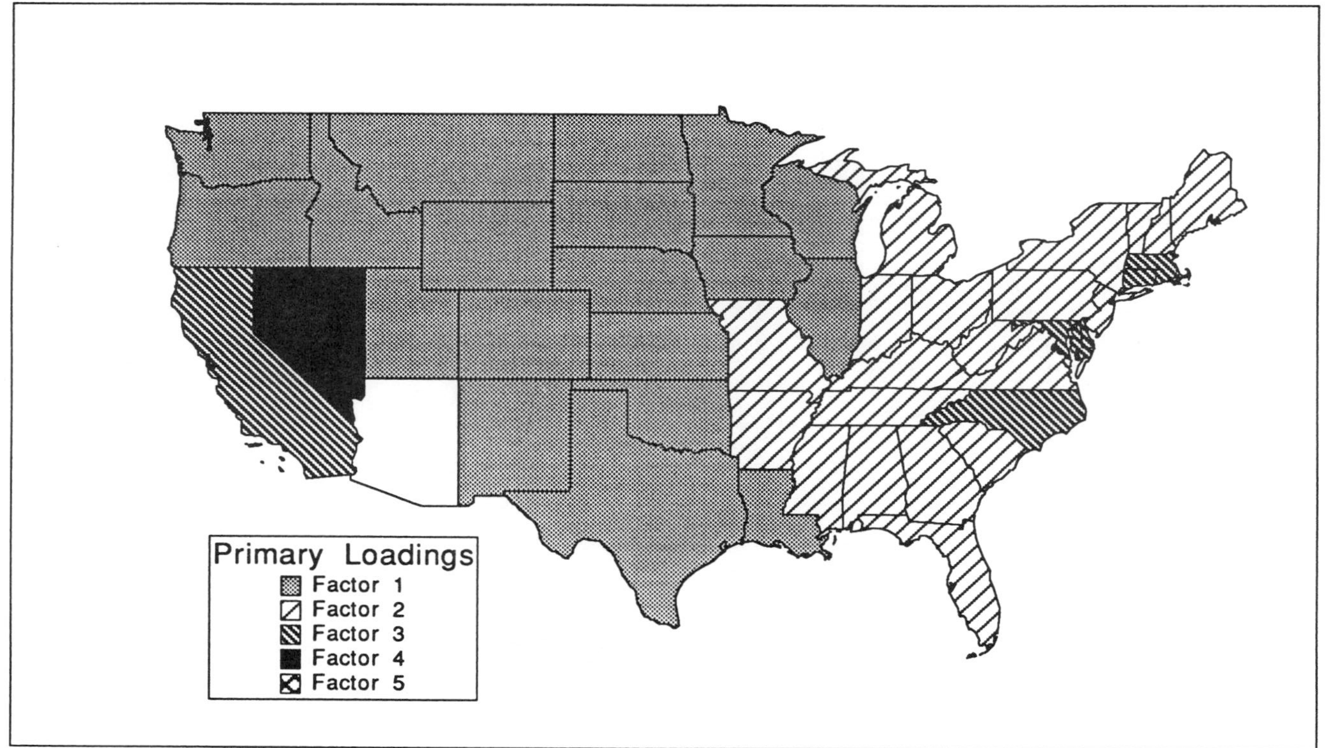

Figure 15.9 Regional Patterns in Time Trends for In-Migration Streams to Arizona

correspond to the more typical maps of migration *topologies* or *subsystems* (see, e.g., Pandit 1994; Plane 1995) based on analyzing the structure of single-period flow matrices.

A final question regarding the correlations of state-level trends is the extent to which the inflows and the corresponding outflows tend to be positively or negatively correlated. To begin to explore that question I computed fifty such correlation coefficients from the California subdatabase and fifty more from Arizona's. The California streams, probably because of the migration flood-inducing events of the early 1990s, had more negative correlations (42 out of 50) than the Arizona streams (32 of 50). As shown in Table 15.7 California also had more statistically significant correlations between its inflows and outflows than did Ari-

Table 15.7 Correlations[1] of Inflow and Outflow Migration Streams for California and Arizona

California				Arizona			
Negative		Positive		Negative		Positive	
Georgia	−0.9662	Connecticut	*0.6297*	Tennessee	−0.8139	New Mexico	*0.6234*
Iowa	−0.9595	Maine	*0.6261*	Washington	−0.7999	Florida	*0.6184*
Illinois	−0.9150			Idaho	−0.7989	Virginia	*0.5769*
Colorado	−0.9124			California	−0.7943		
Montana	−0.9094			Montana	−0.7918		
Tennessee	−0.9038			Oregon	−0.7845		
Nebraska	−0.9021			Nebraska	−0.7460		
Indiana	−0.8705			Kansas	*−0.5955*		
Idaho	−0.8702			South Dakota	*−0.5907*		
Minnesota	−0.8658			North Dakota	*−0.5499*		
Oregon	−0.8403			Hawaii	*−0.5489*		
Kentucky	−0.8245			Wisconsin	*−0.5282*		
South Dakota	−0.8134						
Alabama	−0.8120						
Arizona	−0.7943						
Wyoming	−0.7915						
Washington	−0.7845						
Ohio	−0.7732						
Wisconsin	−0.7572						
Texas	−0.7551						
Delaware	−0.7401						
New Mexico	−0.7210						
North Carolina	−0.6653						
Michigan	−0.6642						
Pennsylvania	−0.6540						
Kansas	*−0.6395*						
Washington, D.C.	*−0.5240*						

Note: 1. All correlation coefficients (R) shown in the table are significant at the .05 level based on a two-tailed test; coefficients in italics are not significant at the .01 level.

zona. Only a few of the positive correlations between in- and out-migration streams were statistically significant. Once again, more work is needed to explore such correlations for the other states throughout the U.S. migration system.

Conclusion

Time series perspectives and physical geography analogies can provide some useful insights about how internal migration systems evolve over time. In this chapter I attempted to provide a definition of migration floods. I also introduced the concept of a population migration time series. An examination of unusually high levels of flows in origin-destination-specific gross migration streams highlights the impacts of particularly significant events on migration patterns. In future work, frequency distributions other than the normal could be explored to more accurately define the recurrence intervals of extreme flow events.

Unlike hydrologic floods, which tend to be associated with highly spikey rainfall events, migration floods (and droughts) tend to play themselves out over several years. More work is needed on the correspondence between such migration pattern changes and business cycles.

This research also demonstrates that all of the inflow and outflow streams for a particular state do not move synchronously over time. A complex web of interregional linkages and complementarities underlies and mediates how the impacts of economic and societal events differentially experienced in one region of the nation are felt throughout the remainder of the system. This chapter has only begun to explore the correlations of the 2,550 (population benchmarked) interstate migration series now available. As the IRS–Bureau of the Census time series continue to grow, the database will become increasingly useful for exploring the evolving dynamics of the U.S. migration system.

Note

I am grateful to Richard Reeves for pointing me to some of the hydrology–physical geography literature on flood frequency analysis. Thanks also to the participants in the Advanced Quantitative Methods Seminar in the University of Arizona's Department of Geography and Regional Development during the fall semester 1996 for stimulating me to think about the parallels between migration and hydrologic and other physical geography systems.

References

Chow, Ven Te. 1964. *Handbook of Applied Hydrology*. New York: McGraw-Hill.

Clark, William A.V. 1986. *Human Migration*. Scientific Geography Series, vol. 7. Beverly Hills: Sage.

Dunne,Thomas, and Luna B. Leopold. 1978. *Water in Environmental Planning*. San Francisco: W. H. Freeman.

Engels, R., and M. K. Healy. 1981. "Measuring Interstate Migration Flows: An Origin-Destination Network through Internal Revenue Service Records." *Environment and Planning A* 13: 1345–1360.

Glavac, Sonya M. 1995. *Return Migration from Australia*. M.A. Thesis, Department of Geography and Planning, University of Queensland, Australia.

Greenwood, Michael J. 1975. "Research on Internal Migration in the United States: A Survey." *Journal of Economic Literature* 13: 397–433.

———. 1985. "Human Migration: Theory, Models, and Empirical Studies." *Journal of Regional Science* 25: 521–544.

Greenwood, Michael J., Peter Mueser, David A. Plane, and Alan M. Schlottman. 1991. "New Directions in Migration Research: Perspectives from North American Regional Science Disciplines." *Annals of Regional Science* 25: 237–270.

Isserman, Andrew M., David A. Plane, and David McMillan. 1982. "Internal Migration in the United States: A Review of Federal Data." *Review of Public Data Use* 10: 285–311.

Ledent, Jacques. 1991. "The Notion of Natural Migration As a Basis for Measuring the Relative Contributions of Push and Pull Factors to Interregional Migration." Paper presented at the North American Meetings of the Regional Science Association International, New Orleans, November.

McHugh, Kevin, and Patricia Gober. 1992. "Short-Term Dynamics of the U.S. Interstate Migration System, 1980–88." *Growth and Change* 23: 428–445.

Milne, William J. 1993. "Macroeconomic Influences on Migration." *Regional Studies* 27: 365–373.

Nord, Mark, and John B. Cromartie. 1997. "Rural-Urban Patterns of Income Migration in the United States: 1992–94." Paper presented at the Annual Meetings of the Association of American Geographers, Fort Worth, Texas, April.

Odland, John, and Adrian J. Bailey. 1990. "Regional Out-Migration and Migration Histories: A Longitudinal Analysis." *Geographical Analysis* 22: 158–170.

Pandit, Kavita. 1994. "Differentiating between Subsystems and Typologies in the Analysis of Migration Regions: A U.S. Example." *Professional Geographer* 46: 331–345.

———. 1997. "Demographic Cycle Effects on Migration Timing and the Delayed Mobility Effect." *Geographical Analysis* 29: 187–199.

Pickles, Andrew R., and Richard B. Davies. 1985. "The Longitudinal Analysis of Housing Careers." *Journal of Regional Science* 25: 85–101.

Plane, David A. 1984a. "Migration Space: Doubly Constrained Gravity Model Mapping of Relative Interstate Separation." *Annals of the Association of American Geographers* 74: 244–256.

———. 1984b. "A Systemic Demographic Efficiency Analysis of U.S. Interstate Population Exchange, 1935–80." *Economic Geography* 60: 294–312.

———. 1992. "Age Composition Change and the Geographical Dynamics of Interregional Migration in the U.S." *Annals of the Association of American Geographers* 82: 64–85.

———. 1993. "Demographic Influences on Migration." *Regional Studies* 27: 375–383.

———. 1994. "The Wax and Wane of Interstate Migration Patterns in the U.S. in the 1980s: A Demographic Effectiveness Field Perspective." *Environment and Planning A* 26: 1545–1561.

———. 1995. "Fuzzy Set Migration Regions." Paper presented at the International Conference on Population Geography, Dundee, Scotland, September 1995, and at the Annual Meetings of the Association of American Geographers, Charlotte, N.C., April 1996.

Plane, David A., and Christopher Bitter. 1997. "The Role of Migration Research in Regional Science." *Papers in Regional Science* 67: 133–153.

Plane, David A., and Peter A. Rogerson. 1989. "U.S. Migration Pattern Responses to the Oil Glut and Recession of the Early 1980s: An Application of Shift-Share and Causative Matrix Techniques." In P. Congdon and P. Batey (eds.), *Advances in Regional Demography*. London: Belhaven.

———. 1991. "The Ten Commandments of Migration Research." In David E. Boyce, Peter Nijkamp, and Daniel Shefer (eds.), *Regional Science: Retrospect and Prospect*. Berlin: Springer-Verlag.

Ravenstein, Ernest G. 1885. "The Laws of Migration." *Journal of the Royal Statistical Society* 48: 167–235.

Rogerson, Peter A. 1984. "New Directions in the Modelling of Interregional Migration." *Economic Geography* 60: 111–121.

———. 1987. "Changes in U.S. National Mobility Levels." *Professional Geographer* 39: 344–351.

Tobler, Walter R. 1976. "Spatial Interaction Patterns." *Journal of Environmental Systems* 6: 271–301.

———. 1987. "Experiments in Migration Mapping by Computer." *American Cartographer* 14: 155–163.

———. 1995. "Migration: Ravenstein, Thornthwaite, and Beyond." *Urban Geography* 16: 327–343.

Waldorf, Brigitte, and Adrian Esparza. 1994. "A Parametric Failure Time Model of International Return Migration." *Papers in Regional Science* 70: 419–438.

16

Conclusion: The State of the Art

Suzanne Davies Withers and Kavita Pandit

The chapters in this book attest to the fundamental changes under way in the economic and demographic restructuring of the United States and their crucial connections with migration. They further highlight the pivotal role of the geographic perspective in understanding these links; both restructuring and migration, although evident on the global scale, vary enormously in their regional and local articulations. From specific research questions to methodological debate, this volume illuminates several prevailing challenges for migration scholars. In this chapter we first present the major substantive themes that emerge from this book, then we address methodological approaches and data availability, and we conclude with emerging questions related to the geographic nature of migration and restructuring.

Substantive Themes

Five overarching themes prevail throughout this book: (1) the links between restructuring and uneven development-polarization, (2) the role of migration as an equilibrating mechanism, (3) the role of migration in ethnic assimilation, (4) the life-course dynamics of migration and restructuring, and (5) the impacts of public policy. Each of these themes represents challenging avenues for future research.

Repeatedly, the chapters suggest that economic and demographic restructuring is associated with income inequality, social polarization, and spatially uneven development. Flexibility of capital, along with the deskilling of the labor force that reinforces this flexibility, inherently leads to spatial disparity in opportunity and economic development. The chapters by Cushing and by Morrill and Falit-

Baiamonte reveal the tendency toward income polarization at the regional and metropolitan scales, respectively. Brown and colleagues similarly note that even within a region of general economic decline, significant economic polarization emerges as a result of the heterogeneous response of localities to larger economic changes. Clark's chapter reveals uneven development that arises from differences in skill levels between native-born Americans and new immigrants and draws attention to the significant spatial differences in the impact of immigration.

The second theme resonating throughout this book is the role of migration in equilibrating spatial heterogeneity. The implicit assumption that migration minimizes regional differences is at the heart of traditional migration theory. This assumption is based on the view that decisionmaking by individuals and households is economically rational. Thus by choosing to move, for example, from regions of lower wages to those of higher wages, individuals narrow the differential in per capita income of origin and destination regions.

Several chapters, however, challenge the assumption that migration is an equilibrating process and found, on the contrary, that migration led to increased spatial polarization. Cushing argues that given housing costs, kinship ties, and social networks, it is fairly rational for people in the impoverished parts of Appalachia not to migrate from their jobless environment to places of employment. Their actions, however, serve to further concentrate poverty rather than equilibrate income over regions. Similarly, within metropolitan areas Morrill and Falit-Baiamonte found increasing concentrations of poverty in certain parts of the city caused by the selectivity of intraurban mobility patterns. De Jong showed in detail that not all residents use the same criteria in deciding to move or choosing the destination.

Ethnic assimilation is closely related to spatial equilibrium. Historically, assimilation has been an important defining concept for this nation of immigrants. Pervasive images of the United States as a melting pot attest to the power of this dominant ideology. Yet as the chapters in this book suggest, assimilation is a complex term; it can be variously used to refer to behavioral similarities between the foreign-born and native populations, the structural integration of immigrant workers within the economy and labor markets, and the geographically even distribution of immigrant populations. Like the concept of equilibrium, assimilation connotes a leveling of differences—socially, economically, and spatially. Further, there is an implicit assumption that processes of internal migration facilitate the assimilation of immigrants and other ethnic minorities.

The authors note that despite the faith of Americans that assimilation is inevitable, actual differences between migrants and native-born Americans have tended to persist if not widen. Clark, for example, notes that the characteristics of the current wave of immigration flows are widening the polarization between wealth and poverty in America. Similarly, chapters by Frey and Liaw and by Gober note that internal migration often reinforces the spatial concentration of immigrants. Frey and Liaw, for example, found that Latino and Asian immigrants continue to settle in traditional port-of-entry cities, and little evidence shows internal migration creating a dispersal away from these centers. Gober, too, found evidence of such polarization among some ethnic subgroups. She cautioned, however, that the "foreign born" do not constitute a homogeneous group and that although internal migration serves to concentrate some groups of the foreign born, other groups did show patterns of spatial dispersal.

Taken together, the previous observations on restructuring, uneven development, and the role of migration suggest an interesting paradox: economic and demographic restructuring is associated with uneven development, which then stimulates population redistribution, which, in turn, frequently leads to further polarization and uneven development.

A fourth theme emerging from this book is the manner in which life-course dynamics shape the nature of migration and restructuring. The relationships between migration and life-course events (such as entry into the labor market, family formation, and retirement) are well established in the migration literature. Consequently, the interconnections between migration and restructuring are in constant evolution and are played out over time. This life-course theme was most evident in chapters by Rogerson, Waldorf, and Moore and McGuiness. Rogerson details how contemporary migration patterns are shaped by the interplay among three successive generations: the parents of the baby-boom generation, the baby boomers themselves, and the children of the baby-boom generation. Clearly, the nature of demographic restructuring caused by migration changes with the progress of generations through their life courses. Waldorf's chapter highlights another life-course dynamic—fertility. She illustrates how contemporary immigration patterns modify fertility rates, which, in turn, may impact population size and future migration. Geographic restructuring caused by population aging and by elderly mobility was highlighted by Moore and McGuiness. These and other chapters emphasize the role of time and the importance of the life course in understanding the migration-restructuring relationship.

The geographic expression of public policy is the final overarching theme throughout this book, with virtually every author addressing the impact of public policy either implicitly or explicitly. Public policy at the national level has witnessed fundamental restructuring that has enormous implications for future migration. The current downsizing of government, coupled with the trend toward greater state and local control, has far-reaching and often unpredictable implications for migration patterns. Espenshade and colleagues, for example, demonstrate the intended, as well as the unintended, consequences of the 1996 Welfare Reform Act and the Immigration Reform Act on immigration. Their projections suggest that although these policies may reduce the level of legal immigration, they are likely to increase the volume of illegal immigration. Moreover, implementation of policies at the national level also has specific and varying outcomes for restructuring at the regional and local levels. Thus the projections by Espenshade and colleagues portend significant economic and demographic restructuring for border communities and port-of-entry cities. Cushing challenges the transferability of national social welfare programs to the local context, noting that the local impacts of these policies may be rather different from those intended by policymakers. Clearly, public policy initiatives must be assessed carefully to identify possible unintended outcomes and reveal their differential regional and local impacts.

Methodological Approaches

The chapters in this book also highlight diverse methodologies in migration research. The methodologies differ with respect to (1) analytical approach, (2) scale of analysis, and (3) data utilization. Traditionally, geographic approaches to migration research have been dominated by the systems approach, which focuses on the spatial pattern of population flows. This emphasis is evident in chapters by Brown and colleagues, Morrill and Falit-Baiamonte, Clark, Moore and McGuiness, Gober, and others. In contrast, the behavioral perspective is employed by Cushing, De Jong, and Watkins, for example, who emphasize the role of individual and household decisionmaking in shaping migration outcomes.

Several chapters underscore the importance of a life-course perspective and longitudinal analysis in understanding the dynamics behind migration and population redistribution. De Jong, for example, argues that understanding choice processes in migration behavior can benefit from individual migration histories and individual experiences in migration. Watkins uses a creative approach to understanding migration by examining personal narratives. His chapter also uses the life course as an important analytical construct. Plane suggests that a longitudinal perspective can also be useful in the study of migration flows. He explores the utility of analogies from the physical sciences to further our understanding of the evolution of specific migration streams over time. These chapters highlight the powerful connection between spatial and temporal dynamics.

Geographic scales evident in this book range from the national (Espenshade and colleagues, Waldorf, Rogerson, Moore and McGuiness, Newbold, Plane) to the regional (Cushing, Brown and colleagues, Clark), and metropolitan (Frey and Liaw, Morrill and Falit-Baiamonte). Clearly, the choice of the appropriate scale and unit of analysis is dictated to some extent by the theoretical context of the research. Yet these studies collectively demonstrate that the interconnections between migration and restructuring are evident at different scales and that patterns at the macroscale often mask complex realities at the local level and vice versa. Thus, for example, macroscale studies have established that economic restructuring triggered a Snowbelt to Sunbelt migration in the 1970s and 1980s that improved the economic fortunes of the South and West at the expense of the Northeast. Yet the chapters by Brown and colleagues and Morrill and Falit-Baiamonte suggest that the picture is much more complex at the regional and metropolitan scales. Brown and colleagues note that even within the old industrial region of the Northeast, some areas continued to thrive economically whereas neighboring regions lost industry and population. Likewise, Morrill and Falit-Baiamonte revealed that within the Sunbelt city of Atlanta, significant pockets of poverty and net out-migration persist.

Turning to migration data, many authors used some form of census data. Of these the majority (Brown and colleagues, Morrill and Falit-Baiamonte, Moore and McGuinness, Rogerson, Cushing) used statistics reported for geographical units, such as county- or state-level migration flows. Several others (Clark, Frey and Liaw, Gober, Newbold), however, used individual-level data provided by the U.S. Census in its Public Use Micro Samples files. These data not only provide detailed socioeconomic and ethnic information of migrants but also contain geographic information that allows spatial analysis.

The census, however, is not the only source of migration data. Plane used statistics reported by the Internal Revenue Service (IRS). Although these data may have some biases, as he discusses in his chapter, they are a unique source of state-to-state information on an annual basis. Other alternative data sources are becoming increasingly available as public and private agencies now gather and store individual and household data in an electronic format. Espenshade and colleagues and Waldorf use yet another type of data—simulated data. Such data, based on clearly stated assumptions, enable researchers to make projections into the future based on alternative scenarios.

Not all migration data, however, are suitable for rigorous statistical analysis. Watkins's chapter shows how detailed interviews can provide insight into the factors that encourage or deter mobility that cannot be gauged through secondary data sources. Such ethnographic analysis can play a useful role in analysis of migration and restructuring.

Overall, the state of the art in migration research clearly employs a wide breadth of approaches, a broad spectrum of spatial scales, and a wide assortment of data sources. The diversity of perspectives underscores a vibrant intellectual community of migration scholars. At the same time, further methodological development is warranted in at least two areas. The first is the refinement of methodology to more explicitly link microlevel and macrolevel perspectives. By design, the theme of migration and restructuring presupposes a link between microlevel and macrolevel perspectives. Economic restructuring and demographic restructuring are large-scale structural changes in U.S. society. Yet the impacts of these structural changes on migration and population distribution are evident at different scales, from the individual and household to the community and from the neighborhood and locality to the state and region. The current challenge for migration scholarship is to recognize the complementarity of these approaches and to develop more effective approaches to link microlevel and macrolevel analysis.

The second area of development is related to the refinement of migration data.

The current availability of data sources is both enabling and constraining migration scholarship. Particularly since the advent of access through the Internet, secondary data sources are more readily available now than ever before. Yet many substantive and theoretical research questions are frequently constrained by the format in which these data are reported. For example, for the past few decades geographers have increasingly taken a life-course perspective in the analysis of migration. Yet few of these longitudinal research efforts examine explicitly the geographic aspects of migration and restructuring, focusing instead on aggregate trends in household formation or on the components of local population redistribution. One reason for this is the challenge of obtaining detailed longitudinal data with sufficient geographic resolution. There clearly appears to be a trade-off between the detail of individual and household profiles and the fineness of the geographic resolution available. Given severe budget constraints at the Census Bureau, there is little promise that this situation will change in the near future. Given this context, the challenge facing migration scholars is to secure the kinds of data needed to address the truly pressing questions. The use of IRS data, simulation, and personal interviews represents an effort toward this end, but unless we rise to the challenge, the absence of appropriate data will continue to confine our theoretical and empirical endeavors.

Geographic Perspective and Future Questions

The chapters in this book suggest that a geographic perspective greatly facilitates understanding of migration and restructuring. This is natural since the national-scale processes of economic and demographic restructuring are translated into migration outcomes through spatial imbalances. On the other hand, the imbalances caused by migration processes recursively influence the restructuring of the economy and the population. The geographic perspective also permits the design of national policies that take into account varying outcomes at the local and regional scales. These ideas are illustrated repeatedly throughout this book.

Our exploration of the role of geography in understanding the links between migration and restructuring has only begun. Characteristic of good scholarship, the contributions here have raised stimulating questions for further research. For example, provocative issues emerge when we recognize that migration does not always equilibrate differences over space. How will the continued polarization of wealth affect the sustainability of neighborhoods, cities, and regions? What does the geographic concentration of immigrants and certain ethnic groups portend for the future of the United States as a melting pot? Will age- and generation-specific migration patterns increasingly segregate the elderly from the rest of the population?

In the area of public policy, the current trend toward greater state and local responsibility appears to allow policies to be increasingly tailored to specific needs. Yet it raises an interesting debate regarding the relative roles of national versus state and local decisionmaking. A particularly sensitive debate is over immigration policy, which has always been articulated at the national level—often in the context of national security—yet its outcomes vary enormously over space. Future research could explore intermediate policy options that address both national and local concerns. A similar national–local dichotomy exists in the articulation of policies that affect the elderly. Current policy is centered at the national level and focuses almost exclusively on issues related to Social Security and health costs. Yet it is clear that aging populations pressure services at the local level. Once again there is a need for policies that are sensitive to issues at different geographic scales.

Ultimately, we may find that our very conceptualization of migration and restructuring needs to be reconsidered over time as residential options yet unknown to us become available and what we consider today to be fundamental economic and demographic changes become routine. These questions will continue to challenge migration scholars in the decades ahead.

Index

About the Contributors

Jessica L. Baraka is a doctoral candidate in the Department of Economics, Princeton University.

Lawrence A. Brown is professor, Department of Geography, Ohio State University.

William A. V. Clark is professor, Department of Geography, University of California, Los Angeles.

Brian Cushing is professor, Department of Economics and Regional Research Institute, West Virginia University.

Gordon F. De Jong is professor, Department of Sociology and Population Research Institute, Pennsylvania State University.

Scott Digiacinto is a doctoral student, Department of Geography, Ohio State University.

Thomas J. Espenshade is professor, Department of Sociology, and faculty associate at the Office of Population Research, Princeton University.

Anthony Falit-Baiamonte is a doctoral student in the Department of Geography, University of Washington.

William H. Frey is Research Scientist, Population Studies Center, University of Michigan, and Senior Fellow of Demographic Studies, Milken Institute.

Patricia Gober is professor, Department of Geography, Arizona State University.

Gregory A. Huber is a doctoral candidate in the Department of Politics, Princeton University.

Kao-Lee Liaw is professor, School of Geography and Geology, McMaster University, Canada.

Linda Lobao is professor, Program in Rural Sociology, Ohio State University.

Donald L. McGuinness is data planner at Southeastern Ontario District Health Council, Canada.

Eric G. Moore is professor, Department of Geography, Queen's University, Canada.

Richard Morrill is professor emeritus, Department of Geography, University of Washington.

K. Bruce Newbold is assistant professor, Department of Geography, University of Illinois.

Kavita Pandit is professor, Department of Geography, University of Georgia.

David A. Plane is professor, Department of Geography and Regional Development, University of Arizona.

Peter A. Rogerson is professor, Department of Geography, University of Buffalo.

Brigitte Waldorf is associate professor, Department of Geography and Regional Development, University of Arizona.

John F. Watkins is associate professor, Department of Geography, and research associate, Sanders-Brown Center on Aging, University of Kentucky.

Suzanne Davies Withers is assistant professor, Department of Geography, University of Washington.